FENGSHUI IN CHINA

FENGSHUI IN CHINA

GEOMANTIC DIVINATION BETWEEN STATE
ORTHODOXY AND POPULAR RELIGION

Ole Bruun

Foreword by Stephan Feuchtwang

UNIVERSITY OF HAWAI'I PRESS
HONOLULU

Published in North America by
University of Hawai'i Press
2840 Kolowalu Street
Honolulu, Hawai'i 96822

07 06 05 04 03   5 4 3 2 1

First Published in Denmark by
NIAS Press
Nordic Institute of Asian Studies
Leifsgade 33
2300 Copenhagen S
DENMARK

Library of Congress Cataloging-in-Publication Data
Bruun, Ole.
   Fengshui in China : geomantic divination between state orthodoxy and
   popular religion / Ole Bruun.
         p. cm.
   Includes bibliographical references and index.
     ISBN 0-8248-2672-8 (alk. paper)
     1. Feng shui—China—History.   I. Title.
     BF1779.F4 B78 2002
     133.3'337'0951–dc21

                                                                    2002007832

Typeset by NIAS Press
Printed in Singapore
Jacket design by Nanna Bild

Contents

FIGURES

Foreword

Fengshui has been globalised, but its centre of activities is still China. It is fashionable abroad because it is 'complementary', like acupuncture: another Chinese body of knowledge and practice. As fashion, trickery or trustworthy truth, its practise in urban interior and garden design in the rich cities of Euro-America as well as China has been added to its traditional use for the siting of graves, homes, and public buildings. But it is important to treat it as a kind of knowledge, rather than as a phenomenon. Fengshui certainly stands the test of being so treated. It is substantial, has a long history, and can be shown to have affected the way Chinese people see and treat the world. One of the ways fengshui is known is through stories of the perfidy of its practitioners. But to ask what kind of knowledge it is and to what uses it has been put gets behind the immediate and practical questions of trust that anyone attracted to it as a client, in China as anywhere else, understandably asks.

Others may go to China to learn the art and cosmology of fengshui in order to become practitioners. Ole Bruun did not. He is interested in fengshui as a kind of knowledge. So am I, and so probably are you, the reader. But there are many available ways of treating and understanding fengshui as knowledge. Fengshui has been studied by historians of science, by historians of religious cosmology, and by landscape architects. But for a closer emphasis on practice and social context, it is best done by anthropologists. My own study, which began nearly forty years ago, combined the exposition of Chinese texts with reports of fengshui in practice. But Ole Bruun concentrates on practice and has interviewed a great many fengshui specialists and their clients, something I did not do. Ole starts with the records of other Western observers as I did for the second half of my book but only after I had given an exposition of Chinese fengshui manuals[1]. He then adds his own much more systematic observations a century and a half later.

The outsider is never neutral. It may be of some interest to compare the difference between the nineteenth-century observers and Ole Bruun as a late twentieth-century observer of fengshui in China because it is also an indication of changes that fengshui itself has undergone. The outside observers of the nineteenth century were missionaries and other representatives of great imperial powers. Ole Bruun is a different kind of outsider, in another time and kind of global economics and politics. He has less direct interest in China as a market or as a field for salvation or for any other mission than they had. He is a European who has used his knowledge of Chinese, years of experience in China and decades of studying it, to make of himself a well respected academic researcher. He is a professional exponent of different kinds of knowledge, how they are embedded in political and economic contexts and extended in social practices. True to this calling as an anthropologist, he describes how the politics of the immediate past, the years of Cultural Revolution, affected his field-work, and he has a very interesting take on the effect that his nine-teenth-century predecessors' quite different preoccupations in China had on the politics of fengshui.

Fengshui was always proscribed, amongst other reasons because of the unfilial delay in the burial of ancestors that geomancers or geo-mantic dispute could cause. Yet it was also supported by the imperial state, as an art for the siting of imperial tombs and the design of the imperial capital. To this was added the privilege and duty of the emperor to produce the annual calendar. On the other hand this imperial duty and privilege had from the seventeenth century been transformed by highly respected scholars' criticism of the correlative thinking behind fengshui in which any thing can be linked to every-thing else. To widespread agreement among the ruling elite learned critics pointed out awkward facts that did not fit and had their own conditions of existence that the correlative systems could not elucidate. They and their successors to the present day could nevertheless not explain why such thinking persisted (which is what the anthropologist tries to do). Now, in the last half of the nineteenth century, a further twist was added to this ambivalence. Fengshui became a useful tool for the mobilisation among the subjects of the state to place obstacles in the ways of the projects (mines, roads, railways, buildings) of

---

1. My main interest was in fengshui as a way of putting into practice a cosmology but first of all I wanted to be able to say what that cosmology is. I have just revised the publication of that study. The new edition of An anthropological Analysis of Chinese Geomancy is published by White Lotus Co Ltd, Bangkok, 2002.

Western imperial incursion into China. In the same way, beliefs in demons and the means for fighting against them could be turned against foreigners to whom the imperial court had been forced to concede privileges. This happened in the Boxer Rebellion in the last years of the nineteenth century.

Imperial ambivalence blew apart in the course of the republican revolution, with republican states turning to science, progress and atheism in their urban bases. Continued use of fengshui seen from the cities was considered to be a backward 'peasant' superstition. The state of the People's Republic of China led by a professedly atheist Party continues this condemnation. But in the last quarter century, official ambivalence has returned. Mao had promoted a policy of walking on two legs, advancing Chinese traditional knowledge in several spheres, including medicine, and at the same time learning and developing scientific knowledge that had started in the West. Traditional Chinese medicine was taught in universities, including reconfigurations of traditional cosmological concepts that are also basic to fengshui. But walking on two legs definitely did not include fengshui or traditional religious practices. Then in the last two decades of the twentieth century, Chinese physics and other research disciplines investigated the scientific value of exercises for cultivating *qi*, the basic energies of bodies and all other physical forms in the universe. Official promotion of such exercises for preventative health fed a craze. Many methods of cultivating spiritual and physical health were born and flourished. They threatened to go out of state control a number of times, particularly in the mid-eighties and the late nineties, when those not registered with state authorities were severely suppressed. At the same time there was a resurgence of religious practices. In many instances they are cultivated officially as local custom and as tourist attraction, in many others they are condemned as superstition, fraud and disorder, and in most instances they persist on an uneasy middle ground.

Popular religion includes Daoist rites, which share with fengshui a conception of the emergence of things from a great unity, through the fertile balances of Yin and Yang. It is elaborated in a cosmology of flows of *qi* energies and substances, of destructive as well as constructive interactions of the Five Elements, and of the astrological influences of stars, likewise harmful or benign. But it is also true to say that geomancy is a completely distinct practice and tradition. The same is true of Chinese medical traditions. I do not think either fengshui or Chinese medicine is a religious system. Fengshui practitioners are primarily diviners, some of whom also perform cures. Others conduct ceremonies at graves and for public buildings. But they do not invoke deities. Nor are they trained in the performance of scriptures and liturgies. Nevertheless, fengshui and other kinds of divination have shared the fate of popular religious practices at the hands of republican governments. Fengshui has persisted, gone underground and resurfaced along with them.

Now in the new ambivalence of the current regime anthropologists and cultural historians, including Chinese as well as those like Ole Bruun writing in English and outside China, study Chinese religious practices, the cultivation of qi and fengshui without condemning them. Notions of scientific progress still prevail, but are questionable. Culture has become a valued concept. So this book is written in a different kind of opening than that provided by the forces of imperial ambivalence and imperialist trade, mission and force. It is the opening provided by an academic international, a network of personal and institutional linkages, and the opportunities provided for it by the new ambivalence of a PRC government that has opened China to world trade and investment, research and development.

Ole Bruun's direct observations of fengshui in two provinces, Sichuan in western and Jiangsu in eastern China, are the most detailed and extensive that have been made in these new conditions. He is well placed to say what fengshui has become in the dramatically changed circumstances of its homeland. Among those circumstances is the huge growth in the numbers and sizes of urban centres, and the rapid change agriculture is undergoing in most parts of China from subsistence to commodity production. These processes have changed the landscape of China, which is the subject of fengshui. The same processes have also produced equally dramatic social changes, which are just as significant for fengshui. I would single out the huge boom in house building for married couples to live separately from their parents, the loosening of intergenerational ties of obedience, and the increased geographical and social mobility away from the places where ancestors are buried. Fengshui is a self-centred use of Chinese cosmological tradition. But in its dynastic life it was for a sense of self that desired and was much more firmly a part of a male line with many strands into the future. Ole Bruun notes that the growing orientation of fengshui to cities and domestic privacy removes divides it into two kinds of ritual. One is public ritual for the orientation of buildings. The other is prescribing ways to adjust interiors and deal with chance events in individual biographies and careers. There is far less concern with the graves of ancestors, because in cities cremation has replaced burial for so many families. It seems now to be more often confined to the shorter-term future of a lifetime plus perhaps one generation.

Fengshui was always closely linked to other systems of divination using the same cosmology, as well as with Daoist rituals. But Ole Bruun extends this point qualitatively. Fengshui has become a much more contested practice, politically and scientifically. So fengshui experts act as mediators between much more widespread domains of knowledge, aspiration and activity – domains of economy, of status aspiration, and of state-sponsored rationalism with the uncertainties of life that give rise to divination in the first place. This is surely an effect of the politicisation of fengshui, the universality and standard-isation of schooling, and increasing expectations of material well being alongside increasing uncertainties of success.

Finally, this book deals with the actual effects of fengshui in practice. This includes, in chapter 6, a fascinating discussion of feng-shui's placebo effect. A fengshui cure relies on an image of the physiology of your body-mind and what can go wrong in it and in its interleaving with more general conditions, physical, spiritual and social. The action prescribed by a geomancer mobilises expectations organised by such an image, and stimulates physiological responses to those expectations. These may be particularly strong in a culture that somatises social and psychic anxiety.

But Ole Bruun's main investigation of effects is an appraisal of fengshui's environmental impact. Here we return to official ambi-valence: fengshui could be a native Chinese science of the environ-ment. Western afficionados of fengshui are certainly inclined to think it is a way of preserving as well as tapping the harmonies of Nature and their enthusiasm has filtered back to China. But here fieldwork comes into its own. Do those who consult geomancers preserve well-balanced environments, according to the aesthetics of fengshui? The rather disconcerting answers can be found in chapter 7.

However disconcerting they are, Ole Bruun has sympathy with the many people he met in Sichuan and Jiangsu who resorted to what he calls 'an archetypical mode of thought and explanation' in a 'high-tension, low-trust environment'. That is the position from which he gained their trust and from which we in turn can share the knowledge he has gained about fengshui in its homeland at the end of the twentieth century.

Stephan Feuchtwang (London, December 2001)

Acknowledgements

The present book has been several years in the making and parts of it have been presented at seminars, both at my shifting places of work and elsewhere (Chapter 7 was presented at the AAS meeting in Honolulu in 1996). In particular I want to thank researchers and staff at the Nordic Institute of Asian Studies in Copenhagen and the Center for Chinese Studies at the University of California at Berkeley for their inspiration and support and for providing an accommodating atmosphere.

The fieldwork and research for this book was chiefly funded by the Nordic Institute of Asian Studies and the Danish State Research Council of the Humanities, which latter has also subsidized its publication.

I am also indebted to my Chinese assistants in the two fieldwork areas, who helped me out in their spare time and went through considerable hardship and mud as we roamed the villages in Sichuan and Jiangsu. I shall also use this occasion to express my deepest sympathy for the rural Chinese geomancers, who still navigate the dire straits of Chinese religious politics, and for the countless rural villagers, whose exceptional hospitality and straightforwardness I always enjoyed.

A number of anonymous writers have provided valuable criticism and suggestions to several versions of the manuscript, greatly improving its quality and securing its consistency with other works in the China field. I especially want to express my gratitude to Stephan Feuchtwang, who has provided lengthy comments at several stages of the work, and in whose spirit it was originally conceived.

Finally I shall acknowledge the invaluable contribution of my desk editor, Leena Höskuldsson of the Nordic Institute of Asian Studies, who has prepared the book for international publication.

Much work has gone into the creation of this book and spending so much time in front of the computer has at times detracted me from my family. I hope the result will merit the efforts.

To Philip and Esther

Some Notes on Transliteration

When Europeans first examined Chinese fengshui in the mid-nineteenth century they translated it as 'geomancy', primarily for want of a more precise term. The Chinese encyclopedia *cihai* gives an account of fengshui as follows: *'Fengshui*, also called *kan yu*. A superstition of the old China. Considers wind directions, water streams and other topographical features in the surroundings of a house or a grave site in order to indicate the inhabitants' disaster or good fortune. Also a way of directing residences and graves'.

Obviously fengshui is very different from medieval European and Islamic geomancy,[2] which has induced several writers to suggest better translations. Stephen Skinner distinguishes between 'divinatory' and 'telluric' geomancy (Skinner 1980: 5), with fengshui belonging to the latter category, while Stephan Feuchtwang has suggested that it is more accurately defined as 'topomancy' (Feuchtwang 1974: 224). Nonetheless, for the sake of simplicity most writers have accepted the old term 'geomancy'.

Some semantic considerations are imperative in rendering feng-shui in any non-Chinese work. *Feng-shui* is composed from the characters for 'wind' (*feng*), also referring to scenery or landscape (*fengjing*), and 'water' (*shui*), also meaning 'liquid'. The term *feng-shui*, apart from its specific meaning, has entered everyday Chinese to mean the general impression of the qualities of an environment. For instance, when viewing beautiful scenery with tree-clad mountains and streams of running water, someone may find an outlet for his feelings by saying that its 'fengshui is very good' (*fengshui hen hao*). Similarly, due to the structure of the Chinese language, a number of other combinations of two simple characters form a nexus as they are imbued with strong sentiment or intricate meaning, for instance

---

2. Geomancy may be defined as 'a form of divination based on the interpretation of figures or patterns drawn on the ground or other flat surface by means of sand or similar ground materials'. The Western form was of importance in medieval Europe, closely linked with astrology and alchemy (Eliade 1987).

shan-shui (mountain–water), meaning landscape and traditional landscape painting or *tian-di* (heaven–earth), meaning universe.

For variation, fengshui specialists are sometimes called geomancers in the present text, just as the adjective geomantic is sometimes used as a referent to fengshui.

1 Fengshui: A Challenge to Anthropology

Fung Shui means literally 'wind (and) water'; but monosyllabic languages have a constant tendency to multiplication of syllables, and the Chinese language, though in great measure tied to its monosyllabic nature by its ideographic literature, contains many duplicate expressions which might with truth be classified as dissyllabic; Fung Shui is an instance of this; as an expression conveying an idea from the mind of one man to that of another it has entirely lost its literal significance, and is expressive only of an abstract idea ... Luck or ill luck arising from any supernatural causes through the medium of conspicuous objects: the baneful influence of exactly opposite doors or straight walls in buildings; are instances illustrative of Fung Shui. We too have our Fung Shuis; we smile at them but act as though we believe in them, provided expenditure of money is not thereby called for; the Chinese smile at theirs, but attend to them, with little more faith (I speak of Chinese with some erudition) than we have in ours, even though at the cost of their purses. (*Notes and Queries* 28 February, 1867)[1]

Chinese fengshui – or geomancy – has been of considerable interest to Western laymen and scholars for more than a century, first in sinology and later in several other disciplines, including anthropology, geography, architecture and ecology. This does not mean that it has been researched in any profound way or that any consensus has been reached as to its interpretation or even its proper disciplinary placement as a topic of study. The lack of penetrating studies can partly be explained by the confusing mass of old text material, popular manuals, practical techniques and endless local interpretations that constitute fengshui, as well as the inaccessibility of China for long periods of her modern history. But equally significant is an absolutist bias in the methodology. Many efforts at definition forced fengshui into Western intellectual conceptions. Depending on the writer's objective we find descriptions of fengshui as primitive psychology, proto-science, pseudo-science, environmental concern, practical techniques for utilizing winds and waters, primitive magic, the essence of Chinese folk religion or simply superstition.

Although we can outline several early concepts and ideas, trace much of its history and suggest what role it has played, we cannot give a definite answer to the common question of what fengshui 'really is'; the mere fact that the fengshui practised in China today deviates significantly from the fengshui practised during the late nineteenth-century colonial rivalry among Western powers obstructs such endeavours. Besides historical change there is also geographical variation: an immense regional and local diversity is evident despite the fact that many classics and manuals are universally used. The current fengshui in Chinese villages is radically different from the direction that it has taken in Chinese metropolises such as Hong Kong and Singapore. To make matters worse, fengshui has now become subject to the influence of cultural globalization. In recent decades a Western version has emerged, but its environmentalist interpretation and free style of application make it substantially different from its native forms.

This is the starting point of the present book: inquiring about fengshui in very narrow terms will merely provide a vulgar portrait of a complex tradition. The more relevant issues are how fengshui is perceived and practised locally, how it is linked to other ideas and institutions, and why this particular tradition gained such significance in Chinese society.

Grasping its total significance also allows us to find parallels in our own world. This is the main point of my argument: fengshui cannot be fruitfully investigated as a system in itself, but forms part of a meaningful whole only when seen against the totality of its cultural set-up. As a broad popular tradition it makes use of the Chinese classics and includes both ancestor worship, ritual and moral interpretation, which constitute common values that allow any Chinese to recognize familiar principles despite endless local variation. But more important-ly fengshui conveys an alternative vision of human existence pertaining to a specific context. During late imperial China, when greater cultural consistency was achieved, it rose to prominence in interaction with other currents of thought, including a complex of intolerant state rationalism and Confucian values on the one hand and a vast ag-glomeration of popular culture on the other. It thrived during the era of Western missionary activity and gained new significance under Chinese Marxist rule, frequently as a manifestation of heterodoxy. Both Western missionaries and Chinese authorities have described fengshui as a many-headed monster: it embraces an infinite repertoire of interpretation that may be brought into the service of all classes of people, but particularly its rural form conveys a defiant antithesis to absolutist ideology, which strives to control meaning, values and perception of reality. Fengshui symbolizes the unifying forces of Chinese culture as much as insists on its alternative interpretation.

The present book is intended to contribute to the anthropological analysis of how various perceptions of reality and currents of knowledge and thought interact in the local society. A no lesser ambition is to provide a comprehensive account of fengshui in China to the readership taking a general interest in the matter. The book pursues these aims by means of two interacting approaches. One is historical: I shall trace the history of fengshui practices since 1850, linking it to major events and the general course of Chinese history until the present, accounted for in Chapters 2 and 3. The other approach is modern anthropological fieldwork in two selected rural areas, one in Jiangsu in the east and another in Sichuan in the west, presented in Chapters 4, 5 and 6. During recent decades, Western theorists have attempted to link fengshui to environmental ethics; the origin of the environmental reading of fengshui as well as its actual environmental potential will be dealt with in Chapter 7.

SOME CHARACTERISTICS

In very simple terms, the essence of fengshui is that configurations of land forms and bodies of water are seen to direct the flow of the universal *qi*, or 'cosmic current', which with the help of a specialist can be brought to optimum advantage for a person's wealth, happiness, longevity and procreation; similarly, a malicious flow of *qi* may bring disaster. The flow of qi is influenced by all natural bodies and human constructions, which may either repulse, redirect or catch the *qi*.

Fengshui is applied to the siting of two forms of dwellings, *yang* dwellings (houses) for the living and *yin* dwellings (tombs) for the dead. The correct siting of both is essential for people's well-being and success in life, whereas any kind of failure may be attributed to malicious fengshui. The common characteristics for a good house location are open, unblocked access to *qi* in front of the house, some shielding at the back, correct orientation of especially doors relative to compass directions or landscape topography and well-considered placement in regard to winds, watercourses, rocks, other buildings, gates, chimneys, pillars, trees and so forth. Tombs are most auspiciously located on higher ground, midway up hill slopes and mountains, and best protected by hills in an armchair position with open access in front. On flat land peasants will allot a corner of the field to their family tombs, frequently marking them with small mounds. Fengshui thought stipulates that if an ancestor is unhappy with his grave, serious repercussions may fall upon his descendants. Fengshui specialists are commonly consulted for siting, for adapting sites and for burial preparations, including calculation of the right moment for interment according to astrological data and the projections of the traditional calendar.

The specialist is commonly known as fengshui master (*fengshui xiansheng*) or yin-yang practitioner (*yinyang duangong*). When inspecting a site, he 'sees fengshui' (*kan fengshui*), scrutinizes his geomantic compass (*luopan*) and consults the traditional calendar (*nongli*). He determines the location of the White Tiger (*bai hu*) and the Green Dragon (*qing long*) as represented by topographical features in the landscape. He usually calculates the birth data of the owner of the house to see whether, by means of the Eight Trigrams (*ba gua*) and the associated Eight Characters, his elements correspond to those identified in the surroundings of the house. The actual techniques involved in rural fengshui-seeing are simple. Usually the specialists rely on experience and intuition more than on books of learning.[2] Seeing fengshui also involves ritual, for instance the killing of a cock and the sprinkling of its blood on a building site, which is supposed to drive away evil spirits.[3]

The geomantic compass is the specialist's most important tool and the key to determining the cosmological correlations of any given site. It consists of a circular wooden disk, usually four to six inches across, flat on the top and rounded at the bottom. In the centre is placed a small compass needle protected by glass. Around the compass needle the flat surface is inscribed with symbols and characters in concentric rings, numbering between nine and twenty-four (occasionally even more), depending on the degree of refinement.[4] All rings are in a fixed relationship, permitting the compass to be turned only around the compass needle. The innermost ring contains the Eight Characters (based on the eight trigrams of yin and yang combinations), with the consecutive rings indicating, most importantly, the Twelve Branches (denoting compass directions as

well as years, months, days and hours), the astrological cycle of the
Twelve Animals, the Twenty-four Mountains and the Sixty-four
Hexagrams (all combinations of the eight trigrams). The Five Phases,
moving from Water to Wood to Fire to Earth to Metal, are represented
in a number of combinations with the seasons of the year, the 360
degrees, and the 28 Lunar Mansions. The geomancer strives to
establish the cosmological correlations in the surroundings and their
impact on a given site, avoiding harmful influences and generally
striking a healthy balance, considering yin and yang aspects and the
five phases. In a sense, fengshui embraces and puts into operation the
entire Chinese cosmology, which was built up during centuries of
agglomeration and competition among the great traditions (see the
Appendix).

Two schools of fengshui are prominent on the Chinese mainland,
although both draw much of their philosophy from the Neo-
Confucian learning that arose with Zhu Xi and his contemporaries in
the twelfth and thirteenth centuries. The School of Forms, also called
the Jiangxi School,[5] is primarily concerned with the 'influence of
forms and outlines' (*jing shi*), including mountains, hills and watercourses, taking primary notice of surrounding land forms and configurations, both the natural and the man-made. The School of
Orientations or 'directions and positions' (*fang wei*), also termed the
Fujian School, grants principal importance to the Eight Characters
and their derived constellations on the geomantic compass, and thus
attaches more importance to compass alignment.[6]

If fengshui merely consisted of such concepts and schemes as
outlined above, it could easily be systematized and perhaps even
denoted as a proto-science. But it is in the active process of application to a specific social context that fengshui acquires its most
distinguishing features. One glance at the geomantic compass is
enough to inform us that interpretation is inevitable since any
direction will disclose a formidable array of symbols and constellations,
all with indefinite bearing on the human condition according to
traditional cosmology. Although fengshui limits itself to certain
classes of phenomena, concentrating on daily life events and life-cycle
concerns of ordinary people, its scale of application is endless, as will
be seen in the fieldwork chapters. In addition to the standard services
of siting, fengshui specialists are consulted in connection with illnesses (both physical and mental), common mishaps, deaths, accidents, family rows, career opportunities, missing persons and
objects, lack of prosperity or offspring, lucky days for various under-

takings and more. To understand Chinese fengshui we must examine it within the total context of its practice. Fengshui verbalizes popular attempts at organizing experience, which retain strict cosmological immanence by the refusal to distinguish between natural, social and psychical domains. Moreover, while interpreting forces in the immediate surroundings and their significance for human satisfaction it frequently employs a controversial and potentially anti-authoritarian language, while at the same time embodying universal Chinese values and articulating essential aspects of Chinese religion. This is the very purpose of the fengshui specialist – he is not part of the state and formal establishment of Chinese society, which is geared to deal with any legitimate human concern, but stands decisively outside, where rational and spiritual domains entwine.

FENGSHUI AND CHINESE STATE RATIONALISM

Fengshui is among the universal elements in Chinese culture, found in the People's Republic, Hong Kong, Taiwan, Singapore and overseas Chinese communities. Yet it remains considerably more outspoken in popular culture than in the Chinese literary self-identity. There is good reason to examine more closely its interaction with, and possibly propelling forces among, the major unifying structures of Chinese civilization such as the family system, including its religious aspects, and the state bureaucracy, building on the historical complex of Chinese state rationalism and social morality.

Although the fengshui mode of thought has a long unbroken history intimately connected to the development of Chinese cosmology, it only rose to prominence during the latter part of Chinese imperial history. This period was commonly associated with increasing cultural integration due to new media of communication, growing capitalist networks and increasing social mobility deriving from growing literacy and urbanization (Rawski 1985), but also by implication marked by the expanding reach of the state. We observe a familiar paradox: a heightened transmission of cultural stuff and greater cultural compliance, while popular resistance to domination increases simultaneously (Gates and Weller 1987: 3). Thus both compliance and resistance may utilize a common frame of reference in an intensified dialogue over culture; it is very likely, however, that such a process of increasing alignment of values and beliefs, and the increasing role of literacy in transmitting them, mould popular consciousness in a way favourable to the ruling class (Johnson 1987). Cultural integration itself did not achieve political unity. During the most recent centuries it was accompanied by tightening social control, purges on religious groups and cults, the state gradually expanding its domain and literary production being increasingly controlled and squeezed into a set paradigm. The enforcement of orthodoxy was carried out not for the sake of a nominal order, but with a large measure of spiritual alignment for the sake of maintaining a specific social order. It culminated in phenomenal endeavours at controlling people's minds and imposing on them a narrowly defined, but initially rational and secular worldview – endeavours which eventually failed.

Hence, instead of searching for the roots of fengshui in Chinese antiquity and ancient intellectual history – traditions like the one in question had their influence on all major civilizations – I shall focus on the far more important questions of why it continued and even gained prominence in the later era of Chinese history and why it remains so prominent today. Chinese popular ideology cannot be studied fruitfully without taking into account the crucial importance in China of attempts by the state and powerful classes to dominate, and attempts by subjects to resist domination (Gates and Weller 1987: 8).

Living traditions change over time. We must refuse to see the survival of the fengshui tradition as merely an unconscious act on the part of the people who use it, such as is implied in the Chinese term 'feudal superstition'. Instead, I contend that it has continued because it serves a purpose, one for which each generation finds it relevant. Insofar as the socio-political context changes, so does the fengshui tradition. The increasing intolerance of Chinese state power and its penetration of local society are crucial factors in the rise of fengshui ideology over time. A fundamental parallelism operates between the unifying and rationalizing efforts of the Chinese state on the one hand and fengshui ideology synthesizing a series of fragmented pieces of natural philosophy into a vast agglomeration on the other – they follow each other neatly in time. The omnipresent state orthodoxy is met with an alternative spiritual order, where a multitude of natural forces, spirits and ancestors are attributed comparable powers. They engage in a form of dialogue, maintain their respective advocates, specialists and supporters, carve out their independent domains and spheres of influence, but at a general level act as competing rationalities offering alternative explanations of causes and effects. In a sense, one is centralized in geographical space, the other ego-centred with reference to an invisible metaphysical space; one preaches social morality, the other sanctions egotism; one locks the individual into a predetermined hierarchical position, the other individualizes fate and inspires activism.

Fengshui can be seen in the perspective of an encounter between traditions of thought, knowledge and action in the widest sense, including competing modes of comprehension, with state and peasantry as the main *structural* carriers of such conflicting traditions, without pinning individuals to such structuration and without postulating a rigid two-tier scheme of interpretation. Despite fundamental divides in Chinese social experience in real life we observe a continuum of religious beliefs and practices between state and society, with many different religious groups and specialists competing among themselves to gain followers beyond their own kind and thereby implicitly mediating across social boundaries (Naquin 1985: 289–290). Much of the recent insight into Chinese 'popular religion' (a theme we shall return to later in this chapter and in Chapter 6), brought about by a shifting focus towards exploring religion as fully embedded in society and culture, applies to the study of fengshui.[7]

While simultaneously transmitting cultural values and attempting to resist domination, the popular ideology, of which fengshui is expressive, also serves less obvious purposes. Cultural integration implies intensified transmission of cultural values and ideals and the increasing ability of social groups to appropriate them by their own means and adopt them into social structures. Popular religion and ideology may potentially support the appropriation of idealized values otherwise out of the reach of common people by providing functional reinterpretation in a local context, including recasting, selection and resistance, all forming part of a continuing cultural dialogue. At some stage, what from an external perspective appears as cultural unity within a greater framework of common terms may well incorporate re-interpretations radical enough to challenge the elite, whose lifestyle and outlook formed avant-gardist cultural models. Fengshui epitomizes this challenge, being essentially Chinese, but conveying radically different versions of common ideals for a good life than emerges from the high-culture literary tradition.

It is beyond doubt that cultural conflicts have been intensified by the expansion of the modern state in China. This implied the penetration of state rationalism, centralism and modernity, including an exceptional developmental fanaticism whereby the pressure on the local society and on the household rose tremendously in recent history. I shall not attempt to outline the development of the modern

8

state in China, but to show a remarkable continuity in the state's attitude to the mode of thought propagated by fengshui.

For this and other reasons we should not overestimate modernity as a unique factor in Chinese history; to distinguish between traditional and modern forms of fengshui or other cosmologies tends to be trivial or even misleading, because the local and the extra-local have always interacted. Mental trafficking across all cultural boundaries is part of the human condition (Howell 1995: 165), but the production of difference rather than alignment is today regarded as a likely outcome of cultural encounter (Appadurai 1990). Marshal Sahlins summarized anthropology's position at the turn of the millennium by asserting that culture is *not* disappearing, despite countless theories to the opposite during the last century (Sahlins 1999: i–xxii).

In the Chinese local society, a complex, mostly secular, outer world always manifested itself in the form of a powerful state attempting to influence, pressurize, moralize, assimilate and integrate the individual by whatever means possible. The outlook of this larger dominant world was once Confucian, became communist, and is now capitalist; yet the concurrent processes of unification and differentiation, or homogenization and cultural fragmentation, bridge them all in common modernization (Friedman 1994: 102). Fengshui is a complex outcome of both remarkable historical unity and great cultural diversity, affecting a radical encounter between state rationalism and popular cosmology, and thus both diffused and in a continuous process of change. By implication, 'traditional fengshui' as a single system of theory and practice has never existed, except perhaps, in intellectual pursuits. A wide range of studies of Chinese religion, from J.J.M. de Groot to Marcel Granet to C.K. Yang to Maurice Freedman to Stephen Feuchtwang and onwards (cited in the next chapter), have attempted to find system, uniformity, order and coherence in the vast terrain of Chinese religious beliefs and practices. Fengshui always played a dubious part in these schemes. Below I will review previous anthropological studies on the subject and from there build up a framework for analysing the material from text and fieldwork.

ANTHROPOLOGY'S CONTRIBUTION

The discipline of anthropology, in theory, could be expected to encompass and examine fengshui as a cultural whole according to the premises of its methodology, but in fact it responded sluggishly.

Anthropologists have been inclined to carve out convenient segments from the entire fengshui complex for their studies, in which
functionalist, structuralist, environmentalist or other epoch-bound
biases clearly shine through.

Some of the earliest studies in anthropology paid attention to
Chinese geomancy. James Frazer, for instance, in his huge exposition
of how primitive culture could throw light on our own society, picked
a few secluded examples of fengshui as 'imitational magic' from the
equally sizeable work of the Dutch sinologist J.J.M. de Groot (Frazer
[1890] 1966, Vol. 1: 170; Vol. 3: 239). A few decades later, but also
mainly using the work of de Groot (1892–1910), Emile Durkheim and
Marcel Mauss discovered that the basic cosmological principles
incorporated in Chinese fengshui could be used as a case to prove a
crucial point for the rising social sciences: a fundamental parallel
between social and natural classifications, the social model in their
conception being the archetype, and the natural model merely a
derivative (Durkheim and Mauss [1903] 1963). They argued that the
Chinese symbolic classifications of space and the countless correlations
(as expressed in the geomantic compass) were essentially instruments
of divination and that the knowledge of diviners did not form isolated
groups of things, but rather groups bound to each other to form a
single whole and a unified knowledge (ibid.: 77). Thus Durkheim
and Mauss could point to the purely speculative purpose of
classifications – as of religion itself: 'The centre of the first schemes of
nature is not the individual; it is society' (ibid.: 86–87). Notwith-
standing conspicuous blunders in their use of data, primarily derived
from their faulty understanding of the elaborate Chinese cosmology
as developed from a single core in an evolutionary process, and their
strategic postulate of the prototypical state of social classification as
compared to natural classifications,[8] Durkheim and Mauss paved the
way for a new understanding of cosmological classifications with
reference to nature: such systems could fruitfully be searched for
social analogies, resemblances and metaphors. It was in their work
that Claude Lévi-Strauss (1967) much later found inspiration, although he modified their strategic assumption by showing that the
social organization of people into groups took place simultaneously
with the classification of nature.

Max Weber, writing almost contemporaneously with Durkheim
and Mauss, also took a keen interest in Chinese cosmology, although
from an entirely different angle. In his highly original comparative
scheme of Confucian and Protestant rationalism he focused on two

primary 'yardsticks', namely the degree to which religion had divested itself of magic (*Entzauberung der Welt*) and the degree to which the relation between God and the world had been systematically unified – the state of tension with the inevitable irrationalities of the world (Weber [1920] 1951: 226–227). While ascetic Protestantism represented a 'last phase', where all forms of magic had been eliminated and ethical rationalism defined conduct according to God's commandment, Confucianism was characterized by the preservation of a 'magic garden of heterodox doctrine' (in his conception primarily represented by Taoism) and the reduction to a minimum of its tension with the world. Within this typology Weber accounted for the coincidence of Confucianism and various forms of magic and superstition in an entirely new way (as to his theory on the origin of fengshui and other magical systems, see the Appendix). In this magic garden, nursed by geomancers among other 'magicians', the development of a rational economy and technology was out of the question, while, as a paradox to the unintended riches of the Puritan, the Confucian economic mentality blessed wealth: 'In no other civilized country has material welfare ever been so exalted as the supreme good' (ibid.: 237). By focusing on the magical stock of popular religion as both cause and effect of a lacking rationalization in technical disciplines, Weber brought explicit cross-cultural comparison into the study of Chinese religion. Although his conception of a religion's 'tension with' or 'adjustment to' the 'world' has remained much debated,[9] Weber provided a shrewd alternative perspective to the exoticism and historicism of his predecessors in the study of Chinese religion.

Hence, in the first decades of the twentieth century, both Chinese culture in general and popular religion as a specific field seemed open to inquiry within the emerging discipline of anthropology. When the fieldworking anthropologist became common (in fact pioneered in the China field by de Groot) fengshui was no longer a strong political force in China's relationship with the imperial powers (see Chapter 2). As far as local community life and politics were concerned, however, it was still an institution worthy of note. Had it not been for the impact of two separate but equally forceful factors, substantial anthropological studies of fengshui in pre-Communist China would most probably have been carried out. One such factor was, of course, the Chinese experimentation with Communism that soon brought anthropological studies to a complete halt and eventually sealed off the country.

Another equally important factor relates to personal elitist biases among educated Chinese, who tend to 'bear the responsibility to lead their civilization away from superstition and towards enlightenment' (Teiser 1999: 110). The lack of attention that the early Chinese sociologists and anthropologists such as Fei Xiaotong, Francis Hsu, C.K. Yang and Godwin Chu paid to fengshui came close to deliberate negligence. These scholars, despite being trained at Western universities, appeared so deeply immersed in a Chinese elite identity that they could not escape the age-old conviction of Chinese men of learning: the religion of the masses was hardly a worthy subject of study and even less a basis for literary pursuits. Wing-tsit Chan commented in 1953 that 'When it comes to the religion of the masses, one is appalled at the neglect by Chinese writers' (Chan [1953] 1978: 144). Or as put by Maurice Freedman, 'the most interesting aspects of Chinese religion and thought were closed off to them by their own ideological resistance to "superstition"' (Freedman 1979: 316). Some strong cases in point are Francis Hsu's *Under the Ancestors' Shadow* (1948), referring only sporadically to the subject, and C.K. Yang's *Religion in Chinese Society* (1970), which even more blatantly avoids it. To Yang, geomancy, together with other forms of divination, was merely a 'religious aspect of Confucianism', to which he devoted two pages. As pastimes of the Confucian gentleman, forms of divination functioned as 'imparting confidence, offering consolation, and giving guidance during a crisis' (Yang 1970: 261–262). As a consequence of these inclinations, Chinese anthropologists had little to offer in the study of fengshui: the most important general information on popular cosmology remained to be found in Western works.

It took several decades and a non-Chinese anthropologist to bring back fengshui as a subject worthy of study. Maurice Freedman, who lived and worked while the structural functionalist school was still unchallenged in British anthropology, produced two essays on Chinese geomancy; one drew on his fieldwork in the New Territories in 1963 (Freedman 1979: Essay 10), while the other was a Presidential Address to the Royal Anthropological Institute in 1968 (Freedman 1969: 5–15). His articles on geomancy derived from his seminal work on Chinese popular religion (inspired by C.K. Yang, among others), in which he introduced a new systemic approach emphasizing overarching structures, order and unity of some sort. He later articulated this in the way that 'behind the superficial variety there is order of some sort', deriving from what he termed 'a Chinese religious system, both at the level of ideas ... and at that of practice

12

and organization', in which elite and peasant religion 'rest on a common base, representing two versions of one religion that we may see as idiomatic translations of each other' (Freedman 1974: 352).

According to these premises Freedman treated fengshui as simultaneously being a standard system of metaphysics and a form of divination, the elements of which were 'transposable' into Chinese religion (Freedman 1979: 331). In his first essay he mostly discussed the connections between the geomancy of tombs and ancestor worship, arguing that they together form a system in which ancestors are worshipped on the one hand and manipulated for the selfish benefit of their descendants on the other hand. Also prominent among Freedman's conclusions is that fengshui forms a system of amoral explanation of fortune as an alternative to Buddhist and other ideas of a moral order in the universe. The second essay, which will receive some further attention in Chapter 7 since it played with ideas of fengshui as ecology, shifted its focus towards graves and houses as members of a single class, forming 'one system'.

Despite its wealth of detail and insight, Freedman's interpretation of fengshui remained predominantly functional, finding in it an institution that sets the rules for social competition while maintaining village solidarity and harmony – in other words an instrument of competition (ibid.: 329). This analytical inclination inevitably led Freedman to consider only a fragment of all significant statements and practices contained in rural fengshui. But undoubtedly as a positive quality of his functionalist presumptions, Freedman's essays embraced a variety of themes with many open ends, all formulated with scholarly shrewdness and made ready to pursue for other China anthropologists.

A few years after Freedman's Presidential Address the American anthropologist Jack Potter wrote a short essay on the religious life of Cantonese peasants (Potter 1970), which took up Freedman's approach to Chinese religion as a whole, but carried it even further by attempting to show peasant religion as a consistent philosophy of life. At the base of this cosmology, argued Potter, was a belief that 'the universe contains as its essence an impersonal supernatural power' (Potter 1970: 140). The occult pseudo-science of fengshui was built up to handle and regulate this power and the geomancer mediated between corporeal and supernatural affairs; although fengshui in principle deals with impersonal forces, it will always be merged with considerations of a range of supernatural beings. Potter stressed, however, much in line with Freedman, that an important effect of the system was that it regulated envy and jealousy: 'The magical and impersonal explanation for differential success ... softened to some extent the effects of great social differentiation' (ibid.: 147). Peculiar to Potter's work was the notion of peasant religion as only one cognitive model out of several, which allowed the villagers to switch from one to another. Since Potter presented this view as a conclusive statement rather than pursuing it in his analysis, it was inadequately developed – but still in perfect resonance with my argument. In fact a long line of early works on Chinese religion had emphasized the lack of individual commitment,[10] which is discussed below.

Freedman's identification of fengshui as a worthwhile subject of study for understanding Chinese religion as a whole was acknowledged by others. Stephan Feuchtwang, a student of Freedman, finished his dissertation on the subject almost simultaneously with Freedman's lecture (Feuchtwang 1974). In addition to a meticulous translation and examination of the symbolism of the rings of the geomantic compass, Feuchtwang set up his integrated interpretation of fengshui along four lines: first, a structuralist interpretation of its natural classi- fications as parallels to social classifications; second, a psychological interpretation of its projections of the imagination, including symbols; third, an analysis of the possible functions of fengshui as divination; and fourth, an interpretation of the perception of reality contained in the system. Although he deplored the lack of detailed information on fengshui symbolism and practices in contemporary Chinese society, he made a significant contribution to the under- standing of fengshui as a conglomerate tradition. Several of his suggestions are important to the present work.

Inspired by Durkheim and Mauss and not least by Lévi-Strauss, Feuchtwang investigated fengshui as a means of self-identification of social groups as well as of individuals. The fundamental question is whether the supernatural world disclosed in fengshui beliefs is a mirror of Chinese society. Chinese religion in general shows a num- ber of characteristics that emphasize a hierarchical order, which may then be equivalent to the social structure, but fengshui is somewhat different. Durkheim and Mauss had taken for granted that fengshui cosmology developed in an evolutionary process, in which the elaboration of classification from simple dualism to complex forms found a parallel in the development of a social hierarchy, where a multiplicity of categorizations at one level were combined into larger groupings under more general classifications and eventually led to unity (a similar point was made by Max Weber in his sociology of

14

religion). With Lévi-Strauss's qualification to this scheme, namely that natural and social classifications arose simultaneously, some crucial events in the course of Chinese history and the development of Chinese cosmology at a very general level could be searched for correlations (ibid.: 239–40).

Feuchtwang points out, however, that the single unified hierarchy conceived in religion may not necessarily be found in the self-identification of social groups. Lévi-Strauss's work on totemism showed that the animal emblems used by social groups came from a level series of categories corresponding to a series of social categories, which were not unified into a hierarchy. By maintaining that fengshui beliefs are a means of self-identification, Feuchtwang finds the resemblance, since 'one is differentiated from others by choice of location on the ground' (Feuchtwang 1974: 240). With fengshui a person or a group (a kinship group) is identified as an ego-centred universe, which by including burials and ancestor worship may be extended both back into the past and forward into the future: the geomancer's compass is oriented from the centre of the dwelling site, the centre of the defined area of one's self-interest. The site itself is a projection of the compass, a miniature universe, and at its centre is the Heavenly Pool and T'ai Chi.

Sites are subject to location within a natural hierarchy, with strong emphasis on the political centre:

> Centralization is the principle upon which the Chinese empire was organized and it was as its centre but not as its top the emperor was equated with the T'ai Chi. In a classification where the criterion is amount of authority, the structure is, however, definitely a hierarchy with the emperor as top. The structure of the natural universe must be distinguished from both the supernatural hierarchy and the social, on the two counts that it is not articulated either by authority or by Confucian ethics. As a convenient over-simplification we may say that the natural structure is a conception of the way power is distributed from a central source, as opposed to the way authority is delegated from a source above. (Ibid.: 241)

These suggestions are supportive of my overall argument and are pursued later on. If by means of fengshui people express self-identification as individuals or as social groups and if this self-identification involves the establishment of small ego-centred universes, fengshui in this way may engage in a dialogue with the moralizing political centre. Social hierarchies are contested as the natural, supernatural and social classifications may contain different statements about the position of the individual. The last element of Feuchtwang's interpretations also tends to support this approach. He sees fengshui as a way to perceive or conceive reality, but also as a way of dealing with this reality, that is an activist approach to this world. Fengshui operates like a cosmological model, applied to reality to serve specific interests. Having previously accounted for fengshui symbolism, which is a discourse with language as the analytical model, and combining this with the natural cosmological model composition contained in fengshui, Feuchtwang sees these two closely linked in a simple scheme of a model, 'its application or exposition progressively more embodied, first in the physical environment and then in social fortunes' (ibid.: 249–250). Thus the same model is used to explain two fields of reality, the natural and the social; in the first it is used as an ideal reconstruction and explanation of the natural environment; in the second, the physical environment of the site is extended as a model for the analysis of social fortune. Yet since fengshui metaphysics is a self-defining set of concepts, it is not open to contradiction or to being checked with reality – thus geomancers always have a line of escape. Since it is flexible and lacks strict logic, any one part of the metaphysics may be applied in the analysis of a social situation and, in the case of a conflict between its principles, fengshui can be used to express both the conflict and its resolution. Nevertheless, the metaphysics constitute an explanation of natural processes that could be believed explicitly by all Chinese.

As a model, fengshui is perhaps best perceived as an explanatory device that functions as an analogue theoretical model (in contrast to an existential theoretical model), which allows for the widest variety of content and a great scope of interpretation. It furnishes plausible hypotheses, not proofs. Since it is analogical, one of its essential instruments is the metaphor: the physical environment and theories about it are used as metaphors for the fortunes of people. It involves a number of cliche images, such as the Green Dragon and the White Tiger, which altogether become something like an archetype: 'an understood field of reference which provides the imagery for describing the original unknown field for investigation' (ibid.: 253). As an archetype it tends to become a self-certifying myth as those aspects of the analogy that are rich in implication will last and have a following. In the course of centuries of metaphysical speculation these aspects, or root metaphors, become 'mythologized', they become 'clichés in the stock of proverbial knowledge which constitutes the metaphoric system by which life is described' (ibid.: 254).

Other anthropologists have accounted for Chinese fengshui in a less thorough manner, mainly as an aspect of fieldwork with other foci (for instance Baker 1965). Several examples of anthropologists treating fengshui in terms of its possible ecological regulatory function are given in Chapter 7. Furthermore, a number of anthropologists have dealt with fengshui in Taiwan, notably Emily Ahern, David Jordan, Robert P. Weller and Steven Sangren. Since Taiwan lies outside the scope of this work, both geographically and thematically, I shall not dwell on this case. Fengshui and similar traditions are prominent in China, Taiwan, Japan, Korea and Vietnam, and material from the entire region would provide an exciting basis for comparative studies.

More recently, Rubie Watson has showed in an interesting paper how residents in the New Territories of Hong Kong use fengshui as a framework for expressing local identities with a number of specified groups struggling over the right to define and maintain such identities (Watson 1995). Here fengshui has a privileged status as a vocabulary or mode of explanation offering both a critique of and a remedy for environmental ills. Although Watson primarily interprets rural fengshui as a means of harmonizing with the physical environment, she still admits it has mystic, cosmological, asocial, technical, and individualistic strands. But concluding largely in line with my own argument, she notes that people in the setting of today live multiple lives that defy easy categorizations: 'The anthropologist can only hope to understand let alone represent or translate these complexities by grounding her or his work in the lives of these people' (ibid.: 25).

Summing up, anthropological contributions to the study of fengshui in China have been sporadic and often lacking in depth. For decades Maurice Freedman's essays have stood unchallenged as the authoritative anthropological interpretation of the matter, with Feuchtwang's work as a second generation exploration, and many later professionals have perhaps felt that there was little more to say. It is a fascinating fact, however, that despite the very limited professional anthropological attention paid to fengshui, scores of anthropology students around the world have continued to write essays on the topic. How can this be? I suggest that the answer is to be found in a combination of an absolutist bias and an inappropriate methodology for the study of popular traditions.

METHODOLOGICAL OBSTACLES

For centuries we have mirrored ourselves in strange and exotic cultures. But in our search for authentic otherness we have attempted to distil the authentic culture from the complex concoction of contemporary life we observed. We identified or perhaps invented a clash between 'traditional' and 'modern' cultural forms. Anthropologists have continually sterilized their material to extract culture pure and unspoiled.[11] For decades, anthropology's major thrust was in the interpretation of small-scale societies and relatively small-scale issues. Alleged Western influence and 'modernity' as recent factors modifying otherwise traditional societies far too easily become a shield for static analyses: they provide the uncertain element that the anthropologist can always point to when his constructed still-picture of a fieldwork area cannot hold.

Moreover, it has been argued that anthropology in general has only had limited insights to offer in the analysis of complex civilizations (Barth 1989), particularly those of East Asia. The possible impact of Christianity on social science must be considered: the concept of culture that developed in the early parts of the twentieth century, carrying strong connotations of system, structure, integrity and essence, inadvertently fitted the Christian world view like hand in glove. Many writers have taken up this issue, for instance Anthony Giddens, in relation to the very general quest for 'system' in anthropology. This methodological flaw has had a specific influence on the study of fengshui.

Doing fieldwork in China one is constantly aware of the radically different nature of our own morality and outlook – and also our propensity for systemic unity and universal order. Christianity, in its wealth of denominations and competing interpretations throughout history, insisted on exclusiveness, absolutism and all-pervading truths as common points of reference. Closely aligned with the Christian monotheistic rationalism was a strong urge for intellectual persistency and integrity of mind. Although religious dogmatism has subsided and exclusionism has generally been replaced by religious pluralism, inherent notions concerning the conscious integrity of the individual are apparently still penetrating science, politics, religion and the arts: one should not waver in the faith – or at least not let it be shown. These are of course truisms – some would say impermissible generalizations – yet their significance in cross-cultural comparison remains. From an external perspective, the Western world may still seem religious in intention, despite being secular in essence.[12]

Modern anthropology has struggled to distance itself from essentialist definitions of culture, which immersed individuals in a uniform culture, but which also in the broader sense implied seeing

18

man and ideology as linked together in a firm and intimate relationship – in a sort of moral order. Yet these premises still tend to influence our perception of the individual's relationship to religion, politics and identity.

In the case of Chinese religion, the empirical multiplicity was incorporated into constructed concepts such as Confucian rationalism, a religious system of radical world optimism (Max Weber), the Chinese religion (Marcel Granet), great and little traditions (Robert Redfield), Chinese religion as a whole (C.K. Yang), a Chinese religious system (Maurice Freedman), a Chinese popular religion, and so forth, all approaches that attempted to extract an essence from or to find a unifying design in the cultural stock encountered. Although these learned works mostly distinguished between textual and practised forms of religion, a certain reductionism was tempting. Why is systemic pluralism so inconceivable as a principle in itself – is this another spill-over from monotheism? Worse are the countless popular works on Chinese philosophy, religion and geomancy, seeing in them simple techniques to be followed.

At the root of this search for unity and systematics in other cultures was the excessively secularized universe of anthropology, which retained a mechanical type of causality far beyond the demands of science.[13] This is obviously a caricature of the discipline, since anthropologists have also been aware of the existence of alternative explanatory systems, for instance in the form of magic or witchcraft. Further, a large body of literature recognizes the composite nature of religion in non-Western civilizations, for instance the duality between a supreme being and lesser gods in African religion, the 'syncretism' conjectured for Southeast Asian religion, the preservation of various *jin* and acts of possession in Islam, the competition between world religions in India and the historical coexistence of the Three Learnings in China.

Within the last couple of decades, a more composite conception of culture has resulted in studies of Chinese religion recognizing how both differences and unities are constantly generated as intrinsic to the dynamics of culture. Furthermore, the holism of culture is neither seen as a shared level of social interaction nor as a diffused set of normative ideas, therefore not representing a single ideology or a shared group identity. Instead, culture is described as the relationship of the parts to the whole, a relationship which produces meanings and constructs communities and their history. This is what Catherine Bell has outlined as the 'third stage' position in the study of Chinese religion – as opposed to a first stage of distinction between elite and folk religion and a second stage focusing on popular religion as a medium of diffusion of values and practices among all classes and thus providing a basis for unity below distinctive forms (Maurice Freedman was a prominent example of a second stage position). Rejecting a priori bifurcations of religion as well as synthetic entities mediating between them, this approach does not look at religion and religious institutions in isolation, but see in them symbols, rituals and practices in which the dynamics of culture are played out (Bell 1989: 42–43).

Yet, to my mind, the systemic propensity in our common apprehension of the culture–religion complex continues to be an obstacle to our sensitivity to coexisting forms of knowledge, reason and religious thought. We must go further than just recognizing religion as a fully embedded 'cultural system' (ibid.: 43), particularly when studying the great Asian civilizations, where a persistent social and political complexity is further entangled by elements of nationalism, globalism, migration and diaspora in recent history. In any fieldwork situation, our informants are seen to engage in a complex of 'multiple lives' that defies easy categorization. In the words of Rubie Watson, 'Anthropologists must learn to reinvent the parameters of fieldwork just as people are reinventing their lives ... East Asia challenges the anthropologists to think creatively' (Watson 1995: 25).

THE EAST ASIAN CHALLENGE

The East Asian challenge to anthropology is anything but new and in an odd way surprisingly parallel to East Asia's challenge to nineteenth century Western civilizing efforts and missionary work. Centuries of cultural encounter in trade, missionary work and diplomacy brought severe epistemological problems to its Western participants. A fundamental relativism and adherence to complementarity and religious pluralism on the part of the Chinese has continually bewildered us. For instance, the controversy about how to deal with Chinese converts' attempts to merge Christianity with ancestor worship was deadlocked into the so-called Rites Controversy, which lingered for 300 years (Mungello 1994). Similarly, in missionary literature a debate over the correct translation of the concept of God dragged on for just as long, never reconciling the Protestant concept of *Shangdi*, the Catholic *Tianzhu*, the Moslem *Zhenzhu*, the Buddhist *Fo* and the Taoist *Shenxian*, just to mention a few of the terms in circulation (*CNA* 17 December 1965: 4). From the time of Matteo Ricci (1552–1619) the absence of transcendent and eternal truths among the Chinese had bewildered missionaries (Gernet 1985: Chapter 2). The vague Chinese distinction between the status of various forms of learning is well captured in the old story about the missionary who found himself utterly perplexed when asking a Chinese about which of the three old systems of learning was true and receiving the answer that they all were. But this is far more than an anecdote and acutely relevant to a diversity of situations across Asia – without imputing any sort of unity into this massive continent. A young Indian student of mine told a story of a more recent encounter between individuals seemingly worlds apart. As a student in India he was working as an interpreter for a European missionary. Once the missionary was visiting a common peasant family and attempted vigorously to explain the concept of God to the head of the household. At first the peasant showed no sign of understanding, whereupon the imaginative student changed to another translation of the term 'God'. Then it slowly dawned upon the peasant and finally he nodded approvingly: 'Oh, but don't you have a picture of him so I can stick him on the wall together with the other ones'. On the wall were pictures of Gandhi, Nehru, Hindu goddesses, Buddhist warrior-gods and Hollywood film stars.

Chinese village life has embraced this position for centuries. Consider, for instance, C.K. Yang's description of worship in a south Chinese village, characteristic of a polytheistic tradition: '[T]he worshippers had no permanent or exclusive connection with any single temple or priest, but visited temples or priests of different faiths as personal occasions demanded' (Yang 1959: 193). Chinese religion encompasses all the possibilities of the totality of religious life and experience. This is a crucial point in preparing for a fuller understanding of Chinese fengshui as of any other aspect of cosmology and religion.

The missionary literature, which we shall return to in Chapters 2 and 3, is in fact highly instructive in spite of its obvious devotional inclination. The old reverends were for the most part honest men, who continuously published and debated the problems of their task. An early observation, which ought to be known by all scholars in the field, was that the Chinese language did not include a general term for 'religion', which the missionaries took for proof of the ungodly nature of the Chinese civilization. Until the late nineteenth century, Confucianism, Buddhism and Taoism were together called the Three Learnings and the unwitting translation of them as the Three Religions in Western languages had caused many controversies with Chinese scholars. It was only under Western and Japanese influence that the concept of *zongjiao* was adopted in the late Qing reform era (Paper 1994). If we link the historical observation of the missing concept of religion with the view of many anthropologists with intimate knowledge of the field (particularly prominent among early Chinese anthropologists) that Chinese religion is not about 'faith', we arrive at the core of the problem: how can we have religion if there is no faith? It is of course a moderating factor that the established Chinese religions have had their own professionals in the form of monks, nuns, priests, scholars and so forth, all of whom may have had a stronger devotional life than the average person. A lesson that remains, however, is that any study of Chinese 'religion' must consider the questions of belief and devotion as integral parts of its premises – I shall return to these questions in the fieldwork chapters. There is certainly a point here in stressing the impact of anthropological authority itself unjustly assuming or creating homogeneity in the re-presentation of culture.

At the same time, modern anthropology has been the antithesis to Christian missionary work. While the mission used the Christian God to moralize among men in the non-Western world, anthropology, by means of the sacred concept of culture, exploited material from the outer world to moralize among ourselves. Their synthesis, so to speak, is a universal compulsion towards systemic integrity, operating at the level of the mind as well as of society as a whole – and perhaps the Western constructions of both God and Culture failed for the same reasons in the East Asian context.

UNDERSTANDING COMPOSITE CULTURAL SCHEMES

We need a new approach that allows us to look more closely into why and how individuals use diverse traditions to interpret common life events and social acts as they unfold in the local society. Common to much of the recent anthropological work with differentiating identities, positions and cultural orientations within a given community is the acknowledgement that culture can hardly be studied as a single entity, homogeneous and uniform. Renato Rosaldo (1989) pointed out that in the multiplicity that characterizes our lives, each view is necessarily positioned, without a unifying 'truth'. Yet we should not stop at this exploded view.

A field of studies which has contributed to our rising awareness of the composite character of culture is that of self and cultural identity. The classical view of Western selves as autonomous, integrated 'entities, 'pristine unities', set against both social and natural backgrounds,[14] was until quite recently a prominent tenet in anthropology. Also derived from classical theory was the distinction between Western and Other selves, the latter appearing divisible, relational, multiple and contextual. From Emile Durkheim, Marcel Mauss, Max Weber, Karl Marx and others came the envisioning of non-Western nations as becoming increasingly like us as they were swept into revolutionizing capitalism and modernization. But whereas classical theory induced us to believe in the necessity of homogenizing human culture, we are today realizing a counter-current of proliferating difference (Marcus and Fisher 1986). Rita Smith Kipp, writing about an Indonesian community, notes that what we commonly see as social change expressed in the identities of people, is in fact more due to a change in our own theoretical conceptions allowing us to see dissociation (Kipp 1996: 10). Another classic endeavour has been the contrasting of Asian and Western selves, in which writers on both sides have participated with great passion.[15] Asian individuals as collectively and communally committed as opposed to the Western individualism is a view that is now often promoted by various Asian elites in the form of 'Asian values' as a counter-current to democracy and human rights (Jacobsen and Bruun 1999).

There is a close parallel in the study of selves and the increased attention to the actor, including the meaning of social acts in their cultural context. For the actor approach really to produce new insight into a specific field such as fengshui it is necessary to reflect on some of the basic sociological concepts. In fact much of the recent actor-oriented anthropology, from Anthony Giddens to Fredrik Barth to Pierre Bourdieu and so forth, makes us far better prepared for analysing Chinese social reality than was the case with functional or structuralist approaches. In particular, the modern readings of the inherited sociological concepts of time–space, structure, system, knowledge and agency have come a long way to meet the requirements of China scholars. Look, for instance, at the definitions provided by the master of timely eloquence, Anthony Giddens, of these critical terms. Giddens' theory of human agency (Giddens 1994) includes assumptions on the acting subject as well as on the situation of action in time and space as a continuous flow of conduct. A stratification of human consciousness into the unconscious, practical consciousness and discursive consciousness, with special emphasis on the practical consciousness, supports his main idea that 'every social actor knows a great deal about the conditions of reproduction of the society of which he or she is a member' (ibid.: 5). While simple enough

23

as a critique of functionalism and structuralism, it has potentially much greater impact on our analyses of social 'systems' as well as on the relationship between object and subject. A basic premise for this line of thinking is, again in all its simplicity, that individuals, not society, are carriers of reason: 'Social systems have no purposes, reason or needs whatsoever; only human individuals do so. Any explanation of social reproduction which imputes teleology to social systems must be declared invalid' (ibid.: 7).

The question of structure can accordingly be resolved by pointing to a central duality replacing those of individual versus society and conscious versus unconscious modes of cognition. By duality of structure is meant the essential 'recursiveness' of social life, as constituted in social practices: 'Structure is both medium and outcome of the reproduction of practices. Structure enters simultaneously into the constitution of the agent and social practices, and 'exists' in the generating moment of this constitution' (ibid.: 5). Though seeing structure as non-spatial and non-temporal, being simply an aspect of practice, and postulating the interdependence of action and structure, the question of time–space is nevertheless crucial. Contrary to common social theory which tends to repress time, Giddens points to the importance for a theory of agency of grasping the time–space relations inherent in the constitution of all social interaction: 'Our life passes in transformation' (ibid.: 3). He is inspired by Martin Heidegger's treatment of being in time and its echoes in William James: 'The literally present moment is a purely verbal supposition, not a position; the only present ever realized concretely is the 'passing moment' in which the dying rearward of time and its dawning future forever mix their lights.' (ibid.: 3). We here get a sense of a holistic trend in anthropology that even has faint echoes of Taoism. But what Giddens brings back to anthropology is perhaps a strand of organismic philosophy from Heidegger and Wittgenstein that steadily conveyed a certain awareness of, or even inspiration from, Chinese thought. This perception of time is crucial for an actor-oriented approach: people act exactly with a view to participating in the relentless passing of the moment and benefiting from acting to change things or to control change. Any action stretches across a span of time, within which things have already changed, even without the active participation of the actor. Chinese popular ideology, which is highly activist is outlook, would not make sense without appreciating the uniqueness of the moment and the aspect of eternal cosmological change – clearly analogous to relentless social change.

Another debate essential for this study relates to the old anthropological distinction between magic, science and religion and to a derived distinction between knowledge and belief. Stanley J. Tambiah (1990) has brilliantly pointed out how problematic it is to accept these heavily charged and historically distinct Western categories as meaningful domains in all societies. In Chapters 2 and 7 we shall see that the phenomenon of Chinese fengshui has in fact been categorized as pertaining to all three during the relatively short period of Western attention to the subject. Further to this rising awareness, and much influenced by Rodney Needham's (1972) criticism of our habitual way of disregarding native systems of thought as 'belief' as opposed to our own scientific knowledge, many writers have pointed out that the conception of knowledge is a more pertinent concept than that of 'belief', presently also a very popular notion in medical anthropology as well as in the rising field of local and indigenous knowledge. That this concept is felt to be relevant in anthropology, while being totally inadmissible in theology, induces us once again to consider distinctions between monotheistic and polytheistic, or religious and atheist conceptions.

It will be shown in the fieldwork chapters that the concept of belief in relation to fengshui is indeed misleading, partly for generic reasons and partly because the concept has become immersed in political discourse: belief in 'superstition' is defiance of the Chinese state.

'SYSTEM', KNOWLEDGE AND TRADITION

Many concepts in conventional anthropological use, such as culture, society, modernity and complexity, are embedded in notions of shared knowledge, values and cognition, which make up a meaningful pattern – a system. The common understanding of a system tends to imply either a conscious construction that ensures the harmonious operation of certain functions or a method of structuring certain aspects of the world that is shared by a group of people. Fengshui may, of course, be subject to theorizing in terms of a system, but as will be shown such methodology induces us to ask the wrong questions: whether this system is sustained consciously or unconsciously, it would require a separate description of its origin, purpose, function, dynamism and so forth – the system itself assumes the role of an agent instead of being an ongoing cultural construction. We would focus on how the system represents the culture as a whole rather than on how individuals and population segments use fragments of a whole in particular contexts.

Most importantly, however, to use the term 'system' for any aspect of ideology would make us believe that there is only one such system in this particular sphere of culture: one social system, one kinship system, one political system, one religion and almost by implication, one culture. Real people in living communities act discordantly: they argue, debate, struggle, weigh and evaluate among themselves, express uncertainty and scepticism, manipulate kinship, claim allegiance to this or that vision of life until further notice, link ideology to their current purposes and interests and make strategic alliances. This does not happen in a state of anarchy but is carried out within a repertoire of meaningful patterns of speech, debate, consideration and action. This is obviously a defence for the deliberating mind as a common virtue of any human being and the basis of any society. Human actors not only embrace differentiation, they also produce it in order to try out intellectual possibilities, which with some caution may be described as 'archetypical'. People divide the world into orderly segments of sex, association, morality and persuasion in outer appearances, but tend to embrace the entire repertoire in their hearts. Is not this exactly the case in complex civilizations, one could ask. Such a repertoire is presumably greater under some social conditions than others, but it abides as a spontaneously generated fact of human society.

The above does not mean that all individuals will act as village philosophers, but rather it emphasizes that a fairly large intellectual repertoire is ever present in a local community and a customary ingredient in everyday interaction. As such, people make use of distinct lines of reasoning, drawing on, for instance, local knowledge, vocational experience, proverbs, natural metaphors, world religion, state propaganda and global learning. There are personal preferences and dominant traditions at any given time, but seldom an intimate relationship between a person and a specific tradition. It has become habitual in anthropology to account for such practice under the heading of cultural complexity. Needless to say, real culture *is* complexity: 'it is ubiquitous in the analysis of any social reality rather than a phenomenon that has emerged recently' (Friedman 1997: 269). Despite his functionalist persuasion Maurice Freedman, when writing about 'Chinese religion as a whole', seemed well aware of this issue when he stated that 'to use the word system systematically would be to run the risk of imposing an order on it which it manifestly does not have' (Freedman 1979: 352).

As a replacement for system to denote an assembly of imaginative human thought and knowledge as contained in fengshui, 'tradition' tends to be a better approximation. It is less formalistic and more alive, differentiated and localized. Traditions are something humans constantly produce and reproduce; particularly after the works of Benedict Anderson, Eric Hobsbawn, Edward Bruner and many others we have sharpened our awareness of constant historic reappropriation, if not invention, in this field. Thus tradition in this sense denotes a body of cultural stock, containing, for instance, information, knowledge and customs, that is carried by population segments and potentially conveyed from one generation to the next.

Using the term 'tradition of knowledge', as does Fredrik Barth, raises another issue. Some new meanings of knowledge have appeared in anthropology as well as in religious and environmental studies.[16] References to local, indigenous, folk, traditional, environmental and other knowledges have become commonplace, and in many cases knowledge has replaced belief as the identified object of study. Changing the terms in this way is obviously done in order to stress the conscious role of the actor – as opposed to an account of his passive beliefs – and to open for a new understanding of the contextuality in the relationships between actor and currents of thought. These diverse types of knowledge just mentioned are often used interchangeably, to the effect that in their meanings there may be recognized a 'shared inter-subjective understanding', as put by Roy Ellen (2001: 3). In many ways fengshui fits into the broad characterization of these types of knowledge provided by Ellen, that it is local, usually orally transmitted, a consequence of practical engagement in everyday life, fluid, fragmentarily distributed, functionally organized and situated within broader cultural traditions (ibid.: 5–7). Yet we must keep a distance. Many studies concerned with local knowledges recognize their rational outlook and practical applicability, although some convey naive views of native wisdom. Our purpose is not to test the truth or usefulness of fengshui in scientific terms, but to investigate its broad social implications. Also, most accounts of local knowledge presuppose a dualism between native and scientific knowledge or between local and global systems as an outcome of modernization. As Edward Said has pointed out, we tend to forget that the distinction between local and global could have been applied almost at any time during the last two to five hundred years (Said 1993), and in the Chinese context the opposition between local and central is perennial. These distinctions tend to carry traces of dualism, essentialism and spacial metaphor, which may not be ascertained empirically (Fardon 1995: 2).

COEXISTING TRADITIONS AND MODES OF THOUGHT

The background for the present work is a conviction born out of reflexive anthropology that we cannot represent culture as, in the words of James Clifford and George Marcus, a 'unified corpus of symbols and meanings that can be definitely interpreted' (Clifford and Marcus 1986: 19). A pattern of reflexivity emerged to bring the discipline away from the 'pseudo-objectivist stance of naive empiricism'. This essentially means constantly questioning our categories of thought and treating ourselves as objects of study on a par with the people of our fieldwork areas, realizing that 'the construction of knowledge means building a bridge from two ends at once and calculating hopefully that the parts will meet in the middle' (Strathern A. 1993: 153).

There are several consequences of this stance. First, instead of depicting unified culture we must identify which bodies of thought and knowledge are actually seen to exist in the fieldwork area, that is to identify certain cohesive traditions. Second, we should look closer into their coexistence: are they really arbitrarily represented in the local community or are there meaningful cultural patterns or models in how they divide and perceive the world, that is, do they represent alternative or complementary modes of thought?

Concerning the theme of coexisting traditions, Fredrik Barth has offered some interesting insights. His concept of 'traditions of knowledge'[17] is obviously an explicit criticism of an inherited localizing and totalizing perception of culture in anthropology. Barth's position is particularly developed in 'Balinese Worlds' (1993: Chapter 10), where he most forcefully argues for a shift away from the metaphor of society as a system of articulated parts and towards focusing on relatively disordered processes of reality construction, centred on individual people – quite similar to Giddens' rejection of society's innate meaningfulness.

Barth's analytical starting point is Max Weber's distinction between 'event' and 'act' and the common assertion phrased by Weber, among others, that 'meaning is something conferred on an object or an event by a person, not something enshrined in that object or event – that is, it arises in the act of interpretation' (ibid.: 170). Barth strongly objects to the way 'meaning' is implanted in culture in the works of many early anthropologists, who tended to totalize and localize culture in a specific setting. He criticizes what he calls their basic ontological premise of a supposed congruence between the formal rules of social institutions, the observed patterns of behaviour, and the purposes and priorities of the actors, i.e. their consciousness. In other words, he opposes the simple-systems approach to culture, where minds, language, acts and institutions are seen to merge into a cultural whole.

Barth further argues that there is no way the anthropologist can frame a unit of study in terms of a determined locality, community or society and yet capture the full set of connections that constitute social acts. Therefore a major task is to account for how acts are placed in particular contexts, frameworks, or worlds in which people themselves embed those acts through their interpretations. An assortment of modern anthropologists have argued that the relevant connections for understanding the meaning of social acts do not necessarily have a form as a localized 'community', but instead form 'delocalized' culture. Barth has moved in the opposite direction by seeking to identify the separate cultural streams that are played out in a given setting:

> Most culture – knowledge, values, skills, and orientations – is embedded more specifically in a particular context of related ideas, a tradition of knowledge: ideas cluster and are tied to a set of social relations, a circle: and syndromes of them are learned and largely exercised in a particular pattern of activity, a practice ... To grasp these connections, we need a framework that allows for more complexity and specificity. (Ibid.: 172)

Barth points to possible determinants, which he describes as 'cultural stock' of knowledge, concepts and values (ibid.: 159). Apart from the obvious fact that such cultural stock is individually constituted and necessarily continuously developed and modified, Barth's argument is that they cluster around specific historical traditions or streams, which in themselves constitute internal discourses and distributions of knowledge and authority, but which nevertheless may be distinguished and named.[18] Barth's explicit aim is, of course, to put the anthropological analysis of complex civilizations on a better footing.

Another consequence of this approach, which is less conspicuous at first sight, is a sharpened scepticism towards a society's self-depiction – particularly where harmony and communality are stressed as the society's virtues and social institutions are defined as working in support of these – a disjunction between cooperative institutions and divisive factionalism: 'formal organization is not *what* is happening' (ibid.: 160). Although this statement is developed specifically in opposition to the accounts of Balinese culture by Belo, Mead, Bateson and Geertz, pursuing it categorically is potentially controversial in anthropology: what right do we have to interpret what our informants say, think and feel? Bearing in mind the current criticism of the way anthropological text is created and the challenged authority of located anthropological fieldwork, we must be aware of the limits to our analyses.

Seeing events and acts as rooted in specified traditions of knowledge is nevertheless useful in the case of Chinese rural society, but we need to further analyse and specify their correlation in local life. Even though at a macrolevel they may form an open competitive field, they are certainly not to be seen, as one critic of Barth has mocked, as 'a supermarket of ideas for the Balinese consumer in pursuit of what is consonant with his experience' (Valeri 1997: 825–826). These traditions cannot be fully understood apart from the social organization that reproduces them through the socialization process and one should not, of course, ignore asymmetries of power among them.

Traditions coexist, and manifestly continue to do so over a considerable period of time, invalidating simple classifications of societies. Instead, we should focus on the complex interplay between dominant and subordinate ideologies – not in crucial historical instances of change and not at the level of society as a whole, but in the continuous interaction between local and extra-local currents and with the conscious participation of the individual. We are back to the basic premise, that seeing individual and ideology linked in an intimate and exclusive relationship is a questionable ideal, rather a fraud.

Almost anywhere, certain traditions attain dominant positions at the expense of others. State power may attempt to reduce heterogeneity, to the effect that a limited number of traditions remain active, conceivably in antagonistic relations. There is a great likelihood that the fewer traditions that remain, the more antagonistic their mutual relations will be, because they acquire greater weight and intensity and cover a wider ideological span. Particularly when local and national elites appropriate and actively support a specific representation of the world and use law, sanctions or physical force to eradicate other representations, some kind of reaction by means of stronger emphasis on an opposing representation is almost inevitable. Conversely, dominant traditions of knowledge are in themselves tools for establishing powerful positions in the local community by drawing on external forces, authority, public sanctions and so forth; in our

Chinese context all directly or indirectly derive from state power. In the wider context, there is a close correlation between elite culture and the means of dominating the public representation of cultural matter, morality, religion and so forth.

In any real-life community, however, fieldwork will immediately reveal the complexity of ideology and reason. Power has many facets and can be exercised along many paths, allowing for a multiplicity of parallel hierarchies. Within one domain a village geomancer may rule, in another the successful entrepreneur, in a third the Communist party secretary, and so forth. Furthermore, although one particular tradition, namely that of the state ideology, may formally rule at the levels of politics and public administration, it is substantially modified, questioned or even opposed at the ground level of individuals manning the structure. We are back to the main argument, that I do not for a moment believe that any single strand of reasoning will ever achieve a genuine dominance, apart from pro forma expressions of compliance, sanctioned by convention and fear of reprisal.

With regard to coexisting modes of thought, David Olson, in the introduction to a book on the subject, argues that the possibility of pluralism in cognition offers an obvious but puzzling notion, considering the ultimate 'psychic unity of mankind' (Olson and Torrence 1996: 1). He argues against a single exclusive way of knowing and for a diversified perception of thought and knowledge, with different modes of thought corresponding to discourses or genres. Such local 'domain-specific contextualized knowledge, which is interpretive in nature and socially or collaboratively constructed' (ibid.: 3), fits well with the role that fengshui is observed to have in the fieldwork areas. Instead of attempting to reconcile traditional and modern forms of knowledge, such as attempted by Robin Horton and Ruth Finnegan in the rationality debate some decades ago (Horton and Finnegan 1973), we are moving towards identifying separate cultural domains or even realities, compelling us to sort out the relations among them and the conditions for their formation in relation to a dominant modernist rationality. Bradd Shore has viewed these trends as an unfolding cognitive revolution, where cultural models, as socially mediated forms of knowledge, are an essential characteristic not only of human social life, but also of human nervous system functioning (Shore 1996: 11) – a theme which is likely to attract much more attention in the future.

31

Despite the death sentence that has recurrently been given to Chinese fengshui by Western scholars, generations of Chinese intellectuals and the entire Chinese Communist partystate since 1949, it is still alive and flourishing in the Chinese countryside and even making a slow comeback in the cities. Also calling for attention is the derivate Oriental wisdom–form of fengshui now widely practised in North American and European cities – we shall see how this has come about in Chapter 7. Instead of pinning our identities either on the dominant line of reasoning that any society obviously conveys, not least because of its dominant strata of professionals setting the terms for public expression, or on alternative gospels competing with mainstream thought, we should pay more attention to the inevitability of diverse currents of thought. Their coexistence need not be systemic, nor arbitrary, but continual products of deliberate acts of identification, driven by mankind's restless intellect. Particularly in the Chinese context, cultural traditions tend not to divide individuals into permanent categories and attach to them exclusive ideologies. Jack Potter hinted at the implications when he accounted for Chinese folk religion as only one out of three possible explanatory systems at work (the others deriving from Confucianism and Buddhism):

> Most cultures are a complex of different cognitive models that interrelate in complex fashion and are often mutually contradictory. The contradictions in Cantonese culture are no more inconsistent than the Calvinist ethic which held that the only way one could know whether he was among the saved was his success in doing God's will in his calling on earth. (Potter 1970: 152)

NOTES

1 *Notes and Queries* was a monthly journal published by the China Mail Office in Hong Kong from 1867 to serve the foreign community.

2 While de Groot sees the learned form of fengshui as 'cobwebs of absurd speculation, hardly worthy of study', he describes common fengshui as a practical art, 'its theories, as expounded in the books, are seldom taken notice of, even by the most distinguished professors' (1897: 938).

3 Since 'ancient times' the cock has been used as a demon-expeller (de Groot 1897: 965).

4 For a fuller examination of the compass, see Feuchtwang 1974; Weller 1987: 177–184; de Groot 1897: 959–975.

5 The distinction between the 'Forms' and 'Orientations' schools of fengshui is discussed in the Appendix. A number of terms for the two schools are discussed in Stephen Skinner 1982: 7–10. Another distinction used is *San He* and *San Yuan*, each with their own compass, discussed in Weller 1987: 177–184.

6   The two schools may use different compasses (Weller 1987: 178).

7   Bell 1989; Teiser 1995; Shahar and Weller 1996; Dean 1998.

8   For a specific critique of these points, see Feuchtwang 1992: 13–16.

9   A thorough criticism is presented in de Bary 1975: 1–37.

10 Two important examples are H. Maspero (cited in Smith H. 1968: 172), and Yang C. (1959: 193).

11 For instance, Bronislaw Malinowski (1935: 480) admitted to having idealized his description of the Trobriands, eliminating considerable European influence.

12 An interesting discussion of religious pluralism in the West as seen from an Islamic perspective is provided by Aslan 1998.

13 One reminder is provided by Murphy 1980: 43–44.

14 For a discussion, see Kipp 1996: 7–10.

15 A highly original exposition of this view was developed by Francis Hsu (1971).

16 A commonly cited meaning of knowledge, that it has 'the capacity to change perceptions', is provided by Marilyn Strathern 1995.

17 The concept of 'traditions of knowledge' is really an approximation to the Scandinavian term 'kunnskabs-tradition' (the word 'kunnskab' bridges knowledge and proficiency), which Barth has expressed is closer to what he has in mind.

18 In his specific Balinese study Barth identifies as the major traditions of knowledge the great religions of Hinduism and Islam, the modern current transmitted by education, mass media, nation-building, the traditions of the old kingdoms including ideas of rank, cast and authority, and lastly a tradition of knowledge modelling social life on a sorcery-based view of agency and responsibility.

2 *Fengshui Practices and Policies, 1850–1949*

A number of confluent factors in Chinese history relatively unrelated to colonialism account for the growing significance that we may attribute to popular cosmology in the Qing dynasty (1644–1911), particularly the divinatory practices. First of all, in the long-term perspective divination lost some of its political functions after the Song dynasty (960–1279), and increasingly became a private practice during the Yuan (1271–1368) and Ming (1368–1644) dynasties. It was privatized in a double sense: while it became open to individuals growing numbers of private diviners served the public as a means of subsistence. The Qing heterodoxy and anti-rebellion law bears witness to the intense state vigilance against popular divination and derived forms of 'deluding the people'. Second, the destitution of increasingly large parts of the peasantry, particularly during the course of the Qing period, is a factor of intrinsic importance to the role that folk-religious practices may have played in local communities and to the number of rural specialists attempting to extract a living from such practices. Yet we must be aware that the relationship between poverty and beliefs in supernatural forces is a complex one. Third, and intimately connected with these other trends, was a sharply rising number of rebellions in the Qing, met with increasingly intolerant state power. While military operations in the early part of the dynasty were targeted at non-Chinese peoples, after the middle of the eighteenth century they were turned against internal religious rebellions. During this period nearly all rebellions had religious gathering points and most were staged by blacklisted sectarian organizations with religious emblems (Yang C.K. 1970: 207, 219). Much evidence points to divination becoming increasingly powerful in late imperial China, particularly during the Qing. A massive Qing encyclopedia from 1726 devotes over 2,000 pages to fortune-tellers and mantic techniques,[1] while another index is Yuan Shushan's monumental *Biographies of Diviners*,[2] of which about one-third are from the Qing period. Western sojourners constantly commented on the prevalence of divination in the Qing. Despite their hostility to all kinds of 'superstition' and possible exaggeration of the situation to justify their civilizing mission, the general picture may hold. Richard J. Smith concludes, 'where evidence exists from the Chinese side, whether in the form of official documents, letters, anecdotes, proverbs, popular fiction, or scholarly indictments of fortune-telling, it almost invariably confirms the accuracy of Western accounts' (Smith R. 1991: 6). Taken together, Chinese and Western sources indicate that divination was a social phenomenon of extraordinary importance.

The present chapter is concerned with historical change and its aims are twofold. One is to trace how the Western view of fengshui has changed radically through modern history, briefly looking at the early period from around 1600, but with an emphasis on the period after 1850. We shall see how Western scholars, missionaries, sojourners, travellers and imperial employees have accounted for fengshui, but also a number of Chinese sources will be consulted, indicating Chinese opinions and sentiments. The other aim is more complex: through these sources we catch glimpses of the changing orientation of the fengshui tradition itself over the historical period covered. I shall assemble these scattered fragments into a larger portrait, pursuing the argument that people's images of the non-rational to a large extent reflect the vital political and social issues of their time: when the overall conditions of life change and new challenges occur, fengshui is among the important means for people to reflect upon everyday experiences, create meaning and attempt to manage the unknown. Yet increasing foreign presence in China and the growing attention that foreigners granted to fengshui through the 1860s is in itself a crucial factor in the formation of fengshui as a critical element of the Chinese national identity in the later part of the colonial era. While the most important conditions for a general growth of popular cosmology were found in the Qing dynasty – despotic state power, attempts to force uniformity and epidemic destitution among the lower classes – the ruling elite retained a sceptical attitude to metaphysical speculation and mostly suppressed it in public. In the later colonial period, however, the Chinese imperial government adopted fengshui as a means of fighting the colonial powers by playing on popular anti-foreign sentiments as well as taking note of the foreign respect for 'native religion'.

THE PERIOD UP TO 1800: LITTLE AWARENESS

When the Portuguese settled in Malacca in 1537 as a result of European seaborne expansion, direct and lasting contacts were established. In the following decades a host of missionaries from all the Roman Catholic countries of Europe flocked along the south China coast to convert the Chinese; as the German missionary and frontier scout Charles Gutzlaff later reported, these eager missionaries included a great variety of characters (1833: 318). It is illustrative, however, that Gutzlaff himself gladly worked as an interpreter on British opium boats in the 1830s, handing out religious tracts on one side of the boat while opium went out over the other (Fairbank 1969: 70). Surely the most able agents of the West were the Jesuits, deliberately schooled in the revolutionizing disciplines of mathematics, physics, and astronomy in order to penetrate a civilization obsessed with celestial analogies (Bernard 1935: Chapter 2). When they gained a foothold and established their missions in south China in the late sixteenth century, a long encounter between contesting cosmologies was initiated: an intolerant monotheism occupied with issues of absolute faith, although in practice showing a wealth of denominations, was confronted with a pragmatic state cult worshipping heaven, although simultaneously engaged in a holy battle against all spiritual deviation.

When the governor of Zhaoqing near Canton, perhaps just out of curiosity, violated the imperial edict not to introduce foreigners inland and invited the Jesuits in 1583, he was taking a great risk; presumably he mistook them for Buddhist monks (Cameron 1976: 156). Moreover, when he later allotted them a piece of land near the public construction site for a pagoda on which to build their house and chapel, the general populace was intrigued by the Jesuits' appearance and their displayed paintings of Christ and the Virgin Mary, but also doubtful about the effect of their presence. Right from the start there were fengshui-based objections to the Jesuits' settlement, but under the 27-year-long leadership of Matteo Ricci (until 1610) the Jesuits themselves apparently knew little about the true nature of their interference. The committee in charge of the pagoda construction was enraged, since the mission was believed to disturb the meticulously calculated fengshui effect of the pagoda. The committee soon engaged in an open confrontation, in which they were determined both to evict the foreigners and in practice oppose the governor. Ricci and his companion Ruggieri soon had to admit their defeat and move the buildings outside the pagoda limits (Cameron 1976: 154–157).

Ricci's journals reveal that the Jesuits came into contact with countless diviners and other religious practitioners who, according to Ricci, abound everywhere: 'This obnoxious class is a veritable pest in the capital cities and even in the court'. With reference to fengshui, for which he has no term but calls its practitioners 'geologists', he comments:

> Many of their most distinguished men are interested in this recondite science and, when necessary, they are called in for consultation, even from a great distance. This might happen when some public building or monument is to be erected and the machines used for that purpose are to be placed so that public misfortune might be avoided. (Ricci 1953: 84–85)

The Jesuits' intrusiveness and calculating use of the new sciences brought them closer to power than any other Westerners before or after. During several decades leading up to the anti-Christian movement of the Kangxi era (1662–1722) the Jesuits Adam Schall and Ferdinand Verbiest controlled the imperial Directorate of Astro-nomy, where their work brought them into the intricate political games relating to the interpretation of omens and divination. An important incident prior to the anti-Christian movement was the burial of an infant prince in 1658, on which occasion court officials erroneously translated the details of the burial divination into Manchu and thus had the prince buried at the wrong hour. Critics seized this opportunity to attack the Jesuits, both on grounds of the burial and the '*Hong fan* orthodox divination' methods they used. What is of major importance to us, however, is that when the Jesuits seized control over the Directorate they intro-duced modern European astronomy for the sake of precision, but they used it entirely for traditional purposes of divination for the imperial court in order to optimize their political influence (Huang Y. 1991: 1–20). The Jesuits' writings on China continued some of this knowledge in the following century; J.B. du Halde's standard work on China from 1736 devoted one page to 'Fong choui', termed the 'most ridiculous invention' of an otherwise rationally disposed nation (du Halde 1736, vol. 3: 48–49).

1850–70: THE FORMATIVE PERIOD

After Westerners had been expelled from Chinese territory for more than a century leading up to the opium war and little first-hand knowledge of the country thus was available, it was the classical tradition and the ramifications of established society that were in focus. Many Europeans became acquainted with translations of the Confucian classics, from which China stood out as a rational and secular society, whereas popular travel literature presented a contrasting picture of a remote and fabled country. Descriptions of odd Chinese superstitions of everyday life, mostly by missionary writers, appeared in journals and magazines. The self-confidence and chauvinism that bolstered the new industrial-age European identity laid the ground for the contemporary view of China as backward, obscure and inaccessible. Revolutionary writers such as Karl Marx and Friedrich Engels embodied this spirit when depicting China in terms of an 'embalmed mummy at the end of the world'; China had already long been used as a standard against which to measure the Western stature (Hamilton 1985: 187).

The intimate knowledge of Chinese divination that the Jesuits had acquired appeared to be forgotten, although it might have proved advantageous to later colonizers of a Protestant persuasion.[3] Charles Gutzlaff, writing in 1838, described only the established religions of China (Gutzlaff 1833: 299), as did his contemporaries. Those very few individuals who stayed in China long enough to learn the language became aquainted with odd Chinese beliefs. In a careful account of Chinese religion from 1848 Wells Williams[4] mentions how burial places are selected by geomancers according to the 'doctrines of the *fung shwui*, ... as ridiculous a farrago of nonsense, superstition, and craft, as have ever held sway over the human mind in any country or age' (Williams 1848: 264). Other short refences to the use of geomancers or necromancers in funerals are found in contemporary literature on China (for instance Davis, J. 1845; Fortune 1847).

The Chinese Repository was the first missionary journal established in China, exploring every aspect of this new ground for Christendom. During its 20 years of existence (1832–52), fengshui is only mentioned a couple of times in connection with burials and pagodas, mainly with reference to the works of Davis and Fortune (*CR* vol. 6, 1837: 190; vol. 17, 1848: 537; vol. 18, 1849: 372).[5] In the 1837 volume, the editors refer to the superstitions of '*fung-shuy*, fully to elucidate which will require much more information than we can now command.'

Around 1850, in connection with preparations for the burial of the Daoguang emperor (reigned 1821–50), we find another early reference to divination when Gutzlaff describes 'Fung-Shwey' professors, 'whose sole business it is to find out the propitious piece of ground desired' (Gutzlaff [1852] 1972: 92). Otherwise, strikingly few foreigners sojourning in China before 1865 paid any attention to fengshui or were even aware of its existence, but the relatively small population and the commercial outlook of their communities partly explain this. It is still a striking fact that fengshui was never mentioned as an ingredient in Chinese foreign relations during the time of the opium war and subsequent establishment of Treaty ports.[6]

Depicting native Chinese customs was largely left to missionaries. The missionary outstations that were slowly spreading inland in the late 1840s and early 1850s as a result of the opium war had nevertheless encountered fengshui related resistance as one among many obstacles. In 1850 an American mission was denied a particular site to build on in Nantai in Fuzhou on account of the undesirable effect it would have on a family graveyard (Carlson 1974: 14). In a widely reported case in 1851, a Methodist mission in Nantai was met with both popular and official opposition when attempting to build an extension on a newly acquired plot. Popular opinion was that the presence of foreigners had already increased the number of deaths in the neighbourhood and that having more foreigners in the area would cause disturbance since the 'good luck' of people would be adversely affected. From detailed accounts of the case, however, it seems likely that some locals who wanted to extort money from the foreigners played a leading role in staging the protest (ibid.: 38–39). These experiences from Fuzhou were to be repeated in many other provinces as anti-foreign sentiments increasingly surfaced, for instance in placards stating that foreigners and Chinese could not live together, that Chinese who rented to foreigners would be treated as traitors, or threatening foreigners with death if entering certain cities (ibid.: 38, 117).

Though fengshui had not yet become a dominant theme in the encounter of the Chinese with foreigners, the seeds of popular protest on these grounds had been sown. The popular hostility and official obstruction to all foreign enterprise was often coupled with local opportunists' attempts to extort money from the intruders. On the missionary front, anger and frustration were building up when every single step forward was countered by official Chinese obstructionism, while simultaneously missionaries were being criticized at home. Many contemporary accounts reveal how controversial the missionary question really was. G.W. Cooke, a British correspondent in China in the late 1850s, challenged the missionaries' monopoly on depicting the 'superstitious' character of the Chinese; he comments that despite the 'glaring inconsistencies' of the Chinese mind, 'in their universities and in their public examinations ... they teach no superstition' (Cooke 1972: viii).

This was indeed a formative period in the encounter between Chinese pragmatism and Christian reformist devotion. Some material shows that in the following period fengshui gradually became a convenient weapon in the struggle against foreign penetration and in particular what was seen as the rebellious activity of the intruding foreign missions. In his two-volume work on 'The Social Life of the Chinese' published in 1865, the American missionary Justus Doolittle briefly describes 'geomancy' as one out of the six distinguishable methods of fortune-telling among the Chinese, albeit the 'dearest and most tedious' (Doolittle 1865: 339). While using the English term geomancy, he identifies it as divination 'by an inspection of the earth and scenery, in order to fix upon a fortunate burial-place'. What is of key concern to us is that out of the hundreds of pages of Doolittle's reporting on the immense arsenal of Chinese customs and super-stitions of everyday life, he devotes only a few pages to the subject. It is also a remarkable fact that Doolittle, despite just having returned from fourteen years as a missionary in Fuzhou and having been involved in the 1850 incident mentioned above, does not seem to be aware of the fact that fengshui may relate to houses as well as to graves. How can this be? Chinese local sources tend to indicate that the most important application of fengshui during the Qing was for identifying proper places for burial, and for reburial[7] in south China (Smith R. 1991: 151). After devoting two pages to describing the geomancer's work and consideration as to determine a good site for a grave, Doolittle comments: 'The above remarks ... show how willing the people are to deceive and delude themselves, and at their own expense. All of these kinds of fortune-tellers are very fluent in speech ... They all have a very patronizing manner' (Doolittle 1865: 339).

Not much foreign attention seemed to be paid to fengshui. A straightforward answer would be that very few foreigners really had intimate relations with the Chinese as only a handful of them had knowledge of the language and most contacts went through the mandarins. In other matters, however, the inquisitive Western mind left few stones unturned. In 1850 the weekly *North-China Herald* was founded to serve the Shanghai foreign community (it was published almost continuously until 1941). The journal probed into Chinese administration by translating and commenting on the official Chinese organ, 'The Peking Gazette'; it commented on Chinese foreign policy and brought news about all matters relating to foreign sojourners; it broadcasted independently gathered information about political affairs in China and the numerous popular uprisings through the 1850s and 1860s; and it published small series on Chinese history, culture, religion and so forth. But it is striking that during the journal's first eighteen years of existence fengshui was not found to be a noteworthy matter. We can only assume that it simply was not yet a matter of any significance in Chinese–foreign relations, at least not from the perspective of the Shanghai community. We get the overall impression that although fengshui was obviously important, and many incidents were reported in Chinese local gazetteers, apparently it was not a concern so central in Chinese society that it merited foreign attention. It was not until the foreign occupation of Beijing (Peking) in 1860–62 and the concurrent foreign interest in opening the Chinese interior that fengshui became an issue in the Chinese–foreign encounter.

The revolutionary impact of steam power in Europe served as a model for the foreigners' vision of progress for China, but another great invention of the day which was about to revolutionize long-distance communication, the telegraph, had changed the prospects for enterprise in the Chinese interior. It was exactly this potential for irreversible and foreign-dominated change throughout China that many Chinese reformers and intellectuals sensed and attempted to counter by internal mobilization. Fengshui was inflated in the tense field between the foreign drive for the interior and the Chinese self-strengthening movement, searching for new national symbols that were easy to read for the general populace.

An early reference to the subject is found in the journals of Robert Hart, who, shortly after he had joined the Chinese imperial customs service in 1863, reported that in private conversations members of the foreign community in Beijing express that they see the 'fung-shway superstition' as their greatest obstacle as regards plans of introducing telegraphs and railways, without the matter seemingly being discussed in any detail (Smith R. *et al.* 1991: 198). We shall return to this issue later. Little by little, as the cultural interface broadened, fengshui became a component in the demarcation of difference between foreigners and Chinese, until someone eventually expressed in public his wonder about the strong Chinese pre-occupation with interpreting forces of good or bad luck. In 1867 a reader of the new Hong Kong journal *Notes and Queries* asked in the queries section under the heading 'Fung Shui – What is it?':

> Most of the residents in China, particularly those who have any know-ledge of the language, are aware of the importance attached by the Chinese to the Doctrine of Fung-shui, or the spiritual influence of wind and water. In traversing the country the traveller sees Pagodas and on enquiry as to their origin and title is told – that the first is unknown, and the second has reference to Fung-shui. ... Most of the Chinese have very hazy notions on the subject. Many, however, not professionals in the art, but who study Geomancy as a science, have some distant inklings of the truth, and after repeated conversations, enquiries on the subject, and on inspection of the Geomantic books, which, indeed, I could make little of, I have come to the conclusion that Fung-shui is simply terrestrial magnetism ... Perhaps some of the contributors to 'Notes and Queries' could throw some further light upon the subject. (*NQ* 31 January 1867: 6–7)

The query sparked off what appears to be the first public debate on the subject. In February another contributor signing himself Shui Song commented as quoted in the opening of the first chapter, '... Fung Shui means literally "wind" (and) "water"...' (*NQ* 28 February 1867: 19–20), while someone signed Deka observed, 'The outline of a hill is fancied to resemble a dragon ... I have seen a broad ditch dug on a hill side so as to break the continuity of the curved outline and thus injure the "Fung Shui" of a neighboring village' (*NQ* 28 February 1867: 19). Other contributions to the discussion included a passage from an imperial edict denouncing fengshui (*NQ* 31 May 1868: 69) and the following description of the geomancer's work in connection with burial rites, yet another topic often alluded to in the journal:

> These gentlemen ape a certain amount of mystery, respectability and independence, in which respects they much resemble some of our own quack doctors and quack lawyers; they generally object to any external indication of their profession, as savouring of plebeianism, and when consulted go through the common quack formula of de-claring their incompetency and unwillingness to take upon themselves such a great responsibility as the selection of a lucky spot for a grave, in the hope of leaving a strong impression of the wonderful ability of the fraternity, and the important advantages to be gained by securing the services of a renowned member thereof. The length of time required to determine the Fung-shui aspect of a proposed grave is regulated very much by the willingness and ability of the applicant to pay for the requisite inquiries ... (*NQ* vol. 2, no. 7, 1868: 110)

Again in 1869 the same question popped up on the pages of the journal when a reader signed as 'Sceptic' asked, 'Does any one know on what principle Feng-shui acts?' with reference to the disturbances Westerners were supposed to cause: 'If it takes offence at Telegraph posts, how can it look complacently on Mandarin poles ... It seems so coquettish that I must appeal to the initiated to unravel the mystery' (*NQ* vol. 2, no. 8, 1869: 122).

In the next few years things developed quickly and soon every foreigner involved with Chinese affairs either through missionary, commercial or diplomatic activity would become intensely aware of the importance that ordinary Chinese evidently attributed to the matter.[8] Rather than a product of the Western world's late discovery of fengshui, the escalation of conflict must be seen as a consequence of fengshui being adopted in a rising anti-foreign discourse, which in turn gave new vitality and support to the fengshui tradition. It increasingly stood out as the cosmology of the entire nation, radically divergent from Western modernism – it all happened in the single decade of 1860–70.

RISING IDEOLOGICAL CONTRADICTIONS

After the so-called unequal treaties with the foreign powers in 1842–44 and 1858 and particularly after the Anglo-French occupation of Beijing in 1860, the Chinese interior lay open to traders, travellers and missionaries. During the rest of the century, both Catholic and Protestant mission stations spread into every province of the empire, and their scope of activity also expanded rapidly. Besides the church, each station would contain residences, usually a school, sometimes an orphanage, and if possible a small hospital or dispensary. Although their converts were too few to matter in the colossal Chinese population, they could still form small communities, enjoying certain social privileges and turning away from the Chinese order under some degree of foreign protection. Outside the treaty ports, these many hundreds of mission stations embodied the most profound cultural contact between China and the West; the missionary hospitals and dispensaries alone provided an immense interface with the local people as they each provided treatment for thousands of patients every year.

Almost by definition the Protestant missionaries in China were reformers at heart,[9] deeply engaged in a theologically informed scheme of modernization. They called for the reform of Chinese thought and institutions, particularly those informed by Confucianism, through the adoption of what they saw as the salient elements of Western civilization: science, technology and Christianity. Missionaries engaged in economic, social and cultural affairs in their districts. In the latter part of the century they struggled to learn the language, engaged in debate with the local gentry to challenge their cosmology, philosophy and social practices. They wrote in Chinese or translated thousands of works and had them printed and disseminated locally, thus resuming the work of the Jesuits in the seventeenth and eighteenth centuries. Their aim was to have a complete set of scriptures, church manuals, school books and life guides for teaching purposes, while at the same time opposing Chinese ancestor worship and superstition (as early as 1871 Charles Hartwell of the American Tract Society issued a small book to oppose fengshui[10]). Of equal importance to their Christian missionary zeal was the dissemination of knowledge about the outside world among the Chinese as well as a critical outsider's view of the empire. The first modest attempt to publish a Chinese language periodical on the mainland was made by Gutzlaff in 1833–37. It was not until the 1850s and 1860s that these activities were resumed, when nine periodicals were founded in Canton, Hong Kong, Shanghai and Ningbo – as was also China's first daily news-paper in Hong Kong in 1858 (Chang Kuo. 1968: 61–63).

In the 1870s a further ten publications were established, of which several were daily newspapers. An outstanding example from this period was a weekly magazine, *Wanguo gongbao* (Chinese Globe Magazine),[11] written in the finest classical Chinese to report on world affairs to the Chinese scholarly class. The native Chinese chronicles had long been barred from bringing other than trivial matters concerning the state of the empire such as official memoranda, transcripts, appointments and so forth. The imperial government was put under tremendous pressure from missionary and non-religious forces working together to expose the impotence of the Chinese ruling class and promote an alternative vision of the world among the Chinese. The outcome was a fierce battle over the control and dissemination of knowledge among the Chinese, a battle which has continued until this day. An prominent missionary and reform advocate who strove to introduce modern science and technology in order to develop the Chinese economy was Timothy Richard, who published a number of articles in the *Wanguo gongbao* in the 1870s and 1880s. On the presumption that famine had an economic cause, and not a natural cause as conjectured by the imperial government, he offered a far-reaching scheme for modern economic development, including railways, mines, expanded inter-province traffic and trade, extensive public works and machine manufacturing to feed and provide labour to China's destitute masses (Bohr 1972: 140–148).

The imperial government extended to all printed media its monopoly on worshipping heaven and on interpreting its will in the future of the empire – and there were no printed news media other than the central government's gazette. Any prophesy concerning state affairs was an open challenge to authority, whether expressed by a geomancer or a journalist. As if the printed Chinese language media were not enough, several foreign missions ran specific programmes for reaching the Chinese mandarins. By their aggressive and provocative style of work missionaries of all denominations certainly made their contribution to the increasing awareness of an alternative social order, which just a few decades later was heard as a strong call for reformation across the empire (Cohen 1978: 586–588).

Against this background it was only natural that the Chinese imperial government was terrified at the prospect of telegraphs and railways spreading into the empire. Much of its ruling elite feared the foreigner as much as his technology and culture, with their zeal to revolutionize the world in the image of western liberal-democratic society. But exactly how and why fengshui came to play such an important role in Chinese foreign relations in the 1870s must be seen as a product of this cultural encounter as much as a natural im-plication of inherent Chinese beliefs. Apart from numerous attacks on missionary stations where fengshui accusations played a part, it was not until 1867–68 that, quite suddenly, fengshui arguments were introduced in the imperial government's policy towards foreign enterprise. One of the first such incidents, concerning a coal-mine near Nanjing, made headlines in the *North-China Herald*.

Along the Yangtse north of Nanjing (partly in the fieldwork area of Baohua, Jiangsu) the British Consul had found some coal mines, which had been abandoned ten years earlier by their Chinese proprietors because the pits were being filled with water. After several specimens of coal had been examined in Shanghai and found very promising, the mine was envisioned as the opportunity to finally open the Chinese mineral resources to foreign exploitation. The initial Chinese response was that it was 'feared' that the presence of foreigners in inland districts would lead to riots and other dis-turbances. As the matter was calculatingly pushed aside a furore broke out in the foreign community: Why was it not being exploited when China was in such desperate need of foreign capital and employment for a starving population? Did the government possess the right to restrict the industry of its people and thus take bread out of their mouths? On the specific reference to the danger of riots, the *Herald* commented that when the Chinese needed foreigners to drill their troops or to manufacture munitions of war, this cry of danger was never heard (*NCHM* 28 March 1868: 13).

Several workable coal mines had been found in other parts of the country. At Zhaidang near Tianjin in the north several large coal mines were operated by local Chinese owners, who had profited from earlier suppliance to the treaty port. They were nevertheless unable to meet large orders because of the poor road conditions. It was suggested that a foreign company build a road to Catting and the Chinese mine owners, supported by their local mandarins, sent a memorandum to the government to plead for construction of the road, declaring that the people of the district would be grateful. Since the issue was so widely reported in the foreign community and the request had been pursued through diplomatic channels, the Chinese government felt pressurized to take a stand. After having sent a commission to investigate and report on the matter, the Chinese government delivered their answer through the British resident minister, Sir Rutherford Alcock, stating that the road could not be made 'first on account of engineering difficulties, secondly because the popular feeling is against it, and thirdly because its construction would injure the Feng-shuy'.[12] It looked like a safeguard. Sir Rutherford then declared that 'no progress should be looked for by diplomatic action'; with specific reference to fengshui he stated that the 'argument is unanswerable, and the objection therefore insuperable'. The *North-China Herald* commented that the Chinese had sent out a commission, not to find a practicable road, but to discover Feng-shuy: 'Experience has taught them that any objection, however flimsy, is sufficient to gain their purpose – under the present regime; so they advance the flimsiest of all arguments – Feng-shuy, and Sir Rutherford acknowledges [it]'.[13] Also in this respect the Chinese had been quick to play on any wavering of their opponents. Under the leadership of E. W. Gladstone (1869–74) the British government was occupied with a fiery reform programme at home and in Ireland, while at the same time the Franco–German War attracted attention, and the colonies were being governed with considerable indulgence.[14]

The Chinese government took note of the uncertainty that the whole question of fengshui raised in British diplomacy. By endorsing what was perceived as the unquestionable faith of local populations and their rulers (very unlike the Jesuits' approach two centuries earlier), perhaps born out of a combination of naivety and deep scepticism towards Christian missionary activity, British diplomacy undoubtedly contributed to raising the standing of fengshui among Chinese and foreigners alike. The Chinese conservatives were looking for a negotiable path to a specific aim: containment of the foreign community and prevention of foreign enterprise stretching further inland. Fengshui had been introduced in foreign relations by the Chinese government as a shrewdly constructed buffer mechanism to ward off foreign expansion, and clothed in democratic oratory alluding to the undesirability of changing the faith of the people. By gaining acceptance for the argument, perhaps only out of Sir Rutherford's disinterested attitude, the Chinese government had come in possession of a new ideological weapon, which it turned against both the holy and the mundane representatives of the West. It will later be shown how Western sinologists in this period played their part in elevating common Chinese fengshui considerations to the level of genuine 'faith' among the Chinese.

The following years were marked by several parallel trends; the Chinese self-strengthening movement was gaining momentum with a broad support for certain reforms of mainly ideological nature among the mandarinate and intellectuals. At the same time the Chinese government was obviously in want of a means to unite the Chinese nation, severely battered by endless rebellions and rampant public discontent through much of the nineteenth century. Without a clearly identified cause, but presumably with an indirect link, untold numbers of attacks on missionary stations as well as other foreign property occurred in the following years.

Throughout Chinese history since the Song dynasty religious groups were effectively cut off from political influence and the major religions as well as religious sects that posed a potential threat to the regime remained under firm control. Some, such as the White Lotus sect, were consistently persecuted. Religious policy apparently had hardened because the Qing dynasty was in decline through the nineteenth century, but despite defeat to the English and massive rebellions evidently still capable of restoring national integration and instituting significant reforms (Naquin and Rawski 1987: 236). Almost every decade of the nineteenth century had seen all-out persecution of heresies, while almost every rebellion was intimately connected with a heresy (Weber 1951: 214).

For the educated Chinese, who bore the Taiping Rebellion well in mind, the Christian missionaries' activities clearly trespassed on this borderline between religion and politics. Particularly when viewed against the imperial monopoly to interpret heaven, missionary promises of heavenly rewards for the faithful were outright blasphemy. Moreover, the Christian rejection of ancestor worship, following the papal orders of 1715 and 1742 to end the so-called Chinese Rites and Names Controversy (Mungello 1994), threatened the cardinal virtues of politics since the obedience of the subjects and the discipline within the formal hierarchy of offices somehow depended on the principle of filial piety. A foreign religion which emancipated the subjects from belief in the exclusive power of imperial office and the eternal order of filial piety was 'unbearable in principle' (Weber 1951: 216). Thus, for the Chinese central government as much as for the gentry, the Christian mission was a political institution which mostly represented the ideological arm of foreign aggression. The Chinese bewilderment over the true motives of missionaries, who devoted their lives to working far away from home in hostile surroundings, and the various Chinese attempts to explain these motives, concentrated the Chinese reluctance to accept 'spiritual truth' or 'faith' itself as a driving force (as was discussed in Chapter 1). Apart from the obvious imperialist motive, which included the viewing of missionary schools, orphanages and hospitals as deliberate bribes to secure converts and thus break up Chinese society from within, there was the personal motive. One version was that the comfortable life of the foreign missionary in China, which to the common Chinese must have been sumptuous, was the real attraction, perhaps surpassing the reward which his talents would have brought him at home (Lutz 1988: 14). Another personal motive suggested was that the missionary was out there to seek his own spiritual blessing; a humorous anecdote is provided by Pearl S. Buck, who describes how her father's audience began to slip away under a lengthy sermon, whereupon an elderly woman stood up to admonish the dwindling congregation: 'Do not offend this good foreigner! He is making a pilgrimage in our country so that he may acquire merit in heaven. Let us help him to save his soul!'[15]

If there was scepticism about the missionary's cause, then there was deep suspicion of the Chinese converts' motives. They were under heavy fire from the gentry and accused of being either traitors or simple criminals seeking foreign protection. A common term indicating an economic explanation for their motive was 'rice Christians', who had 'eaten' Christianity, since they were accused of being baptized in exchange for food, employment or protection at the missions. As nationalism grew in China during the last decades of the century, the attacks on Christian converts grew more violent.

The stated purpose of missionary activity was 'salvation' for China through distinguished elements of Christian civilization: science, industry, spiritual truth and the relationship between material progress and Christianity.[16] Many conceptions were foreign to Chinese thought, for instance the radical exclusiveness – the concept of a lifelong worship of one religion, to which the individual assigned uncontested faith. But it may with equal truth be said that the Protestant missionaries were excellent Confucians, competing with the Chinese local authority, perhaps even setting up an example aimed at mocking the gentry on their home ground. They strove to learn the language and exploited every bit of new knowledge for their cause and published locally. They studied the Classics and learned the Confucian ideals of social responsibility and a just and orderly society; they cared for the needy by accommodating beggars and setting up orphanages. During the catastrophic famine in north China in 1878 Christian missionaries, particularly under the leadership of Timothy Richard, organized famine relief of greater scope and efficiency than the native administration, which was frequently accused of misappropriation. The missionaries took note of the Confucian principles of personal integrity and impartiality of officials and criticized corruption and interfered with local jurisdiction and court cases, particularly in favour of Chinese converts. They concurred with the Confucian emphasis on bookish learning to socialize the individual and set up primary schools locally, but employed instead modern education. By competing in the fields of public responsibility and moral obligation towards the ordinary citizenry, missionaries very consciously undermined the status of the gentry-scholar class and did not refrain from questioning the true spirit of Confucian ethics.

To the tension that arose from missionary activity and intensified cultural contact must be added the Chinese gentry's deliberate attempts at undermining missionary work. The real contention behind the gentry's furious denunciation of the relatively modest and small-scale missionary activities, however, was the battle for control over the rural Chinese, who until the arrival of foreigners had mostly conducted a life in political oblivion and increasing social neglect, as the weakening Qing rule was cutting down famine relief, public works and all forms of public spending – the missionaries' arrival made the Chinese countryside publicly visible. Obviously it was the Confucian-schooled gentry class that stood to lose the most (Cohen 1978: 564)

It was in fact in the outstations that missionary work was most successful as the traces of dissolution spread across the rural areas.

A continuous trend throughout the nineteenth century, which might have stimulated the growth of popular cosmology, was the spontaneous militarization of the countryside (Kuhn 1970). The Qing government strove to maintain control over both local militia and a growing and recalcitrant rural populace, capable of political revolution: the White Lotus Rebellion from 1796 to 1804, the Eight Trigrams Uprising in North China including an attack on Beijing in 1813, and the Taiping Rebellion of 1851–1864, nearly overthrowing the imperial government, all conveyed the hopes of millions of destitute peasants. The period 1850–1875 was particularly marked by a long series of rebellions affecting most parts of the empire; in addition to the Taiping there were also Muslim rebellions in the west, the Miao rebellion in Guizhou and the Nian rebellion in the northeast.

Rebellions had drained the resources of the state and could only be put down by the establishment of local militia forces all throughout the country. The gentry played a crucial part in organizing these part-time soldiers, not because this was an ideal solution in the eyes of the imperial government, but because it was the only solution. The militia, which was under official supervision and gentry management, could be employed against internal disorder, but they could also be turned against foreign intruders and, in principle, any threat to their interests that the gentry might see.

Being without formal power to interfere because after 1860 the missionaries enjoyed the rights of extraterritoriality, the Chinese gentry took to another time-proven weapon – that of intimidating commoners and inflaming public opinion against foreigners by playing on latent xenophobia. During the 1860s a steadily growing number of attacks on missionaries and Chinese converts as well as destruction of mission buildings and churches took place. Hundreds of mission stations were targets for attacks, culminating in 1868–69 and continuing through the 1870s. The majority of attacks took place in the missionary outstations, where personnel and property were less protected and antagonism between missionaries and gentry far more serious. In the province of Fuzhou alone, nearly a hundred attacks on missionary outstations involving destruction of property or bodily harm were recorded between 1860 and 1880 (Carlson 1974: 174–175).

Also at the political level this period saw substantially changing relations. While colonialism in the early period, termed the 'first phase' by John K. Fairbank, was signified by 'imperialism of free trade', a second phase was begun in the 1870s (Fairbank 1992: 205). The Anglo-Qing dominion of the China coast gave way to imperialist rivalry among the great industrial powers of Britain, Russia, France, Germany and Japan, who all invaded Chinese territory. While establishing an alien hegemony in their possessions and granting extraterritoriality to their citizens, the foreign powers placed the native Chinese elite in the situation they most abhorred: ruling under alien hegemony, reminding them of both the Manchu dominated Qing rule and the Mongolian dominated Yuan dynasty. The Imperial government's reaction to foreign domination was the movement for self-strengthening and restoring 'wealth and power' (*fu-qiang*).

As missionaries settled further and further inland, imperial rivalry was somewhat paralleled in missionary rivalry and jealousy, greatly detracting from the reputation of the otherwise admirable social activity of missionary stations. Missions of all denominations widened their scope of activity significantly, which again resulted in reported incidents of conflict rising dramatically. Also for the Chinese mandarinate Western interference was becoming a real nuisance, especially the increasing criticism of the imperial 'minimalist' government. Missionaries and other foreign sojourners concurrently spoke and wrote against the established type of local self-government, which involved a poor sense of evidence, common use of torture, the exploitation of official position for financial gain, false reporting to higher levels and other customs strongly contrasting western ideals. Quite outspokenly, most Westerners in China supported the position of the weak against the power-holders and through all possible channels they disclosed corruption, torture, misgovernment and low moral standards as a contradiction to the Chinese elite's claim to high civilization. John H. Gray wrote that 'the mandarins of China ... have plunged this fair land into that deplorable anarchy, confusion, and misery, for which it is now conspicuous amongst nations' (Gray 1878: 26–27).

When Westerners engaged in social work among the weak, they provoked the response of local governments. The Catholic orphanages, for instance, which simultaneously taught and converted the children, were commonly accused of kidnapping them; perhaps the feeling that the missions drew the children away from their community fostered the metaphor, developed into a common Chinese saying, that the 'foreign devils eat children' (many missionaries and

51

travellers in this period reported that wherever they went people were hiding the children at their arrival). A Chinese pamphlet printed in the late 1860s with the title 'Death Blow to Corrupt Doctrines', and almost certainly of official origin, was first ridiculed by foreigners but soon believed to be instrumental in stirring up hostility and real atrocities (NCHS 12 May 1871: 333–334). Contemporaries described China as being seized by a frantic fit of superstition as the little book disseminated descriptions of how the professors of Western religion tore out the eyes of the dying to form a nauseous paste to make proselytes among men, tore out the eyes of the living to make photographic lenses, captured and mutilated Chinese children, buried people alive to secure the foundations for their churches, bewitched all kinds of people and much more (NCHS 27 July 1872: 61). Ignorance about the outside world was easily manipulated into gross superstitions by a ruling elite who rarely held aspirations for civil enlightenment, but instead promoted the kind of all-embracing metaphoric thinking typical of Chinese popular ideology.

The missionary question developed into a major point of conflict between the colonial powers and the Chinese imperial government. The extent of this can be seen when in 1871 the Chinese side distributed a Memorandum on Foreign Missions[17] to all diplomatic representatives of the treaty powers, apparently its first independent foreign policy action since 1858 and also the first incident of fengshui becoming an explicit element in foreign policy. The memorandum singled out an unrest in Guizhou in 1870 as especially serious, when missionaries and Chinese Christians, after a dispute between a Chinese and a Chinese Christian had received an unfavourable verdict, had 'seized the yamen (magistrate's office) and compelled the local authorities to reconsider the verdict' (Monina 1983: 277). The memorandum, which played on Western criticism of missionary activity – frequently likened to the import of opium[18] – generated much debate and disagreement among the foreign community. It concluded that the missionaries 'demanded the same authority wielded only by the emperor'. But there was much more at stake. Considering the persecution of hereditary sects that had been carried out in the previous decades of Qing rule, even against much smaller threats to power than the Christian, there could be no question of how serious the Qing rulers took any religiously founded opposition. Moreover, the Taiping rebels, who had barely been prevented from toppling the dynasty a few years earlier, had employed messianic-Christian spiritual support in their cause. Now foreign religion supported by aggressive colonial powers was penetrating deep into the interior, a clear breach of the Chinese policy of containment. Several previous internal memoranda had in fact recommended strict control or even prohibition of all missionary activity, but the government feared impinging upon the interests of the colonial powers (ibid.: 278).

In the note accompanying the memorandum the Qing government complained about the social aspects of the missions. By concentrating on getting converts among the poor, the missionaries assertively violated Chinese traditions and ignored Chinese authority. This is probably as close as we get to the heart of the issue. When beggars were being fed, orphans getting work and education, and women allowed to attend churches just like men,[19] it was all part of a deliberate effort to secure converts among the impotent. To the Chinese imperial government, which largely ignored social injustice and showed little concern for marginalized groups such as beggars (Hosie 1890), and to the local gentry, who exploited the scarce land resources to the utmost and enjoyed almost unlimited authority over their serfs, missionary activity was not merely a thorn in the flesh: attempts to mobilize the poor might erode traditional forms of domination and fan a glowing fire of social rebellion.

Objections to the siting of churches and mission stations grew stronger as the missionaries were accused of contravening the rules of fengshui; apparently at times they deliberately defied these rules, considered 'pagan superstition' (Chesneaux 1973: 51). A massacre in Tianjin in 1870 and disturbances in Yangzhou in 1871 demonstrated the sturdy resistance to foreign missions particularly among the Chinese literati and from time to time also among common Chinese. The missionaries themselves accused the literati of being the real instigators (*CRMJ* September 1871: 111), something which in the late 1860s had become ever more conspicuous. In the case of the Tianjin massacre, for instance, it was beyond doubt. According to several concordant reports and a later Blue Book, the massacre, in which a French consul, several Catholic priests and missionary staff nurses were killed, was organized by a number of local officials including a military mandarin (possibly with consent from the Chinese government), who deliberately played on the talk of local people that a hospital run by the Belgian Sisters of Charity was kidnapping and mutilating Chinese children. Fire-gongs were used to call people to arms at a pre-arranged time and the killings were committed in broad daylight in the presence of the mandarins. Moreover, some missionary staff were tortured in the *yamen* where they had been detained allegedly for protection.[20]

The Chinese memorandum, consisting of a note, eight articles and a conclusion, would in effect bring missionary activity to a halt. Orphanages should be abolished (Art. 1), women were not allowed in churches and the Sisters of Charity were not allowed into the country (Art. 2), missionaries should be subject to Chinese officials, any teaching must be in accordance with Confucianism (Art. 3), indemnities for future attacks on missionary property were refused (Art. 4), missionaries were subject to stricter immigration rules (Art. 5), mandarins were empowered to forbid any Chinese to become Christian (Art. 6), and missionaries must observe Chinese ceremonies (Art. 7). Of special interest here, however, is Article 8, providing local mandarins and inhabitants with the means to prevent the opening of new chapels. Although the Qing government in general attempted to check the art of geomancy and formally condemned it, this article proposed to legalize fengshui as a justified veto against the opening of foreign missions.[21]

Geomancy thus appeared a convenient means of manipulating popular sentiments and particularly aggression towards foreigners. In the years following the 1871 memorandum on countless occasions both Chinese central and local government authorities would refer to fengshui disturbance to postpone undesirable matters or simply oppose everything foreign with diversionary issues and bureaucratic obstructionism. They argued that local people were worried about fengshui interference and that the missionaries had to consider public opinion. Similarly, they held that officials could not change the opinions of the people (Carlson 1974: 117), although for centuries the persecution of heretic sects had involved rectifying the beliefs of the people. Such arguments even went against Qing law, which was very restrictive about geomancy and all sorts of magic. The Qing rulers exhibited great skills in sensing contradiction among their enemies; in this matter they could play on the common criticism of missionary activity among the missionaries' own governments and in the foreign communities in China. Reverend J.S. Burden, writing in 1872, ascribed the Chinese allegations to the British Foreign Minister's expressed contempt for both 'opium and missions', which conceivably had inspired the Chinese government to issue the said 1871 missionary circular (Burden 1872: 264).

In a single case illustrative of hundreds, Chinese authorities supported the local gentry's claim that the missionary presence on a hill in Nantai (Fuzhou) had caused natural calamity in the form of terrible fires in the city, in consequence of which the missionaries had to abandon the site to avoid the violence of the crowds. Such arguments were designed to make an impression on the British consul (Carlson 1974: 137). The actual attitudes to missionary work among ordinary Chinese is nearly impossible to judge; the missionaries repeatedly claimed that their relations with common people were good.

A variety of interpretations were offered about possible causes for the hostility. The contemporary debate quickly became entangled in the controversy in Europe over missionary activity in the colonies, in which those who were against such activity accused the missionaries of disrespect for other religions and therefore interpreted the clash to be a matter of conscience. Missionaries in China, however, generally repudiated this as sheer nonsense. J.S. Burden, for instance, argued with reference to the 'non-religious' character of the Chinese people: '[W]e no more outrage the feelings of the people by delivering a Christian address in a Buddhist or Confucian temple than we would at home preaching in the market place' (Burden 1872: 264). Instead, he saw the Chinese government's attack on Christianity as first of all based on a Chinese view of Christianity as a political institution, primarily owing to the fact that the French Roman Catholic church was supported by the French government, which furthermore had extended its protection to everyone belonging to that church (the issue of possible Chinese criminals converting to Christianity for protection was frequently brought up). Another reason was ascribed to the hatred towards all foreigners on the part of the Chinese educated class, who saw their presence as a threat to their own authority and privilege. So the missions had come under attack from both sides, simultaneously bearing the brunt of the hatred of the Chinese literati towards foreigners and being put under political pressure from home to check their activities.

FOREIGN ATTENTION TO FENGSHUI

The sporadic queries and comments regarding fengshui in contemporary journals, as well as the aggravated political climate in general, evidently inspired some to make more thorough inquiries into the subject. In 1872, *The Chinese Recorder and Missionary Journal* published a series of small articles on fengshui, written by Reverend J. Edkins. Like most of his contemporaries, he was outraged by the now massive influence of fengshui:

Every thing can be made plainer by investigation ... The Feng-shui of the Chinese deserves to be examined for it is one of the great obstacles to the progress of civilization. It interferes with commercial enterprise. It checks the efforts of missionary zeal. It interrupts the free thought of the people and keeps them wrapped in the mummy folds of ancient prejudices. Within the last few years this peculiar system of native geomancy has been made the ground for refusing the establishment of electric telegraph poles at Shanghai; of railways; of a road from Tianjin to the Catting coal mines, and I do not know how many more manifest and desirable im-provements, all of which could have been of the greatest advantage to the people of the district. (Edkins, March 1872: 274–275)

As in numerous other instances of Christian ministers introducing aspects of Chinese culture to a Western readership, Edkins' account of fengshui was remarkably precise and sincere, explaining both its practices, symbols and etymology. In 1873 the first treatise on Chinese geomancy in a Western language, *Fung-shui – or – The Rudiments of Natural Science in China*, was written by E.J. Eitel, the German clergyman and longstanding school-inspector in Hong Kong. He too set out to answer the question 'what is fengshui'. Eitel's approach was of course influenced by his work as a professional in the Hong Kong administration, as seen from this celebrated quotation:

When the Hong Kong Government cut a road, now known as the Gap, to the Happy Valley, the Chinese community was thrown into a state of abject terror and fright, on account of the disturbance which this amputation of the Dragon's limb would cause to the Feng Shui of Hong Kong; and when many of the engineers, employed at the cutting, died of Hong Kong fever, and the foreign houses already built in the Happy Valley had to be de-serted on account of Malaria, the Chinese triumphantly declared, it was an act of retributory justice on the part of Feng Shui. (Eitel [1873] 1984: 2)

A distinguishing feature in Eitel's account is his treatment of the matter as a serious means of structuring the world and bringing order to human experience; 'Feng-shui is, ... as I take it, but another name for natural science' (ibid.: 4–5), albeit a rudimentary and misled science, totally lacking practical tests and experiments, and instead based on an emotional conception of nature. Following a division of 'Chinese science' into four branches, Eitel works his way through the basic cosmology to which fengshui refers. Still Eitel finds his search for Chinese proto-science futile. Concerning the common conviction of some contemporaries that fengshui was terrestrial magnetism, he comments that geomancers use the magnetic compass as a matter of course, 'but I am sorry to say that I have not been able to find even the slightest empirical knowledge of ... inclination, declination and intensity of the magnetic currents in the earth' (ibid.: 34). Eitel concludes in the same vein; what he had 'hitherto, by a stretch of charity, called Chinese physical science is, from a scientific point of view, but a conglomeration of rough guesses about nature, sublimated by fanciful play with purile diagrams' (ibid.: 78). Yet he does not see fengshui as a barrier to the introduction of foreign civilization in China because of its extraordinary flexibility. Rather, in an evolutionary scheme of events, 'Feng-shui, ... based as it is on human speculation and not on careful study of nature, is marked for decay and dissolution' (ibid.: 84).

Needless to say that Eitel's account reflects the Western self-confidence derived from the rising prominence of modern science and technology. Yet this famous quote from Eitel should now be seen in a new light. First of all, out of a vast terrain of Chinese heterodox religious practices Eitel's account introduced fengshui as a subject worthy of study in the Western world. Secondly, behind his account of fengshui can be traced a certain sympathy for Chinese nationalistic sentiments, which were constantly surfacing in this period and with increasing frequency turning into open resistance. Conceivably many sinologists introduced fengshui to a Western audience in a manner designed to heighten the respect for the common Chinese, depicted as uncivilized heathens throughout the nineteenth century; here was a complex system of cosmological thought that the Chinese really believed in. Although distorted by emotion, it recognized the universality of natural laws as well as the numerical proportions of nature and taught man how to rule nature and his own destiny; it was the 'foolish daughter of a wise mother' (ibid.: 49, 68). But there was much controversy. The practical people behind the *North-China Herald*, for instance, were scornful about sinologists, whom they accused of being out of touch with reality.

During the 1870s Western accounts of fengshui appeared with increasing frequency in the wake of its aggravated political implications. In many ways the contact between Western and Chinese culture was intensified in this period and if Westerners saw Chinese officials as obstructionists, the Chinese power-holders undoubtedly viewed many Westerners as villainous revolutionaries. The more notice foreigners took of fengshui the more it became a showpiece for Chinese resistance and a gathering point for patriotic sentiments – something it had evidently never been before.

In Europe fengshui was quickly gaining recognition, often described in terms hinting that now had been found the true faith of the

Chinese, a kind of animistic nature worship. In 1879, the German missionary Hubrig spoke about fengshui in the Berliner Gesellschaft für Anthropologie, Ethnologie and Urgeschichte, and to a large extend repeated Eitel's description of the Chinese (obstructionist) beliefs in the bad influence of mining, railways, and telegraph lines: 'How can it be, that the Chinese as a people always so hardheaded cut themselves off from the religion and culture of the West [Das Abendland]' (Hubrig 1879: 34). Hubrig argues that an answer to the question why the Chinese do not exploit their resources must include their belief in fengshui. Turning to the definition of fengshui, Hubrig's account reflects the theological debate in the China mission at the time:

> Since it deals with how nature is generated and continued, it could perhaps also be called science, particularly in our times, when unproved and unprovable assumptions too often are designated with the word science. The knowledge of God's existence, which alone forms the foundation for all existing learning, fails the Chinese, though they recognize an invisible divine force in Nature, and thereby ascribe Godly attributes to natural forces. Nature appears to the Chinese as a living and in all its individual parts animated organism, which emerges in the self-consciousness of man. To be human is the highest stage of development which can be reached; thus all Chinese gods are earth-born. It demonstrates itself here, that defection from God leads to self-deification or deification of one's own kind. *Eritis sicut Deus.* (Ibid.: 36)

In spite of growing tension, Hubrig and his contemporaries delivered remarkably factual reports. Though seeing the strong adherence to geomancy as the greatest obstacle to the introduction of Christianity, Hubrig presented a clear account of the ideas and elements in fengshui. He explained the concepts of *qi* (cosmic breath) and *li* (ritual), the component drawn from the classic *Yi jing*, the Five Phases, the entire complex of Chinese astrology, the organic universe and the configurations in the landscape identified in fengshui; everything is sensibly interpreted as belonging to the Chinese 'anthropocentric' pattern of thought. He even scrutinizes the geomantic compass. Reflecting prevailing attitudes of his time, however, Hubrig dealt with fengshui in terms of derailed religion or misled science. As regards the final question as to the nature of fengshui, he concludes:

> It is a fantasy-painting with many successful ideas, which we would ascribe to a practical mind. It is a blend of science and a degenerate religion, from which the purer impulses of theism have disappeared to be replaced by service to spirits and deification of Man. It is the quintessence of taoist mysticism, buddhist fatalism, and confucian, or better Chu Hsi'an, materialism. *Fengshui* comes from the elevation of inquiry and loses itself in the depression of superstition, where it en-

slaves its adherents, both high and low, educated and uninformed in all aspects of life from birth to death and cripples all progress. (Ibid.: 42)

It was the outstanding Dutch sinologist J.J.M. de Groot (1854–1921) who offered the first comprehensive study of Chinese geomancy in his monumental work *The Religious Systems of China* (1892–1910). In contrast to his predecessors, who employed merely the common sense of a 'rational' mind, de Groot's work offered sophisticated ethnographic analysis based on systematic fieldwork as well as study of the classics. In his analysis de Groot identified the roots of feng-shui as belonging to two different areas of thought: firstly, veneration or awe for nature, and secondly, ancestor worship – both being inherent patterns of thought in Chinese civilization. J.J.M. de Groot also specifically sets out to answer the familiar question, 'what is fengshui?', since it 'holds the nation in its grip and reigns supreme in the empire, through its whole length and breadth'. He immediately suggests a definition,

> a quasi-scientific system, supposed to teach men where and how to build graves, temples and dwellings, in order that the dead, the gods and the living may be located therein exclusively, or as far as possible, under the auspicious influences of Nature. (de Groot 1901: 935)

By linking fengshui to the evolution of ancestor worship in Chinese civilization, de Groot's approach came to play an immense role for the emerging social science of his time. Both his sophisticated analysis and his ability to show the universal relevance of his topic for the study of human society served as a model. Yet his study had the uncompromising tone so common for early ethnography,

> Fung-shui is a mere chaos of childish absurdities and refined mysticism, cemented together, by sophistic reasoning, into a system, which is in reality a ridiculous caricature of science. But it is highly instructive from an ethnographic point of view. The aberrations into which the human mind may sink when, untutored by practical observation, it gropes after a reasoned knowledge of Nature, are more clearly expounded by it than by any other phenomenon in the life and history of nations. (Ibid.: 938)

J.J.M. de Groot's exemplary fieldwork and his immense exposition of ethnographic detail raised his account to a level of timeless authority, but his analysis remained hampered by two conflicting sets of ideas. One was the evolutionary perspective on religion and culture, in which the passionate development of ancestor worship in China played a crucial part in his scheme of interpretation, often to a degree incompatible with facts. At a very general level my own fieldwork material suggests that fengshui has little dependency on veneration of ancestors. Another was the common standpoint of sinology that China had degenerated from antiquity, and through his career he gradually moved from viewing China as an alternative civilization on a par with Europe to seeing the Chinese as a semi-civilized people: 'Many rites and practices still flourish among the Chinese, which one would scarcely expect to find anywhere except among savages in a low state of culture' (de Groot 1892: xii). Perhaps even a third notion running through his work was that 'China never changes'.[22]

FENGSHUI AS CULTURAL ENCOUNTER

In the Western accounts fengshui had slowly emerged as a type of religious system and an issue of faith. In step with Western writers taking it seriously as an authentic cosmology, proto-religion or other system occupying a prominent place in people's consciousness, the more important it may have become for the Chinese as a common shared tradition. It gradually acquired the guise of an anti-foreign discourse, a national emblem justifying an obstructionist set of practices.

In China clashes between Western enterprise and Chinese government interests were increasingly cloaked in popular cosmology expression. An interesting article in a Shanghai newspaper from 1875 refers to an instance of the now 'well-known superstition of Fengshui', where a district in the city of Hangzhou suffered an unusual number of deaths. A geomancer was called in and soon discovered a range of buildings belonging to the American Missions which stood on a hill overlooking the district. Instead of organizing a mob, such as had happened in many earlier incidents, a number of gentry were commissioned to proceed to Ningbo to approach the United States Consul. They suggested that the buildings were moved to another location to be agreed upon at the local authorities' expense. After communication between the consul and the mission they apparently agreed to let the station be moved, because the article closes at the time when this arrangement is being carried out (Dennys 1876: 66).

Another fengshui-related incident of Chinese resistance was the famous destruction of the Shanghai–Wusong railway in 1878. Ambitious railway schemes for China, including a line from Calcutta to Canton, had been suggested by foreign merchant interests from the 1840s, but had been abandoned because of rebellion and Western exclusion from the interior. In the 1860s a new comprehensive railway scheme for China was drawn up by a British company, but a

Chinese government official replied that 'Railroads would only be beneficial to China if undertaken by the Chinese themselves and constructed under their own management' (Fevour 1970: 107). Foreign enterprises insisted and Jardine's organized a company to build a little tramway from Shanghai towards the Wusong port, completed in 1875, in defiance of the Chinese authorities. Despite the first section being only a few kilometres long it was given tremendous symbolic values since its proprietors, who included Chinese shareholders, hoped that once the little railway had proven its worth it would end the Chinese reservations about railways. It had been built with an oddly winding track to avoid accusations of interference with the fengshui of the region and disturbance of graves and spirits. The imperial government, on the surface, chose not to get involved. The railway operated at a profit until 1876, when the death of a Chinese on the line was announced by the Chinese authorities in Shanghai; this was followed by a number of official protests and disturbances along the line, openly supported by the local gentry, who accused the line of ruining fengshui. As part of the Chefoo Convention the Chinese government agreed to purchase the line. But instead of continuing its operation the line was dismantled in 1878 and the rails and rolling stock sent to Taiwan, while the Chinese officials supervising the destruction work moved about in sedan chairs 'as an expression of their abhorrence of mechanical locomotion' (Chang K.N. 1943: 24).

It is possible, however, that practical considerations among the peasants were equally important to superstitious beliefs. The later nationalist Minister of Railways, Chang Kia-ngau, wrote of this incident that the Chinese peasants, 'like home-loving peasants everywhere', were unwilling to suffer expropriation of their land for railroad purposes and the locomotives were feared as a danger to cattle and pedestrians (Chang K.N. 1943: 25).

Considerable regional variation in the political setting was evident from coastal and riverine areas to the interior. Yet one should not underestimate the internal cohesion of the empire and the gentry's ability to mobilize across regions to confront a perceived threat to their interests – that of preserving the imperial social order. From Sichuan in western China we hear of missionaries being turned away by local gentry when attempting to build summer cottages in scenic mountain areas (Service 1989: 105–107).

At least some reports suggest that fengshui difficulties could be overcome in the interior. G.E. Morrison writes about his meeting with a Danish engineer Jensen, who, while working for the Great Northern Telegraph Company that established the first telegraph lines in China proper in 1881, built up a reputation for solving conflicts with the local population. He superintended the construction of more than 3,000 kilometres of telegraph lines in Yunnan and Guizhou, the more undisturbed hinterland. His account hints that practices conventionally ascribed to superstition could have a pragmatic aspect, if not be of an entirely worldly nature. When, for instance, in western Yunnan a group of villagers saw the telegraph as a menace to the good fortune of their district and cut down the poles – and sold the wire in compensation for their trouble – the engineer called for civic action:

> An energetic magistrate took the matter in hand. He issued a warning to the villagers, but this warning was unheeded. Then he took more vigorous measures. The very next case that occurred he had two men arrested, and charged with the offence. They were probably innocent, but under the persuasion of the bamboo they were induced to acquiesce in the magistrate's opinion as to their guilt. They were sentenced to be deprived of their ears, and then they were sent on foot, that all might see them, under escort along the line from Yunnan City to Tengyueh and back again. No poles have been cut down since. (Morrison 1895: 157)

As an increasing number of Chinese reform-minded officials advocated railways, mining and telegraph lines as inevitable means of modernization and national defence, following the advocacy of, for instance, Li Hongzhang, Zuo Zongtang and Ding Richang, the Qing court gradually eased up. In 1881 it permitted the construction of a 10 kilometre railway line from a coalmine near Tianjin to the river, but using only wagons drawn by horses and mules. The American engineer in charge of the line secretly built a locomotive from scrap materials and ran it on the line. Again, the court officials protested on the grounds that the rumbling locomotive disturbed the ancestral spirits and that the smoke polluted the rice fields. After a lengthy discussion the locomotive was finally sanctioned and as it proved its worth China soon entered a phase of native railway construction; public opinion was quickly diverted from the theoretical issue of the benefit from railway construction to the practical question of which railway to build first (Chang K.N. 1943: 25). As a matter of greater importance here, however, since it seems to confirm the argument, fengshui-based protests to railway and telegraph construction apparently died out soon after their nativization. An example of local magistrates' resolute handling of public protests was given above, while the same source states that by 1890 objections had been overcome everywhere (Morrison 1895: 157). Dyer Ball wrote in 1893:

> [I]t is not an insuperable obstruction, for whenever the Chinese government has made up its mind to the introduction of any of the inventions of Western science, Fung Shui is not allowed to be an obstacle, for, while pandering to its absurd ideas as far as is practicable without hindering the feasibility of their scheme, yet the populace, if obstructive, is soon made to feel that the will of the rulers has to be obeyed. (Ball 1893: 206)

Around the turn of the century the cultural encounter between China and the West acquired a new dimension. Despite immense difficulties, new nations had joined the Christian crusade to convert China. Soon most European nations had their own missionary societies in China and the powerful American Protestantism became a major force in the Christian enterprise. During the last decades of the century the number of missionaries posted in China grew rapidly and the missionary expansion continued into the 1910s and 1920s. Roman Catholics listed approximately 1,100 personnel in 1901 and over 2,500 in 1920. The number of Western Christian evangelists increased from approximately 1,300 in 1889 to 3,800 in 1906 and to 6,600 in 1919; having their backing in the wealthiest nations, the Protestant missions not only surpassed the Catholic in numbers, but far more so in significance. Only 106 out of China's 1,704 counties were not reached by Protestant evangelic activity (Lutz 1988: 2). The new dimension in missionary work was schooling: more than anything else, Protestantism in China came to be engaged in modern education as opposed to traditional Confucian learning. In a formal sense, conversion had been a failure although it began to pick up in the beginning of the twentieth century. As an example, an Australian traveller to Yunnan in 1890 describes the personal results of what he sees as narrow-minded and uncompromising men of the China Inland Mission, whose dispatch to China he sees as a mere farce: 'In a population of five to seven millions of friendly and peaceable people, eighteen missionaries in eight years ... have converted eleven Chinese; how long, then, will it take to convert the remainder?' (Morrison 1895: 179). Conversion to exclusiveness had obviously failed.

Both in the foreign community in China and back in the home countries, education was endorsed as the most legitimate among the missionaries' activities in China and the chief means to civilize her population. By 1900 there were some 2,000 Protestant schools in China, including six institutions claiming the status of college or university. Particularly after the abandonment of the Confucian examination system in 1905, the Protestant institutions converted their new-found favour into larger and better equipped schools able to accommodate a rapidly increasing number of students.

Still both Western teachings and particularly Western technology remained under heavy charge, the latter often compared to machine-breaking, or 'Luddism' in industrializing Europe (Chesneaux 1973: 50). High factory chimneys were often opposed due to the polluting fengshui influence of smoke (Morrison 1895: 175). Modern weaving and spinning machinery was destroyed in rural districts near Canton in the 1880s, and attacks on factories, now termed 'factory-smashing' in Chinese (*da chang*), continued until the end of the century. Peasant resistance to modern textile industry was widespread in towns, which had attracted thousands of impoverished peasants in search of work. Unlike similar movements in England, motivated by purely economic aims, Chinese resistance typically combined a number of sentiments: modern technology was rejected because it was foreign as much as because it was seen to create unemployment. Factory-smashing and attacks on missionary property and personnel often occurred simultaneously. In some cases, as for instance in the 1891 anti-Christian riots in the Yangtze valley, local gentry incited the peasants against the foreigners and provided both arguments and arms. When the Yellow River went over its banks in the late 1890s and impoverished thousands of peasants in Shandong, Zhili and Henan in the northeast, foreign churches and missionary personnel were accused of having caused the disaster by their malicious fengshui influence (Davis, F. 1971: 15). Revolts raged over the three provinces. This increased tension climaxed in the Boxer Uprising in 1897–1900 aimed at destroying everything foreign.

Thus, in the late nineteenth century, fengshui concerns had acquired a new role: its all-embracing categories without clear distinction between natural, social and psychological phenomena, and much depending on the situational interpretation of a geomancer, could easily accommodate expressions of proto-nationalistic sentiments and frequently even provide a justification for infuriated attacks on anything associated with foreign dominion. Particularly anti-foreign resistance around the areas of foreign influence gave a boost to fengshui as a means of expressing nationalistic sentiments. Its capacity for accumulating odd pieces of philosophy and in practice everything that matters for a good Chinese life made also it a convenient means to express the factors seen to inhibit such harmony: capitalist economy challenging social structures, Western technology producing unemployment, new communication lines changing local power structure, and missionary activity causing division between fellow Chinese. Fengshui was continuously nourished and developed as a separate idiom and an art of cultural performance in, for instance, Hong Kong – presumably further stimulated by the continued presence of foreigners and the willingness of the British government to take it seriously.

CHINESE IMPERIAL GOVERNMENT POLICY ON FENGSHUI

Not only did the popular support for geomancy seem to grow during China's later dynastic history, but also the Confucian literati appeared to have become less critical towards it. In city planning and the layout of city walls geomantic considerations were evident from early times, although rarely spared from scepticism (Wright 1977). A seventeenth-century manual for local magistrates, for instance, advises fengshui considerations in the construction of ditches for defending cities against bandits, but at the same time it strongly recommends action to rectify people's beliefs in heterodox religions and their charlatans that promise riches, power and long life (Huang L. 1984). Edward Farmer writes of the early Ming government that it is difficult to determine to what extent fengshui was taken seriously in the choice of a new capital; someone had warned against the choice of Beijing on account of the Mongols having ruined its fengshui, but later this kind of thinking was criticized as superstitious deception which ought to be punished (Farmer 1976: 42–43). Through the Ming, however, emperors increasingly used fengshui against enemies (Wang Y. 1991: 292); at the end of the Ming records show that the emperor and a peasant leader used fengshui against each other (Hong 1993: 10). Around 1600 Matteo Ricci wrote of the Chinese that 'many of their most distinguished men are interested in this recondite science' (Ricci 1953: 360). Despite imperial policy denouncing fengshui, the historical records abound with anecdotes concerning the private employment of fengshui specialists by the throne, and despite a profound ambivalence on the part of the elite high officials there was much concern with finding auspicious locations for tombs (Smith R. 1991: 156, 159). C.K. Yang writes of late imperial society that 'some Confucians did not believe in geomancy, but they appeared to have been in the minority', which according to Yang was testified in common family genealogies. One read: 'Although we should not completely believe in geomancy, yet if a location is damaged, those involved seldom escape from the harmful effect.' Similarly, according to Yang, few major public buildings were constructed without advice from geomancers and Qing law provided for these services (Yang C. 1970: 263–264). Also a smaller number of Chinese officials, some even high-ranking such as Zhao Zhixin (1662–1744), Li Wentian (1834–1895) and Zhang Zhidong (1837–1909), practised *fengshui* during the Qing, together with a number of office exam failures (Smith R. 1991: 148).

The fengshui mode of thought operated at a point where elite and common outlooks interacted. If the early Western sojourners in China had a patronizing attitude to beliefs in fengshui and other traditions of thought among the populace, they were indeed echoing the Chinese imperial government and large parts of the literati. Yet a striking difference in opinion existed among the Chinese rulers, whose shifting policies demonstrated the common ambivalence toward divination. The Kangxi emperor (reigned 1662–1722), for instance, took a clear stand against divination when in 1681 he wrote,

> Siting experts have a great deal to say, not from books about how the great sages and worthies of ancient times made their selections, but rather from books fabricated by people later on to suit themselves ... There is no such thing as a definitive opinion. It is true, however, that such techniques cannot be completely dispensed with. (Huang Y. 1991: 16)

By contrast, the following emperors did not share this scepticism, but instead strove to guard orthodoxy. The resolute Yongzheng emperor (reigned 1723–35) explicated his father's policy in a decree called Amplification of the Instructions of the Sage Edict, intended to exclude heterodoxy in order to elevate the study of orthodoxy:

> The accomplishments of the sages and the principles of the sovereign are all founded upon orthodox learning. As to the writings that are not those of the sages, and those unclassical books which arouse mankind and alarm the populace, causing disorder and confusion of views and gnawing at the people and their wealth as corroding insects – these are all heterodoxy and ought to be excluded. (Yang C. 1970: 194)

The decree goes on to state that 'the misleading of the people... is a thing which the law does not pardon, and against the heterodox practices of leaders and priests the realm has constant punishment' (de Groot 1904: 245–247). Another imperial edict from 1735 prohibited the postponement of burials for long periods, a common practice if the best geomantic position for a grave was not immediately available. It also prohibited the moving of bodies to other graves believed to be better (Lee 1959: 93).

Clearly the late Qing state was not arguing against popular cosmology on theological or philosophical grounds (Yongzheng was a Buddhist believer), but merely attempted to safeguard the state against popular rebellion and other disturbances and challenges to its authority deriving from religious specialists 'deluding the people'.[23] Politics were more important to the state than cosmology. The late Qing dynasty penal code (*Da qing lü li*), published in 1805, was remarkably harsh on all sorts of magic,[24] stating that 'all persons convicted of writing and editing books of sorcery and magic, or of employing spells and incantations, in order to agitate and influence the minds of the people, shall be beheaded, after remaining in prison the usual period' (Cadell and Davies 1810: 273). Thus a strong incentive to express fengshui calculations as soberly as possible was provided. Yet, the same law has no less than thirteen clauses on disturbing graves, showing the imperial concern with preserving the peace of graves, coffins and corpses. Apart from a single clause against practising incantations on opened graves, the rest are concerned with breaking into graves and coffins in order to rob belongings or destroy the graves. Most serious are offences such as 'destroying, mutilating, or casting away, the unburied corpse of an elder relation', which were to be punished with death (ibid.: 295). A foreign account from the mid-nineteenth century provides insight into the intense conflicts that may arise over dead bodies: it mentions the practice of creditors seizing the coffin of a deceased debtor to force the family to pay (Williams 1848: 264).

The above-mentioned 'Sacred Edict' of the Yongzheng emperor, later published among the Imperial Paraphrases, also denounces fengshui in a blunt formulation:

> Taking a prominent part in deluding the people with false doctrines of any description, obtaining money by false pretences under the guise of official authority, believing in the false stories of the necromancers and geomancers ... all these are punishable with death.[25]

What has often been said about fengshui, that Confucianism despised it while mandarins would use it privately, is certainly substantiated by the ambivalent stance towards grave manipulation in official documents. While forbidding fengshui, legislators obviously held the view that great harm could be inflicted by putting objects, characters or signs expressing evil into an enemy's family grave. To the Ming dynasty law code on sorcery, which obviously recognizes sorcery as a means of hurting or killing people, a legislator added a commentary in 1817,

Whoever, cherishing a grudge, clandestinely puts a stake of peach-wood into the ancestral grave of another, with intent to frustrate the fung-shui of the same, shall be punished as if he had used spectres in subjection, written charms, or spells, with intent to render others ill or miserable, that is to say, two degrees less severely than the law would demand if he had planned a murder and begun to execute the crime, yet without inflicting any wounds – viz. with banishment for two years. (de Groot 1907: 913)

The perfunctory character of many Imperial Chinese laws and regulations has often been stressed and particularly in relation to religious matters their enforcement would vary according to the political situation. The imperial circular from 1871, which proposed to legalize fengshui when turned against foreign missions, has already been mentioned. According to C.K. Yang, historical records show that many laws would be enforced in critical situations but tacitly ignored in normal times (Yang C. 1970: 181).

The ideological motivation for religious persecution, on the other hand, appears relatively unchanged over the centuries. If we follow C.K. Yang's argument for a while, there is much testimony to the Chinese state ideology being of non-secular construction. Traditional government strove to demonstrate its mastery over supernatural forces, that is, to make the belief in supernatural forces instrumental to the exercise of power. There followed logically a strict hierarchical pattern of supernatural powers, the highest of which only the state could seek to control. As supremacy was assigned to heaven, there was an exclusive imperial monopoly over the performance of rituals in the worship of it, which was clearly stated even as late as in Qing law: 'Those who make private appeal to heaven and worship the Seven Mansions... shall be punished with eighty strokes of a stick.' (Yang C. 1970: 183). Worship of heaven was left exclusively for political purposes, with the ruler as the only legitimate intermediary between heaven and man, and any interference with interpreting the will of heaven was defined as heresy. When this had a private character punishment would rarely ensue, but when connected to any kind of public statement or to associations, established religions or secret religious movements, persecution would follow. Even though the law was very general in formulation, its spirit was clear: any use of spiritual agents for political purposes was a challenge of authority, to which the proper state institutions would react with whatever means they saw fit. The government monopoly on interpreting heavenly omens served to prevent dissenting groups from linking unusual natural phenomena or societal ills to heavenly responses to imperial government. Violation of the anti-heresy law was met with the severest punishment: 'Those who make up heretic apocryphal literature, and circulate heretic talk to deceive the public, shall be punished by decapitation' (Yang C. 1970: 185).

Any religious belief or activity divergent from the state orthodoxy of Confucianism (including its 'syncretism'[26] with Buddhism and Taoism) might be regarded as heterodoxy, with possible subversive influence. In 1813 the Jia Qing emperor (reigned 1796–1820) declared in the suppression of a sectarian movement: 'No so-called religion exists beyond the Three Basic Relations ... and the Five Constant Virtues ...; and there is no quarter from which happiness may be sought after, other than the Way of Heaven and the laws of the monarch' (Yang C. 1970: 193).

This largely echoed the above-mentioned decree from 1724, which continued to be widely circulated. Throughout the nineteenth century countless sectarian movements were crushed, amply described by J.J.M. de Groot, C. K. Yang, J. K. Fairbanks and others. Some examples are the suppression of the Eight Trigrams society in 1813, a sect lead by a single person in Shandong in 1837, the Long Hua sect in the 1840s and the demolition of numerous local so-called heretic temples through the 1820s and 1830s (de Groot 1904: 223). Far from being on theological or philosophical grounds, argues C.K. Yang (1970: 193), this served the specific purpose of defending the Confucian state, evidently in crisis long before the Opium War and the Taiping Rebellion. All major persecutions of organized religious movements were connected with political rebellion or the imperial government's fear of such, in addition to those mentioned above for instance organized by the blacklisted organization such as the White Lotus, whose rebellion was crushed in 1805, the Heaven and Earth society, the Triads and many others. If the frequency of these persecutions is taken as an expression of political pressure on the imperial government, the Qing dynasty was drawing towards its end.

During the tumultuous nineteenth century the issue of civil and military officials, either as individuals or groups, converting to heterodox religions came up repeatedly. A study of Viceroy Yeh Ming-ch'en in Canton shows that diviners were used for public affairs on certain occasions in the 1850s, but mainly in relation to the suppression of the Taiping Rebellion (Wong 1976: 15). Geomancers were among the groups of people to which Qing law was particularly sensitive: 'Sorcerers of the Yin-yang school are not permitted to enter the homes of civil and military officers of any rank and make disorderly talk on the good fortune or calamity of the state. Violators are punishable by one hundred strokes with a long stick' (Yang C. 1970: 186).

What did all this mean to the practising of fengshui in late imperial China? First of all, in accordance with the broad conception of all cosmology, divination and religion as contained in heterodoxy, state policy related to potential threats rather than to strict categories of institutions. The message conveyed to geomancers and other diviners by Qing law was clear enough. Only Buddhism and Taoism were tolerated as congregational religions and countless restrictions applied, such as each priest being licensed; only priests over forty being allowed to proselytize and only having one proselyte each; every temple in principle having to be approved of by the local authority; only deities lesser than heaven being worshipped and so forth – even though these rules may not have been widely known (Welsh 1968: 134–35). For the diviners such as geomancers public appearances, proselytizing, running conspicuous shops and inter-fering with state affairs were a risky business, which the state could crack down upon at any time and accuse participants of heresy. Even if fengshui had the intrinsic potential to develop into a formalized institution comparable to congregational religions, for instance by the establishment of academies, this would hardly have been allowed in the Qing. Instead, the imperial government preferred to see geomancers and many other diviners and popular religious specialists acquire roles comparable to that of artisans. The common geo-mancers generally remained restricted to the village community, where they certainly were influential, but held a dubious position in which they should make sure that people would come to them privately to acquire their services. Over the centuries, most Chinese power-holders from the imperial government down to clan leaders turned against untamed popular ideology. Even rebels such as the Taipings and the Boxers, who themselves used magico-religious symbolism, attempted to destroy rural beliefs in supernatural forces because they were either taken as a sign of weakness along with opium smoking and foot binding (Shih 1967: 226–227), or as obstacles to mobilize the peasants around worldly causes. But at the same time there should be no doubt that the authorities' close guarding of popular cosmology contributed to its unruly and disobedient char-acteristics.

There is another matter of importance. Countless imperial edicts had emphasized Confucian orthodoxy, rooted in the ancient classics and the neo-Confucian synthesis of the Song. To support the sacred faculty of the classics and of official documents, a decree forbade the destruction of paper with writing on it except in imperially sanctioned kilns. But behind the same imperial edicts we also see the contours of a ceaseless and nation-wide battle to delineate orthodoxy according to specific interests. Even within the imperial government orthodoxy was contested, as the Jesuits discovered in the seventeenth century. Outwardly state power defended a rigorous reading of orthodoxy in all matters, while independent forces strove to give it a much broader scope and character. There ensued a veritable battle to find historical origins of dubious literature, controversial heroes and popular figures, questionable ideas and unauthorized religions, in an abstract sense to raise their authority in competition with state orthodoxy, but as much in a very concrete sense to pursue their legitimate status and escape persecution. The Board of Rites supervising religious affairs was constantly on guard and ready to 'destroy heretic religions to correct the customs of the people', which involved the burning of illicit books and printing blocks.[27] Even popular works of fiction were not exempt; one example was the thirteenth-century novel *Shui hu zhuan* [All Men are Brothers], depicting an unjust empire in collapse, which by an imperial mandate as late as around 1800 was strictly forbidden to be printed, sold and even read (Buck 1933: vi–vii). Along with other philosophers, fengshui philosophers through the ages pursued exactly this matter when they traced their leading ideas back to archaic times, placed themselves in a long unbroken literary tradition and sometimes even backdated their own works. Who did they delude? Hardly themselves or their contemporaries, but perhaps some of the later sinologists feeding on the ancient roots and authenticity of Chinese civilization. With the gradual degeneration of the Confucian state two issues came to dominate. One was that heterodoxy rose in a myriad of representations, among which those commonly associated with popular cosmology were prominent. Another was the escalated state oppression of heterodoxy, either as a response to its uncontrolled growth or simply reflecting the state power's own dwindling heavenly mandate. Although a majority among the literate classes may have approved of the general ideas behind fengshui cosmology, their application in a myriad of interpretations by semi-literate practitioners who struggled to scratch a living from serving a destitute peasantry hungry for magic, was at the same time opposed.

71

THE STANCE OF THE NATIONALIST GOVERNMENT, 1911–49

More than anything else, it was China's disastrous 1895 defeat to the Japanese that awakened the Chinese nation to the bankruptcy of the Qing dynasty. Young intellectuals joined by scores of reformists among the official ranks called for radical reforms if not the overthrow of the dynasty. The following years have been called the golden age of the Chinese press, as the number of native Chinese publications exploded. The Manchu Court responded by ruthless suppression of all publications inspired by the outside world and by prohibiting students from working for, writing for, buying and possessing newspapers (Chang Kuo. 1968: 17). Although the Manchu dynasty fell in 1911 and the remarkable 'Chinese Renaissance', or 'New Culture' movement began in 1917, press censorship and suppression persisted until 1949, when the People's Republic took over.

British parliamentary democracy became the model, albeit short-lived, for the establishment of the new republic under Sun Yat-sen in 1912. The new modern-educated ruling elite took a hostile stand against popular cosmology and religion. The young Sun Yat-sen, inspired by both the Gospel and his impressions from his stay in Hawaii, where the white man's assault on local 'superstition' made a major contribution to his obsession with the idea that the breaking of Chinese 'superstition' was a condition for progress (Sharman 1968: 16), confronted his fellow villagers when he returned from his studies in 1883:

> And what does the Son of Heaven do for you in your village? – Nothing. It is you who establish the schools; it is you who build bridges and take care of the roads; it is you who do everything. The Manchus even neglect your moral development, for they allow you to linger in the ignorance of Fengshui. I do not blame you; the fault lies with the Son of Heaven. (D'elia 1931: 10)

Even closer to the Christian stand was his war against idolatry, presumably also inspired by his knowledge of the course of the Taiping rebellion, starting as a war against 'superstition' with iconoclasm as its method. He saw this as a necessity to make an entrance for new ideas: 'No progress is possible for China as long as the people offer incense to idols. Superstition inspires fear. Ere China can become a progressive nation, it will be necessary to destroy all these paintings and all these statues, for all superstition stands for fear and ignorance' (D'elia 1931: 11).

But progress for whom? For half a century elitist biases had induced Chinese modernizers to perceive the toil and taxes of the peasantry as resources in the progress of the nation rather than

72

viewing progress as a means for improving the livelihood of the peasantry. The early decades of the twentieth century were a vibrant time in China with a plethora of innovative thinkers. Yet there were relatively few 'liberal' thinkers (in the manner of John Locke, Bertrand Russell and John Dewey) and the China League for Civil Rights of the 1920s was shortlived (Huang M. 2000). There were few intellectuals (in the manner of Karl Marx and Friedrich Engels) to oppose national chauvinism and promote international class struggle, and there was not yet a rising social science to point out that it was perhaps fear that inspired superstition rather than the other way around. Despite a richly faceted debate on China's predicament and her potential role in the modern world, many modern-educated Chinese of the new century were unduly ashamed of their rustic compatriots; astonishingly, all references to the pillars of rural society – family, ritual and popular cosmology – disappeared from intellectual debate. Even the peasant associations which developed out of the renewed resistance to foreign domination and the growth of actual nationalism soon adopted the rulers' national administrative and integrationist concerns and turned against geomancy (Chesneaux 1973: 92), thought to be one of the traditional fears from which the peasants should be liberated. The republican period saw a deepening conflict between modern-educated elite intellectuals, with whom the leadership rested, and the common people, who were under the persistent influence of religion (Yang C. 1970: 341). C.K. Yang has suggested that the continued civic strife, economic deterioration and social disintegration of the Qing empire, continuing into the Republican period, represented circumstances conducive to the development of popular movements stemming from notions of superhuman powers, miracles and a host of supernatural ideas (Yang C. 1970: 354).

Foreign sojourners' accounts from the early years of the Republic are a stunning imitation of the Chinese republican elite's modernist outlook – or the other way around. It was noted in Chapter One how the new generation of Chinese sociologists disregarded popular cosmology in their social and religious studies, related to the increasing extroversion among young Chinese intellectuals. To a large extent both parties saw a common aim in a thorough Chinese reformation. Foreign universities were established at the beginning of the century. Typical of the early republican years is an account of Chinese superstitions by Professor Isaac T. Headland of Peking (Beijing) University. He foresees 'monstrous difficulties' in the reconstruction of China, which he doubts the Chinese will be able to cope with alone: 'Among these difficulties there will be none that will be harder to overcome than superstition' (Headland 1914: 257). He claims that the principles of fengshui, which he describes as 'a scientific system of superstition' embracing everything that its founders know and do not know about nature, is believed by high and low alike (ibid.: 259–263). Paul Myron, writing at the same time as Headland, expresses a similar determination that the ways of the Chinese people must be changed. Although the Revolution did wonders, he argues, the people uphold this 'winged dragon monster ... which has ruled China for a thousand years or more ...' allegedly with a religious faith, that tends to surpass the reverence held for the three religions (Myron 1915: 24–26). A story from Beijing around this time is quite humorous: alterations to the square in front of the Qianmen to make room for modern traffic were met with violent public protests, particularly concerning the two stone lions in front of the gate that had to be moved and therefore would be displeased. A 'Chinese' solution was found: the lions were blindfolded with blue bandages and then dragged, unresisting, to their new positions (Bredon 1931: 49).

Another aspect of both Headland's and Myron's descriptions is of great significance, since it contrasts the naive endorsement of feng- shui so common to their time, for instance in Dyer Ball (Ball 1893: 269–271). Headland traces the fact that so many fengshui difficulties occur between Chinese and missionaries to widespread Chinese superstitions about foreigners: they were foreign devils, who took out the eyes of Chinese and used them in medicine or photography, they cut off the queue of the Chinese to ridicule them, they put a Chinese child under every tie of the railroads they built, and so forth (Headland 1914: 267). Missionary sources add another very common superstition, namely that foreigners ate Chinese children. Yet an- other one concerning Chinese children was that in the missionary orphanages they were killed to prepare 'fiendish medicine' (Monina 1983: 281). All these tales spread across the country like wildfire as soon as they originated in one place (pre-sumably with official backing) – something which the Boxers had exploited when they put up placards and circulated outrageous accusations against the foreigners. Missionaries in many localities were the primary or only representatives of foreign races, and had to bear the brunt of anti- foreign sentiments, prejudices and convenient projections. Myron also speculates that the encounter between Chinese and foreigners affected popular uses of fengshui:

There is a tendency on the part of foreigners to exaggerate the pre-valence of superstition and particularly Feng Sui. There is even or has been a tendency to exaggerate Feng Sui by the anti-foreign Chinese themselves, who after the Boxer outbreak sometimes invoked that ancient custom merely as a part of their Boxer political propaganda. (Myron 1915: 30)

Many contemporary writers indeed referred to incidents of the 1870s, relocated into the present as proof of the Chinese faith in geomancy, which, for instance in the words of Dyer Ball, 'played such an overwhelmingly important part in Chinese life' (Ball 1893: 269–271). We are back to a theme which modern anthropology has paid considerable attention to: performance in ritual, overstating differ-ence and playing with the stranger's indignation. A growing body of literature shows how the construction of national, minority and indigenous identities has built on elements that derive their mean-ing from their impact on the perceived enemy, not least 'Western imperialism', and that these identities were in fact built in close interaction with Western historians, anthropologists and activists. In a larger historical perspective, Westerners' sudden at-tention to native traditions such as fengshui may well have con-tributed to their rising significance on the domestic front. We shall return to this question in Chapter 7, dealing with the construction of fengshui as environ-mental discourse in recent decades, since these sources provide a better opportunity to pursue such argument.

In 1915, after two remarkable decades comparing in intensity to those of the 1840s to 1860s, the nationalist government became more draconian with abuse of power and constant persecution of political opponents, gradually laying the foundation for civil war. China entered the era of war-lordism 1916–27, while at the same time the Communist movement was gathering strength. One remarkable out-come of the rise of the Republic was most certainly a rising dis-crepancy between rural life and the new urban lifestyle,[28] particularly in the increasingly metropolitan cities of Shanghai, Canton, Hong Kong, Tianjin and Beijing. Chinese politics became centred on the city, where religion was losing its hold on all major social institutions.

The Republic gave rise to a new urban elite and with it the New Culture or Chinese Renaissance movement. At the close of World War I Chinese intellectuals were of the conviction that science and demo-cracy were the keys to the success of Western civilization. They were particularly convinced that modern science was of the leading influences that reduced the power of religion: a vision that the outlook of science, founded on scepticism and empirical knowledge,

75

could prove a powerful transformative power also in China. The writings of many Western scientists were quoted to glorify science and devaluate religion, increasingly depicted as primitive ignorance (Yang C. 1970: 364–365). Praising the omnipotence of science instituted a logical correlative, that of religion being an obstacle to progress for China. Movements to revive Buddhism and Confucianism as national religions were silenced.

Despite paying lip-service to democracy the diverse political ideologies that sprang from this movement still shared a strong urban elitist outlook. The new urban elite constituted the common roots of both the nationalist party and the Chinese Communist Part (CCP), also sharing a negative stance towards Christian and native religion. The leading intellectual figures of the New Culture movement such as Hu Shi, Luo Longji and Chen Duxiu strove to popularize language and literature, but it was in a manner that was intended to revolutionize Chinese society according to a preconceived scheme – nationalist and elitist in outlook – more than it took notice of the expressed needs of the destitute classes. Sun Yat-sen's nationalist revolution bore the imprint of traditional absolutist power; only his own death in 1925 highlighted the contrast between his dream of national unity and the 'brutish' fact of China's territorial, social, cultural and political disunity (Fitzgerald 1996: 16). For him, as for his successors, Chinese politics to a very large extent meant 'managing the affairs of the crowds' (Fitzgerald 1996: 17), that is, managing society.

The new enthusiasm for science together with rising nationalism were the basis for the anti-religious movement of 1922, first targeting Christianity. A broader current of the Chinese Renaissance movement emerged in the mid-1920s, including the battle cry of 'Down with superstition' along with the cries against imperialism and warlordism, resulting in widespread demolition of temples and sacred objects as well as conversion of temples into secular uses and confiscation of property. The nationalist government, staffed with many new-culture radicals of the Renaissance movement, instituted a number of decrees intended to curb beliefs in 'magic, fate and the supernatural'. In 1929 came the promulgation of the 'Procedure for the Abolition of the Occupations of Divination, Astrology, Physiognomy and Palmistry, Magic and Geomancy', followed in 1930 by a decree ordering those who sold 'superstitious merchandise' to change their occupation, but without effective enforcement (Yang C. 1970: 266–267).

As missionary activity again declined in many parts of the empire in the 1920s and 1930s due to political unrest, and a major power realignment slowly emerged in China with the rise of the new Western-educated urban elite, fengshui was gradually transfigured. It became more commonly rural than urban, despite many urban intellectuals taking an interest in it and some practising the academic forms.

In the wider perspective, cosmological ideas were undergoing change. When those in power ceased to use the heavenly factor to consolidate the political system, its cultic symbols and rituals were perhaps also losing their influence on the popular mind. Yet popular religious cults associated with the moral and political order in local communities still flourished (Yang C. 1970: 372, 375). It is incorrect to conclude that fengshui was dormant, but it seemed to disappear from the political scene and primarily be practised in circumstances far removed from foreign onlookers. We can only speculate that with fewer Westerners around to describe, study, theorize and wonder about fengshui, perhaps it became less of an issue, at least in the form that we knew from the second half of the nineteenth century. It would take more than the present study to prove this point on a general scale, however.

We can conjecture from the tone in nationalist government policy that popular modes of thought continued to constitute a potential threat to established authority. The late nationalist government attempted to suppress the 'superstitious worship of spirits' allegedly performed by fortune-tellers, astrologers, geomancers, magicians and other categories of local practitioners receiving money for doing services and curing the sick. A decree issued in 1948 shows once more the plasticity in the legal system, enabling local governments to interfere at will. The decree concerned

> [t]hose who operate unorthodox religious houses to delude the people; those who contribute to spirits of impurity to obtain riches; ... those who build shrines for the spirits...; all who initiate or participate in those processions in which idols are carried to thank the gods; all who invoke superstition in their actions; other illegal movements and secret societies. (Bush 1970: 383)

The nationalist government continued with more than just imperial policy on popular cosmology. The local administrative control of religious affairs was also kept in place in most localities until the Communist takeover in 1949; this was the case in the Sichuan field-work area, for instance, where a number of the present geomancers recalled the general meetings in these guilds. All practitioners of the

Yinyang School, including all forms of divination and astrology but with geomancy as the most important, were under the control of a special officer elected by the practitioners themselves in every local department of administration. In addition to controlling the yinyang specialists, his duty was 'to prevent them from misleading the populace with imaginary and false talk, and to use them properly for public ceremonies, for selecting locations for major construction works, and for divining propitious days and hours' (Yang C. 1970: 190).

Summarizing the century that passed from the 1840s to the 1940s, we must first of all realize that Chinese society was thrown into a process of transformation with few parallels elsewhere. Millions and millions of people were killed in internal turmoil and strife, a fact which modern historians like John K. Fairbank will only admit to foreign aggression having played a minor role. The Chinese state simultaneously expanded its sphere of authority dramatically, with rising militarization as a consequence. There was a growing gap between the educated elite, ashamed of their rural compatriots' beliefs, and the vast rural population, largely unable to enjoy the fruits of modernity. The 'one culture, one China' syndrome led to the persecution of heterodoxy that rose to near-paranoia in the latter period of the Qing, and it was carried into the new republic in the form of a self-assured urban elite's attempts to modernize society, while largely ignoring the demands and convictions of the peasantry.

Despite anti-religious legislation all conditions for the continued prominence of popular cosmology and particularly its divinatory aspects were at hand in the latter part of China's modern history: a miserable peasantry, either landless or heavily indebted from outrageously high land rents and lack of public protection, a ruthless gentry who enjoyed wide-ranging protection and frequently re-presented the government in the villages, and a general hardening of policy and abuse of power justified by civil war.

NOTES

1 'Imperially Approved Complete Collection of Writings and Illustrations, Past and Present' (*Qinding gujin tushu jicheng*). Quoted in Smith R. 1991.

2 Yuan Shushan, 'Biographies of Diviners in China by Period' (*Zhongguo lidai buren zhuan*), 1948. Quoted in Smith R. 1991.

3 When Elizabeth came to the throne of England in 1558, she changed the language of worship from Latin to English. In 1570 Pope Paul V excommunicated Elizabeth, declared her not the lawful queen but rather a suitable target for assassination. The Jesuits were outlawed, but for many years thereafter

(beginning in 1580) the Jesuit seminary at Douay in France sent a steady stream of priests (secretly educated and ordained Englishmen) to England, where they celebrated Latin Masses in secret, subject to death for treason if caught.

4   Samuel Wells Williams, originally a printer, was sent to Canton in 1833 by the American Board of Commisioners for Foreign Missions and lived in China for 12 years. Williams was co-editor of *The Chinese Repository*. He finished his career at Yale University as occupant of the first American chair in Chinese studies.

5   A list of the journals cited is provided after the references in the back of the book.

6   The few references to the significance of fengshui for the Chinese during this period, for instance for the Hong merchants in Canton, were written at a later date.

7   Exhumation and reburial of bones was commonly practised i south China.

8   An early inclusion of fengshui in a standard work on China is found in Nevius 1869.

9   This is despite the fact that missionaries commonly were conservative in personal and religious outlook (Cohen 1978: 543).

10   The book is listed in 'Catalog of Protestant Missionary Works in Chinese' (Lai 1980: 110).

11   Published in Shanghai from 1875 to 1904.

12   'Editorial Selections: Mining in China' *(NCHM* 19 June 1868).

13   See note 9.

14   Sir Rutherford Alcock's statement was remarkably weak considering the reputation for resoluteness that he acquired during his time as a consul in Shanghai in 1846–49 and considering his subsequent professional experience in south China.

15   Buck 1954: 199, cited in Lutz 1988: 14.

16   Expressed, for instance, in the writings of Timothy Richard (Bohr 1972).

17   The *Zongliyamen* Memorandum of 9 February 1871. The memorandum followed several secret memoranda from Qing dignitaries to the emperor and from the emperor to the *Zongliyamen* concerning the missionary question, but was as much expressive of internal discontent with the Qing government's 'tractability' to the foreign powers after officially apologizing for the Tianjin massacre in 1870. See Monina 1983.

18   The Chinese Prince Kong is reported to have said in a conversation with the British Foreign Minister Sir Rutherford Alcock after the latter had raised the tax on imported opium: 'If you could only put a check on the importation of missionaries, China would be eternally your debtor' (Burden 1872: 266).

19   There was a law against permitting women to worship in Buddhist and Taoist temples and monasteries where they might come into contact male priests and worshippers. This law was rarely enforced, for womed were typically in the majority among worshippers in temples. Immorality and sexual promiscuity were frequently brought up in the persecution of religious

organizations, however, as one of the undesirable features of heterodoxy (Yang C. 1970: 203–204). There were separate nunneries in China and lay Buddhist ascetic associations (*zhaijiao*) had also admitted both men and women since the Ming.

20 For instance, *NCHS* 15 February 1871; 29 April 1871; 5 May 1871.

21 Most of the memorandum is translated in MacNair 1927: 448–452, and discussed in *CRMJ* September 1871: 111.

22 A thorough criticism of de Groot's work, including an account of his intellectual development and the complete transformation of his view of China, is offered in Freedman 1979: 25–31.

23 Also missionaries were of the opinion that the Chinese government was guided by political motives in attacking sects. See, for instance, J.S. Burden 1872.

24 The last dynasties saw a gradually tightening penal code, seen for instance in the dramatically rising number of offences leading to capital punishment (Bodde 1981).

25 As translated by 'A.B.C' in *NQ* 5 May 1868: 69.

26 A certain syncretism between the three doctrines became fashionable from the end of the Ming period (Gernet 1985: 64)

27 One example is the persecution of the Buddhist Lo sect and several others in the seventeenth century. See, for instance, Overmyer 1976, Chapter 6.

28 Contemporary Chinese books discussing social issues strongly advocated a modern lifestyle as a basis for national progress; one example of many is Chen C. 1922.

3 Fengshui Practices and Policies after 1949

Ideology was put into practice only gradually after the Communist forces took control and established the People's Republic in October 1949. It is debatable whether the Communists were sincere when they initially conceded religious freedom on the condition that it did not interfere with their overall revolutionary programme,[1] strongly atheist in word and deed. Three major trends were important for the development of both popular cosmology and policy responses under the new regime.

First of all, atheism had been on the rise in the previous decades when many young Chinese were eager for modern education, on which Protestant institutions had a firm grip. They grew up with the Protestant critique of traditional Chinese society and Confucian values, which they largely accepted, but soon began to look for alternative readings of modernity than that promoted by, in their eyes, imperialist foreign churches. A whole generation of Chinese reformers, whether liberal or Marxist in orientation, hence came to share an equal contempt for Chinese popular religion and Christianity. During the half century of republican government a solid anti-superstition movement among large segments of society had also contributed to a distinct drift towards secularization of social life in the cities. Thus, overall, what we usually see as secularization and a modern materialist approach to life had gained considerable ground, particularly among the elite. Yet, as has been argued previously, secularization of the state and social institutions in general did not prevent individual convictions from being fused with alternative modes of thought, although public expression of religious thought had been restricted. Evidence from throughout the revolutionary period suggests that not only common people but also party secretaries and even state officials frequently trespassed on the border between acceptable and obsolete ideas.

Secondly, as modernization took a firm grip on the urban elite and intellectuals were increasingly oriented towards modern science and international politics, religion and religious symbolism were losing their influence on leadership and government. On the other hand, common people in rural areas were persistently influenced by religion, indicated, for instance, by the ubiquitous presence of all sorts of diviners and the widespread sale of the old almanac, containing chronomantic guidance for the conduct of life and other religious material (Yang C. 1970: 341). We can conjecture the increasing divide between rural and urban people through the republican period, generating tension, at times actual conflict, and most certainly a growing disdain for each other's lifestyle and outlook.

Thirdly, a long-term trend was the increasing ability and determination of the modernizing state to reach out and interfere with the life of common people in the vast rural hinterlands. Even though the Communists built on a deep-rooted Chinese inclination towards centralized totalitarian power, and even though they continued a progressive control-extending trend in Chinese history, the type of interference with local culture they imposed was new. The Communist rulers were to carry to an extreme all previous rulers' schemes of ideological alignment in their attempt to realize a new vision of the old Confucian doctrine of 'oneness'. The new means was to deal a final blow to 'feudal religion' and to the entire mindset that thrived in the countryside, which the Communists referred to by the single concept of 'superstition' (*mixin*), a neologism borrowed from Japanese in the late Qing era. Pluralism in public expression was ruled out from the beginning – but personal ambivalence remained a constant factor in the party ranks, perhaps even responsible for much of the paranoid policy reactions towards alternative modes of thought.

After attacks on institutional religion, ancestor worship, monastery and temple buildings and religious objects, only the most diffused, disorganized and locally anchored elements of rural cosmology survived, without any potential for becoming the emblem of religious rebellion. As a result of this process, in many places fengshui stood out as the most important vehicle for an alternative, religiously informed mode of thought in the countryside. Since Chinese policy was indiscriminate as regards rural 'superstition', we shall not yet draw a clear line of distinction between fengshui and popular religion – this will be discussed in Chapter 6.

THE EARLY POLICY RESPONSE TO POPULAR IDEOLOGY

The writings of the young Mao Zedong in the early phases of the revolution echoed Dr. Sun's attack on rural superstition a generation earlier. Only gradually did he sharpen his attacks on rural people's deplorably 'darkened' minds, 'soaked' in superstition, depressed by 'feudal thinking' and easy victims to 'spiritual pollution' and 'dangerous ideas' that 'poisoned' their minds. His policy was strongly action-oriented with violence as a justified means to preconceived ends. Mao was brought up with a strong Buddhist influence, which apparently remained throughout his life (Li Z. 1994: 113, 302), and stories have circulated about his continuous visits to a rural diviner. Admittedly having been 'superstitious' himself before he was exposed to modern ideas (Snow 1973: 197), the young Mao epitomized much of his generation; he soon cast his lot with the reformers of his time.[2] In 1927 he wrote against the peasants' subjugation to the 'three systems of authority', constituted by the state, the clan, and the supernatural:

> If you believe in the Eight Characters [bagua], you hope for good luck; if you believe in geomancy, you hope to benefit from the location of your ancestral graves. This year within the space of a few months the local tyrants, evil gentry and corrupt officials have all toppled from their pedestals. Is it possible that until a few months ago they all had good luck and enjoyed the benefit of well-sited ancestral graves, while suddenly in the last few months their luck has turned and their ancestral graves have ceased to exert a beneficial influence? (Mao 1982: 46–47)

Mao was well aware of the forces he was up against; in the same document he mentioned that if too much effort is made prematurely, the 'tyrants and evil gentry will seize the pretext' to turn such into counter-revolutionary propaganda, for instance by accusing the new peasant associations of having no piety towards ancestors. Curiously enough, he did not simply state that fengshui did not work; he argued within the logic of the tradition itself, trying to prove its said effects wrong, something that could easily be interpreted in the way that the Communist interfered with the local fengshui, bringing either good or ill luck depending on your place in society.

The social theory of the new regime was firm and the leadership hard-headed; only was the implementation from the outset cautious and calculating. The theories and basic conceptions were readily available, having been developed in the West, and there was plenty of practical experience to be gained from the Soviet Union, Eastern Europe and Mongolia, where sweeping purges during the 1930s had killed millions of priests and lamas. The Marxist perception of religion as an opiate of the people – in Friedrich Engels' terms 'the fantastic reflections in men's minds of those external forces which control their daily life' – was uncritically taken over by the Chinese Marxist theorists and further illustrated with references to Chinese ancient history. With specific reference to the *Spring and Autumn Annals* the theorist Chi Yuchang writes in a typical article from the early 1960s:

> Imploring gods and consulting oracles ... and exorcism of evil spirits to cure diseases ... were all designed to tell that the life or death of a man or the consequences of a certain thing were all determined by gods and spirits, and that nobody could change them. Accordingly, they tied many people down, delayed the proper execution of many things, put off until it was too late many cases of illness that could have been cured ... and killed a great many people.[3]

He argued that fortunetelling, physiognomy and geomancy were the superstitious activities continuing this trend. It quickly became clear that the new regime did not intend to distinguish between religion, superstition and theism, although some debate over the correct handling of them recurrently arose,[4] since it saw all of these as stemming from the same core of oppressive forces. As a consequence religious leaders of all denominations, practitioners of popular religion and all kinds of diviners were regarded as parasites carrying out political and economic oppression 'under the cloak of religion' and were in principle to be treated as a single category. In the drive to determine class status in the countryside the new government announced that everyone who for three years prior to the liberation had derived the main part of their income from professions as those of geomancers, priests, monks, fortunetellers and so forth, were to be classified as religious or superstitious practitioners (Bush 1970: 384). They were singled out for future persecution. Another debate of signal importance that sprang up spontaneously concerned the possible link between religion and rebellion. In the Marxist conception peasant revolts were the main motive-power in Chinese history, but the role of religion in these movements was controversial: particularly the Taiping Rebellion, which left millions killed and nearly toppled the Qing dynasty a century earlier, had evidently grown out of a religious movement, a fact that could not be denied even by party historians (*CNA* 346, 1960: 4–5). The wording of the new Constitution of 1954 had special significance for the practising of fengshui. The Constitution contained separate paragraphs stating citizens' rights of religious belief (Article 88) and their freedom of speech, assembly, demonstration, etc. (Article 87), apparently to the effect that while freedom of religious belief was guaranteed, freedom of religious worship and practice were not. As a consequence, religious activities outside temples and churches were prohibited. The nominal difference is obvious: organized religious congregations had their temples and churches as a last resort, while the practitioners of popular cosmology, usually operating in public or in people's homes, were in principle outlawed. On the other hand, the established religious communities were seen as a much greater immediate danger, not least due to their real or imagined foreign connections, and their worship was easier to challenge than the elusive practices of popular cosmology, drawing on scattered literature, local interpretation and masses of mainly unorganized rural practitioners. However, again in principle, popular cosmology could be cracked down upon at any time without a change of policy, while established religions were subject to decisive purges, the legality of which could be criticized both internally and abroad; these purges were therefore much more sensitive matters.

The attacks on established religions and popular religious practices, or to employ C. K. Yang's terms 'institutional religion', including both established religions and those aspects of popular religion forming independent social institutions, and 'diffused religion', meaning the religious aspects of common institutional and community life (Yang C. 1959: 192), came to follow somewhat different patterns despite the indiscriminate Marxist classification. Moreover, in the countryside the extermination of one could well have contributed to the silent growth of the other. It should be pointed out in this connection that even though Yang saw fengshui specialists as belonging to institutional religion since they continued aspects of classical religion and were part of public life – and presumably aspired to elite status as professionals – the practice of their art certainly catered for the 'diffused' religious aspects of everyday life.

Both deteriorating foreign relations and very concrete obstacles to implementing a Communist societal order after the initial division of land into private plots contributed to a gradually hardening policy through the 1950s. Village militia and regular troops came to play an increasingly conspicuous role as socialist construction went from Mutual Aid Groups to Agrarian Production Cooperatives to Collective Farms to entirely party-controlled People's Communes in 1958 (*CNA* 246, 1958: 1).

HARDENING POLICY RESPONSE

The collectivization programme of the new regime met pervasive resistance expressed in the popular religious idiom. The Chinese press reported countless incidents, particularly in 1957. In a county in Hubei masses were reported to riot in front of the party headquarters when a cadre had a Buddha image removed from a temple and other articles report resistance to the destruction of ancestral halls (*CNA* 189, 1957: 6). Another example was an incident at a shrine in Hubei province, where people customarily visited the tomb of the goddess Ma to heal the sick. For some years the shrine had not been too popular,

> but in 1957, when rumours spread that 'the other world is drafting new recruits for its armed forces and those on the call-up list will not survive', people crowded around the tomb in large numbers, usually about three to four hundred a day with as many as six hundred a day. On grounds that agricultural production would be affected by such absenteeism, local party cadres dispersed the crowds and began to dig up the tombstone. The people were incensed and threatened to attack the party men, whereupon the latter called the police ... Wiser heads finally prevailed and conducted an investigation which showed that the public health department had done a poor job in dealing with measles, meningitis, and influenza, which had attacked the area, leaving the old people no recourse ... The author-ities therefore arranged for scientific explanation of the cause of disease and made the necessary medicines available to the people. Upon the arrival of the medical team the number of devotees dropped to one hundred, and in three more days declined from sixty to thirteen, and finally to zero. (Bush 1970: 393)

Another incident concerned a temple in Guangdong where the Lady Xitai was venerated. The temple had been destroyed after liberation, but when an epidemic of influenza broke out thousands of people flocked to its former site. The word was spread that Lady Xitai would come back to save the country from the Communists, the leaders of the collective would be killed and the Guomindang would soon come back. A revolt followed but was soon put down by the police.[5]

Then in 1958, following widespread rioting, a new massive crackdown on all religious sects was staged; this happened almost simultaneously with the establishment of the People's Communes.

Taoism was specifically identified with the nationalists and Taoist priest were accused of being reactionary leaders, but this time the authorities also hardened the line over other popular religious practitioners. During the summer ancestral cults, traditional burials and a variety of religious practices were suppressed in the villages. Several articles in the *People's Daily* denounced popular religion as reactionary and conveyed reminders of wrong thinking, for instance when rural people attributed a good harvest to the 'Old Man in Heaven' who gave them good rain and favourable wind (a fengshui allegory), but imputed failure to the people's communes.[6]

Just before the onset of the Great Leap Forward in 1958 the *People's Daily* brought the first warnings of a coming stop to traditional burial practices. An article argued in a matter-of-fact style that the expenditure on funerals, including coffins, offerings and dinners, was a waste just as the plots of land occupied by graves were unproductive. The author, a party secretary, argued in an unusually sympathetic tone that the peasants were aware of the problem, but that they were 'perplexed by the absence of new rites that will replace the old'. He went on to say that cooperatives had adopted slogans like 'Let us compete with heaven; let us save land from graves and tombs; let us fight against nature; let us rely not on gods and heaven, but on our own hands, for more production!' After some practical suggestions to change burial habits he recommended cremation to be introduced gradually.[7] The party was really desperate to increase agricultural production, in the eyes of the rural populace perhaps the only true measure of its success. When yields could not be increased, cultivated acreage had to be expanded.

This was the most severe attack on the popular religious complex including fengshui. Ancestor worship was now condemned and villagers were forced to do away with graves and objects such as gravestones, coffins and altars. A massive party-guided and army-backed movement dug up the remains of several million ancestors and carried them up in the mountains. A rich symbolism was simultaneously employed, for instance when ancestors were 'collectivized' in common graves (*CNA* 240, 1958: 2). A party secretary attempted to express the villagers' own interest in the *People's Daily*:

> Ancestral tombs long regarded as sacred have been removed by the masses themselves. In many localities, family altars, gods of the city, gods of thunder, local gods, and the Queen of Heaven have been eliminated ... Grave stones, coffins, etc. are used by the collective farms for building irrigation works, pig sties, latrines, carts, manure buckets,

sheds, small water gates ... Many temples which formerly housed images have been turned into pig sties or processing plants.[8]

Still the party journal *Red Flag* admitted that these things were not always done voluntarily. When some villagers near Xian were forced to level the graves they offered prayers to the spirits at the same time, saying 'Spirits, spirits, I am not the one who wants to move you. It is the cadres who want to do so'. The journal maintained that the revival of ideas concerning spirits and ghosts was the work of counter-revolutionaries.[9] It is of specific interest here that the journal mentions the *revival* of popular religion – whether this is expression of propaganda or a true observation is impossible to determine, but it is in accordance with my own argument. The Great Leap Forward from 1958 put an end to compromise. Peasants were if necessary forced to level all graves occupying farmland and to establish public cemeteries on non-arable land. Crematoria were built in many rural areas and cremation enforced where possible.

The closer the new authorities got to the domestic sphere of rural people, the sharper became the contradictions – quite foreseeable if we recall the close correlation between family organization and popular cosmology mentioned in Chapter 1. For a regime that deliberately fought the clan and family organizations of the old society, ancestor worship could only be seen as the ideological super-structure of this system. Thus Communism and traditional authority embodied in spirits became highly antagonistic entities in the competition for controlling both power and reason itself. Ancestor worship represented the faith in invisible, strictly local powers, while Communism demanded subjugation to external powers, equally invisible. Rural study groups which had been established all over the country continued to discuss the ridiculing of ancestor worship and popular cosmology, depicted as ignorant superstitions and psycho-logical comforts for cowardly people (Bush 1970: 400).

Communism and ancestor worship were competitors also in a moral sense. In the rural, Confucian-inspired tradition filial piety demanded satisfaction of elderly parents' material needs. As an extension of this, funerals for elderly parents were critical public testimonies to the moral worth of the family, and intense mourning and lavish feasts usually involving the entire village were both moral obligations and prestige-awarding investments. In the new Com-munist tradition, however, thrift for the sake of the public interest was a cornerstone in resource redistribution within an egalitarian materialist ethos. Many rural people and their local party secretaries strove to accommodate the two and enable them to coexist, but gradually hardening means of implementing centralized socialist control made it risky for the local party leadership to be lenient in these matters.

The seizure of lineage temples and prohibition of ancestor worship in public in the early 1950s had had little effect on rural burial practices; in fact, in many cases the relative prosperity deriving from the newly won peace and well-being of the nation provided the means for elaborate and costly funerals. Moreover, the new Labour Insurance Regulations of 1951 and 1953, extended to rural areas in 1956, guaranteed workers ample funds for their own and their family members' burials, which, when combined with private savings, could finance extravagant public burials, rich in Taoist and Buddhist rituals (Davis-Friedman 1991: 60–62). Thus, in the mid-1950s, cremation was rare and regarded by most elderly Chinese as a barbarous invention, depriving the deceased of an afterlife and being detrimental to the most valued sphere of civilized Chinese life.

In many ways the CCP policy on burials embodied the move from a rural to an urban lifestyle experienced by most of the party veterans. In 1949 many urban families had already adopted a lifestyle where temple and home worship did not play a part and the entire complex of traditional religion was in general much weaker in the cities than in the villages. Such urban-style cultural renovation, expressive of Chinese modernity, was envisioned as a precondition for genuine socialist reconstruction for the whole nation. What the rural people would not voluntarily comply with in this project, became items of enforcement in the party's programme of action through the 1950s. Equally revealing was the style of language employed in public and the party media, now commonly referring to party members 'descending to the villages'.

After 1958 geomancers experienced harder times. They could no longer work safely in public; signposts outside their homes were removed if still in place and the geomancers' small stalls in the temple access areas or at temple fairs were closed. Any one of them would now come in constant conflict with the law since he invariably would recommend a corpse be buried intact for a wholly auspicious effect on the descendants.

The quick collapse of the Great Leap Forward and the ensuing national disaster from 1960 also resulted in a return to open popular religious practices in the villages, but only briefly. Already in 1962 the Socialist Education Movement, which gradually intensified to merge

89

with the gathering Cultural Revolution, attacked this retrograde step and cremation was again enforced everywhere. At the same time, information became scantier, even to the point where, in the mid-1960s, the course of events in China could no longer be followed from the outside. Although reliable reports were scarce, both Chinese press reports and reports from refugees noted that geomancers continued to play a role despite the state's determination to watch over and intervene in village affairs. Maurice Freedman points to various references to fengshui in the Communist press in the early 1960s, particularly from rural Fujian and Guangdong. Several letters to the editor ask for advice on matters relating to declining family fortune and fengshui. One writer asks about the possible connection between his father's death and his own failure in examinations; another writer tells that his family connects a poor grave with the fact that the family line has only one male descendant in four generations and asks how to deal with 'these country people' (Freedman 1966: 182–83). The *Chinese Youth Daily* in 1964 laments that geomancy is still practised in the villages, even though '[it] is wrong and it is futile to ask its advice on building a house or orienting a grave' (*CNA* 25 February 1966: 4). Almost simultaneously the *People's Daily* writes that cremation in order to save land is 'common' and that public cemeteries are urged (since the Great Leap Forward), but admits that the peasants grumble, complaining that this disturbs their fengshui. A number of other sources narrate stories of deceased party members whose families wished to give them traditional burials, obliging the party to interfere *(CNA* 25 February 1966: 4).

Several sources suggest that the Communist power was far from absolute in the villages during these years and that the party cadres sent down to the villages were often in a vulnerable position. A study by Doak Barnett identifies three groups of influential individuals deriving their authority from non-Communist sources: old farmers with special agricultural skills, old ladies forming the core of informal networks in the villages while being impervious to controls, and finally geomancers and other religious specialists who guarded and spread the belief systems of the old society (Barnett 1969: 168–169). Local variation must have been tremendous in these years, however, particularly when seen in the light of the highly localized patterns of popular thought reported both before and after the Communist era. From Chen village in Guangdong we hear that just before the Cultural Revolution in 1966 the Four Cleanups workteam (installed to eradicate the Four Olds: old thinking, culture, customs and habits) carried out an anti-superstition drive as their last task (Chan *et al.* 1984: 87–88). Though geomancers no longer plied their trade openly and popular religion had disappeared from the public scene, religious practices and rituals had survived in the households. Special attention was paid to a group of female spirit mediums, who would drive away evil spirits by means of burning strips of paper with magical characters, falling into trance in the sickroom and making the sick drink *shengshui* (holy water: a bowl of water stirred by the finger of a religious specialist); these are in fact very similar to the tasks still performed by geomancers in the fieldwork areas.

In the years immediately prior to the Cultural Revolution a shift in government policy was again seen, replacing education of the peasants with more direct action. Education alone had not brought about the desired effects; both peasants and workers, quite in accordance with Chinese religious conceptions, refused to be submerged in a single exposition of moral truth and social reality. The 1962 publishing figures from the People's Literature Publishing Company showed that by far the best selling works were the three classical novels, *Water Margin, Romance of the Three Kingdoms* and *Monkey*, together selling over 2 million copies, as compared to only 10,000 copies sold of *Chairman Mao on Literature and Art* (Moody 1977: 116).

The evidence we have from this period tends to support the main argument that the resolute promotion of any one system of thought is an implicit comparison, both for the sender and the receiver of ideological messages: it channels attention onto its adverse modes of thought as much as it conveys its own subject matter. The campaign against Confucius in 1973–74, for instance, unintendedly served to familiarize an ignorant generation with his ideas, and his *Analects* were reissued during the campaign, albeit with politically correct annotations demonstrating his feudal ideas.

It has been claimed that since the Chinese constitution of 1954 guaranteed freedom of religious belief, the party did not engage in religious persecution as such, but only guarded society against 'counter-revolutionary activities under the cloak of religion' (ibid.: 117). But at least in public the Communists practised their atheism with a seriousness quite unprecedented in a Chinese context. The Four Cleanups campaign in 1965–66 eventually criminalized all expressions of popular culture. Fengshui along with popular cosmology as such could be classified under any one of these. There was to be no more incense or religious objects in the markets, weddings and funerals must be cleansed of all non-Communist content and all popular beliefs relating to 'superstition' should cease: 'Superstition is dangerous', as one official commentator held, 'One cannot wait until it disappears of itself' (*CNA* 17 December 1965: 4). There followed resolute attacks on all popular religious practices including attempts to transform the traditional festivals. The implementation of the tougher policy relied on increasing involvement of the Communist Youth League and young people in general.

Concerning the Spring Festival, those practices most obviously deriving from popular religion were at first discouraged and then forbidden. They were the offerings made to the ancestors while the family gathered, including the use of candles, joss sticks, paper money, red paper, religious images and clay figures, as well as the practice of 'sending the Kitchen God to Heaven to report'. As communes and work units attempted to control the use of religious paraphernalia, the media simultaneously brought stories to ridicule the practices and calls from commune members and other readers to transform old customs. Also the handwritten couplets placed on either side of the door were to change from religious contents and lucky characters to revolutionary messages.

The fact that all the religious objects and images mentioned above were still available when the Cultural Revolution was launched demonstrates that the authority of the Communist regime was far from absolute. The producers were small cooperatives, which both religious institutions and private persons depended upon to support themselves, but they were 'assisted' to change their production. The places at which such objects were sold, usually squares and alleys in front of temple gates, were also common places for geomancers and other practitioners to offer their services. News reports reveal that these, too, were still in existence, although the public display of religious activity was drawing to a halt. In 1965, groups of young people could be seen to give lectures against superstition to people buying things or acquiring services, and occasionally to hinder their access. Soon the access ways were cleared of people and booths (*SCMP* 16 February 1965), resulting in the rapidly declining economic role of most temples.

Also the Festival of the Dead (*Qing ming*) in April, during which graves were cleaned and offerings made, suffered a gradual incrimination and elimination from public life. Still in 1966, however, a reconciliatory atmosphere induced the party to infuse the festival with new meaning; it was changed to become National Memorial Day in order to commemorate heroes of the two revolutions that had taken China from imperial rule to Communism. Posters and banners were seen everywhere, telling people to 'abolish old superstitions', 'replace old harmful customs with new', 'believe in science, not superstition', 'cremate the dead to save money', and so forth.

RESISTANCE TO ABSOLUTISM

The party's policy towards Christianity was particularly resentful: it was composed of equal shares of hostility and jealousy. Christianity had been the closest rival and most determined alternative to Marxism-Leninism in the battle against the old social order, and they shared between them a great number of revolutionizing concepts and virtues: equality, humility, sincerity, self-discipline, frugality, hard and devoted work for a future paradise and, not least, the idea of a strong integrity of convictions on the part of the individual. One can indeed argue that even though the entire missionary enterprise had limited success, it undoubtedly prepared the ground for another Western intellectual construct, namely Marxism. As a historical irony of considerable proportions, Marxism became China's first substantial, nation-wide encounter with Christian civilization – and perhaps with ideological exclusionism. To preclude any comparison of ethics, the party developed a policy that you cannot be a Christian and a Marxist. Unlike Moslems, who were allowed into the party as a recognized minority group, Christians were excluded. Anyone who denied that religion was basically a class question was ruled out. Marxism is modern, religion is of the past, was the common argument, based on crude evolutionary thought.

While contemporary Chinese accounts were limited, many foreign observers from this period shared the Communists' view that the popular religious complex had determined people's lives and obstructed progress. Accordingly, they expected these aspects of Chinese culture to dwindle as socialist modernization made headway. Around the time of the revolution Isabel and David Crook reported from a North China peasant community that previous mystical practices of diviners had largely disappeared as a consequence of a never-ending series of political campaigns and local struggle sessions tearing the social fabric apart; worst of all was the order to fill a twenty-five percent quota of class-struggle objects (Crook and Crook 1959: 166–167). In contrast, the Chinese anthropologist C. K. Yang (who emigrated to the USA in 1952) argued that in his area of study, a suburban village to Canton, as well as in Chinese society as a whole, 'diffused' religion, of which ancestor worship was the strongest ingredient, represented the structurally stronger and more pervasive force in the lives of the common people (Yang C. 1959: 192). Another Chinese anthropologist, Fei Xiaotong (who remained in China after the revolution), simply noted a general tendency towards the diminution of religious and superstitious beliefs and activities, particularly the three previous main focuses consisting of ancestor worship, the Kitchen God and the Goddess of Mercy (Fei 1983: 242). From Chen village we learn that the party deliberately strove to replace folk religion with Mao thought and a socialist world view: 'The power and glory of Mao Zedong's thought was supposed to fill the void left by the destruction of traditional religious practices' (Chan *et al.* 1984: 89). Piece by piece, kitchen gods, family altars, front door posters and so on were replaced by Mao pictures or Communist symbols and slogans; the means were a mixture of persuasion and coercion. The local party people quickly realized, however, that the final battle between popular religion and Mao Zedong thought would be decided in the agricultural production figures.

This is the point where we should briefly return to the main argument. Throughout the twentieth century foreign and Chinese modernizers had concurrently carped at the Chinese peasant for being despairingly immersed in supernatural beliefs, thought to control his entire existence. Now, when it came to improving his very existence, the same modernizers – whether of a Christian, a purely democratic or a Marxist conviction – had to realize that in terms of agricultural skills there was very little or nothing they could teach him. Motion pictures were introduced into the countryside in the early 1950s, disseminating agricultural knowledge on depth ploughing, insect control, sanitation, common literacy for technical literature and so forth, but after initial curiosity 'fatigue from the monotony of the political propaganda soon set in' (Yang C. 1959: 191). The Communist party in particular was faced with this fact: supernatural beliefs did not preclude solid agricultural knowledge. Beyond land reform and an extended range of medicine its actual contribution to the peasants' material well-being quickly faded, or were even seen to be gradually reversed by aggressive political campaigns conducted by the centre. The three cornerstones in the Marxist tradition of knowledge, rising standards of living, modern medicine and the popularization of science, were already wearing thin.

Lack of positive results in agriculture at several stages of the collectivization process, and certainly from the time of the Great Leap

Forward and onwards, presumably added to a gloomy political atmosphere and rampant power struggle. There followed attempts to spiritualize ideology in order to create a new justification for suffering – instead of pointing to material circumstance as the cause of the agony, the idea of suffering as a political ordeal was introduced. Chinese Marxism gradually emerged as a politico-religious creed when it was adopted as state ideology, developing into an utterly inquisitional form, departing from the broader-minded and more pragmatic Chinese religious traditions of the past. As the spiritual justification of Marxism rose at the expense of a purely materialist rationality, it became even more expedient to stamp out any current of potential opposition – real or imagined.

While Christian, democratic and Marxist forces had shared a predominantly evolutionary perspective on religion, the social scientists who started fieldwork in Chinese rural areas in the 1930s saw it in a primarily functional perspective. To them, the superstition of the Chinese peasant alleviated his fears: it arose from his demand for confidence and strength in the face of humanly insurmountable circumstances in the struggle with nature and adjustment to a social order beyond the peasant's control. But both reformers and intellectual observers had to recognize that most superstitions lay outside the reach of science and technology – they began where a materialist approach to life ended. An intense activism prevailed among the Chinese peasants, who wasted few human or material resources. In the eloquent wording of C. K. Yang, writing about his village in the early 1950s,

> although superstitions were numerous, they did not vitiate the peasants' realistic view of their struggle with the natural and social environment. There was strong traditional insistence upon the injunction: 'Do the utmost within human power, but accept the ordinance of Heaven', and there was general social pressure against and popular contempt for those who did nothing but appeal to the spirits and gods for help. (Yang C. 1959: 192)

Such conception would seem at odds with any single-system perception of reality such as promoted by Christianity, Marxism and to a certain extent also the early social sciences – as argued in Chapter 1. It was neither a question of working hard *for* heaven to fulfil a sacred contract, nor a question of working hard to *surmount* heaven's impediments to human existence; to the peasant, heaven's impact on human enterprise was arbitrary – heaven had a will of its own.

Similarly, popular cosmology had a truth of its own. Despite the gigantic totalitarian project of Chinese Communism, rural people hung on to popular perceptions of the world – nothing like exclusive truths, but rather a large conglomerate of statements and ideas, which all were equally meaningful for the style of comprehension among rural Chinese. When foreign missionaries were expelled, Buddhist, Taoist and ancestral temples closed or deprived of their function, only 'diffused' religion, divorced from institutions as well as from all objects of worship, remained to serve this purpose: in a relative sense its magnitude grew. Of equal importance, and in some ways parallel to the move from institutionalized to diffused religion, was the individualization of religious worship. When public and communal manifestations of popular religion were restricted by the new authorities, worship was confined to the home and possibly the family tombs. Increasingly, geomancers became the main exponents of Chinese popular cosmology and people's links to the past since in many places in China they were the only specialists remaining active – particularly after the Cultural Revolution. In the absence of Taoist priests and in some areas also spirit mediums, who had previously engaged in curing the sick or probing remedies for infertility, mental disorders and personal problems (Doolittle 1865: 331–337), geomancers acquired this new function; when Buddhist monks were eliminated, geomancers became more prominent in life-cycle rituals and ceremonies, not least in funerals; when altars and ancestor halls were destroyed and worship of ancestors impeded, people could resort to letting geomancers check their homes to see whether the ancestors were content. Another consequence was that the distinction between fengshui and popular religion became further blurred.

THE FATE OF GEOMANCERS AND THEIR GUILDS

What actually happened to the geomancers after 1949? First of all we must be aware that geomancers were not a single group of professionals but belonged to various social strata. We may use either institutionalized–diffused or urban–rural distinctions to point out differences. To some extent they overlap since many urban geomancers were monks in Buddhist or Taoist temples, but by far the largest number of rural geomancers were independent livelihood practitioners. There were independent practitioners in the cities, too, but their numbers had been declining in the twentieth century. Those linked to temples shared the fate of other monks in the campaigns to organize, control and eventually eradicate religion. An example from Jiangsu will be given in Chapter 5.

Only to a limited extent did the fate of the rural geomancers resemble that of common religious specialists from pre-revolutionary society. As the Communist party established a single category of 'religious and superstitious practitioners' including priests, monks and diviners, which were anyway seen as a transitional phenomenon, pressure was built up in 1950 to make them transfer to other activities, first in the cities and gradually disseminating to the countryside. As a result, fellow villagers would periodically hesitate to acquire the geomancers' services, but the demand for them never ceased.

Some geomancers voluntarily gave up their professions. This presumably applied to the younger people and the apprentices rather than to the old 'masters', who were left with fewer choices. Geomancers were typically landless, which narrowed down their opportunities to either adopting petty trade, acquiring the skills of artisans or working for the new regime. Quite a few of the younger geomancers eventually joined the party and became village cadres, of whom some even rose to prominent positions. Other geomancers, presumably the majority, kept practising their trade, adopting new strategies for survival. They worked inconspicuously and with fewer clients. The signboards outside their homes and advertisements in public places were pulled down and they would usually take care not to announce their arrival in the villages when performing jobs; for instance, several geomancers in the fieldwork areas reported practising only at night.

The policy towards particularly Taoism had hardened considerably during the first two years of the new regime, with confiscations of temples, criminalizing of Taoist associations, registration of their members as reactionary elements, and a series of accusations of counter-revolutionary activity and connection to the nationalists, which culminated in the mass liquidation of religious leaders in late 1952. The policy towards geomancers, on the other hand, was softer and to a large extent left implementation to local party organs. Of equal significance was the fact that geomancers were not yet subject to mob violence to the same extent as Taoist and ancestral temple personnel in the early years of liberation, when they were attacked by anti-religious groups acting on the constitutional freedom to oppose religion.

There was a clear and persistent tendency throughout the Communist era of ancestor worship and traditional burials (including reburials in the south and southeast) not being criticized as severely as other elements of the old social order. Several factors may have been prominent in this matter. First of all, a genuine fear of mass riots among peasants if their most cherished rituals were eliminated counted for the calculating attitude as to how far the party could go in the early period. It was not until all discussion of 'winning over' the peasant had ceased, probably at the time of the Great Leap Forward and the construction of people's communes, that harder measures were taken and regular troopers were deployed to clear graves. Judging from reports throughout the 1950s to 1970s, another prominent factor was that the rural party members often wanted traditional burials for both their deceased family members and themselves, even though they would be reluctant to engage in any kind of worship of the former. Another very plausible cause could have been that ancestor worship inspired both hierarchical thought and a respect for the traditional authority that conceivably could be transferred to party loyalty. Despite the peasants being encouraged to oppose 'feudal' authorities, a very convenient term for the new regime, they were never invited to oppose authority as such and take matters into their own hands – political participation was only permitted in accordance with the theory of the mass line under guidance of the party (Burns 1988: 14).

As compared to Taoism and Buddhism, which were seen as a greater immediate danger as secret societies employed them well into the 1950s (Lieberthal 1980: 14), geomancy appeared more harmless since larger, organized rebellions never had used it as a focus. Geomancers also seemed to derive a certain protection from their prestige in the villages. They were not members of secretive or segmentary professional associations, but worked in public selling their services to anyone willing to pay. They had their own 'secret' knowledge which they guarded and strove to keep within the family line, but this did not separate them from common artisans in pre-industrial society. Furthermore, they were often among the better educated rural people, having acquired basic literary skills through their apprenticeship with master geomancers. In many cases they were the only literate individuals not belonging to the gentry and they could offer services to their fellow villagers on this basis, for instance by acting as scribes and even as village headmen. Thus geomancers and their art seemed to enjoy a certain respect among all rural people and extended well into the ranks of the party – a clear testimony to the unifying aspects of fengshui as communicating common Chinese values. Still geomancers operated under severe restrictions.

Reports from several localities in China, including the two fieldwork areas, suggest that geomancers, along with most other groups of religious and divinatory practitioners (*duangong*), had been organized into guilds at the level of the township, apparently with a superstructure at county level and in principle at provincial level. William Hinton's report from a Shanxi village in 1948 conveys a picture of local gentry actively supporting traditional institutions, such as geomancy, which could be used to explain the differing fates of the gentry and the impoverished:

> The rich were rich, so their tenants were taught to reason, because they were born under a lucky star; and the poor were poor because the heavens were out of joint when they emerged from the womb ... The rich prospered, it was said, because their fathers were buried in auspicious places in relation to flanking hills, flowing water, and prevailing winds ... Since the rich, with the help of professional geomancers could often pick their spot while the poor had to be content with whatever sorry ditch they were thrown into, this fate had an inevitability that was hard to beat.
>
> The squires of Long Bow did not leave the propagation of such attitudes to chance. They actively supported all the various ways and means by which the 'right thinking' could be impressed upon the people. A village school for that small minority able to attend emphasized the study of The Four Books and the Five Classics of Confucius; operas at New Year's drove home the theme of the contrasting rewards of virtue and vice; a Confucian Association promoted ancestor worship and provided mediums who could converse with the spirits of the dead; a temple society kept Buddhism, with its passive acceptance of fate, alive. (Hinton 1966: 48)

We should not be led to believe that inequality can be ascribed entirely to ideological factors, however, and particularly not of such an elusive kind as propagated in Chinese rural traditions. It is beyond doubt that the ruling strata employed all possible explanatory devices to justify their power, but at no point in history have these devices been able to rule people without the simultaneous use of force. Quite the contrary, people below the gentry would conceivably use exactly the same devices, but for adverse purposes.

Many accounts from the first decades of Communist rule, both Chinese and foreign, either foresaw the rapid disappearance of fengshui or emphasized that 'superstitious' beliefs played a decreasing role in people's lives. These observations were mainly built on the fact that such beliefs 'no longer govern their lives' or 'their impact on the lives of peasants, and the obstacles they pose to social change, seem diminished' (Parish and Whyte 1978: 289).

THE CULTURAL REVOLUTION

If the policy towards popular religion and fengshui had hardened during 1964–65, it became fanatic at the inception of the Cultural Revolution in 1966, although the change was only piecemeal when seen from the villages. Much has already been written about this macabre chapter of Chinese history. There are only meagre references and scanty evidence available concerning fengshui practices and the fate of geomancers during this period, when China was virtually secluded from the outside world. The foreign missionaries and other sojourners were gone, ordinary travel and tourism had become impossible and the customary flow of people from Hong Kong into south China during festivals ceased completely in 1966. Some personal narratives from the fieldwork areas in Sichuan and Jiangsu are presented in the following chapters.

The religious aspects of Chinese Communism were intensified after the inception of the Cultural Revolution: study sessions on Mao's Little Red Book came to resemble Bible study sessions, Mao was elevated to a divine figure demanding cult-like worship, and politics incorporated spirit and devotion as equally important to material life. Yet in 1966 *China News Analysis* commented that sixteen years of Communism had had little success in curing the 'national character': 'What the party is attacking in every campaign appears again when the campaign is over with what looks like historical necessity' (*CNA* 25 February 1966: 3). Serious unrest was visible in the villages in early 1967, following the Red Guards' campaign in late 1966, with protest allegedly finding expression in traditional religious practices. Repeated shock treatments had not been enough to cure rural people of their 'beliefs': religious objects and other objects of worship were destroyed and replaced with Mao pictures and slogans, but pictures of the Old Man in Heaven and Buddhist warrior-gods were returned after a very short interval. As early as 1967–68 the mainland Chinese press abounded with references to the need to repress 'feudal superstitious practices' and many press reports complained that 'the Four Olds are revived' (*CNA* 19 July 1968: 4–6).

The great assembly halls – a cornerstone in the party's 'scientific education' of the rural masses – were built during the Cultural Revolution by the 'cultural teams' (*wenyidui*), who viciously fought religion and assembled the peasants to make them 'do away with superstition' (*poxu mixin*). During the land reform 'culture stations' (*wenhuazhan*) had been set up and study groups organized among the peasants to make them ridicule ancestor worship and popular cosmology, invariably depicted as ignorant superstitions and psychological flights for a weak and cowardly people (Hu 1960: 131). But now the means hardened. Geomancers and other remaining specialists were drawn to the fore, aggressively reproached and forced to confess to having backward ideas and intentionally deluding the people. The personal accounts of geomancers told during fieldwork were presumably typical for anywhere in China: their homes were ransacked and books and implements were burned. The most prominent were paraded through the streets and senselessly beaten by the mobs. Many of the old geomancers practising today bear physical evidence of the molestation they went through in this period. Some were killed, either deliberately or by relentless beating.

One report by a young Chinese tells that a geomancer who was 'almost beaten to death' during the Four Olds campaign was employed by a school already in 1968 to locate collective graves for groups of young who had died in factional warfare between young students in Amoy (Xiamen) (Ling 1972: 362–363).

All material culture associated with the old society was destroyed in this period, including copies of the classics, almanacs, geomantic manuals, compasses and so forth. Attacks on local lore and sacred objects in the villages was simultaneously carried out, including chopping down sacred old trees known for their beneficial fengshui effect on the surroundings, along with pillars, tablets, gates, tombstones, statues and whatever symbolized other than Communist values. Far from being eradicated, popular ideology acquired new meaning and persisted underground. With the perpetual uneasiness and fear for future campaigns that could tear people's lives apart overnight, alternative reasoning was nourished. Steven Mosher, commenting on a peasant believing in fleas as an evil omen of a political campaign or a bad harvest, writes:

> Westerners may find this explanation ludicrous. This is to miss its significance. Lest reason become impotent, experience fail to make sense, and life itself approach absurdity, any explanation for the inexplicable, however unreal it may seem to the initiated, is better than none at all ... the state orthodoxy propagated by Beijing, except for a few vague pronouncements in the Maoist canon concerning the necessity of 'continuing the revolution', has flagrantly failed to help Chinese to cope with the endless merry-go-round of high-pressure movements. Given their lack of alternatives, it is perhaps not at all surprising that Chinese peasants grasp at fleas to convince themselves that God is not mad. (Mosher 1983: 283–284)

CLASS STRUGGLE IN THE SPIRITUAL WORLD

Geomantic punishment was not a new invention (de Groot 1897: 1052), but it was somehow unexpected that the Communist regime would employ, as seen in retrospect, the most concentrated collection of fengshui-related means of punishment ever experienced in Chinese history. In the hands of the Communist regime it developed into a demonic means of securing power for some by destroying the fengshui of others, included breaking their group confidence and uprooting their social identity. During the Cultural Revolution the peasants' links to their ancestors and clans were broken when graves were wrecked and ancestor halls, shrines and tablets demolished. While forbidding fengshui, the authorities themselves used anti-fengshui: they imposed attacks to punish people and inspire fear in a way that suggested their own perverse belief in it.

We cannot prove that the Chinese regime actually thought of fengshui as a means of punishment, but the consistency with imperial policy in this field is indeed striking. As a first reaction to organized popular movements such as the Taiping rebellion came the destruction of the graves of rebel leaders in order to destroy their fengshui fortunes, as well as the destruction of graves where good fengshui had generated rumours of a new emperor being born (Smith R. 1991: 157). When old peasants in the fieldwork areas reported that they themselves saw their fengshui shattered by these vicious attacks, it suggests that the aggressors must also have been aware of the significance of their acts.

People belonging to the four stinking categories were punished by publicly destroying their ancestors' tombs and burning the bones to symbolically wipe out their family lines.[10] In Shanghai, which was thrown into a revengeful reign of terror in 1951–53 and hit hard again in the 1960s, the descendants of a former wealthy industrialist reported that after the slaying of their father his dead body was removed so his family could not honour him, the family graves were sought out and destroyed and his name was forbidden to be written or spoken.

With the ransacking of people's homes came the smashing of all ancestor tablets and tombstones, as if the new authorities, at least symbolically, wanted to sever the peasants' links to their ancestors, clans, and native earth. As especially the older geomancers would see it, the assaults reflected the aggressors' own beliefs – fengshui became a means of breaking the fortune of others, while secretly cultivating their own. An intense struggle over buried human bones arose. The Red Guards smashed tombstones, tore coffins apart and scattered the bones to the absolute horror of onlookers. At night, the women would sneak out to collect what bones could be found and hide them elsewhere around the house. Geomancers were involved, giving advice on temporary places for these remains to be stored until political turmoil had died down and proper graves could be re-established.

The Communists' clash with popular religion in modern times had provided inspiration to the Chinese scholar C.K. Yang, now working in the USA. In his influential work, *Religion in Chinese Society,* first published in 1961, he presented a general theory on religion and political rebellion in Chinese society, arguing that religiously motivated uprisings occur in times of severe oppression, for instance as a consequence of political unrest or famine. Whereas the ruling class deprecated the role of religion, the common people always maintained religious beliefs and clung more tenaciously to them in times of increased oppression. As classical examples he gives the increasing imperial intolerance in the first half of the nineteenth century, which eventually led to the Taiping Rebellion, and the Communist takeover, resulting in an upsurge of popular religion in the 1950s. In 1968 a *China News Analysis* commentator inspired by C.K. Yang accordingly sees 'a clearly distinguishable revival of ancient religious practices' as a reaction to the brutality of the Red Guards in 1966. Speculation aside, it is a matter of fact that serious unrest in the villages in 1967 was only quelled by emergency orders and deployment of regular troops – plus the public media's raging against mostly unspecified 'feudal beliefs', 'superstition' and 'superstitious activities'. Also foreign reports mentioned increasing activity at the Festival of the Dead in April (*CNA* 19 July 1968: 5).

An account of a burial in south China in 1970 conveys a clear message: as soon as the social control of the Cultural Revolution faded away people would anxiously resume their native practices. Resisting all attempts to align rural universes with the Communist world view, the traditions of ancestor worship and fengshui continued to play a part in Chinese villages:

> Wu Chenlong, the father of a brigade level CCP party secretary, died at the age of eighty ... and in preparation for his funeral he had secretly consulted a geomancer, who chose an auspicious gravesite for both the old man and his wife on a hillside located just outside the village proper ... Local custom dictating the appropriate dress faithfully reflected the earthly inequalities between men and women. Men wore

103

three rather than two sets of clothing; their shoes were embroidered in
a distinctive fashion; and their jackets had additional pockets in order
to carry more money into their afterlife ... A middle-aged villager
instructed the younger men how to carry the coffin from the village to
the grave, so that they could alternate pallbearers and never let the
coffin touch the ground. At the grave there was additional instruction
on how to lower the coffin properly and cover it with earth. When the
last spadeful was thrown in, a shovel filled with candy was offered to
those who had helped so that they would leave with only the sweetest
thoughts for the deceased ... In the home of the widow and in that of
her elder son, one member, usually the mother, would burn incense
on the first and fifteenth of the month in honor of all deceased family
members ... If conditions still allowed, seven to ten years later, the
family would have a second burial. They would hire a local expert to
exhume the body, clean the bones, and rebury the remains in a small
funerary urn. (Davis-Friedman 1991: 64)

During the Anti-Confucius Campaign of 1973–74 filial piety and
traditional burials were again attacked and probably with good
reason; from the Communist takeover in 1949 to the end of the
Cultural Revolution rectification campaigns appeared to be the only
effective means of government when unpopular political programmes
were implemented. In between campaigns, people would cautiously,
but surely, slide back to their old practices. Thus, based on interviews
with refugees in 1973–74, William L. Parish and Martin King Whyte
reported that in only one village out of forty-one had cremation
been generally adopted (Parish and Whyte 1978: 261), and in the
mid-1970s Gordon Bennett wrote of a people's commune in south
China, that although officials told visitors that cremation was
common, emigrants reported that burials, and even second burials,
were almost universal (Bennett G. 1978: 155).

The cremation policy introduced a sort of devoutly formalized
'burial hierarchy' hingeing on political status, the significance of
which culminated in the Cultural Revolution, when class enemies
were again to be eradicated and heroes sanctified. After 1958 the
burial hierarchy started with the cremation and dispersal of the
remains of counter-revolutionaries, continued with the prescribed
cremation of commoners but legal worship of cremation urns, and
ended with the burial of revolutionary heroes at the designated burial
ground at Babao Mountain in Beijing (Wagner 1992: 412). Only
when the embalmed chairman himself was installed in his mauso-
leum after his death in 1976 was it complete.

THE OPEN DOOR POLICY: FENGSHUI MARKETED

Let us jump a few years ahead to the comeback of Deng Xiaoping in 1978 and the declaration of the Open Door Policy in 1979. The triumph of pragmatism and the economic revitalization through the 1980s steadily altered the power balance between party and people. The newly won economic surplus in many rural areas plus the relaxed political atmosphere led to a boom in ancestor worship and burials, now reappearing as public events. All over China millions of old family graves were restored and new ones were established. Innumerable families dug up the hidden bones of family members, who had died during political turmoil or were killed in political campaigns, and put them in proper graves in geomantically auspicious surroundings.[11] The new wealth inspired people to polish their ancestors' glory and boost the family lines' prestige.

The open door also allowed the anthropologists back in the field. Steven Mosher, doing fieldwork in Guangdong in 1979, reported harshly on the Communists' total failure to institute other than a faint shadow play of collectiveness. Despite all public evidence of religion being destroyed, peasants worshipped gods according to convention, preserved ancestor tablets in hidden places, invited Taoist priests, married and buried their dead on lucky days and even performed reburials after seven years (Mosher 1983: 7).

When rural areas are industrialized and an increasing proportion of the population engages in wage labour, the basic structure of village communities will inevitably change. It has often been said that what the Communist party never attained through policymaking was quickly devised by the market, just outside the reach of centralized control. The economic reforms brought higher standards of living, but also rising expectations and new images of the good life, including modern housing, altered consumptions patterns and, to some extent, changed social values. The following chapters will discuss how modernity has effected an individualization of fate and worship. However, in line with the remarks in Chapter 1 concerning the sturdiness of cultural production, popular modes of thought are not driven away from local community life, but are seen to change and adapt into new forms, in which political ramifications are still manifest. A somewhat contradictory trend will also be shown in the fieldwork chapters, since the tradition itself is affected by accelerating social transformation. While the tradition has been allowed to return to public life, at the same time it is further privatized as many people avoid using fengshui in public for fear of being thought 'backward'.

There is a close resemblance in the paradox that ancestor worship as such may be declining (Chu and Ju 1993: 226–227) even though tombs in many localities are becoming increasingly conspicuous. Recapitulating the Communist era we observed that fengshui persisted as a separate current of thought and was even strengthened in a relative sense. The popular religious complex emerged invigorated, but at least initially concentrated around fewer strands. The multitude of traditional practitioners such as astrologers, *bagua* diviners, soothsayers, necromancers, geomancers, shamans, wizards, exorcists, soul-searchers and Buddhist and Taoist priests had been narrowed down in most localities to a few sturdy practitioners, among whom the geomancer would almost certainly be represented and commonly also be the most prominent. The surviving geomancers would incorporate a range of techniques known from former colleagues and rivals in the villages and broaden their scope of activity, particularly in relation to curing disease and mental disorders. Yet modernity, Chinese style, transcends rural areas and leaves a highly diffused pattern of revolutionized rural communities mixed with largely unaffected villages. As the Chinese state is currently on the retreat in favour of highly individualized efforts and rewards, a broader scope of experience is fostered within and between village communities. The three cornerstones of CCP ideology, which together were thought to eliminate superstition and religion in rural society – a higher standard of living, modern medicine and the popularization of science – have been seriously eroded by conflicting interests. Inequality is now tremendous and poverty widespread in rural areas, modern medical personnel have left rural areas on a massive scale since the reforms, and science is perhaps important in agriculture, but access to knowledge is restricted by government and party interests, for instance in the environmental field, where quantitative knowledge of pollution levels is guarded as a state secret. The highly differentiated experiences of contemporary peasant communities, spanning both revolutionizing riches and desperate destitution, have polarized the peasants in their approach to religion. C.K. Yang's theory of popular religiously informed reaction to pressure is no less relevant in contemporary China than it was in the 1950s to 1970s, only loyalty to the modernizing efforts of the Chinese state is perhaps greater today in those areas where new wealth proliferates.

FENGSHUI IN THE MEDIA

Until recently all modern Chinese sources on fengshui tended to paraphrase the definition given to it by the regime: an old superstition, which some people belonging to backward segments of society still support. It has been government policy since the 1950s that all matters relating to religion must be monitored and central authorities maintain a strict censorship on local media to ensure that news items only convey clean and correct messages in this field. A more lenient policy on religion prevailed from the early 1980s, but with occasional setbacks including mass arrests of religious leaders of all denominations. Today, countless religious societies have their own journals and newsletters, still censored, but important for the societies' formation and expansion. This is not quite the case with popular cosmology. Anything relating to fengshui has been subjected to a nearly total ban in the public media, which tend to ignore both its very existence and its increasing conspicuousness since the reforms.

Although book publishing in the spiritual field has gained considerable ground, newspapers and magazines evidently remain under much stricter control. Only occasionally do fengshui-related news reports slip through the official ban on news items that contribute to the 'dissemination of feudal superstition'; sometimes they are deliberately disseminated as a pre-warning of renewed government action against them. Commercialization of local authority, as will be shown in the fieldwork chapters, is but one of the challenges to the Communist regime in recent decades. Another is the magico-materialist worldview of the new rural entrepreneurs, who tend to be more than slightly inspired by powerful overseas Chinese business communities. Everywhere new entrepreneurs extend the limits for private business and personal achievements, sparing no effort to investigate new fields, as was evident when a notice placed in the Shijiazhuang Daily (Hebei province) by municipal authorities stipulated that anybody wanting to place stone lions in front of buildings must apply for a permit. Although they are traditional decorating items, stone lions are attributed obscure powers:

> Battles have been fought over stone lions. One interior decorating company placed a pair of them before its gates so that they faced the salesroom of a nearby transportation company and a refrigerating plant. This made the sales staff angry. 'The lions are trying to swallow us', they complained. 'We have to smash them!' When a restaurant put two stone lions beside its entrance, the residents across the street sued. Some hung mirrors opposite the statues to reflect the evil effects. The manager of a printing and dyeing mill found that their gate was facing

northwest, which was considered unlucky, so he put two lions in front of the gate to counteract the ill luck. But the residents in the complex opposite his became furious. Hundreds of residents, hammers in hand, threatened to shatter the lions because of the deaths that had occurred since they had been put there. Endless complaints have been lodged, enough to prevent the officials from doing their normal work. (*CF* 1 October 1994: 7).

Since fengshui is still banned in the media it seemed like a veritable break-through when the first officially printed books on fengshui in China since the liberation appeared in the bookstalls in 1989–1990.[12] One book, written by a young scholar at the Southeastern University in Nanjing, 'Exploring the Source of Fengshui' (*Fengshui tan yuan*) from 1990 opens with a definition of fengshui, which by using terms like *xuewen* [learning, knowledge] decisively departs from its official denouncement: 'The central content of fengshui is the *learning* about people's selection and handling of the environment of their dwellings.' The book quickly sold out and was reprinted several times; even geomancers are seen to use it. Trying to establish a compromise between official policy persistently stigmatizing fengshui as 'feudal superstition'[13] and a vast public demand for alternative reading material, a number of popular books have cited the title above in their depiction of fengshui as 'knowledge' (He X. 1990: 1).

The printing of the first few books was taken as a signal of legalization by other publishers and many ensuing publications referred to these precedents as a defence against accusations of propagating superstition. A scholarly compendium also appeared quite early, including translations of several Western works on the subject (Wang Q. 1992). Within the next few years the number of volumes addressing fengshui cosmology as well as ancient and modern practices simply exploded. For several years they were available everywhere,[14] although more prominently in the bookstalls of Xian, Chengdu, Chongqing, Wuhan and other cities of the interior than in Beijing and Shanghai. They were displayed alongside books on a variety of other spiritual subjects such as meditation, *qigong*, various types of divination, yinyang health theories, longevity, the Book of Changes and *bagua*. Another new market for Chinese fengshui books is the international airports, where both overseas Chinese and other foreign travellers are eager buyers.

Torn between its policies to vitalize Chinese culture[15] and to permit publishing only in fields officially recognized as being in the best interest of the public, central government must constantly be on guard. Editors must work within narrow limits in the spiritual field

Figure 3.1: *Illegal booklet of divination circulated in Sichuan*

because manuscripts are severely censored and vital sections are often cut out by local representatives of the State Education Commission. As the young editor of religious and philosophical studies at the Sichuan University Press noted after the publication of a title on fengshui (Yeji 1993), almost half of the manuscript had been cut out by censors and immediately burned. Abandoned were all parts related to 'superstition', including the influence of grave positioning on descendants, gate orienting as a means of securing wealth and fortune, the relationship between the shapes of rooms and dwellings and people's careers, and so forth. Moreover, the censors set a limit to the number of copies printed.[16]

Apparently such works represent a new wave of interest in fengshui, the underlying catalyst of which we shall return to in Chapter 7. Apart from the masses of rural people practising fengshui, Chinese intellectuals and a large number of other city people conceive it as something comparable to *qigong*, *bagua*, *falungong*, reincarnation or psychoanalysis. Accordingly, the number of books on fengshui printed in mainland China continued to grow at a steady rate though the 1990s until another religious trend, that of *falungong*, became intolerable to the regime and the entire book market was subjected to stricter supervision. In May 1999 regular police reportedly emptied bookstores in the major Chinese cities of volumes on fengshui along with all similar publications, but in the following period most titles were instead made available on the internet.

NOTES

1   Commonly expressed in the 1950s to 1970s. See, for instance, Yang, C.K. 1959: 194; Smith, D.H. 1968: 162; Moody 1977: 117.

2   As told to Edgar Snow (MacInnins 1972: 6–7).

3   'Oppose Superstition'. In *ZQB*, cited in *SCMP* 1963: 11.

4   Only in the early 1960s did a debate break out over the possible distinction between these terms, although the aim was merely the application of 'correct policies' for their eventual eradication. See Bush 1970: 25–29.

5   *RR* 9 August 1957. Quoted in Bush 1970: 394.

6   *RR* 15 October 1959. Quoted in Bush 1970: 398.

7   *RR* 17 June 1958. Quoted in Bush 1970: 401.

8   *RR* 12 May 1958. Quoted in Bush 1970: 399.

9   *HQ* 16 August 1958. Quoted in Bush 1970: 400.

10 As reported to me by descendants of wealthy entrepreneurs in Shanghai.

11 As I have heard from peasants and people with relatives in the countryside during my extensive fieldwork and travels in China.

12 Previously, illegal copies of overseas Chinese publications were found in both urban and rural markets, for instance *Zhuzhai fengshui qin jixiong* [Attendance to good or ill luck in dwelling fengshui] along with simple copies of the traditional calendar (*nongli*).

13 Public authorities still follow Mao in this respect; as a recent example, the Beijing journal *Fazhi ribao* [Legal forum] urges the curbing of 'rampant superstitious activities' (*FBIS* 8 March 1995: 39).

14 A few common books are Wang Y. 1991; Gao 1992; Zhou W. 1993; Yang W. 1993; Zhang H. 1993; Yi *et al.* 1996; Kang *et al.* 1998.

15 In the mid-1980s, the public media emphasized that 'Confucianism can combat moral decline' (*SWB* 15 May 1995: FE/2303 G/8) and that education in traditional cultural values is the answer to 'moral degeneration' (*SWB* 19 May 1995: FE/2307 G/8), although 'backward stuff' must be filtered out.

16 In 1993, however, it was felt that rectification was under way. The year of 1994 indeed became a year of purification in the printing business as over 1,000 book titles were removed from the Beijing wholesale market (*CF* 1 October 1994: 7) and a large number of papers and periodicals across the country were allegedly rectified (*CF* 1 February 1995: 7). Among the books were illegal titles on various aspects of 'superstition', including fortune-telling, physiognomy and fengshui. Complaints over the publishing of books 'propagating superstition' continued in the centrally controlled media throughout the 1990s.

111

4 The Fengshui Revival – Fieldwork in Sichuan

Ever since my time as a student in Beijing I had wanted to investigate the state of the fengshui tradition in contemporary China.[1] Occasional reports in the Chinese press had stimulated that interest, for instance when the *China Daily* in 1986 published a small article about a geomancer in a remote Shanxi village who had urged the entire village population to jump into a creek to avoid a natural calamity, the jump having caused the loss of many lives. Whether true or false, the story was used by party authorities to justify renewed action against 'rural superstition', but for me it was more of a signal that something was still there to be studied now that Communism was waning.

In the early 1990s I had the opportunity to start research in the broad field of rural Chinese perceptions of nature and the possible role of popular religion in that respect – something I imagined permissible for fieldwork. I contacted my previous associates at the Sichuan Academy of Social Science (SASS), which had been the official counterpart in my previous fieldwork in China (Bruun 1993). After the Tiananmen incident (mass demonstrations were staged by students in Chengdu before anywhere else in China and eventually quelled with extreme brutality), the SASS had not really recovered: research efforts had almost ceased, several important staff had left and the most conspicuous activities in the buildings were private consultancy and business undertakings out of the individual research staff offices.

112

In 1992 I organized the first stint of fieldwork with the SASS as counterpart, carried out in a rural area near Yaan in western Sichuan. Both the villages we visited and the processes of social and spiritual change that were taking place were indeed fascinating. The circumstances of the fieldwork – travelling in a huge Shanghai motorcar, a long trail of SASS staff, local officials and drivers following me into every household, excessive fees paid to the SASS, and the unscrupulous financial practices of some SASS associates – were, however, not conducive to positive results. After a few weeks I decided to arrange things on my own and prepare for a longer period of fieldwork the following year.

I came back to Chengdu in the spring of 1993, prepared to stay in the countryside for a three-month period. I had decided to focus more specifically on fengshui beliefs and practices in a rural township; my plan was to combine the Sichuan case study with similar studies in other provinces, instead of staying in one place for a 'full' anthropological fieldwork. Through acquaintances I found Xiong, a Ph.D. student from the medical college in Chengdu, who was willing to work for me as an assistant. He was the perfect choice: being born and raised in the countryside he had intimate knowledge of the peasant way of life, including popular cosmology, and from his medical studies he knew the basic vocabulary of Chinese cosmology and the macrocosm–microcosm analogies, which repeat themselves in fengshui thought.

With an assistant in place only a suitable rural setting remained to be found. The criteria for the selecting the fieldwork areas in Sichuan and later in Jiangsu were the same. I wanted a location with varied topography, featuring flat paddy land and hilly patches, for instance the borderland between a mountain range and a basin. Another parameter related to rural development. Rural industrialization had begun in the villages and in 1992–93 many more Chinese villages opened up for visitors and investors, while at the same time wresting loose from stiff party domination to get their share of development and modernity. I wanted an area in the cross-field between old and new, containing both modernizing and relatively unaffected villages. In sum, I looked for an area thought to be 'typical' for contemporary rural China.

Also accessibility mattered. Without a proper research permit in the Sichuan case I could not be sure that my assistant and I could actually live in the area, so we depended on the possibility of staying overnight elsewhere and getting to and from the area every day. After some map studies, checking of bus routes and initial touring around to get visual impressions I decided on Longquan, an hour's bus ride from Chengdu. We began the fieldwork by simply taking our bicycles on the bus to Longquan in the early morning and back again at night; once in the fieldwork area, our bicycles were a useful and inconspicuous means of transportation.

LONGQUAN

Longquan, meaning Dragon Spring, is an area southeast of Chengdu, the provincial capital of Sichuan. Longquan lies where the fertile Chengdu plain borders the scenic Longquan Mountains, rising to approximately 1,000 metres. A mountain range, a city, a county and a rural township all take their name after the Dragon Spring. The new City of Longquanyi, just a decade ago a small town untouched by industrial development, is now in the rapid process of developing into a modern city with a new road connecting it to Chengdu, new industrial development zones and large-scale housing development aiming at attracting foreign investors and wealthy people from the provincial capital. Due to its diverse landscape with rich green valleys, plenty of rivers and streams, and the steep south-facing hills rising to snow-clad peaks beyond, the Longquan Mountains have been a famous site for final resting places since early times. A number of ancient tombs are still to be found in the mountains along with those few Buddhist temples that survived the Cultural Revolution.

Longquan township (*Longquan xiang*), the focus for the fieldwork, is a rural area located approximately 30 kilometres southeast of Chengdu, bordering on Longquanyi on the one side and stretching into the mountains on the other; one small part of the township is in fact involved in the new housing programme of the city. The 28,000 inhabitants of the township are still exclusively rural people, with average land holdings of 7–8 *fen* per capita, which is just safely above the minimum for survival. With mostly good soil and a growing season stretching all year round, a household can support itself on as little as 5 *fen*, or half a *mu*,[2] per person, provided that ecological conditions are stable. For decades the township has been desperately poor, while only most recently has fruit growing for urban markets brought higher living standards. Approximately 70 per cent of the arable land is now grown with fruit, mainly peaches and grapes. Average recorded income is 900 yuan per capita, but actual income is estimated by the local government at well over 1,000 yuan.[3] Especially the nearby markets of Longquanyi and Chengdu provide the peasants with a nice income, particularly from the peaches, which are prudently nursed and guarded through the growing season and only allowed to ripen on the tree while wrapped in paper to shield them from insects. Administratively Longquan township was formerly a People's Commune. In 1980 the Commune was dissolved and transferred into a civil administrative structure. The Commune became a township (*xiang*), the eighteen former brigades became administrative 'villages' (*nongmin weiyuanhui*), and the 200 'teams' (*nongmindui*) were maintained as the lowest units of administration, frequently coinciding with what is discernible in the landscape as small hamlets. Some villages now have small shops and tea houses, but the township has preserved its sturdy rural appearance. Only the road from Longquanyi passing through the administrative centre of Longquan town (*Longquan zhen*) and heading southeast is paved, and here a bus route serves travellers. Otherwise the township has only rough gravel roads and small footpaths into the remoter hamlets. Several of the poorer hamlets located in the hilly zone towards the east can only be reached by foot, although some hamlets now struggle to give access to trucks by clearing steep rocky tracks.

Recent history has left its clear imprint on Longquan and particularly the period called the Three Hard Years (1959–61) proved fully worthy of its name in her villages. Being a fertile but sensitive area with great ecological variation from village to village and even from plot to plot, featuring dry patches, swamps, groves, mountain slopes and many small watercourses, it was absolutely unfit for the type of rice monocropping imposed by central authority. Both for ecological and political reasons production declined and eventually halted when people no longer had seeds to sow. Starvation and suffering of unbelievable proportions followed. People died in their thousands and corpses were left to rot outside. In the poorer mountain villages, survivors estimate that half of the population perished. In other villages on more fertile lands, a quarter to a third of the inhabitants reportedly died. Parents abandoned their children to barely survive themselves, children left their parents to scrounge for edible plants and roots in the mountains, and the weak and the sick were just left to die. 'In the end, when we could find no more food, we all sat silently indoors waiting to die', an old woman said, 'I don't know how we survived'. A large proportion of the population in Longquan are still heavily marked by their struggle for survival through this period as well as during the Cultural Revolution, not to speak of the effects of the unbearable mental strains that the starvation and deaths have caused. In the poorer villages countless people, young and old alike, are still unusually bony, crooked and bent, with grim toothless faces. These people are a living testimony to the perverse political experiments that lasted twenty years from the late 1950s onwards. No wonder that Longquan was closed to foreigners until recently; its villagers would have rendered a sombre portrait of a proletariat under central dictatorship, if not scaring off visitors prematurely.

Figure 4.1:
One of the few pre-liberation books on feng-shui that survived the Red Guards' book-burning

The intermediate period between the Three Hard Years and the Cultural Revolution was not only signified by pragmatism in the economic field. Economic freedom was immediately followed by an unfolding spiritual life in the village. Soothsayers and especially geomancers slowly began to reappear on the public scene, some even putting up their old signs in front of their houses. When the Red Guards entered Longquan in early 1966, the targeting of religious groups and specialists had come only second to rectifying the local leadership. Moreover, the number of religious practitioners (*duan-gong*) in all fields was far too great to allow them to be rounded up. Comprising nearly 200 people in the county, the majority of geomancers, soothsayers, priests and monks were landless and had no other professions to turn to. So the Red Guards first went for the most famous of geomancers, primarily those masters with literary training and collections of old classics, such as master Chen and the Xiong family. Others, who were practising at the level of artisans with smaller compasses, a simple traditional calendar and maybe a few odd books, were dealt with by means of the systematic ransacking of private homes. Mao's four 'overthrows' of the early revolution, intended to remove old religion, government, concubinage and clans, were the guiding principles for uprooting the old rural society. The notable geomancers were publicly forced to admit that they had been cheating people and to denounce everything relating to 'superstition', a new broad category including the entire spiritual life of the villages. They were paraded through the streets of Longquan village, where the new government had installed itself in the compound of a departed landlord, with dunce caps and humiliating signs around their necks, and brutally beaten up. Apparently none of the geomancers was killed during this campaign. Some were paraded endlessly through every village and hamlet in Longquan to be shown to the populace. In the following years they were forced to study like everyone else, but with greater efforts, stigmatized by their background.

The fearful spirit of that period lingers on, especially among those segments of the population least in contact with modern society, for instance the elderly and the people in remoter villages. Years, decades or even centuries of religious persecution by the Chinese state and an equally long tradition of monks, priests, soothsayers and religious specialists of all types attempting to extort money from a destitute population have had a considerable bearing on the common perspective on religion: together they have set the scene for religious practices in the local community. Thus, Chinese popular religion is quite accurately characterized by eclecticism and pragmatism. When people in pre-revolutionary rural society were likely to uphold a simultaneous confidence in Confucian-type social values and popular religion, so in the early days of the revolution people saw no conflict between, for instance, Communism and ancestor worship – quite similar to the Christian missionaries' experience in the previous century.

Today the fengshui tradition is again flourishing while subject to public exposure. In Longquan, as in all other rural localities I visited in Sichuan, the fengshui situation of a building site is now routinely considered. Almost anyone who had recently built a new family house, buried a deceased family member, or restored an ancestor's grave, would freely declare that a fengshui specialist was consulted; the few exceptions were likely to be merely formal denials on political grounds. Fengshui is used by all strata of rural society: government officials, the new rural entrepreneurs, labourers in the new rural industries and ordinary peasants, the only recordable distinction being perhaps the reputation and fee of the specialists used. The prevailing use of fengshui for building layout is hardly controversial. Far more contradictory to Chinese state policy, however, is the increasing authority that rural people grant to fengshui with regard to disease aetiology, mental disorders, accidents, the sex of unborn babies, business affairs, and a host of daily-life occurrences, on which geomancers are now consulted. This chapter will describe the various uses of fengshui in Longquan as well as introduce the specialists and the local people who acquire their services. An analysis of a large body of fengshui-related incidents will be presented in Chapter 6.

TRACING THE FENGSHUI SPECIALISTS

The very first part of my fieldwork aimed at tracing all the active fengshui specialists in the township, simply to find out what kind of people they were and what precisely they were doing. In this way my Chinese assistant and I also became acquainted with all the villages and hamlets in the township, randomly scattered across the landscape and with very few accessible roads. Bicycles proved by far the most convenient transport, since they could take us almost anywhere in the township, or they could easily be left behind if we had to walk. Our first meetings with people and visits to their homes were deliberately 'casual', since the visit of a foreigner to these villages had not had a precedent for some 50 years. It caused considerable astonishment, but was taken as a positive sign of the village community opening up to the outside world. Even though the word of our presence travelled fast and everyone quickly became acquainted with the stated objective of our study, no one for a moment believed this to be the true purpose. In the eyes of the local government we were potential investors, to many common people we were more specifically industrialists seeking a building site for a factory to make use of the cheap labour, and to many house owners in the hilly areas with favourable fengshui locations we were city people out to buy a nice house in the country. Investigating rural fengshui was considered a good joke, though a bad cover for our activities. My assistant showed sensitivity to the issue and during the fieldwork he gradually learned to introduce me as a foreign author interested in

Chinese culture, which was somehow comprehensible to most people – after all, they thought, China had something to offer to the world in this respect.

As a stranger you cannot simply ask if there is a geomancer around; the question would arouse scepticism or fear. You need to present yourself and your objective carefully in order to inspire confidence, particularly among people having experienced such atrocities. The method used in the first phase of fieldwork related to housebuilding. Since new wealth was starting to flow into the township after many years of depression, a large number of modern-style houses had been built (these houses are described later). There had been a total lack of building activity for decades and houses were clearly distinguishable between the old and dilapidated and the very new. We thus traversed the entire township to visit all the new homes and their owners. We simply called on the households, expressing an interest in their new house, including land questions, permissions, building costs and so forth, and only later during the course of the conversation did we tell them about the purpose of investigating fengshui practices. Despite some initial scepticism, people were most often willing to inform us about the geomancer who had been consulted when building the house and many in addition told us stories about the strange workings of fengshui in their households. Also, despite all previous hardship and suffering, we could still enjoy the friendliness and hospitality so common to rural Chinese people. An elderly woman, Mrs Liu, who lived alone in a house in Longquan town after her husband had been hospitalized, was willing to accommodate us on a day-to-day basis (because of the risk involved), so we did not always have to go back to Chengdu. Admittedly, however, my topic of research remained an obstacle to getting close to many people, who kept thinking that I was fooling them. Throughout the fieldwork I used a two-dimensional approach consisting of a broad series of interviews including everyone of interest combined with repeated visits to a limited number of households with whom we established friendly relations. In this way we could check information gathered from the broad interviewing with people who had deeper and more intimate knowledge of the local community.

Once we knew the name of this or that geomancer it was usually no problem to ask the way to his home, mentioning his name and title such as Fengshui Master Yang (*Yang fengshui xiansheng*). When visited in their own homes none of the geomancers would deny their trade – at least not for very long, although several of them insisted on a different surname – and after just a brief hesitation they were mostly quite proud of being the subject of our interest. Both clients and geomancers now use the universal Chinese term for the geomantic specialist, *fengshui xiansheng* (Mr Fengshui or Fengshui Master). Other common terms are *yinyang xiansheng* or *yinyang duangong* (yinyang practitioner), the latter being a somewhat broader category of religious specialists in rural areas but without much distinction today.

After a fairly fine-combed search it was found that approximately ten full-time fengshui masters lived and worked in the township, which means that local people can always find a geomancer either in their own or a neighbouring village. The geomancers were all extremely busy and hard to find at home. Usually their wives or other family members receive requests for them to perform fengshui inspections. Estimating their significance is not so simple, however. There are several geomancers within any given area allowing some choice for potential clients. It has been the case since liberation, however, and presumably also earlier, that geomancers draw their clientele as much along lines of kinship and acquaintance as among their fellow villagers. Thus, as already noted, they may practise both in neighbouring households and in neighbouring villages, townships, and even big cities. Usually, however, they were found to practise within a radius of 5–10 kilometres from their native villages, a distance allowing knowledge about their skills to spread by word of mouth. Yet, when emphasizing their reputation most specialists would refer to assignments in distant places, for instance in the provincial capital. We quickly detected that there is much competition, jealousy and slander among the geomancers in the township as every one of them strives to build his own reputation as the only 'true' master of the art.

Since they can now practise quite openly, but still do not advertise their trade, they mostly attract customers by such conventional means. Some geomancers from other townships also freely practise in Longquan, but I assumed that the trafficking of geomancers in and out of the township balanced out. From studying the working weeks of several geomancers I estimated that the ten geomancers altogether perform several thousand fengshui inspections per year, which indicate that the 5,600 households of the township on average invite a geomancer at least once every second year. Added to this are the numerous occasions on which people drop by a geomancer's home to ask for advice, to determine correct days for marriages and funerals or to ask him to write posters bearing fortune-bringing characters and symbols. In addition to their common functions geomancers tend to have a range of specialities, from which they derive their individual reputation and prestige, for instance exorcism,[4] magical poster writing, spirit mediation and chanting, advice on marriages, curing infertility, calling people back from madness, and so forth – this specialization was also confirmed for pre-liberation society by the elderly geomancers just as it appears from historical records (Smith R. 1991: 149).

All geomancers are men and by far the majority are elderly, trained as apprentices to fengshui masters in the pre-1955 era. Since hardly anyone was trained after this period, the geomancers' average age was very high at the time of fieldwork. If we do not count Ye, who is the youngest member of a family line of geomancers, the rest of the geomancers will average 71 years of age. Including the only 36-year-old Ye, the average age will be brought down to 66 years.

The modern fengshui master is anything but a scholar, even though he, as anybody else, will have aspirations of social progression either for himself or his children.[5] The common fengshui master is in every sense an ordinary member of the local community. He usually dresses in plain working clothes and lives in an unimpressive house, deliberately avoiding displaying his trade. He has the appearance of a craftsman, most often having acquired his skills through years of apprenticeship with an old master. His level of articulation will support the impression that he is not a scholar, although his vocabulary contains a large number of terms that commoners do not understand, drawn from Chinese cosmology through classical works on fengshui. Some embarrassing situations arose when we discussed fengshui terms with local geomancers and my assistant Xiong, being a medical student, corrected the geomancers' knowledge, for instance concerning the reading of the characters on the geomantic compass. The geomancer is commonly supposed to guard a body of secret knowledge, which he is unwilling to pass on except to members of his own household. A number of the older geomancers, who had practised for a lifetime, expressed that a true fengshui master should be trained by his own father in a genealogical affiliation with their trade. Few of them, however, could prove such ideals upheld for more than a few generations within their own families. It is only recently that circumstances have allowed the training of a new generation to begin, usually youngest sons, grandsons or other closely related youths.[6]

The tumultuous history of modern China finds expression in the older geomancers' life stories; these geomancers lived their lives exactly in the convulsion between the social continuity expressed by popular cosmology and the modernizing aspirations of the Communist state. While they were persecuted by the authorities, they were still requested by their fellow villagers to continue their trade secretly. Many of them thus kept practising, as best shown by their personal experiences.

The very first geomancer whom we encountered also became one of the best informants and a person whose 'homestead' we often visited. Fengshui Master Luo, who is now over 70 years old, lives in a most peculiar collection of houses that serve as a living testimony to the dubious position of the village geomancer. When we first entered his little house on the perimeter of the village, I felt both discouraged and somewhat disappointed, since I imagined the Longquan geomancers to be of greater prominence. The low wooden house is more like a shack with a single room and only one window, which is permanently boarded up. Inside it is pitch-black at first, and when your eyes get adjusted you notice that it is also filthy beyond description. The old couple sleep in a big nest-like bed filled with mostly unidentifiable objects and pieces of clothing with a circular clearing in the middle for the two to sleep in. In addition to the bed there is a small table, which has a history of its own, and a couple of chairs. The old couple are mostly cleaner than their habitat and always friendly, but clearly on their guards towards strangers. What is so peculiar about the homestead is that Luo's little shack is in the middle of a small yard surrounded by three massive two-storey modern houses, which belong to three of his four sons and their families. Altogether their place accommodates an extended family of no less than seventeen members. As it later turned out, much of the wealth that went into building the three modern houses derived from Luo's work as a geomancer. For 'historical' reasons, however, he has chosen to preserve the inconspicuousness of his own little dwelling.

Luo was trained in Longquan by his father from his twelfth year. For many years he went out to work with his father, quietly watching his techniques, and at home he would study the old books under his father's tutorship. When he was 18, he started doing smaller jobs of his own in order to gradually build up his own skills and reputation. When his father died he acquired the roles of fengshui master and head of household. He still lives in his native village and practises both here and in neighbouring areas, and has never in his entire lifetime had another job – except for spending his spare time attending to his small orchard.

Figure 4.2: *Mr. Luo in front of his house.*

After the liberation in 1949, when he was in his late twenties, he kept practising for a number of years without interference from the new regime. Prior to the Great Leap Forward fengshui came under attack together with all other practices branded as superstition. In 1958 the use and practice of fengshui were prohibited in Longquan. Luo never took part in the formal integration of the village into a people's commune and the organization of brigades and work teams. In fact he did not leave his small house for several years. Yet the unfavourable political climate did not prevent him from continuing his trade. Clients would visit him in his small house in order to seek his advice on fengshui matters, and occasionally to ask for exact specifications for house or grave construction. They would draw maps with their fingernails on the filthy surface of his small table, and explain the distance and direction to major hills, groves, and streams. At this time Mr. Luo still possessed a large collection of old books which he had inherited from his father. From such information he would determine the fengshui situation of the site in question, and prescribe the correct location for a new construction. The clients would pay him with a chicken, some rice, or a bit of money. Some relatives and neighbours would provide him and his wife with basic foodstuffs. When the calamities of the Three Hard Years had set back the socialist construction, and more pragmatic policies were adopted from 1962, fengshui was again openly practised.

Not for very long, however. In 1966, with the inception of the Cultural Revolution, fengshui operations were again outlawed, and this time the ban was supported by vicious ransacking of people's homes. Luo saw his precious old classics being burned on the huge sacrificial bonfires in the centre of the village – an experience he shared with most other rural geomancers. Only an old divination compendium[7] and a few calendars survived because, as he says 'the Red Guards did not find them because my house was in a mess'. The period 1965–72 was again one during which Luo hardly ever ventured out of his home. People would still consult him, but they were few and far between. These were quiet years for Mr Luo, and the unspeakable poverty in the village was mirrored in the slight demand for fengshui services. Fortunately his sons were then old enough to contribute to the family's livelihood.

After 1972 the Cultural Revolution lost strength in Longquan, and Mr Luo again ventured out to do fengshui jobs on the spot. Some graves were quietly restored, though kept in an inconspicuous manner, and new ones were quietly placed in auspicious surroundings. Towards the end of the 1970s, when Sichuan led the way to rural reform by dissolving the communes, the open practising of fengshui was again a fact. The new opportunities for market-oriented production, which in the matter of a few years resulted in rapidly improving living standards in the countryside, were also the foundation of a fengshui boom. Through the 1980s, when the new private houses were constructed to replace the old wooden farmhouses and new tombs were built, the demand for fengshui services exploded.

In old age Mr Luo is still very active, going out on fengshui jobs several times a week – in the busy periods every day – and his reputation extends to a number of surrounding villages. Some years ago, he boasts, even a state unit constructing a factory near the town of Longquanyi employed him to select the correct spot and to orient the new building. Mr. Luo is also proud that his own land accommodates a number of tombs, including those of his own family and the remains of a more than 100-year-old landlord's tomb, which is still honoured by the landlord's descendants.

The common ambivalence of both wanting social progression for the next generation and assuring that special knowledge is continued within the family, is also reflected in Luo's family (Smith R. 1991: 152). All his sons are well established, but Luo is now training one grandson to become his successor. At 18, the young man has already been instructed for a couple of years, and has started to do simple jobs on his own. To become a real fengshui master, however, he still has a long way to go. Luo reckons that three to four years is sufficient to train someone having completed senior middle school, but considerably more time is needed for someone at a lower level. Thus Mr Luo considers seven to eight years to be the appropriate length of training for his grandson; obviously Luo's position as head of the lineage cannot permit the grandson to rise to fame as an independent specialist just yet.

Geomancers no less than others are subject to ranking as a result of rising social differentiation in the villages. The common specialists with only very basic knowledge, such as Luo, are usually paid from a few tens up to a few hundred yuan for inspecting a site. Their reputation and the nature of the assignment determine the fee. The most famous of the specialists, however, will ask several hundred or a thousand yuan for orienting a house. The highest paid geomancer in Longquan county is actually considered to be a swindler by Mr Luo and several other geomancers who know his story, but this does not seem to affect his success.

We first heard about the geomancer Li, who is only in his forties, during one of our many visits to the local tea houses, the pride of Sichuanese village culture. Several people told us to go and see Li, since he was commonly ranked the highest among the geomancers. We were never able to get other than brief glimpses of him and to catch a few conversations – both Xiong and I got the strong impression that he avoided us. We also found Li to be immensely busy delivering fengshui services to people throughout the day. He travels long distances and can reach a large number of sites every day, and according to locals he is making a fortune. To accentuate his professional identity he has withdrawn to a beautiful private house on a hillside overlooking the valley, surrounded by nice scenery and many trees. He claims to be trained by an old master, who died only recently. The old Master Chen, who was widely known and respected in the county before the Cultural Revolution, was his neighbour in the village where he used to live.

Local people of the older generation know, however, that Li is self-taught; apparently he stole the old master's books. Politically interested, he knew what was coming when the Red Guards entered their village. The night before their mass raid on people's homes he sneaked into the master's house and stole his books, which he then

125

buried in a secret place. When the political winds blew more mildly and old Chen had died he started studying the old books on his own, and in the 1980s, when the demand for fengshui services was insatiable, he started practising and gradually built up his reputation as a specialist. Today his major professional asset is a 'complete' set of classics, including fengshui manuals and calendars, which provide him with a rich stock of fengshui allegorism.

His style of work is very conscious of the mysterious forces of both fengshui and his own reputation. Of all the specialists in the area he uses the largest compass, of which people say that 'you can only understand it if you know the books'. Recently he inspected a hillside to find an auspicious site for a deceased member of the Zhang family. When the workers were digging into the hill according to his direction, two old stone lions appeared, indicating this to be a gravesite of considerable age.[8] Everyone present was astonished and agreed that this was definitely a sign of wonderful fengshui, to be attributed to Mr. Li's excellent skills. Catching the emotional state of the moment, he declared that the corpse must be buried sideways along the hill, otherwise his own eyes would turn blind – apparently with inspiration from the classics, which contain many stories about geomancers helping others to fortune but themselves being hit by accidents, for instance turning blind.[9] No one dared to inquire about the reason for this strange command, and the Zhang family complied with it.

Yet another geomancer in Longquan township is Yinyang Master Xiong. He was born in year 55 in the 60-year cycle [1919], he says, in a family that allegedly counted five generations of geomancers. He followed his father from quite young and continued alone after his father passed away. He was a member of a yinyang association under the supervision of local government. After liberation, he had to practise secretly just like many other landless geomancers. He removed his sign from the gate of his house, but everybody would continue coming to ask for his advice. In 1965–66 things got worse. When the Red Guards entered the village he was attacked for being a counter-revolutionary. He was brutally beaten up and paraded through the streets with a dunce cap and a sign around his neck saying 'I am a counter-revolutionary, I have betrayed the proletariat' (Xiong shakes his head and his face clouds when telling us). He had to leave the area in search of new places to practise since he knew no other livelihood. The new authorities simultaneously coerced him into divorce. Xiong ended up in Guizhou in the south, where he was able to practise on a small scale in a remote rural area. In the mid-1970s he ventured back to Longquan, where his family maintained a good reputation. The real breakthrough, according to Xiong, came in 1986–87, when two things happened. One was the rapidly increasing income of rural households, enabling many to build new houses. Another was the liberalization of government policy, allowing for freer public expression. Ever since, Xiong has been extremely busy.

Xiong ranks himself as one of the best and most genuinely trained geomancers in the area. He wrote several small booklets for his 'students' to use. Xiong is dressed like anyone else of the rural populace, but wherever he goes, he carries a three-foot cigar tube with brass mouth piece and head. When lighting it, he first ignites his old petrol lighter and puts it on the ground, whereafter he sinks the pipe head with the cigar down to the ground and puffs from the other end. A few young children from the village sometimes study with Xiong, but they tend not to demonstrate a strong commitment. Xiong has long ago given up teaching his own son, who is educated as a schoolteacher and candidly expresses his disbelief in fengshui: 'People should look ahead', he says, 'not backwards to feudal beliefs'.

It is difficult to estimate either the individual income of geomancers or how much money is involved in village fengshui on a larger scale. The various types of relations through which geomancers are invited to do their work affect payment. Within family relations seeing fengshui could involve either free service or some kind of exchange in kind or labour. Since many geomancers traditionally were landless, it was common to pay them in kind: grain, vegetables, pork, chicken or whatever people thought they would need in their households. Today the geomancers prefer money and usually ask for a specific payment, the level of which their customers will have little means of influencing; most clients will say with awe, 'you don't argue with a geomancer'. Also, geomancers see fengshui for a large variety of constructions demanding more or less work; simple advice performed at home may only involve payment in kind. Very important for their income is the fact that the clientele spans all classes in local society and payment is usually adjusted to the capacity of the client. In general the geomancers now enjoy prosperous times after many meagre years and their income will probably easily compare to that of ordinary peasants. Except for the boisterous geomantic entrepreneur Li, nearly all of them still believe that a geomancer showing off his wealth will produce a challenge to local authority.

BUILDING HOUSES AND REPUTATIONS

Along with the unfolding differentiation among rural families, increasing sums of money are involved in rural fengshui. Wealth and power are being matched with a search for auspicious surroundings for houses and graves. According to several geomancers in Long-quan, their trade is more absorbing today than during the times when it was considered a criminal activity, but it has also become more complicated in relation to the clients – we will return to issue of clients potentially shaping the geomancers in Chapter 6.

The number of inspections of sites for houses and graves mentioned previously is merely indicative of the significance of rural fengshui. New houses had not been built for decades and a frantic building activity in rural areas began in the early 1980s, with the later constructions becoming ever bigger and more elaborate in exterior design. As noted by Maurice Freedman in his celebrated essay on Chinese geomancy (1969), building higher or bigger has always been regarded as a challenge to the rest of the community; or as Luo put it with regard to pre-liberation society, 'If you built bigger you should have the means to defend your wealth'. After the liberation in 1949 convention was turned into politics; rural mansions were demolished or seized by public authorities and small standardized housing became a political manifestation of equality. In the old established communities such as Longquan very little building activity was performed at all, and only very basic reparation was done during the times of political turmoil. Now that private construction has been given free reign, an immense production of both houses and symbols is taking place – as a means of demonstrating the position which a family think they deserve in this world. Since this quite naturally is subject to interpretation, fengshui has become an idiom for expressing social relations that are not easy to articulate either in the village or in the reforming society at large: private ambitions, social competition, and manipulation of moral codes. The theme of unity and diversity simultaneously being produced is intensely played out in fengshui applications. As a parallel discourse to common social talk fengshui principles may support social vigilance and make people refrain from breaking community rules. At the same time, however, once households drift apart and social ascendence is consolidated, the same principles can turn into a powerful cosmological backing to social inequality.

In the fengshui mode of thought, the flow of *qi* is influenced by all natural bodies and by human constructions. Moreover, the relation between one's own house and other buildings and constructions in the vicinity has a major impact on the common fengshui situation, since a larger house may catch more of the common *qi* at the expense of others. As a parallel to material wealth, which is seen as a limited resource, also *qi* is regarded as a resource that can only be tapped at the expense of other people's share. But while access to material wealth is restricted by human politics, *qi* flows freely for everyone to catch and with considerably more room for manipulation.

Material wealth and *qi* are two separate things, but people want both. Yet they serve as each other's preconditions: if somebody has good *qi*, material wealth and a good life should come easily and the other way round, if people get wealthy they will immediately strive to have good *qi* in order to preserve their new-found wealth. These are the considerations behind the 'modern' type of family house, built in concrete with some parts covered with coloured tiles and usually rising to two storeys. The new concrete houses have all been built since the reforms and are a curious contrast to the low traditional wooden houses in Longquan. They are powerful symbols of the new wealth in this as in other rural areas, prominently displayed to the local community. They are often very big with more rooms than the household can possibly occupy or furnish. Interior decoration and furnishing are as simple as in the old houses, and at this stage apparently of far less importance than the exterior of the house.

Local government is confronted with an intensified public awareness of the fengshui situation around homes and businesses. When people living in the crammed old villages want to build new houses they must move to the village outskirts where it is possible to build bigger. Local governments usually allocate land for such undertakings. Anywhere within the village confines, a new house towering above others is bound to influence people's fengshui. One example will illustrate this. When passing through the village of Woji on one of our routine interview outings, we see a man supervising the construction of a new house. The man confirms that he is the owner of the house. After some polite conversation we ask him whether he utilized the expertise of a fengshui specialist when the foundation of the house was laid. The man first denies, glancing at us with suspicion, but when we manage to convince him of our harmless undertaking and he learns that neither Xiong nor I have any connection to the local authority, he admits using fengshui as a matter of course.

The man, named Zhao, tells his story. He had lived his entire life in another village. Some years ago he found work in a new shoe factory near Longquan and soon saved up enough money to start up a small business for himself as a wholesaler, working on a contract with his former employer. He wanted to build a new house for his family, but land was scarce and his native village did not have a vacant site. Then local government transferred him to this village for a good fee. He hired a geomancer, whom he says was paid 20 or 30 yuan – but we get the impression that it could have been a lot more. The geomancer took great care in positioning the foundation and particularly the entrance since the site allocated to him by the township government is indeed problematic. It is right in the middle of the courtyard of a low elongated two-winged building that houses five families. This building previously enjoyed a large courtyard, once a communal threshing ground, allowing all front doors to face directly towards the rolling hills around the village. Now the new two-storey house right in front of them has 'broken' their fengshui. The inhabitants think he should have stayed in his own village and they have complained vigorously both to him and to local government, but formally there is nothing they can do. There is not open hostility, but ill-concealed grudge simmers. While talking to us Zhao looks back with uneasiness.

We pursued the matter further by visiting both the families around the courtyard and the local government. The old inhabitants in the compound expressed fury at local government for allotting this plot, accusing government officials of cashing in on it for themselves. But land is public property and people can only acquire land use rights for specified periods. Since there is pressure to get plots for building bigger houses and these ambitions are commonly supported by government, people are frequently allocated plots which are obviously taking away qi from others. Local government, however, formally denies taking fengshui considerations into account, but there are limits to what local people will tolerate, so in reality local government, too, most negotiate their way through trouble. After receiving the complaint above, the local government simply replied that 'you may want to build new houses yourselves one day, and then you can move to new locations and build bigger'. Local government is the staunch defender of modernity and favours rational solutions to conflict. Yet also government demands that certain conventional rules of fengshui must be obeyed, such as doors not facing each other. Compensation is frequently paid despite a local government prohibition, but in cases like this hostility may only be avoided by the active interference of local government. The solutions which people often negotiate emphasize that *qi* and wealth are somehow reciprocally convertible, despite their origin in disparate domains. In the case above, after some time the new house owner had to pay a small compensation to the other families in the courtyard, negotiated individually in each case, in order to attain peace. Until then, people cursed him, the builders were obstructed in their work, things vanished and so forth until the man gave in to the pressure.

The houses now commonly built have much the same layout as many traditional wooded houses, only the rooms are likely to be bigger. The main entrance, which is not necessarily facing south in the 'forms' school of fengshui dominating here,[10] but rather looking towards open landscape and taking the owner's birth date into consideration, leads into the central room. This serves as a living room for the family. There is always a table with benches or stools in this room, which otherwise is sparsely adorned. Here visitors will enter, usually without much formality or courtesy. Bicycles may also be parked here and vegetables or grain may be temporarily stored along the walls. To the right of the central room is the bedroom of the married couple and to the left either children or grandparents may sleep depending on the age composition of the household. The kitchen is usually placed towards the back of the house, sometimes in a small annexe with an entrance through the living room. The kitchen has a sensitive position in the fengshui tradition and used to be placed in a separate building, since the stove chimney is thought to have a bad influence. What turns these new constructions into modern 'western-style' (*xifang*), houses, however, is not the fact that they are built in concrete, but that they have two storeys with a staircase in the central room. For larger families, having an extra floor containing two or more rooms can be a relief. While previously everybody slept in one or maybe two rooms, generations may now be separated. The married couple will usually sleep in the ground floor bedroom and children will be placed upstairs or to the left of the living room. Elderly people are usually allowed to stay on the ground floor, both because they may not be able to climb the stairs and because they commonly refuse to leave the ground floor with reference to custom.

Because of earlier political catastrophes and because childbearing is now restricted, families tend not to be very big. In fact, most families only have three to five members living together, which does not give much incentive to make use of the second floor. When inquiring about the function of this second floor and asking permission to see it, I was mostly met with remarks like 'but there is nothing to see up there, we only use it for storing things' or 'it is all empty, you know we just built the house a couple of years ago and we have not needed the second floor yet'. Houses in this region are not as big as in coastal regions, where farmers may build even three or four storeys although usually for other than purely utilitarian motives. Fengshui ideology supports individualized pursuits both symbolically and instrumentally by focusing on the intimate relationship between the person and the surrounding world; its resurgence corresponds well to the structural changes that the market economy has brought to rural areas. Thus fengshui embodies the egocentric traits that were always suppressed in the Chinese ethos, which rather emphasizes the values of the group and the nation.

Expressions of ambivalence and uncertainty are characteristic of cases where fengshui cosmology is applied, as in a typical case of a family we visited after having heard about their problems in the tea house: 'What do you want – do you want to buy the house?' A woman refuses to chain the dog and let us into her courtyard when we ask permission to see her. 'We don't like strangers here, we usually don't talk to them. We are afraid of their intent.' A bit later, upon hearing what we are after and inspecting us prudently, she says, 'Many people in this village use geomancers, but they will never tell you the truth!' We are finally let into the house and served tea – a researcher seems harmless enough as compared to an official, although the woman maintains her scepticism. One wall is covered with a newly written red paper couplet (*duilian*) and on the floor is an empty bottle and the remains of burnt paper money. Evidently a geomancer has been consulted. After some greeting and tea drinking the women relaxes and tells her story.

> We built this new house in 1988 on land allocated to us by local government. We came from another township. We asked a geomancer, who is a relative's acquaintance, to arrange the plan for the house, including the placement of the kitchen and rooms. We are doing all right, we can survive, but we do have problems. My husband likes to drink alcohol and he spends too much money on it. Also, he sometimes gets violent when he returns home. We honour our forefathers – every time our son is home from service in the army we gather to offer food and wine to our ancestors, light candles and incense sticks, and burn paper money. Yet my husband keeps drinking. Many people urged me to invite a geomancer, so finally I did. He inspected the house, which was all right. Then we walked around inside and outside for a very long time and finally he told me that

some of our forefathers were unhappy. Their tombs were destroyed during the time of the Cultural Revolution, so now we will try to recover them. But maybe it is just my husband's habit to drink and there is nothing to do about it!

In this case, honouring the forefathers symbolizes respect for the entire patriarchal hierarchy and the male head of household. Thus, while both comforting the head of household and submitting to his authority the act also underscores his obligation to uphold the family line. This is of course commonplace. Ancestor worship, filial obligations and domestic hierarchy represent a separate rationale that can be seen and analysed as a tradition of knowledge in itself. That the forefathers are unhappy with their graves, however, refers the matter to fengshui thinking. I shall return to these coexisting explanatory devices, which tend to penetrate all aspects of daily life, in Chapter 6.

HOUSING AND FAMILY GENEALOGY

The desire to have a new and bigger home is shared by everybody and sometimes amounts to public hysteria. For those farming families who have no ability or wish to earn extra money outside farming, however, the goal can only be reached by pruning the family budget. The collective craze for modern housing has made entire village populations tighten their belts to acquire this new symbol of family success and material affluence. Cutting down the consumption of meat at home and selling the surplus on the free market is one common solution. Countless local families are putting their health at risk. For a population which in many respects still suffers from the long-term effects of undernourishment and malnutrition, cutting down on protein is a risky undertaking. After the Cultural Revolution ended and gave way to a new regime in the late 1970s, many people never regained their ability to put on weight and they still tend to be as bony as then. Others are suffering from chronic ailments such as digestion disorders, respiratory diseases and recurring hepatitis. What adds to the health risk is that people are reluctant to spend money on medical check-ups and drugs during this long haul of saving up, which may last for years before the new family house can be built (the general health standards in Longquan will be returned to in Chapter 6).

Differences in income among farming families do not only depend on their agricultural skills and techniques. To a very large extent they also depend on the management of consumption and spare time. Depending on the ratio of working to non-working family members, some families have hardly any surplus labour capacity, while others can spare one member to work full time outside farming. Sons or daughters may work in one of the rising number of private factories in Longquanyi or neighbouring areas, receiving a salary of approximately 150 yuan per month. Alternatively the family may choose to send a family member to Longquanyi or even to Chengdu to sell fruit directly to customers instead of relying on wholesalers. In summer, people take the bus into Chengdu, struggling onto the shabby old bus carrying huge baskets of peaches. Once the bus leaves Longquan with its heavy load of baskets and people sitting on top, there is little room for extra passengers along the route. This is the 'peach express' that despite its humble appearance has brought new wealth to many families.

There are several ways of accumulating enough funds for the construction of a new house. Some households have chosen to start up sidelines such as making hats or baskets, or opening small repair shops. Learning from the big cities, where restaurant owners were among the first to get rich after the reforms, a number of local households have set up small tea houses and restaurants, where even simple meals based on the family's own produce may contribute a considerable extra income to the budget. In the early reform period such families with extra sources of income were probably the first to build, and they still tend to be those who build the largest houses. They belong to a new group of village entrepreneurs, of whom many want to leave farming after establishing their businesses.

Concrete houses may be built for 40,000 yuan[11] if the family does not demand much refinement or tiling. On the other hand, building costs can easily run up to 300,000 yuan or more if the family want three floors, a tiled roof and parts of the facade covered with coloured tiles. In the new building craze the only tiles available at first were those of the green and bluish colours commonly used for public toilets, but now there is more variety. In contrast to traditional houses, which were all built with pointed roofs, the modern-style houses usually have flat roofs. These are cheaper to build, allowing everything to be built with prefabricated concrete elements or made on the spot. This causes problems with water penetrating the roof, however, resulting in the ceiling and part of the walls on the second floor being covered with mould after a few years. The owners of the houses will just shrug their shoulders and state that the house is already several years old. In this sense the new houses share the destiny of their predecessors; they were never built to last, but follow the conventional pattern of every generation building a new house.

In terms of social status it is difficult to distinguish clearly between people in Longquan, even though some lasting differentiation is beginning to be felt. Since the break-up of the commune, land has been allocated according to the number of individuals dependent on farming in each household and reallocation is taking place at five-year intervals. Thus, almost everyone has the same agricultural background and comparable land holdings. It is only the new economic activities such as sideline production, shops and restaurants that for the moment have provided some families with an advantage over others. Conspicuousness is of phenomenal importance in this process, since many families struggle to prove that they belong to a higher social class than that of peasants. There are historical reasons for this immense desire for social stratification. For decades the ruling authorities did not permit anyone to stand out from the class of small peasants, unless they went along the path of party schooling to reach superior positions as village headmen or party secretaries. Today a rising number of people want to try their luck as merchants, restaurant owners and entrepreneurs, and even more people want a lifestyle associated with the new Chinese middle class. Those people who can afford it pay tens of thousands of yuan for permits to move into the new apartment blocks in Longquanyi in order to become city people. They never themselves believed that being a peasant was something honourable and today, when it is no longer a political oppression they are up against but economic exploitation from local officials extracting huge fees, they are affirmed in this belief.

What is the role of fengshui in all this? It could be seen as a motivating force itself, since many people appear to think that other families building bigger houses will ruin their own lives if they do not follow suit, or fengshui could be seen as merely a symbolic resource for expressing essentially materialistic concerns and intense social competition. Such representations cannot be truthfully distinguished and the only logical solution is to rephrase them to match empirical facts.

A crucial fact is that people do not express a positive belief in either of these contradictory representations of reality, but assert their respect for both. This may be captured in a series of common statements: 'you need good *qi* to build a happy family and to become wealthy'; 'in order to have good fortune you need to work hard'; 'if malicious *qi* flows into your house, mishaps will occur'; 'you can perhaps influence your fortune by improving the flow of *qi* around your house'; 'you must honour your forefathers and pay attention to their graves, or something bad may happen'. Various models, or traditions, are in themselves rationally and consistently construed and they tend to enjoy a certain autonomy. Yet even though they belong to different domains they are still bound up in a single, immanent cosmological order and therefore meet and interact – 'just like people do', as some locals would picture it with an anthropomorphic analogy. So the real questions are rather *when* these potential couplings are effectuated, *how* transgressing forces are triggered and *what* the consequences are.

To judge exactly how elements in one model impinge on another is not considered a matter for amateurs, although everyone has a certain knowledge of their interaction. It takes a professional to have sufficient knowledge of each domain, to know the cosmological theory from the old books and to gather the necessary experience for applying it all to a specific case – in short, to know all the subtle connections and to master the refined tuning to make all elements work harmoniously together takes a fengshui specialist. Hence the specialist both maintains a local tradition of knowledge radically diverging from state rationalism and at the same time monopolizes its interpretation. It is perhaps for this reason that Chinese folk literature abounds with references to geomancers: they are common figures in family dramas and in competition for wealth and power, noted for playing with people's frustration when they are caught between the geomancer's potential supernatural powers and his cheating character.[12]

POPULAR BELIEFS AND KNOWLEDGE

It was noted in Chapter 1 that there is only a vague link between religious creed and the individual in China, to the effect that Chinese religion is not primarily a question of faith. Yet this insight has primarily been drawn from people's relationship with institutional religions. Popular, folk or 'diffused' religion, on the other hand, is intimately linked to life-cycle rituals and ceremonies, agrarian production and the basic conditions of rural life, in which family and kinship organization always play a crucial part. It has been suggested that family and popular religion in China really are coterminous, accounting for much of their flexibility; as long as one survives, so will the other (Jordan 1972: 177). One could surmise that publicly denouncing the family would probably be the closest anyone could get to blasphemy in a Chinese setting.

Before going on we should briefly consider the distinction between fengshui and popular religion. It has been shown how successive Chinese regimes as well as Chinese intellectuals in general have refused any such distinction. Fieldwork has also indicated that local people tend not to differentiate purely cosmological thought from religious creeds involving actual worship of gods and deities. For these reasons, the concept of popular cosmology may serve as a convenient generic category until we round up the discussion in Chapter 6.

During fieldwork I explicitly asked a great number of people, first, if they *used* fengshui, and second, if they *believed* in fengshui (*xiangxin fengshui*). It quickly became clear that *using* and *believing* were not the same thing and that there were both political, generational and personal motives for distinguishing between the two. Today almost anyone will admit that they use fengshui in practice in the con-struction of houses and graves. But whereas *using* it could be referred to custom, *believing* it was regarded to be more like an active position, a deliberate and verbalized standpoint for popular cosmology and therefore implicitly against the party authorities that had tried to curb it for an entire generation. Thus, when expressed in public it had attained the role of a quasi-political statement. Chinese experiment-ation with Communism has not made the question of belief less enigmatic than it ever was.

In the process of interviewing I had to admit that the concept of belief was so ambiguous that it really did not serve well to investigate people's perception of fengshui. Apart from its obvious political connotations the term could never be applied to any aspect of Chi-nese institutional religion or popular cosmology. Rodney Needham has brilliantly pointed out how the term 'belief' in European languages has been taken for granted as a common psychological category denoting a human capacity that can immediately be ascribed to all men – and that in many cases of ethnographic description there is really no linguistic or other justification for using the term (Needham R. 1972: 3–4). What is particularly dangerous when we transplant the term into a Chinese setting (or any ethno-graphic context) is its association with truth, faith, evidence, ex-clusiveness, and so forth. Further, belief in 'something' tends to refer to an agent strictly external to the human mind, a separation of human and external nature, whereas in Chinese cosmology their relation is more plastic.[13]

For many people belief had come to denote faith, faith in Communism, confirming my impression that Communism more than any other creed had introduced absolutist beliefs into China. Particularly people of the older generation were strongly influenced by politicized attacks on peasant 'beliefs'. When confronted with this question even the elderly people whom we had come to know well would often clam up, excuse themselves and quickly attend to other matters. Only in strict confidentiality would some expand on the subject, for instance by telling stories of the strange or magical workings of fengshui – in fact this was the most common way of discussing the issue of *belief*, quite pragmatically testing religious creeds with perceived reality; not that the perceived reality was an entirely mundane construction, free from cultural biases, but rather in the sense that the world offered a much larger register of forces and outcomes than accommodated in a single set of *beliefs*. Under the influence of absolutist power, belief becomes a potential classifier, both socially and psychologically.

The older generation tend to avoid discussing the discrepancy between using and believing in fengshui; they will declare that good graves for their ancestors are necessities in order to attain a good life just as the living should pay their respect to the dead at the Festival od the Dead in spring. This is where popular cosmology may be seen to deviate from institutional religion, however, and the issue is tricky. Although not a question of positively stated beliefs, there is a strong and pervasive fear of unfortunate consequences of disbelief, that is if some essential principles are ignored. The younger generation will express all grades of variance between common, unreflective use and scepticism, with the youngest expressing little faith in the 'truth' (*zhenli*) of fengshui, clearly revealing the impact of modern socialist education. Yet neither customary nor modern scepticism has had much impact on limiting the ordinary household's use of fengshui specialists for a range of matters – not grounded in belief, but in common *acceptance* of its cosmological premises.

The situation outlined above – that beliefs are relative and subject to scepticism – is anything but new and to ascribe it to modernity penetrating rural life, such as has often been done in studies of Chinese religion, would be to miss the point. It was shown in Chapters 2 and 3 how the Chinese state has opposed popular cosmology for centuries. Now as before, in their everyday lives people engage in multiple activities which appear to lack common ideological consistency and purpose. Some examples from Longquan illustrate this.

Peasants are rational people who do their utmost to squeeze a meagre existence out of their plots of land and travel long distances to sell their produce at urban markets where prices are higher; but at the same time they may honour their forefathers with increasing vigour at the Festival of the Dead if market prices drop. They employ modern farming methods with chemical fertilizers and pesticides to control production and increase yields, but will call in a geomancer if a sudden pest hits their crops or if their domestic animals inexplicably die from disease. They may spend considerable funds to send a son to town for secondary schooling, with a curriculum strictly controlled by the Chinese state, but if he fails his exams they may call in a geomancer to have their house checked. Young people may ridicule the superstitious practices of older generations, but at their own weddings they will take great care to have their birth dates and wedding dates calculated and matched by a village diviner and they may return to him if they do not fare well in matrimony. If a spouse is unable to have children or drinks too much alcohol, and a geomancer cannot cure the problem, they will refer it to the obscure workings of fate. If seriously ill, people will see a doctor if they can afford to, but at the same time they will arrange for a geomancer to check their house and their ancestors' graves, or their family may call in a spirit medium to chant through the night at their bedside. Some of these people are likely to be Communist party members, but neither in their case is the choice of remedies limited to the type of knowledge disseminated by the authoritarian Chinese state.

Chinese peasants are sensible people, always prepared to improve their existence, and yet evidently subjected to several diverging currents of thought deriving from radically dissimilar authorities, one being a rational and materialist outlook which is further strengthened by the modernizing and coercive influence of the party state and another being 'cosmological' or 'supernatural' forces. It was suggested in Chapter 1 that we may replace the concept of belief with that of knowledge, which better allows us to distinguish and investigate diverse sources, for instance in the form of traditions of knowledge, with links to broader currents of thought. We may then replace the affiliation between the individual and a belief system with a structural affiliation between the individual, a domain and knowledge applied. In the common manner as to how knowledge is applied within a given field of action, little distinction may be detected between purely political ideologies, the other-worldly aspects of institutionalized religions and local interpretations of popular religious cosmologies.

139

Figure 4.3: *Spreading 'road money' ahead of the funeral procession*

For the individual, spanning these highly diverse fields of reference requires knowledge of each individual field – certainly not a comprehensive understanding of every detail, but at least a basic knowledge that enables him to act in a meaningful and purposeful way according to the complex interplay between his own objectives and the demands of the situation. Different people obviously have different approaches to the religious domain, and the application of knowledge merges with common acts of positioning. According to the opinion of several geomancers, local people consider fengshui, or

Figure 4.4: *Funeral procession, carrying a modern-style paper house for the deceased*

Figure 4.5*: Funeral procession – the urn*

yinyang as it is often called in this context, 'the religion [*zongjiao*] of this area'; as such they clearly see themselves as religious specialists or priests. This is somewhat contradictory, but apparently related to positioning. It is not meant to say that they consider fengshui as belonging only to spiritual matters – in fact quite the opposite, since the folk cosmology does not recognize a substantial division between mind and matter (I shall return to that in Chapter 6). More important here are the geomancers' specific interests when they state that fengshui occupies the place of a religion and claim an exclusive affiliation between a local area and one particular religion. Fengshui masters were always puissant men in the villages, often in a state of rivalry with some rising to positions of village leadership. The old geomancers practising today know this from before liberation and now that their trade has such favourable conditions they are obviously trying to regain lost ground. Every geomancer has a unique position in his native community and there are rarely two rivals practising in the same village. Each of them slowly builds up his authority and position in his native village while taking great care to avoid offending the political elite, still chiefly connected to the party. By not only having a standard repertoire of fengshui services to offer but also by developing independent 'specialities', the geomancers are in intense competition with each other, trying to win clients from other villages and districts. But the dividing line between seeing fengshui for a family as a private matter and interfering with village politics is a fine one, particularly when new two- or three-storey private houses are built, and geomancers walk a tightrope between building their own fortune and becoming scapegoats when things go wrong.

Contrary to geomancers most other people agree that no single religion or creed occupies a dominant position, be it Communism, Buddhism or the broad field of popular religion. But again, in public any question of religious or ideological affiliation to other authorities than the party has become a matter of antisocial behaviour or counter-revolutionary activity and public expressions of belief are heavily politicized. This is still of key importance to any situation where the geomancer serves a client. In private, however, or within the confines of the small hamlet, specific traditions play more important roles, very much influenced by charismatic people in the local community. A highly respected geomancer, for instance, is able to build a following in his native village and to control a range of spiritual and earthly matters, including siting of houses and graves, interpretation of fortune or ill luck, curing diseases, condoning marriages, arranging funeral processions and so forth. But that the inhabitants of any single village or Longquan township as a whole should be more permanently devoted to any single creed is inconceivable.

Regarding the geomancers' level of knowledge and skills and the outcome of their work, a wide range of opinions are heard among the clients. The clients respect geomancers and attempt to hire either a local one or the best one available according to reputation. So even if people do not have faith in every aspect of fengshui cosmology, the majority is still convinced that its opposite – a total neglect of geomantic considerations – will have strongly adverse effects on the household. It is often described as a matter of convention, or tradition, which you do not need to consider beyond observing certain principles and as long as everything is well. During one of my observations of a fengshui specialist at work, a young onlooker commented on Chinese fengshui as compared to Western customs, which she knew from a magazine: 'It is like Christmas in the West; you don't have to believe in Jesus to celebrate it!'

COSMOLOGICAL KNOWLEDGE AND GENDER ISSUES

Geomancers are exclusively men, a fact which also holds true for historical records (Smith R. 1991: 149). From imperial times when the interpretation of heaven was the exclusive privilege of emperor and state, authority has been drawn from knowing the cosmos. It was noted in Chapter 2 that after the Song, divination and to some extent also the cosmos itself were 'privatized', to the effect that large groups of diviners served the public. The hierarchical order of society operated in favour of keeping these powers within the sphere of male dominance. Attention to religious matters may vary between the sexes, however. A conventional pattern of women being the caretakers of family rituals and spiritual obligations appears to have survived – in this sense the women are traditionalists.[14] Women make sure that paper money, food and drink are offered to the ancestors and see to the purchase of proper religious objects and services.

To get a clearer picture of gender roles in the spiritual sphere we should briefly look at gender roles in general. Today, most families make use of mixed fruit and vegetable cropping. Vegetables may be planted between peach trees or along the perimeter, or fields planted with vines may interchange with vegetable or rice plots. Not much rice is planted any more since the price has dropped constantly and rice can easily be purchased for the much larger profit that can be had on cashcrops. Grapes alone will bring in several hundred yuan per *mu* depending on weather conditions. In addition to crops most families have one or a few pigs, some chicken and maybe ducks which are fed on whatever is available of waste matter and garbage. Since private land holdings in the area are limited (approximately 0.7 *mu* per person), farming usually offers ample spare time for one or more family members.

When the household has abundant labour there tends to be an unequal distribution of work between the sexes. Women have a fairly constant work load throughout the year since they alone are responsible for cooking and preparing foodstuffs. Their labour is also used in the fields, where they take care of routine jobs such as watering, weeding and spraying the fruit trees. Men, on the other hand, tend only to be fully occupied during the busy seasons in farming. They commonly estimate their average work as eight hours a day in these periods, stretching from six in the morning to mid-afternoon. Between the busy seasons, however, their labour input may drop to just a couple of hours per day, and in some winter periods they may be left entirely workfree. Then there is plenty of time to socialize and visit the humble tea houses in the villages.

The tea houses, which may serve both tea, beer and spirits, are also important in relation to fengshui. This is where people gather to discuss all communal matters and anyone interfering with either the wealth or the *qi* of others is sure to have complaints voiced here. As a public place it is also the locus for the encounter of traditions of thought. Matters relating to new crops, farming methods, sideline opportunities and village leadership are mixed with spiritual matters and daily household occurrences. Here, almost everyone will admit the use of fengshui as a matter of practical concern in all construction work and the men will discuss the qualifications and merits of each of the geomancers in their area. But the question of a decisive belief in fengshui (*xiangxin fengshui*) is rarely brought up. First of all this is because the men prefer to see it only as a partial precondition for a desired outcome, but also because of the political connotations. Party policy is no longer strongly felt in the villages, but the strain of modernity has had an impact on particularly the men's way of talking about popular cosmology in public. The men will gladly narrate stories about the mysteriousness of fengshui, but frequently in a joking manner, while they maintain that 'only the women believe in it'.

We went back to those geomancers we knew best to hear their opinions. Luo, or rather his wife who receives all the requests, confirmed that the large majority of people calling upon them for

Luo to inspect fengshui in their homes are in fact women. 'They invite him on behalf of their families', she said. Luo himself, speaking out of bitter experience, commented that 'it has always been more dangerous for men to invite geomancers, they have to be more careful than women with what they do'. Also geomancer Xiong's household confirmed that it is mostly the women who send for geomancers: 'women can better see the need for it', was one comment. In the household of Wang, another local geomancer specializing in curing the sick, they told us that many people in their village had built a habit of sending the children to call the geomancer after his work had for many years been condemned by the local health station (now closed, but described below).

The question is whether the different attitudes toward fengshui that can be observed between the sexes is merely nominal, or whether they are based on actual differences in terms of perspective, practices or even beliefs. The women definitely tend to be more secretive about spiritual affairs, usually discussing them only among themselves in the confidentiality of their own homes; their public life is much more restricted than that of the men. Since we were both men my assistant and I experienced considerable difficulties in getting access to the discussions of spiritual affairs among the women. They were always willing to talk to us, but appeared cautious when it came to women's talk, joint action and conflicts between the households. Our landlady, Mrs Liu, warned us that many of the local women felt 'obliged to talk to the foreigner', but would frequently change their stories beyond recognition to protect themselves and their families, so we should doublecheck everything. Concerning the involvement of women in spiritual life, her interpretation was that women in general were more responsible for the well-being of their families: they toiled in the fields, cooked, cleaned and took care of spiritual obligations as an extension of these other responsibilities. If the women seemed more committed to fengshui consideration around the home, it was primarily because of their stronger commitment in general. Interestingly, but perhaps peripheral to this study, Mrs Liu also made me aware that modernist and traditionalist positions between the sexes are frequently reversed: in spiritual life women appeared traditionalist, but in regard to educating the young they were most often the modernist, whereas many men preferred to keep their sons in agriculture.

ATTENTION TO GRAVES

Fengshui is routinely used for both *yang* dwellings (houses) and *yin* dwellings (graves). Practically all households have family graves which their preserve, either on their own contracted land or in the nearby hills. Contrary to the argument raised by government, particularly in the 1960s, that graves impinge upon farm land, setting aside a few square metres for family graves rarely strains the budget and it is not remotely comparable to the burdens placed upon the peasants by the regime at any time. Even graves of former landlords, some of whom were slain after 1949, have been maintained by their families, although the tombstones were removed in the 1960s. Graves in Sichuan are usually quite humble in comparison with those in Guangdong and Fujian, but newly established graves or old restored ones are now growing rapidly in size and grandeur. For decades family graves were hidden or restricted to inconspicuous plots in vegetable gardens or insignificant corners of fields. Through the 1980s, however, grave construction followed the development in *yang* dwellings, with increasing demands on family savings. As was earlier the custom in this area, large engraved slabs of flagstone are again erected on the tombs and small trees are planted where possible.

Previously, many graves were just holes cut into a hillside covered with a stone or a small mound with a stone slab on flat land, except for those built for landlords which were either bigger earth mounds or, in rare cases, stone constructions in the mountains. In recent years, people have searched for their old family graves that were demolished during the Cultural Revolution in order to re-erect them or to build new, larger graves for the entire family line. Some recent ones consist of a small, half-rounded brick wall protruding from a hillside or are entirely built up in concrete as coffin-length arched chambers sealed up at both ends. These constructions are plainly meant for burying the dead body without cremation, although unlawful, but they tend to be hidden on private plots with lush vegetation.

Central to the geomancer's work is to locate the most auspicious site for the tomb. Geomancers are also consulted for burial preparations, including the calculation of the right moment to put the body or urn in the ground according to astrological data and the projections of the traditional calendar. Preparations are meticulous and funeral processions lavish, usually involving the entire hamlet

Figure 4.6: *Mr Luo showing the landlord's grave on his property*

and relatives from outside. They begin in the early morning hours, well advised by the geomancer so that the coffin may be taken to the tomb without official interference. Sometimes the coffin is carried to its resting place before the procession starts. First to appear in the procession is a man with a basket, running ahead while generously spreading 'road money' (*malu qian*) – elongated sheets of plain paper – to appease the spirits and open the road for easy passage of the procession. Then comes a number of people carrying gifts and expressions of honour to the deceased, including paper wreathes and garments. Next may follow carriers of large paper constructions, for instance models of houses and automobiles, which will be burned and transposed to the world beyond to make life comfortable for the deceased. Finally come four people carrying either the coffin or a sedan chair with the urn, and after them follow the rest of the procession, easily numbering 50 to 100 people.

A new type of grave construction in the area, which is generally acknowledged for its good fengshui, is that of citypeople who want a peaceful resting place in the country. Some of these people have local relatives or friends enabling them to bury their dead on private land. More and more city people rent small plots from local farmers, however, to get access to auspicious surroundings – an indication that also city people, particularly those from the elite, are paying increasing attention to fengshui. Placing graves on other people's land is illegal in a double sense, both because they are graves and because they involve renting out contracted land. Local government is aware of the problem but tends not to interfere as long as the number and the size of the graves are limited.

SEEING FENGSHUI

There is always an exalted atmosphere around the geomancer when he comes in to inspect a building site or a house, an act which ideally takes place in the morning hours. He is received as an honoured guest[15] and treated to tea and usually a good meal after inspection. Very often his arrival is kept secret to avoid the scrutiny of neighbours and also to secure his uninterrupted work around the site. Many of the concrete acts in seeing fengshui appear ritualized, demarcating the family's move from one location to another and dramatizing the transfer from a situation of distress to one of contentment. The geomancer gives his endorsement to the new home according to traditional knowledge in order for the family to settle down peacefully in a small well-ordered ego-centred universe.

Nonetheless, when the geomancer inspects a site, he 'sees fengshui' (*kan fengshui*), scrutinizes his geomantic compass (*luopan*) and consults the traditional almanac (*nongli*). He determines the location of the White Tiger (*bai hu*) and the Green Dragon (*qing long*) as represented by topographical features in the landscape. He calculates the birth data of the owner of the house to see if, by means of the Eight Trigrams (*bagua*), his elements correspond to those identified in the surroundings of the house. The actual techniques involved in rural fengshui seeing are simple. Usually the specialists rely on experience and intuition more than on books of learning. Seeing fengshui also involves ritual; very significant is the killing of a cock and the sprinkling of its blood on the building site, an act which since 'ancient times' has been used as a demon-expeller (de Groot 1897: 965). When, for instance, Mr Luo works he obviously relies mostly on his own feeling. Apart from using his compass for establishing general directions, he determines the location of the White Tiger and the Green Dragon from experience. He looks for the hills and mountains with the right features on the horizon in order to reach the best possible position, featuring open space in front of the door for the *qi* to flow, maybe low hills in front and always higher mountains and peaks towards the back. If siting a grave, he will look for the approximation of an 'armchair' position, with hills on three sides and perhaps high mountains way out on the horizon in front of the tomb. The location and direction of running streams of water are taken into account, as is specific configuration in the immediate landscape such as small hills, rocks, trees and groves. When people want him to explain the configuration of their land, he may draw a small map, either on paper or on the earth. The final judgement of the correct place, however, is based on his own feeling for the locality's innate condition. Mr Luo employs a number of technical terms when he explains to clients how he sees fengshui on their land; otherwise his style of language is quite ordinary and typical of the rural area in which he lives. Just as his outer appearance is far from that of a scholar, his vocabulary and grammar places him in a category of people with little formal education. Explaining the rings of his compass, he points to the Eight Trigram symbols and the corresponding Eight Characters on the inner ring and says that the rest are aspects of these fundamental symbols. When asked specifically about the meaning of the outermost rings, a touch of embarrassment is seen in his face: 'Ah, they belong to the secret knowledge of fengshui.' He reads the characters of his compass, but in explaining their correlation he does not want to write characters himself in the presence of city people like us.

The technical simplicity and 'poverty' of rural fengshui, which I have often heard asserted by elderly Chinese scholars of the pre-liberation urban elite, is by and large confirmed in the villages, but as will be shown its application is highly creative. When Mr Luo goes out to inspect a site he carries only his geomantic compass and maybe an old calendar. His compass, which is a cheap version produced under the People's Republic, has only nine rings, compared with the old masters' compasses having up to twenty-four. The filthy and worn-out lunar calendars in Mr Luo's possession are for the years 1950 and 1984. A third book contains a calculation of astrological data for birth days for a 50-year period, but all the elaborate information on auspicious days for various activities stated in the calendar are specifically computed for the year of issue, as is all the specific information contained in the almanacs.

To judge from the local geomancers' work there is no interaction with Taiwan and Hong Kong fengshui which has been radically adapted to the modern urban life, including life in huge apartment blocks, busy traffic and a merchant environment. In this context fengshui has taken up many new angles and a voluminous modern literature has been produced. Although an occasional lunar calendar produced in Hong Kong or an illegal copy from Guangzhou is found in rural areas, modern books on fengshui from overseas Chinese communities have not yet generally broken through the official ban.

FENGSHUI AND FAMILY WELFARE

Now as before, the application of fengshui to other matters than placement of dwellings tends to be politically controversial, particularly when involving the geomancers' mediation between earthly and supernatural affairs.[16] Nevertheless, almost every family in Longquan can tell stories related to the mysterious forces of fengshui, either working spontaneously or deliberately applied in households that suffer from diseases, mental disorders, and early deaths. Further common incidents for which geomancers are called in as trouble-shooters are other 'misfortunes' such as accidents and a client's lack of prosperity or desired offspring.

Again, we must consider the socio-economic circumstances to better appreciate people's relationship with the supernatural. The liberalization of the health sector meant that medical personnel could no longer be assigned to work in rural areas. The fact that all doctors in Longquan have moved to the city to work has definitely contributed to the rising prominence of geomancers. A former people's commune health clinic on the main road in Longquan town, on the facade of which is still painted the WHO slogan 'health for all by the year 2000', has been totally abandoned.[17] Despite the prophesy embodied in the slogan, rural people now must to travel to an urban hospital to see a doctor and they generally feel awkward when doing so. They tend to have little confidence in the intentions of city people, and they often claim to be exploited. The peasants in Longquan have very little knowledge of modern medicine and they have no frame of reference regarding payment. Furthermore, hospitals now ask for a considerable collateral before taking in any rural patient for non-ambulatory treatment. For example, people report paying several thousand yuan for the hospital to receive them when their condition is serious. When such conditions threaten to ruin the family a geomancer is frequently called in to inspect their house.

In general people do not choose between a doctor and a geomancer – if they can afford it, they gladly consult both and do not see any conflict in the different approaches to disease and therapy. The doctor inspects the body, while the geomancer is in charge of external forces, including ghosts and ancestors. Earlier, when health care was publicly provided in villages and treatment was inexpensive, people were likely to see a doctor first and a geomancer later if the cure did not work. Now the sequence is often reversed, especially for the lower-income group of peasants. A geomancer is usually much cheaper to consult, he is readily available in one's own or a neighbouring village and he is himself a local whom people trust. Numerous cases were recorded of people with various ailments avoiding medical check-ups for fear of the costs involved. It is of signal importance, however, that which specialist is seen first tends to be a matter of convenience and availability rather than of more faith in one of the therapies.

In common with other concerns of rural people, procreation also finds clear expression in fengshui terminology. Childless women frequently turn to geomancers, who may find trees blocking the flow of qi in front of their gates, chimneys wrongly placed or birth dates and marriage dates being out of tune. Geomancers are now consulted to determine the sex of unborn babies, which has developed into a new specialized branch of activity. This act is prohibited in China by whatever means. The geomancer may calculate birth dates and check elements in and around the house to arrive at conclusions concerning the gender of the foetus. As a consequence, in some instances women are known to have chosen self-induced abortions.

Business and monetary affairs are also of increasing importance. Rural factory owners are among the geomancers' new clients, either for construction works or when sales figures are unsatisfactory. Several geomancers were reported to have advised the changing of the direction of factory gates, whereafter businesses suddenly prospered. Commonly the 'flow of money' is considered parallel to the flow of vital energy or qi in fengshui cosmology, which applies to both business and family finances. An example was a young peasant, whose family suffered from poor health and whose domestic animals died, resulting in heavy expenditures on medicine and replacement animals. He interpreted it as 'money flowing out of the house' and attempted to stop the flow by placing a large flagstone (fengshui-stone) in front of his entrance (see story in Chapter 6).

One afternoon we walked into a small hamlet hidden near the top of a tree-clad hill in the Longquan mountains. Since it has no roads, but only narrow muddy paths almost impassable after rain, the village rarely receives strangers. This is one place where half of the population reportedly died during the Three Hard Years due to fatal rice cropping. Conversation in the little tea house halts immediately when we enter, led by some local boys who have guided us up the hill. After some tea and greetings we tell the group of men about our work. 'Yes', one says, 'we often use a specialist, mostly for houses and tombs, but some people also use him for diseases.' 'I call him every time I catch a cold', the girl serving tea remarks jokingly. Once acquainted with our doings, people are immensely sociable and willing to talk about village affairs. Here in the mountains all houses face west since the wind and dust comes from the east. 'Maybe if everything is well you are not concerned, but it could also be the opposite,' as one comments. One man invites us home for dinner in order to tell his story without others prying into his affairs,

> For some time I had a pain in my chest and breathed heavily. It gradually got worse until I could not work any more. My wife went to Yinyang Master Zang in Yanbao village and told him about my problem. Then he poured water into a bowl and stirred it with his finger. He told my wife that I had reached a difficult gate (*guankou*) and that we had to invite a geomancer to inspect our house, otherwise a disaster would hit our household. Of course she invited him. Some days later he arrived with an exorcist from his own village, called Feng. They arrived in the evening and began immediately to put up pieces of paper with fortune-bringing characters. Then, from 8 o'clock at night until 6 o'clock in the morning the two men chanted and walked around in the nine point pattern, using various instruments to call all our forefathers and spirits. We paid 120 yuan. Afterwards I did not feel any improvement and since I could not work any more I finally had to go down to the local hospital in Longquan. I stayed in hospital for 20 days. They said I contracted three different diseases: pneumonia, water in the lungs, and something else. It was awfully expensive, almost 1,000 yuan, and we are poor people. Moreover, I did not really get well, so they told me to go to Chengdu to be checked for TB and cancer at the Southwest Medical College. I went there, but their equipment was broken. I was checked at another hospital, however, but they found none of these things. I still cannot work very hard. Recently I went to a *qigong* specialist, who studied with a master from the Qingcheng Mountain College. His treatment helped somewhat with the water in my lungs. I received three treatments and paid 100 yuan. Now I cannot afford any more treatments. We have only 4 *mu* of mountain land for four people. We used to have more, but an army unit took some of the village land to build on. And you know, taxes are increasing all the time!

FENGSHUI POLITICS AND LOCAL GOVERNMENT

The indiscriminate application of the fengshui tradition to every-thing that matters inevitably brings villagers and local bureaucracy into close encounter. Laws and regulations concerning the disposal of dead bodies and construction of graves in particular restrain fengshui practices. According to provincial regulations, dead bodies must be cremated before burial. Furthermore, general law stipulates that graves must not be placed on arable land or take up space usable for other purposes.[18] In actual practice, in the numerous cases where people do not have access to hillsides the fengshui specialist is likely to point out a corner of the field to be used for a grave and thereby inspire people to violate the law. Concerning burials, contradiction is even sharper. Any true fengshui specialist will advocate the burial of the intact body, since preparing of the body, selecting wood for the coffin, building the coffin and placing it in the tomb are core elements in traditional ancestor worship without which a burial is incomplete and the ancestor's positive impact on his descendants is amputated. With the increasing wealth in rural areas the demand for all-inclusive burials has exploded.

In real life the penetration of the law is doubtful and its effect is ambiguous, since legal relativism is as much an integral part of Chinese culture as is fengshui. Most people desire to bury the whole body and along with the increasing commercialization of public authority this act can now be paid for. Local government places a fine of approximately 1,000 yuan on anyone burying a body without cremation, so what was originally intended to be a penalty to make people obey the law is now regarded as a levy by both parties involved. Even if people want to make the burial a public event and invite the whole village for the ritual, this levy is just an expense to be reckoned with along with the coffin, the entertainment of the guests, and maybe professional mourners and musicians. Since convention prescribes that the coffin is placed in the grave pointing towards the centre of the hill, only a small opening in the hillside is required, and when the grave is closed it will be impossible to determine whether it contains an urn or a coffin. Usually local authority does not interfere with the placement of graves as long as only inconspicuous sites on privately contracted land are chosen.

The interests of local government and common people may intersect at other times over the issue of graves. Frantic construction activity in rural areas is changing the landscape rapidly. When local authorities seize land for public works such as the construction of roads, bridges and buildings, and in so doing have to remove graves or happen to dig into hidden graves, no compensation is paid. Instead, the local government provides the descendants with a jar in which to collect the bones in order to relocate them. Thus, even though government does not allow tombs and graves to interfere with public works, it still respects the sanctity of human remains, also when their very existence is in obvious contradiction to the law.

After a good deal of tracing and interviewing village geomancers all over the township, I finally ventured to approach local government to inquire about their stance towards popular cosmology. At this point the local authorities knew that I was visiting but were not fully aware of what I was doing. The Longquan township government is located in the main street of Longquan village with easy access into Longquanyi. The compound that accommodates local government is the former dwelling of Fang, the mightiest landlord in Longquan before the revolution. Many times we had passed the old low buildings, which were still pervaded by an aristocratic air in spite of their poor state of repair. Previously we had passed by quickly to avoid attracting attention, but this strategy proved totally unwarranted.

When we visited the local government the porter apologized that hardly anybody was in, but pointed to an office where we might find someone to answer questions. Approaching the clerk only sparked off new excuses for the emptiness of the offices. Apparently everyone had other things to attend to than government work in any strict sense. However, noting my interest in the old buildings, which are known for excellent geomancy, the clerk offered to show us around. The buildings are laid out around two courtyards, an outer, quite large courtyard into which the main entrance opens and an inner courtyard around which the former living and sleeping quarters were located. The buildings around the outer courtyard are all un-damaged, with tiled roofs and windows covered with traditionally ornamented wooden frames, each one in its own delicate pattern. Even inside almost everything is intact, although marked with age. Some beautifully carved hardwood partitions were destroyed in the 1960s. Also during the Cultural Revolution the remaining ornament-ation around doors and under the ceiling was found to be feudal and consequently all woodwork was plastered over and painted white. Through the years, however, the plaster has started to peel off, revealing the beautiful carpentry, and nothing has been done to repair it. So today much of the fine woodwork is again visible in the offices which otherwise look unoccupied, apart from a desk or two in each room. One of the dragonheads under the tiled roof shielding the main gate has also dropped its plaster and now looks as vicious as ever. Apart from these few modifications very little has been done to the buildings since that day in 1949 when the new lords walked in. The rooms leave the impression that no one ever washed, brushed, painted or repaired anything. The cobwebs in the corners of the ceiling could well be as old as the Communist era itself. The inner courtyard is only accessible through a gate in the left hand side of the outer courtyard. This part of the compound is exceptionally beautiful. It is designed to make full use of shadow, vegetation, and water to create a cool and pleasant atmosphere in the courtyard. All beams and traverses holding the roof covering the walkway around the courtyard are elaborately carved in fantastic motives and some parts have once been gilded. When it was built in the early twentieth century, a large number of carpenters were invited to make their personal designs on the traverses so that every single one was unique. This part of the compound had never been subject to the 'purification' drive of the Cultural Revolution, and all ornamentation is untouched. It was the sealed-off headquarters of the commune leaders, who obviously appreciated traditional layout and design. Today the large hall serves as a meeting room and the former bedrooms, all with wooden floors, serve as offices for the township governor, vice governor, and party secretary.

In contrast to so many other landowners, who were stigmatized as landlords for as little as 5 *mu* of land (everyone who had others to work his land was included in this category), Fang had been a real landlord. He was said to have owned almost 300 *mu* (19 hectares), corresponding to approximately a hundred family farms. Since Fang was a modern, educated man of the new republic, he kept few servants and only one wife, whereas his father was said to have had four. Even though no one regarded Fang as a cruel oppressor, Fang was sure to become a victim of the new authorities. Since he was in intimate contact with the Guomindang he also knew when to quit. He left for Taiwan in 1949, just before the arrival of the Communist forces. His former master of servants, now a feeble 96-year-old man, still lives nearby and from him everyone in the village knows the most intimate stories from the Fang household.

Fang was also the Guomindang magistrate in the village and one room near the main entrance served as the seat of the township government. To our astonishment not only his desk was still in place but also the winged star of the republic was still sitting on the wall. The symbol, about four feet across, stands out with bright colours painted on the white wall as if it was done recently. Apparently it was never touched. Seeing my amazement, the office clerk showing us the room, which is used as just another office, comments: 'Yes, it is the symbol of the old government. No one ever bothered to remove it –

during the Cultural Revolution a piece of cloth was hung up to cover it.'

Apart from an arranged meeting with the township governor (*xiangzhang*) and vice governor plus a couple of lower ranking officials, who all thought of me as a potential investor in their region, it was indeed hard to find anyone of the 50 listed local government employees in their offices. Among these, however, are also village leaders, who have official rank but mostly work in their own villages. Of special interest was the section of government called the 'culture station' (*wenhuazhan*), set up in the 1950s and later occupied by the 'cultural team' (*wenyidui*) during the Cultural Revolution. As the unit responsible for educating the peasants they set up a large assembly hall in Longquan village, where they taught revolutionary songs, arranged performances of the plays by Mao's wife, held political speeches, and performed all public political events, including the trials of counter-revolutionaries. Today, a partition traverses the interior of the hall, with a small meeting room for party members remaining on one side and the much larger part being rented by a private contractor for storing vegetables. In recent years the culture station has been responsible for little things such as supervising that proper names are being used for roads, villages and geographical places as well as for commodities. The station is also responsible for supervising religious activities, including the curbing of rural 'superstition'. In addition, the writing of local history and collection of artifacts are placed under its responsibility, sometimes giving rise to bitter irony. Some years ago they set out to collect stories among elderly geomancers, but were met with a well-founded reservation: 'It was the same people who persecuted us during the Cultural Revolution, and now all of a sudden they come out and try to be really nice to collect our life stories', several geomancers accordingly complained. Today only a single official remains in change of the culture station. This woman went to 'study in the city', however, and has not been back for almost a year. In the local government the common impression is that there is not much for her to do any more. The door of the culture station's office is locked and someone has found the space in front of the door a convenient parking place for his motorcycle while at work.

Political reform has come gradually but inevitably to Chinese villages. It was the simultaneous weakening of the local party organization and the election of a young, non-party aligned governor that produced the decisive breakthrough for political pragmatism in

Longquan. The new governor and his staff are devoted modernizers, who never yield to political romanticism in their promotion of local economic interests. Their appearance is unmistakably business-like, being true copies of the business people they want to receive. The current big game in local politics is the intense competition between local governments to attract investors. Their procedures are straight-forward and uncomplicated, often to the point where they are suspected of operating in defiance of higher level government. For instance, during my meeting with the governor and his staff they freely offered me a research permit to be issued by the township government and assistance in finding local accommodation – and this for an area that until recently was sealed off from the outside world due to massive poverty and evidence of political catastrophes.

Their stance towards Chinese culture and tradition is indifferent. The suppression of fengshui-related news items in the Chinese public media stands in sharp contrast to their public importance in rural life and to the quiet acceptance they enjoy with local government. Across the street from the township government compound lies the house of Fu, a retired cadre now practising as a geomancer, for which he was trained before the Great Leap Forward.[19] He practices a version of fengshui that draws heavily on spirit mediation or 'shamanism', including the writing of magic symbols, incantations and chanting and dancing through the night to mediate between the sick and the world beyond. His entire collection of coloured paper, brushes and musical instruments is visible in the front room of his house, which has the appearance of a grocery store, and people freely drop by to acquire his services.

The new local government neither promotes nor inhibits the revival of things Chinese after Communism, but if they may be put to practical use for their overall development ambitions it is another matter. Land development is a vital activity for the local government. New development zones around Longquanyi are widely advertised: an industrial development zone is chosen specifically to satisfy the demand for good fengshui and a huge roadside advertisement for the new housing programme highlights the good fengshui of the area (also a general term for a pleasant landscape) in order to attract investors, primarily overseas Chinese. Further, a new cemetery has been opened on public lands close to a park area.[20] The graveyard is perfectly sited in hills forming the coveted 'armchair' position, featuring a perfect view to high, misty mountains on the horizon. Here, long rows of standardized concrete chambers on the sloping hill are available for prices ranging from a few thousand yuan and upward. If the customer wants an exclusive coffin burial, a tomb in the adjacent hills can be arranged, but the charge is formidable. The cemetery is run by the local government, while privately hired geomancers choose the chambers for their clients, calculate the correct date to place the urn and have the lid to the chamber sealed. The graveyard has a good reputation among the Sichuanese elite for its outstanding fengshui and many official persons are now among the clients.

POWER, POSITIONING AND NEGOTIATED TRADITIONS

In China, no religion, philosophy or political ideology is ever left alone for its trustees and believers to build up their creed unnoticed. In an ambience of intense social activism, to which both rulers and subjects contribute, all matters of persuasion have become heavily charged, unfolding fields of power struggle and domination. Thus there is no religious organization without official scrutiny, no successful religious specialist without fake imitators, and no religious act without a potential domain of exploitation. These are the realities of China yesterday and today and there is no reason to expect any radical change in this resilient pattern in the immediate future. Perhaps as a reaction to the double challenge of control from above and exploitation from below, religion is infused with scepticism to a degree maybe not seen elsewhere – but that is open for debate. To the question (as derived from Wittgenstein) of whether belief is really experience (Needham R. 1972: xiii) China provides us with an example of religious scepticism firmly rooted in the human experience. This is part of a paradox which gives us problems of interpretation: we see a sustained 'credibility' granted to the existence of a broad range of metaphysical forces coupled with a deep distrust in their human agents and interpreters, a hyper-sensitivity to hidden motives.

We have seen how local authority, geomancers and ordinary people respectively regard popular cosmology and specifically feng-shui in the villages. Roughly speaking, local government is now mostly indifferent, refusing to carry out the control measures stipulated by higher level authorities, but always alert to possible ways of using popular cosmology to its own advantage. Geomancers, at the other extreme, readily pronounce fengshui the native religion of Long-quan, positioning themselves as religious leaders and custodians of the local tradition. Ordinary people are the doubtful believers but

potential clients, whom the geomancers depend on for their livelihood and whose behaviour public authorities monitor for the sake of
public order and the maintenance of the political status quo. Among
these parties, fengshui takes on different roles and meanings, not as
a unified system of belief, but as an aggregation of ideas, practices and
pieces of knowledge that derive from various sources: old classics, the
teachings of local masters in pre-liberation times and new constructions by the present generation of geomancers. These elements
are constantly combined in new and unique patterns by the highly
creative agents and forces at play.

Figure 4.7: *Road sign announcing the good fengshui of a public graveyard in
a development zone*

Fengshui obviously constitutes only one among several independent 'traditions', each with its own masters and followers. Other
traditions, such as in the political and economic fields or in organized
religion, take the form of hierarchies, but in popular cosmology this
is hardly the case. Geomancers may have different ratings in the eyes
of the public, but they are not bound together in a common
structure. Disparate bodies of knowledge rule these independent
domains. We could use the metaphor of publishers and subscribers,
since each domain, whether in the political or the religious field, has
its own trustees mastering the intricate language of his field and
drawing his authority from it. A very general distinction between
publishers and subscribers relates to commitment: whereas the

publishers are intimately tied to their own domain, subscribers are not. A geomancer cannot simultaneously pose as a businessman, a township official cannot pose as a geomancer, and so forth. Subscribers, on the other hand, may with ease subscribe to various publications according to their immediate, situational needs. Outside the ranks of the 'publishers' there are no devoted Communists, Liberalists, modernizers, Buddhist believers or fengshui addicts, since there is no exclusive relationship between people and specific traditions and domains. Quite contrary to Western ideals of devotion, it is highly uncommon for people to attribute any exclusive truth to bodies of ideology, knowledge or religion.

There is no doubt that the 'initial stage of socialism' as interpreted and promoted by state power is still the dominant tradition – even though it is gradually turning into Chinese nationalism – and strongly supported by the modernizing complex of public media, schooling and propaganda, as well as by the possible use of ultimate force against unruly individuals and groups. Communist ideology is often mockingly described by the peasants as the 'religion of the masters'. Correspondingly, fengshui is antithetical to public authority, which will be further elaborated upon in Chapter 6. But what may also look like a transgression of barriers to the Western observer is the fact that a government official, who is unreservedly committed to Communist ideology, may well employ a fengshui specialist, even for public construction works. When dealing with the specialist, however, he is compelled to use the distinctive idiom demanded by this situation, thus recognizing the exclusive authority of the geomancer within his domain.

Among these various fields ordinary people move about quite unconstrained, while drawing on, using, comparing and manipulating elements from each in daily-life occurrences and in social interaction. They have learnt a profound scepticism and how to keep a distance by means of a divine pragmatism that does not give in to ideological pressure or alluring promises of heaven on earth. Rather, the old anthropological phrase on culture that 'it does not matter where they get it from, it only matters what they do with it', could be modified to fit a Chinese world-view as 'it does not matter what people say, but why they say it'.

Many local fengshui stories elaborate on the refined art of exploitation, a salient theme in Chinese culture. An example: in the 1940s the old landlord Ye wanted to build an extra wing to his three-winged compound, closing it off on the fourth side. He bought all the building materials and sent for a geomancer to inspect the site. After seeing the spot the geomancer refused to make directions for the construction and told the landlord that it was simply impossible to build the new wing. The landlord then called in another geomancer, who also, upon inspecting the site, refused. This repeated itself with five different geomancers and the landlord had to give up building the wing – so the story goes. Anyway, it is a fact that the building materials were just lying there for years. After liberation, during which the landlord was slain, his land was parcelled out to the peasants and six families moved into the landlord's house. After some years the new inhabitants needed more space and they decided to build the new wing since the building materials were still untouched. Without approval from a geomancer they completed the fourth wing, but took care not to place the passage into the courtyard exactly opposite the main entrance of the old building. 'So you see fengshui does not always work', one of men tells me, 'the geomancers just cheated the old landlord, and you can see that nothing happened to us even though we defied their advice'. The men still express the common sentiment that even though you do not believe in fengshui, you should still respect directions and principles. Talking to the men standing or sitting in a circle near the passageway through the fourth wing, the topic of taxation is brought up. Everybody complains about the flood of new taxes and fees. I venture to remark: 'So now local government is the new landlord.' Several of the men get so excited that it is almost impossible to follow their stream of words: 'They are much worse, much worse, all levels and all bureaus have their own taxes. They just collect and collect and do nothing else.' Everybody seems to hate local government now:

> We have often gathered to protest, but to no avail. And you know, many of them are sons and daughters of the old landlords and officials, because they had the money to educate their children and they had all the connections. And now they only promote their own kind. They say they strive to develop the area, but they really do it to enrich themselves. They take some of the best land to develop, and the geomancers are always willing to help them for a fee.

NOTES

1   As a student of anthropology I had written a thesis on Chinese cosmology and early sciences, which again was inspired by my previous studies in physics.

2   One *mu* is approximately 667 square metres.

3   At the time of fieldwork, 1,000 yuan was the equivalent of 130 US dollars.

4   An early twentieth-century description of Sichuan geomancers mentions that they are found 'in every village, town or city' and that their repertoire includes conducting funerals, practising medicine, writing paper charms, exorcism as well as sending out evil spirits to harm people 'if business is dull' (Graham 1961: 104–105).

5   For an interpretation of the geomancer as a mediator between the masses and the elite, see Freedman 1969. For social mobility of geomancers in traditional China, see Eberhard 1962: 41, 230.

6   Unfortunately this implies that at the time of publication of this work, the entire group of village geomancers will have changed since the elder generation will most probably have died.

7   *Xiu zeng xiang jie tong shu da quan.*

8   According to de Groot (1897: 978) this is an 'ancient practice'.

9   One example is Li Yiqing, mentioned in R. Smith 1991: 152.

10   The distinction between the 'Forms' and 'Orientations' school of fengshui is discussed in the Appendix. Another distinction used is *San He* and *San Yuan*, each with their own compass (Weller 1987: Appendix A: Geomancy).

11   The equivalent of 5,200 US dollars. A family may support itself on a few yuan per day and state workers' salaries in 1993 were in the range of 150–200 yuan.

12   One example is given in Eberhard (1967: 31). In this case, a dead geomancer punishes a little boy for falling into his coffin, but is himself punished by superior spirits and his bones eaten by a dog.

13   I.A. Richards (1932) has brilliantly discussed this issue with regard to Mencius' thought.

14   Both historical and modern studies confirm this, for instance Francis Hsu (1948) and Maria Jaschok and Shui Jingjun (2000).

15   Also this aspect tends to follow customary principles (de Groot 1897: 975).

16   Although fengshui in principle deals with impersonal forces, it will always be merged with considerations of a range of supernatural beings; see, for instance, Jack Potter (1970).

17   Recognizing the consequences of the primary health sector breakdown, central government has promoted health education programmes in rural areas (*FBIS* 3 April, 1995).

18   The Chinese land law remains ambivalent on this issue and leaves room for 'authorization' of such by local government. 'Land Administration Law of the People's Republic of China (*CL* 15 December 1998: 108, 114).

19   Many village geomancers became cadres in the early years after the revolution since they were respected people in the villages; one prominent example was the 'model peasant' Chen Yonggui, who became a Politburo member.

20   New graveyards became lucrative businesses for both public and private investors across China (*CD* 26 July 1995: 3).

5

Another School of Fengshui – Fieldwork in Jiangsu

I came back to China the following summer to carry out another three months of fieldwork in Jiangsu. I believed that eastern China would provide a substantially different setting for fengshui practices on account of the 'orientations' or 'Fujian' school of fengshui[1] dominating here as well as the different type of rural communities, affected by a strong lineage organization and a high degree of wealth differentiation between villages.

My formal access to fieldwork in Jiangsu was easier than in Sichuan. A Chinese friend, who had studied in Denmark, arranged my permission through her own unit, the Nanjing Forestry University, located on the outskirts of Nanjing. Being a technical university, and including a social science unit, the Forestry University was a priority research and educational institute with a totally different atmosphere from the SASS. Here were active researchers and devoted teachers and students, eager to participate in their country's development. The fact that their financial situation was much better than at the SASS also meant fewer problems for a foreign visitor. The university could even provide me with a nice inexpensive room in their guest house, located in the park-like section of the campus adorned with a wide variety of experimental tree specimens. Several of the university teachers were willing to work as my assistants; I chose to make use of two of them in turn, both to make it easier for them to combine it with their other duties and to make sure that I always had somebody to accompany me.

Although formal access to the field thus was easy, working with a large Chinese institution still presented a challenge reminiscent of my long cooperation with SASS. This university was a totally different set-up, but the dubious role of the party in disciplining people, the infighting among staff and the intense striving for privileges experienced everywhere in Chinese society still affected the work and attitude of each individual staff member. Furthermore, just belonging to an academic institution is perceived as a privilege that sometimes impedes scientific objectives. Perhaps because my assistants Liu (a woman in her mid-thirties) and Dong (a man in his late twenties)[2] both came from families of urban intellectuals, their concern for rural life was limited: it was maybe 'interesting', but thought to be without real significance for their country's development. During our work in the countryside, which included many hours of walking along muddy trails in all kinds of weather, there was some reluctance, complaints about dirty shoes and scepticism as to the value of our undertaking. Our relations remained good, however, and in 1996 I returned to carry out a few weeks of interviewing in the fieldwork area as a follow-up, bringing my 4-year-old son.

I chose the Jiangsu fieldwork area according to the same criteria as for the Sichuan case. Also the location of the Forestry University on the northern fringe of the city was important. By choosing an area to the north our access was much easier than if we first had to traverse the city. I came upon Baohua township approximately 30 kilometres north of Nanjing. There were bureaucratic obstacles to staying overnight in the fieldwork area as well as practical ones, since accommodation was difficult to find and my assistants were dependent on returning home at night. Instead, every morning we jumped on the overcrowded minibuses that run on all highways as an alternative to the public buses that are far between. Once in the fieldwork area, walking long distances from the main road into the villages and hamlets was often our only choice. Without the convenience of bicycles I had to modify my approach from that in Sichuan. I first investigated the general ethnographic context and only gradually established an overview of the total number of geomancers and their significance in the villages.

BAOHUA TOWNSHIP

Baohua is partly flat and partly consisting of the Baohua Mountains with peaks rising to 400 metres. The population of Baohua is approximately 25,000, distributed on 15 villages. The total land area of the township is approximately 70 sq. km., of which the larger part is mountains. The farming villages have average land holdings corresponding to approximately 1 *mu* per person, which bring in an estimated income of 1,200 yuan per person. According to local government, the district is economically fairly average; a bit better than the adjacent townships, but considerably poorer than Jurong to the south and Nanjing to the southwest. The main crops are rice (harvested twice a year), other grains, cotton, rape seed, tea, mulberry leaves for silk production, a large selection of vegetables and some fruit. As a matter of course, most families raise a pig and several chickens. Some villages, especially those deficient in land, have specialized in silk production to supplement their income.

Many aspects of the socio-political setup differ from the Sichuan fieldwork area, requiring a brief outline. Situated in a coastal province, albeit inland, Baohua has had more favourable conditions for economic development than the Sichuan fieldwork area. Several transport and communication arteries cut through Baohua: one of the two main roads from Nanjing to Shanghai, the railway between these two cities and a freight line connecting Longtan town with the southward railway. Just a few kilometres to the north the Yangtze River flows towards Shanghai. Until very recently Baohua was a truly rural township with no other industry than a cement factory and some simple workshops and handicraft businesses in Longtan, the seat of the township government. A newly established industrial development zone along the highway, described below, has contributed new jobs and new wealth to some villages, but has left others unaffected. Longtan is a small town that grew up next to a cement factory established in the 1930s, mining the nearby rocks. Today the entire mining and production complex is run as a penitentiary, with an unknown number of young prisoners carrying out the heavy work. One section of the town consists of the prison itself, secluded behind massive walls and barbed wire. Every day brigades of prisoners are marched through the streets to and from work under heavy guard.

Also relevant to understanding the state of popular cosmology in Baohua is the fact that this region of China is politically and socially more complex, influenced by a large number of lineage or single-surname villages (*shicun*), to some extent functioning as independent polities. In each of them, one surname group has dominated village life entirely, either on a lineage basis when recognizing common descent from a given ancestor or on the basis of a number of large families with common surname without clear notions of their interrelation. Some villages have two or three surname groups, usually with each one dominating a section of the village. All villages had large ancestor halls and shrines, where tablets and lineage records were kept, until the new regime either demolished them or forced their conversion into other uses in the 1950s and 1960s. Contrary to Southeast China, where these institutions have been revived recently, religious control remains stricter here. Yet the kinship organization in the villages has tied individuals together in a much closer texture of mutual obligations and has accounted for attention to fengshui on a larger scale, potentially involving more people and frequently effecting conflicts to be played out in public.

Speaking of villages, it must be emphasized that what figures as a 'village' in the administrative organization of the Chinese state is mainly a remnant of the production brigade in the People's Commune and in actual practice embracing a number of hamlets or clusters of houses, which to the eye appear as natural 'villages', each with its own fields and irrigation system. Such entities are nevertheless termed peasant committees (*nongmin weiyuanhui*) in the official jargon, remnant of the production team in the People's Commune. The villagers themselves refer to this entity as the natural unit of social organization and call it a village, corresponding to its designation before 1949. The administrative village of Mudan, for instance, consists of seven hamlets, of which five are single-surname 'villages' (Feng, Zhang, Luo, Xi, Wang) and two contain two surname-groups each (Feng/Zhang and Feng/Luo). Inevitably, however, the in-migration of non-locals in recent decades has added a number of households with other surnames.

Although the kinship organization gradually lost its formal institutions and much of its political power after liberation, the common identity and solidarity among surname groupings have continued to play a role in local politics and social life. Any local party cadre, whether himself a native or an outsider, must take them into consideration, for instance when dealing with skirmishes within or between villages. Because land is scarce and tends to be unequally distributed between the villages, mostly following pre-liberation land ownership patterns, many conflicts over village borderlands and water resources occur. In such cases those local cadres who do not themselves originate in Baohua have served as mediators, since native cadres tend to have bonds and obligations that prevent them from ruling against their own surname groupings. Since the present-day hamlets and usually also their combined land holdings are directly derived from pre-liberation villages, the peasants invariably point to traditional rights when such conflicts occur. Moreover, in many cases the peasants can claim rights that are legally sanctioned because the new regime issued land certificates at the time of the land reform in the early 1950s. Later, however, when the People's Commune was established in Baohua to fulfil Communist goals the original certificates were collected and destroyed, but as Mr Chen, an enterprising cadre faced with a local dispute found out much later, the Commune staff had preserved copies of the certificates. These documents are now consulted by the mediating cadres when conflicts occur.

LOCAL IDENTITIES

The powerful lineage organization of most villages in Baohua together with a Buddhist monastery being a large independent landowner prevented the rise of landlords as in Sichuan. While this type of social organization lessened differentiation and prevented outrageous exploitation among individuals, it still resulted in a considerable wealth differentiation between villages, mainly depending on per capita land holdings (varying between 0.7 and 1.5 *mu*), land fertility and access to water. After the break-up of the People's Commune, which in terms of land policy tended to be a very pragmatic structure in Baohua, village land holdings are basically the same as in 1949. Thus a considerable difference in living standards has been maintained between the villages and has in some cases been enlarged since many of the poorest villages were never connected by roads. As noted, conflicts between villages over border lands and water courses are quite common and they may at times be phrased in fengshui terminology. In recent years heavy land taxes and low prices on rice have encouraged peasants to seek alternative incomes, primarily through wage labour.

Village identities which emphasize customs perceived as different from those of the 'outer' Chinese society have been the basis of a considerable defiance of authority that continues today. A few villages in Baohua have taken their originally lineage-based identities to extremes by publicly resisting party politics and openly claiming their adherence to local custom. The people in the small hamlets of the administrative village of Mudan, among the poorest and only accessible by foot on a muddy trail winding through bamboo groves and over dikes, often claim that they resemble a 'tribe' (*buluo*) when they refer to their rich lore, kinship-based system of organization and open resistance to party authorities in terms of leadership. During the

Cultural Revolution they refused to follow other than their own leaders and resisted the full integration into the Commune, while preserving a large share of their private land. But their internal political affairs are complicated. Mudan has always been dominated by three large families and a common colloquial explanation as to why they have always resisted outside authorities is that they have 'a long tradition of arguing and quarrelling among themselves'. The villagers will commonly point to two separate customs as a proof of their success in maintaining their village identity: avoidance of the one-child policy by having two and sometimes three children and adherence to traditional burials instead of cremation. In fact, from an external perspective, these customs are common in rural areas, except that Jiangsu is among the few provinces that have seriously attempted to institute the one-child policy fully in rural areas.

But these local characteristics – or privileges – are only claimed at a high cost. They depend on a system of payment-for-privilege to township government authorities, which again build on a general consent between all parties involved, including villagers, village leaders and government officials. These payments are a heavy burden to the villagers, who have monthly average incomes of approximately 100 yuan. The sums of money paid vary from a few hundred to many thousand yuan, depending on the type of privilege bought and the channels that need to be opened up. Individuals as well as entire villages have different access to privilege. If a village leader has established a good network he may have easier access to higher-level authority than others – and the other way round, if both a village and its leaders have a reputation for defiance, such as in the case of Mudan, they are likely to pay much more than others.

In the absence of open access to public services this system of petty-corruption forms the most common interaction between villagers and representatives of bureaucracy. When seen from below, the structure of the Chinese state adapts beautifully to a capitalist market society with only minimal regulation. Access to privilege is marketed in the local society and few areas remain sacred when it comes to supplementing the income of local authority. The system inspires countless individuals to act as brokers between government and citizen in order to extract a fee; these are typically village leaders and secretaries, lower government officials and other party members, all of whom have some measure of public endorsement. It may support the party's financial control and political power, but at the same time it inhibits the ideological credibility of the party. In the

Chinese market society, rural folk will only attain at the cost of their purses – today money rules.

Another local characteristic frequently pointed out by the villagers of Mudan underscores the huge difference between old and modern villages and its adoption in local identities. This is the practice of purchasing young brides through middlemen. The village has long experienced a shortage of women available for their young men and what the villagers here point to as evidence of a local identity is really tantamount to necessity. It is a simple consequence of maintaining a taboo on inward marriages and usually on same-surname marriages, while at the same time being a village which others avoid as a home for their daughters because of its conspicuous poverty (as also reported by Chan A. *et al.* 1984: 14). The middlemen consulted by the Mudan villagers take orders for brides and organize their procurement. The middlemen then make contracts with small gangs, operating mainly in Sichuan and Gansu provinces, where they seize the young women in remote villages. Once brought out of their home area the young women will usually be unable to make their way home – and in any case they could not pay for the transportation. Most of them will gradually accept their fate as peasant wives in Jiangsu, which is generally better off than their home areas. The popular ideas of fate embrace such radical acts and tend to make business easier for the kidnappers. According to these ideas one's fate is not simply given and unchangeable, since activism is sustained as much as fate, but significant events and sudden changes of one's life course are still typically examined as the possible work of fate, offering some comfort to the individual. The women themselves are usually quite frank about their peculiar life courses and may eventually smile at it; some will express that they never had much of a choice in life anyway. 'After all', one woman said, 'an arranged marriage in our home area differs little from one arranged through kidnapping, except that we lose contact with our own families.'

INDUSTRIAL DEVELOPMENT AND ECONOMIC DIFFERENTIATION

I chose my two fieldwork areas according to common criteria: they must have fairly good farmland allowing for a conventional Chinese peasant society to be found – conventional, but still allowing for endless variation – and they must have nearby mountains or hilly areas where to place graves. Fulfilling these criteria, I believed, would also provide the type of scenery usually associated with good fengshui. This appeared to hold true, even to an unexpected extent.

It turned out that my two fieldwork areas were also chosen by the two provincial governments respectively as new development zones. It crossed my mind that since attracting overseas Chinese capital has become so critical to industrialization, local government would be highly susceptible to the demands of these investors. The demands are cheap labour, efficient transportation, vicinity to urban centres and a willing bureaucracy, but certainly also good fengshui.

Along the road to Nanjing, the Baohua Development Zone (*Baohua kaifaqu*) was established by the township government in 1991. The idea was to attract foreign investors in order to bolster economic development in the area, which could offer both good transportation, land that was easy to develop, ample manpower and, in addition, a pleasant scenery along the Baohua Mountains. Some local officials had seen this done in a number of other locations along main roads in Jiangsu and thought it could be done here, too. The first step was simply to plot out the area on a map, set up a couple of concrete pillars and signposts along the main road and establish a service centre, consisting of a small parking lot and an information booth manned by officials from the township government. It took but a year or two before the initiative bore fruit. A few industries were established and in the subsequent years new ones followed at an accelerating pace. Today Baohua is a thriving industrial development zone with producers of wooden articles, toys, clothes, hats, water pumps, sanitation fittings, motorcycle parts and more.

Quite early during the fieldwork, my assistant Liu and I entered the small development zone office to look for local maps and to see what they were doing. Two men, seated behind near-empty desks, handed out small brochures of incredibly poor print and provided information to potential investors. As in Sichuan, I was received as one such. Again, my stated purpose of investigating fengshui in rural China remained a kind of coded message to them, a pretext for not revealing the nature of my investments. As one said, 'you can always come back and tell us what you have found'. Still the small office provided an opportunity to speak to local government officials, who manned the office in turn, on 'neutral ground', and it became a place we would frequently return to for information or a chat. Several officials confirmed that landscape and fengshui considerations were in fact important in the choice of development zone. For instance, a large mountain in Baohua named Stone Lion Mountain had both a ring of good fengshui and a resemblance in Hong Kong, which some investors had said inspired confidence. Several overseas Chinese investors were known to have brought in their own fengshui specialists to inspect the site before building, but this was mostly done unnoticed. Later, I had the opportunity to meet a Taiwanese and a Hong Kong investor and to see their plants; they confirmed my impression that a geographical location that appealed to me for the study of modern fengshui uses also appealed to the investor. The common allegory is that good fengshui also facilitated a good flow of money.

The new industries have provided jobs for many hundreds of local peasants and youngsters and have generated unprecedented wealth in the nearby villages despite a very low standard of payment, commonly ranging between 80 and 250 yuan per month.[3] In the matter of a few years it turned farming into a secondary economic activity in a belt along the main road, and at my second visit in 1996 several fields were lying fallow because all adult family members had jobs and no longer wished to till the land. But an accelerating process of economic differentiation has also come about in Baohua, threatening to tear the township apart. The competition between counties and townships to attract investments and promote development in their areas seems to repeat itself at village level, since the exact location of new industries has definite consequences for the villages around. All villages are willing to transfer land to industrial development, since they receive attractive compensation. But after new industries are established, jobs are first offered to the people of the village that provided the land and the networks that build up around new industries will often be narrowly local. So while almost every household has one or more members involved in wage labour in the villages of Jinhua and Jiatou near the road, only one in three households will be involved in wage labour in villages like Bashi further away, and hardly anyone in Mudan. When this is added to the income differences stemming from variance in per capita acreage, the basis for the social differentiation that is seen all over rural China is exposed.

The rich and the poor villages of Baohua are quickly growing worlds apart. The first and foremost symbol of modernization in rural areas, the new family house, is pursued by every family, but the incredible sums of money involved make it a powerful social classifier. Some of the most recent houses constructed in concrete have risen to three storeys, inspired by houses of the new rich in the coastal areas as well as by pictures in Western magazines, which some locals with connections overseas circulate in their neighbourhoods. One of the very first houses we fell upon was a huge construction in the village of Meimu, built by Mr Bi, an old housebuilder who also claims to be knowledgeable about fengshui, thus combining the work of a house-builder and a geomancer. Mr Bi's three-storey house, built recently in an explicitly 'Western' style, cost approximately 120,000 yuan. It is equipped with everything modern a native person can imagine: it is brick-built with a wide doorway, a large rounded balcony, big tinted windows and the facade covered in blue tiles. Inside it has a gigantic central staircase, a fish pond on the ground floor, many more rooms than the family can furnish, several indoors toilets, a huge bathroom with a bathtub and a watertank up under the roof. This is conspicuous consumption at its peak. It was meant to be Mr Bi's masterpiece at the conclusion of his long career, a sort of personal statement to the world, and the dwelling into which he would retire now that he is old.

Since we first went looking for Mr Bi in the big house to question him about his work as a housebuilder, it became clear that things never worked out the way he had envisioned. Mr Bi, who is more than 80 years old, had become too feeble to walk about safely in his new house; he was afraid of stumbling on the concrete stairs and floors and soon after the completion of the house he had moved back into his little old wooden house, which was preserved right next to the new one. This was where we found him. His mansion resembles a monu-ment, with one floor occupied by a nephew and his family and the rest being empty. Quite frankly, to the eyes of a Westerner the house is indeed ugly, devoid of life and lacking in atmosphere.

In this case a geomancer would agree. Mr Bi never had much luck in fengshui although he has an unequalled reputation as a house-builder. The old geomancers, whom we later came to know, regard him as an amateur who has ruined his own life due to his stubborn belief in his own capacities. Mr Bi told us the sad details of his life. In 1950 his two small sons died within a short period and his wife never bore him any other children. He interpreted this in terms of bad fengshui and accordingly changed the direction of his main door (by cutting the edges of the door frame). But it did not stop his misfortune. He always felt weak, eventually diagnosed to be due to diabetes and hypertension, which he had suffered from ever since. Since medicine could not cure him, he again applied his own knowledge of fengshui. Believing he could block the evil that hit his front door, he moved the toilet to a position in the middle of the courtyard right in front of the entrance. That did not help either. Things never went well for him and some years ago he was struck by a heart disease on top of his other ailments. Today he lives in his little old wooden house, too weak to enjoy the fruits of his labour.

According to local lore the village of Meimu has many houses built without the advice of a geomancer, including the house of Mr Bi. A legend tells that in ancient times the emperor passed through the village when a natural disaster in the form of an earthquake occurred so that he was compelled to stay for some time in the village. A local woman, named Mei, took care of him so well that when she died many years later he commemorated her by building a wonderful grave outside the village. The village later came to be known as Meimu, meaning 'the tomb of Mei', and the villagers have since felt well protected by its auspicious fengshui.

DIVERGENT FENGSHUI APPLICATIONS IN OLD AND NEW VILLAGES

The trend towards economic differentiation outlined above is only predictable in the large-scale industrialization that most of coastal China has embarked upon. It could perhaps also be predicted that fengshui practices would lose their significance or perhaps be abandoned with the coming of modernity. Yet this is only the apparent state of affairs; as shown in the previous chapters, cultural traits like fengshui are constantly being revived and adapted to new circumstances. Since Baohua contains both local communities along the main road going through rapid transformation and more or less unaffected communities in the hinterland, we may, for the purpose of examination, distinguish between these two types of communities to get an idea of how cosmological forces possibly acquire changing roles in the modernization process.

As in Sichuan, the old villages have preserved a collection of fengshui allegories and practices that constitute a broad comprehensive tradition, maintained by the continued interplay between clients, fengshui practitioners and written fengshui materials. The 'new' villages, on the other hand, tend to discontinue some strands of this tradition, at least in their outer appearance. First of all, in the newly industrialized communities people will still send for a geomancer when a ground plan for a house is drawn up or a site for a grave is determined, but the various other everyday applications of fengshui thought are muffled. Secondly, people are less likely to admit that they invited a geomancer at all and particularly the men tend to deny it when being among other men – in one instance a woman interrupted her husband during our conversation in order to mediate between self-representation and truth as she stated that 'the geomancer came later with his compass and said the site was OK'. One senses a mounting conflict within the individual in reconciling the competing outlooks of fengshui and modernity. During an earlier epoch it was fear of reprisal that prevented people from admitting to the use of a geomancer; today it is fear of being thought backward. Those among the villagers who had recently abandoned farming as their primary occupation and experienced rapid economic improvement as wage-earners have most conspicuously joined the ambitious modernization enterprise of the Chinese state. The work they perform in the new factories is highly individualized as compared to family farming, and both the type of work and the goods they produce for the modern sector or for export have intensified their ambitions of climbing the social ladder. They have begun to embrace the futuristic ideology of the Chinese media and think of themselves as citizens in a modern state of rising power and ability. In these communities the modern media play increasingly important roles. Also in the old villages people will gather around colour television sets at night, but it is rather for entertainment because what they see is other peoples' world, not their own. By contrast, in the new villages people have started taking an interest in specific programmes and tend to watch them more on an individual basis. They will no longer gather to see, for instance, children's programmes, but let the children watch them alone, and concentrate on programmes that address them personally: as men, women, workers, farmers, entrepreneurs, housewives, pensioners and so forth. With the higher level of interaction with the outside world and the penetration of Chinese modernity, a greater sense of individuality undoubtedly is fostered. Together with an expanding sphere of personal affairs also disease is individualized to a much greater extent than previously. It is no longer ascribable to forefathers being unhappy, one's soul having departed to roam freely or to take residence in another person, the entire household suffering from bad fengshui or foes spreading their evil influence in the neighbourhood. One may still consider these possibilities, and many people evidently do, but they are no longer explicit.

Something else is at work, too. With regard to the old villages it can be said with considerable validity that people view the outside world with ambivalence and often share highly antagonistic feelings towards it. They see the state in a similar fashion to how they viewed landlords in the old society, that is, as a medium of exploitation for certain classes of people with connection to the city – the state and all city people are notorious enemies. Yet they maintain ideas of an intangible interconnectedness of the universe that derive from the mode of thought expressed in fengshui – in this larger scheme the peasants represent everything that the Communists hate. By contrast, to people in the new villages modernity presents a powerful image of mechanical causality and immediate links between the individual and the totality. They see foreign investors set up factories which produce goods for vast export markets and they receive salaries that may again be spent on goods from the outside world. Thus they see not a spiritual, but rather a material interconnectedness in their brave new world. While in the old villages the fengshui tradition has an implicit anti-hegemonic vein, the rising futuristic ideology of the new villages will weaken the barriers between the local community and the wider Chinese state, in which only the cities carry real significance. The inhabitants gradually absorb the Chinese national identity, while simultaneously aspiring one day to become city people themselves.

In Baohua all this is only a recent development, but the reorient-ation that has emerged among the inhabitants of the new com-munities is striking. Obviously a more positive attitude to the state is detected when the economic miracle is realized. But what happens more specifically with fengshui practices in this process and what happens to the fengshui tradition as such?

In the new communities a process of fragmentation of the fengshui tradition has begun, including a cleavage between know-ledge and practice, since knowledge is not immediately lost but actual fengshui uses appear to be narrowed down. What may be called phys-ical fengshui for houses and graves is continued, perhaps in a more ritualized and standardized form, while the 'metaphysical' fengshui, involving the intuitive judgements of geomancers are repressed. This is not the final result of the process of change, however, and it tends to have a stronger influence on public appear-ance than on actual practice. What really seems to emerge is a transfer of the basic tenets of fengshui thought from a public to a private domain. They are subordinated in public, encroached upon by the massive machine of modern 'rational' thought and the market economy combined. In-stead fengshui becomes ritualized when used in public for building-related purposes and privatized in all other contexts. Fengshui uses for illness, bad luck, lack of offspring and other similar matters are reduced, but do not disappear.

As the fengshui tradition as a whole becomes individualized and its expressions are muted in social life, a kind of knowledge schism is created in relation to philosophical reflection: what a person will ponder in private and what he or she may express in public tends to be divorced. While the men previously discussed fengshui matters in the tea house, perhaps in a joking manner, they will now avoid the topic altogether. Besides, people tend to become more self-sufficient in the new villages with greater emphasis on the private sphere than on village social life. Thus, instead of several knowledge traditions complementing each other in the arena of public life and thought, the principal tradition, that of Chinese modernity and state ideology, rises to a truly dominant position. Fengshui, on the other hand, and with it the entire complex of popular cosmology, enters a non-communicative space. In this process fengshui as a body of knowledge is not only fragmented in terms of common, everyday knowledge of its principles, but also increasingly diffused since it no longer interacts with established schemes of interpretation and the judgements of specialists.

These tendencies are presumably comparable to those experienced in the West with the penetration of 'modernity' in the previous centuries, when both established religion and various undercurrents of 'folk' beliefs and practices such as geomancy, astrology, native medicine, crypto-Christian cults and so forth were pushed into the background. Both the rational thought of world capitalism and international socialism were giant bodies of doctrine and custom intended to encompass the full register of human deliberation and to a large extent successful in marginalizing and repressing alternative forms of knowledge. It is, of course, essential to the main argument here to demonstrate that in a long-term perspective these alternatives do not disappear, but reappear in new interpretations or are replaced by analogous traditions when the pressure for alternative contemplation builds up.

Elements of fengshui thought quietly live on, mostly as a tool of the mind which people use to contemplate the nature of disease, bad luck and other everyday occurrences that are intuitively felt not to be rationally constituted, but to a greater extent than before they do so in private. These fragments are reduced to a personal instrument for scrutinizing chance events and perhaps still, at a very personal level, an agent for controlling such. If it is not yet entirely individualized, it stays within the confines of the family, where people will continue quietly to honour the recently deceased, perhaps burn incense and a bit of paper money and place food in front of pictures on certain occasions. Also within the family circle, fragments of soul-searching and fengshui terminology are still in use. Just as fengshui lived on in latency during the years of Communist campaigning, it may also in this case be revived at a later stage of modernization, when people feel more secure both economically and ideologically and they perhaps gain a more critical view of modernity as such. As yet, the newly modernized communities disdain backwardness and 'superstition' and feel a strong urge to distinguish themselves from those who believe in such, usually identified with the people of the underdeveloped villages.

The men play an important role in suppressing fengshui thinking in village community life. As household heads they are eager to advance their family status into the ranks of the 'modern' section of the Chinese population and compare themselves with city people. It is much more difficult for men than for women to admit, for instance, that the family has used a geomancer. As an illustration, a woman whom we visited in Jinhua told the following story:

> Some years ago my husband and I decided to give up our land and open a restaurant on the main road close by. We borrowed some money from my husband's family and had a similar amount of our own savings. The restaurant was quite small, but since we were the first on this stretch of the road we had many customers, particularly truck drivers and army personnel, and we could save up for a new house. We built a new brick house outside our village, but some time after we moved in things started going wrong. My husband repeatedly got sick, our daughter was dragging herself through classes in school and scored the lowest marks and our restaurant lost business to a number of newly established restaurants further down the road. We all felt terrible. You see, we had the house built without the assistance of a geomancer, since my husband said that it was only for the poor peasants to believe in superstition. I was worried right from the start, but my husband refused to discuss it. When things went wrong it was useless for me to suggest that a geomancer searched the house and it was only after my parents-in-law interfered that my husband relented. They demanded that we invite a specialist because they felt the restaurant was also their investment and they would not watch it go down. Finally my mother-in-law made arrangements for an old geomancer from another area to inspect our house. He walked about endlessly, but could find nothing wrong. But when he heard about our nearby restaurant, he suddenly frowned. He walked back and forth between the house and the restaurant and finally told us that the front doors of the two building were almost facing each other, which is very bad. The two buildings belong to the same family, but many strangers feel 'at home' in the restaurant, so one of the doors must be changed. We had the entrance to the restaurant moved a little bit, which also created more space inside. After this, things are going a little better, but we would still like to receive more guests.

In many instances of fengshui considerations one can get the impression that they are really an after-the-fact type of explanation that reverses the course of events. In this case, for instance, one could speculate that perhaps the downward spiral was really set in motion by increasing competition and waning profit from the restaurant, which the entire family responded to mentally. Some examples of this are discussed in Chapter 6.

The process of fragmentation, which fengshui is undergoing in the modern-type village communities is significant in another respect. While it evidently marks the conclusion of fengshui practices as experienced in the old village community, it also prepares the ground for its reinterpretation in a new context, exactly as seen in the overseas Chinese communities. But these are fairly long-term processes. By following the further course of development in the modern-style village communities we shall perhaps be able to establish how fengshui and other comparable traditions are reconstructed through a sequence of losing ground to modernity, fragmentation, infolding, yet being subject to a human yearning for alternative reflection and explanation, reinterpretation and unfolding in a new context, and a new batch of mentors establishing themselves. Obviously, only time can tell if this theory holds true; Chapter 7 will show how the fengshui tradition has been reconstructed in its Western version.

Other studies have shown that entrepreneurial groups play an important role in the reinterpretation of tradition in China (Harrell 1987; Siu 1989). They are often important actors in new religious movements as they seek a path to quick gains and social ascendence. The preoccupation with fengshui for the manipulation of economic fortune in Hong Kong and overseas Chinese communities may be used to show this correlation, but it should not be exaggerated, since multiple other processes are simultaneously at work in these places, for instance cultural performance and the emphasis on a Chinese identity as a common platform in the interaction with other groups. If it is correct that fengshui is individualized and oriented towards chance events instead of the overall link between the individual, society and the cosmos, it is only logical that it gains a stronger commercial and monetary significance. Modern business on any scale embodies the chance aspects in investments, stock holdings, unpredictable markets, sensitive currencies and international political events. It is beyond doubt that many new business communities find fengshui useful and infuse it with new meaning, but this appears to be mostly an urban phenomenon. In Baohua, however, there is some controversy over the use of fengshui services in the new industries and private businesses. Local geomancers for their part claim that the new business community along the main road is an expanding market for their services, while private business owners are reluctant to admit that they invite them. It has become a private affair, just like their earnings, which they find absolutely no reason to advertise.

A number of recent studies have questioned the authenticity of Chinese popular cosmology in its contemporary form. It has been argued, perhaps most incisively by Helen Siu (1989) in the case of a Pearl River delta market town, that the recent revival of popular ritual in rural China is merely new reconstructions of cultural fragments, since for decades powerful state intervention has destroyed the social basis for popular rituals and deprived them of their fundamental values and connecting ideology. This is a tempting conclusion, of course, but historical evidence rejects this: popular cosmology never maintained a life of its own, independent from other traditions, not least Chinese state power. Popular cosmology was as subjected to change as the surrounding society and considering the tumultuous change in China during the last 150 years – the Communist rulers certainly did not have a monopoly on absolutist power, which rather has become an institution in Chinese political culture – the demarcation of 'before' and 'after' Communist rule appears ahistorical and deceptive. Instead, we can trace a direct line from Chinese intellectuals' classical scorn for popular culture to the neglect that Chinese writers on religion in this century have shown towards fengshui to the apologetic tone in contemporary American Chinese writers' accounts of popular culture.

THE GEOMANCERS AND THEIR FUNCTIONS

Getting an overview of the total number of active geomancers in Baohua was more complicated than in Longquan due to our lack of transportation. The networks consisting of the geomancers and their clientele are either narrowly local or entirely personalized and nobody in the township would know more than one or two geomancers. Yet an important generic feature turned out to be a considerably smaller number of active geomancers than in Long-quan. While the two areas have comparable populations, only three or four geomancers were found to practise fulltime in Baohua as compared to ten in Longquan. Several of the old geomancers have died in recent years, leaving only four alive, of whom one was hospitalized during the last stretch of fieldwork. Since there is an evident shortage of practitioners, one or two geomancers from neighbouring townships practise regularly in Baohua. Another differ-

ence is that while the geomancers in Longquan had a virtual monopoly as practitioners of popular cosmology, several other branches
are represented here. Ideas of a human soul, or indeed multiple
souls, that may depart from the body to cause serious illness and
therefore need to be called back, are prominent in Jiangsu and tend
to affect the work of its geomancers. A few elderly women are
independent specialists of *fuji*, soul-search divination, directing
people where to look for departed souls. Also a couple of Buddhist
monks are to be found in the Longchang monastery, although their
activities have been severely curbed since the 1960s.

This should not in itself be attributed to a lesser importance of
fengshui in Baohua, however, but is as much due to the structural
difference between the two schools of fengshui. In fact, as will be
shown, the 'directions' school of fengshui practised here allows for
less flexibility in housebuilding and tends to give rise to much more
serious conflicts. Complaints over other people's acts with a bearing
on the common fengshui situation are definitely of greater intensity
in Jiangsu, particularly in the older villages. Furthermore, the
Longchang monastery, which will be described below, previously
offered fengshui services to the local population and presumably had
a fair share of this market. These former specialists could not be
traced, since none of the many monks that used to inhabit the
monastery were found in Baohua, except for an old man who acted
as our guide in the temple.

In general terms, the designs contained in the 'directions' school
of fengshui are more orderly and predictable, allowing for less
improvisation on the part of the geomancer. Since the directions of
the compass are a primary concern when building a house and the
layout of rooms likewise follows a distinct pattern, the basic principles
of fengshui are known to everyone. Thus from a fengshui perspective
it may be considered safe to build on a site already approved by a
geomancer one or two generations ago, if only the basic layout and
directions of the old house are respected.

Nevertheless, in Baohua as in Longquan most people building a
new family house or a tomb will invite a geomancer to inspect the site,
draw up or approve the ground plan, and calculate the proper day of
action. These are the ordinary activities of the geomancer and the
cornerstone of his profession. Another type of job, for which ordinary
people are used to employing a geomancer, is the correction of
fengshui around houses and graves if the first arrangement has failed
or if the external situation has been altered. Apart from the common

task of siting, people invite or consult geomancers on a number of occasions that in Baohua may also be accounted for by means of the geomancers' own categories of prosperity (*cai*), happiness (*fu*), long life (*shou*), and procreation (*zi*), also representing the popular Chinese fortune-bringing characters. Many instances of such feng-shui uses are quite similar to those already described in the previous chapter and need not to be repeated. Moreover, many cases originating in both fieldwork areas are analysed in the next chapter. Instead, those features of fengshui thought and practice that differ from the Sichuan fieldwork area are highlighted.

Figure 5.1: *Traditional entrance adorned with powerful images*

Stricter rules and less scope for interpretation will also result in greater competition among households. As every house will have its entrance facing the life-giving sun to the south, the layout of villages tends to be fixed and standard. Narrow lanes run east–west between several rows of houses, so that the entrances of the houses on one side of the lane face the backs of the houses on the other side. If all houses were of the same size and nobody wanted to build bigger, harmony could be perpetuated. This is not the case, however. In order to regulate the size of houses so that the *qi* is equally distributed and no household is left in the shade, a strict rule has been effective since 'ancient times', according to the villagers. It states that 'East overlooks

West and North overlooks South'. This implies that people may build bigger and higher towards the north and the east within the village, but never towards the south and the west since this would cause fengshui to be blocked for those households behind. With reference to the historical development of fengshui one may question the perseverance of this rule, but it has been effective long enough to regulate all existing structures in the villages.

East over West and North over South' is zealously guarded and measured out in inches. In the old villages, where most houses have attached gables, the lines of the walls and roofs of houses along one lane will either be perfectly flush or will be broken to allow for slightly bigger houses towards the east. The logical consequences are of course that villages must either have flush lines or be quite small, since houses cannot vary indefinitely. In reality the villages are mostly quite small, usually with two to five rows of houses and with a few or up to ten houses in each row. Political leadership in the individual villages may have determined that lines must be flush at least in some lanes to avoid competition and struggle, while in others each lane will have its own shape with sharp edges and rooftops breaking the line towards the east. To allow for variation in household size according to the number of children and domestic cycles in general, the buying and selling of houses or of sections of houses are common; a large family may be seen to own two houses either adjoined or separated by a lane, while a small household may occupy only a single room in a house.

Now that an increasing number of people want to build new houses, the old rule is felt to be a straightjacket. It still stands, however, and struggle is commonplace when people attempt to manipulate the lines of the old houses or simply build bigger in the hope that neighbours will not respond. The result is that the traditional village layout tends to break up, since nearly every second family moves to another location when building a new house in order to build bigger and avoid complaints. In the modernizing villages along the main road almost all new houses are built individually and spread out from the old village centres, because hardly anyone would be content with a new brick-built house the size of a traditional mud-built one.

It is the duty of the lowest level of administration, that of village leadership, to regulate these matters, lest things get out of hand. Both they and local government tend to support 'tradition' to avoid public

Figure 5.2: *Seeing fengshui, although the circumference of the house is already indicated*

turmoil, since conflicts easily escalate out of control, as in one particular case described below. In the villages where a lineage or a single-surname group prevails local organization and informal leadership will usually assure reconciliation when conflicts arise, but in the villages that accommodate competing surname groups matters are more complicated. These are common occurrences, which may also involve geomancers. For instance, in the village of Nantou two neighbouring families belonging to different surname groups got into a row when one of them built a new house slightly exceeding the lines of their neighbours'. The housebuilders argued that the doorway and rooftop of the neighbouring house had already broken the lines so that fengshui was not disturbed. With the intervention of the village leader it was agreed that a geomancer should be consulted to settle the matter. Each family invited its own geomancer, however, and as could be expected the geomancers proved loyal to their clients and ruled differently. A third geomancer was called in from another district, paid jointly by the two families, but when he heard that he necessarily had to rule against one of his own kind he rushed away and the two families were back to square one. Finally, when the entire village was embroiled through lines of kinship and loyalty, it was agreed that the housebuilders should pay a moderate sum of money as compensation to their neighbours.

It was noted for the Sichuanese geomancers that they were sometimes specialized in branches of fengshui involving exorcism, fortune-telling and so forth, and the link between the various religious practices is equally strong in Jiangsu. Any geomancer who deals with sick individuals must relate to ideas connecting disease with the possibility of a departing or fully departed soul. Particularly in the case of serious, otherwise inexplicable illness or mental disorders, either the household members or a group of elderly people from the village will gather around the bed and chant through the night to 'call the soul back' (*han hun*) in order to restore the physical health of such individuals. This may also involve 'searching for the soul' (*zhao hun*), either in the spiritual world of the forefathers or in the world of the living. Accordingly, some geomancers master techniques to assist them. As noted previously, several old women practise *fuji*; by means of stirring *shengshui* and other forms of divination they will tell which direction the soul has taken and sometimes describe a house or a person in which the soul has taken residence. The relatives of the sick person will then go out to locate and call back the departed soul, or call it from home, possibly assisted by a geomancer or a *fuji* specialist. The geomancers are divided on this issue: some will include soul-finding techniques while others find them 'unscientific' and inappropriate for their profession. Below I shall introduce a geomancer from each of the two categories.

Geography Master Wang (*Wang dili xiansheng*), is a geomancer who kept a low profile during the periods of political turmoil and thus avoided serious reprisal. For years he practised cautiously, either by receiving customers in his tiny house on the fringe of Longtan, or by going out at night to inspect sites. For him as for many other geomancers his life-course has added considerably to his trustworthiness. He never took another job and he never got involved in the formal socialist construction of society, which tended to politicize all personal relations down to neighbourhood level. Since he had always stood outside the formal hierarchy it was easy for people from all walks of life to consult him once the political winds blew calmer. In the late 1970s long-desired changes of graves and houses again became possible.

Mr Wang is the most highly esteemed geomancer practising today. He is in his mid-seventies, but still working energetically throughout

Figure 5.3:
*Rural geo-
mancer with
compass and
book*

the day. He practises fengshui for houses and graves, writes charms or
'couplets' (*duilian*)[4] and has a reputation for knowing how to find
water. He is not involved in soul-searching, but another speciality of his,
which is quite common in the region, is the ability to tell the direction
where missing persons and things may be found. For instance, during
one of our visits a couple from the neighbourhood came to his house
to inquire about the whereabouts of their daughter, who had run away
after they had for some time put her under much pressure to do well
at school. Mr Wang then told them which direction she had taken and
estimated her location, but advised her parents to wait patiently and
foresaw the approximate time of her return. According to Wang
himself, he is frequently consulted on this problem.

Otherwise Mr Wang is nearly impossible to catch at home. His wife and daughter-in-law receive 'invitations' and make arrangements for the old man, who himself spends most days out in the villages of Baohua and in neighbouring townships. He has a special role in his home town, however. He is a kind of spiritual leader of the 'village', which people tend to call their part of the town, and everybody there consults him on lucky days for weddings, inexplicable diseases, forecasts for students, monetary affairs, family problems and so forth. Mr Wang has written the couplet adorning every single door in the neighbourhood and his day-to-day contact with people has given him a tremendous insight into the private life of the villagers; if someone has a problem with his neighbour, Mr Wang will know exactly how that problem is perceived from either side of the fence.

The geomancer who is presently hospitalized is Mr Xu, a former student and nephew of the famous old master Xu,[5] who passed away some years ago at the age of 90, while being out to see fengshui for a client. As a peasant from his village commented sarcastically: 'There you see, fengshui doesn't work, it is only to extort people for money. Old Xu died while he was seeing fengshui for another man's grave.' The younger Xu, now in his mid-sixties, was among the very last to be trained by an old master before the liberation. In 1955, when he was still a young man, he was forced to quit his trade. Since he was among the very few local youth with any measure of schooling, he soon became a work-brigade secretary, not uncommon for those village geomancers who were willing to abandon their trade and work for the new regime.

As a party cadre, Xu had to provide a good example: one way of showing loyalty to the new regime was to denounce the clan and lineage organizations of the local community and even to break up his marriage arranged by these traditional institutions. In his village a group of men would sit together drinking and one night in the heat of the moment they agreed collectively to divorce their wives and the very next day they did so. Both Xu and his present wife, who had had her first marriage arranged already one year after her birth, were divorced in the early years after the liberation and soon married each other. At the outset of the Cultural Revolution Xu voluntarily handed in his geomantic compass and collection of old books, which had been handed down in his family line.

Xu worked devotedly as a party cadre throughout most of his life until he retired in 1990. Since he was always a highly respected man, and since everybody knew that he was 'really' a geomancer by profession, people started inviting him to see fengshui in their homes after his retirement. However, he only had the opportunity to practise a few years before he fell sick. He was taken to hospital for examination and the hospital kept him because of a suspected lung cancer. The doctors feared that he would die during hospitalization, so the family was requested to pay a deposit of 3,000 yuan. The deposit plus additional expenses nearly ruined the family, and two pigs had already been sold. Now his wife has begun to fear for both her husband's and her own future: 'Xu has always been good to people, so we should not have anything to fear', she said, apparently torn between morals and medicine. Xu finally left hospital without a clear diagnosis, but considerably poorer than before.

Uncle Ling (*Ling daye*) is yet another geomancer and fortune-teller practising at the lowest level for a small fee. He is now 80 years old and several nicknames allude to his shaky appearance, senile mind and his comical performance as a practitioner, 'balancing at the edge of the grave'. However, even though he is a common laughing stock in his village, where people show little restraint when joking about others, he is still consulted regularly in his home to have dates computed for weddings or simple couplets written. He is cheap and therefore convenient for many people in his little old village without a single modern house.

Though hard to find at home, geomancer Wang became one of my best informants in Baohua. We learned to catch him in the early morning hours, since he mostly carried out fengshui sitings from mid-morning and throughout the day; or we spotted the sturdy little man with the plain blue working clothes and a black cap elsewhere in the villages when he was out on jobs. On several occasions we were able to accompany him to see fengshui around the township. Despite his customary appearance, he is a celebrated figure whom people address prudently and respectfully. Whether called upon in his home or received in the villages his function as a spiritual authority allows him to rise above the common people. Wherever possible he is transported around by three-wheeled bicycle or motorcycle cab at the client's expense and at every assignment he is treated as a guest of honour. His home is deliberately crude, but his lifestyle and diet are way beyond that of ordinary peasants and workers.

Some of our many talks with Wang concerned the popular view of fengshui in Baohua and his clients' belief or disbelief in his work. He regretted that not every household used fengshui 'according to tradition'. Some people would ignore its principles and others would use it selfishly without care for the malicious effect on others, for instance by building too big and conspicuously. A topic that arose out of our talk was whether everybody was equal before the flow of *qi* and the forces of fengshui, or if some classes of people had a privileged position or were better protected. Just as popular religious ideas in these parts of China speculated that only the rich had a soul, since only they ate meat, there are sturdy popular notions that the common rules of fengshui do not necessarily apply to the rich and the powerful – somehow emphasizing that natural and social phenomena are tightly interwoven.

Both Wang and several other geomancers in Baohua and Long-quan mentioned that their art does not apply to certain categories of people. A powerful official or wealthy industrialist may build his house anywhere he likes and disrespect the rule of 'East over West' without receiving complaints. An example was provided when a provincial government official considered building a new house in a grove outside one of the old villages, but still near enough to the village to disturb the fengshui of other houses. He came by car to investigate the site carefully, but eventually went away because the road was too bad. They do not have to obey tradition because they are powerful, but they are also somehow immune to the forces of *qi* themselves. Geomancers could not give a definite answer as to why such people were exempt from transcendent cosmological prin-ciples, but would rather point to the mystical properties of being rich or powerful, as if these people belong to another world where a different kind of fengshui may apply. Similarly, Mr Wang would interpret fengshui from a narrow local perspective if I inquired about how I could improve my own house at home: 'I don't know if it works for you foreigners', he replied.

Despite being a broad tradition linking the local society to both tradition and the Chinese world in general, I was constantly struck by the narrowly local perspective of the geomancers, resulting from a master–apprentice way of transmitting the fengshui tradition from one generation to the next. Hardly any of the geomancers were aware of an alternative school of fengshui being practised elsewhere in China. A narrow local perspective does not mean that the tradition is static or that historical necessity rules. Rather, an intense dynamism originates in the constant interplay between the geomancers know-ledge and his clients' expressions of their immediate needs, to which the geomancers response with an ever-readiness to incorporate new phenomena, for instance by seeing fengshui for bigger houses, predicting the sex of unborn babies, or dealing with new types of mental disorders among their clients.

SEEING FENGSHUI

Mr Geographer Wang has been invited to see fengshui for a family building a new house in the village of Bashi. He first calculates the correct day to start building, arriving at the fourth day of the month in the lunar calendar. On the morning of the fourth, however, it is raining and Mr Wang sends a messenger to call off the service, because, as he says, 'it is difficult to see fengshui correctly in the rain' (we suspected that convenience also counted). The family once more go to Mr Wang to ask for a new date and he comes up with the eighth – eight being a lucky number with endless cosmological meanings (Eberhard 1988: 91–93). On this day Mr Wang already has a number of appointments, so the family rushes off to find another geomancer. Inquiring among local people they find one in a nearby village, who is also called Wang. This geomancer, a 76-year-old man, is available on the eighth, presumably because his reputation is far below that of the other Wang. My assistant Dong and I wait to follow the event.

Wang arrives a bit before 11 o'clock, carrying an old shoulder bag with his implements. The family have already levelled out the ground along the edges of the building site where the foundation stones are to be placed; already at this stage it seems that there is little scope for interpretation of the 'correct' site. They have also just slaughtered a cock for its blood to be sprinkled on the site by the geomancer. Then Wang takes out his compass to lay out the directions and placement of entrance and rooms. He places a few sticks as markers and starts measuring out the outer edge of the foundation. Sticks are placed with several feet intervals all the way around and when all measurements are correct the sticks are connected by a cord to encircle the building site. This is not only done to mark out the walls of the house, but also to show neighbours and fellow villages that this area is claimed for a new house in case somebody will complain on grounds of their fengshui being disturbed. The above procedures are finished in about half an hour.

At 11.30 the head of household is sent away on his motorbike. His year of birth is that of the Rabbit, while this year is the Cock's, and according to the geomancer these two are not good friends. The man is sent so far away that he cannot hear the firecrackers which are to be thrown on the site. Soon after his departure his young son brings a bag of huge firecrackers. The son and a few relatives his age ignite the firecrackers and throw them into the building site. At this point a number of relatives and villagers have gathered to watch. Then the geomancer digs three ceremonial spits along the edge of the foundation and utters a number of happy spells, and wishes for a good life and a healthy household, while waving his arms in the air. After only twenty minutes the head of household returns. It is close to lunch time.

At 12 o'clock everybody enters the old house, right behind the site of the new. The women have set the table and now bring in the food, consisting of fish, duck's blood sausage, pig's fat, smoked beancurd, eggs, green garlic stems and other vegetables. Only the men, approximately ten in all, are seated around the table. This is a celebration and to go with the food is a large quantity of liquor (*baijiu*). The geomancer is an important guest and he is treated to plenty of refills, while he constantly toasts the health of the household. The big fish, fried in one piece, is placed at the centre of the table. Nobody touches it, however, because fish (*yu*) is a homophone to affluence (Eberhard 1988: 106–107), or to saving money (*yu qian*); to leave the fish untouched symbolizes leaving the family savings intact. Rice is brought in towards the end of the meal. For a short while the wife and daughter join the men, but soon return to the kitchen where the women talk, eat small dishes prepared for themselves, wash dishes, and so on.

It is difficult to attend these services without oneself becoming an important part of the celebration. When I joined the men at the dinner table, the fish pointed at me, indicating myself and not the geomancer to be the most distinguished guest. Foreigners are rarely seen in these parts, and nobody knows of a foreigner having visited this village since a cement factory was established in the 1930s. Sitting next to the geomancer, I inquire about his recent pieces of work. After listening to a story about his successful cure for a women who could not get pregnant (recounted in the next chapter), I ask him to specify the *reason* for this successful cure. He just replies: 'Oh, I cannot tell you, there are so many things. You know, fengshui is like poetry – it has symbols, classics, people, nature, and more – you cannot know exactly *how* it works.' He soon adds: 'But of course, it takes a long time to learn, and still you see only the surface. I write down all my experiences in my little note book, so I can remember all the things that influence the fengshui of the moment.' Some things Wang gets from books, while other things are his own interpretations.

'For instance (he points to a page), those who do not protect themselves in winter will be impotent in spring' (a phrase apparently copied from the Yellow Emperor's Classic of Internal Medicine). Around 3 o'clock, when the men have talked a lot and all have healthy red faces it is time to go. The husband takes Mr Wang aside in order to pay him – Mr Wang asks a moderate 40 yuan for his service. Then he collects his things and puts them back in his old knapsack: geomantic compass, a roll of cord, a note book, a copy of 'The Source of Fengshui',[6] and a traditional calendar, which he has received from a friend in Taiwan. He closes the ragged bag with a huge safety pin, which sparks off a comment from the daughter of the household: 'You should get professional assistance, it would only cost you 9 *jiao*.' Everybody laughs heartily and the old man is on his way home, a day's work accomplished.

FENGSHUI POLITICS AND LOCAL GOVERNMENT

When doing fieldwork in rural China approaching local authorities is a critical point. Almost everywhere the local peasant population is friendly and straightforward, usually just as curious about the foreign visitor as he is about them. Public authorities are less predictable. When paying an unannounced visit to the public security bureau, for instance, my assistant Dong and I were vehemently thrown out, followed by heavy cursing. Such tends to be the procedure when either party or public security interests are at stake. Dong commented that 'It is not because you are a foreigner, they just don't want anybody to see what they are doing'. Local government administrations, on the other hand, are increasingly business-oriented and tend to bother little about other than financial affairs. Any foreign visitor to a rural township with a industrial development programme is now likely to be seen as a potential investor and treated accordingly.

This was certainly also the case in Baohua; asking about local lore and religion as we did was taken as a gimmick, a discrete way of inquiring into the feasibility of placing an industrial enterprise in the area. What some township officials only assumed was spoken out loud by many villagers; in Mudan, for instance, located outside the industrial development area, a woman said: 'You have really come here to invest, haven't you? We need it very much in our village, so we would welcome you.'

A similar accord prevails over the question of fengshui practices, which the civil administration in Baohua does not regard as a challenge as long as they do not become too conspicuous, involve too much money or disturb the public order, for instance by blocking the traffic or causing riots. Quite similar to the Sichuanese case, the local officials are far more concerned with economic development in their area and in actual practice they tend to see popular cosmology as a convenient means of supplementing their finances, be it public or private. The most common instance of payment for bypassing the law involves, as mentioned, a proper burial; in some cases people pay fees to rebury a corpse upon a geomancer's advice. Another instance is housebuilding, when on account of fengshui people must move to a new location where it is possible to build bigger. Permission to build on the outskirts of the village is usually granted without formalities, but a payment in the range of 2,000–5,000 yuan is common. Some of this money is transferred to the village committee for compensation. Another instance involves having more than one child, for which considerable sums of money change hands up through the system, for instance 5,000 yuan.

The common attitude to popular cosmology was expressed by a young official in the technical department, who belongs to the new generation of well-educated staff with neither revolutionary experience nor party affiliation. They are the new professionals, who also differ from their predecessors by not being involved in the power struggles and personal vendettas that characterized party cadres before the reforms. The young official expressed a certain interest in fengshui, but being from the city he was less inclined to use it himself than the older, local breed of officials. As he said: 'Why do you investigate folk religion? There is nothing important about that. Why not big business or international trade? You know, China has only the future to be proud of.'

State and party interests stand in sharp contrast to those of local government in regard to popular cosmology. Local party cells are requested to keep an eye on 'superstition' in their area and respond firmly if a large-scale resurgence of 'superstitious practices' is detected, if religious movements arise or if religious organizations become too powerful. It is questionable, however, whether these party cells are still active and if they are, whether they are still a reliable means of carrying out party politics in this field. It is evident from Chinese press reports that central government authorities have spasmodic reactions to the ideological bluntness and declining party control in rural areas, for instance when party members are found to be members of Magico-Christian, mystical or millenarian movements. What they most fear is public hysteria or 'disorder' (*luan*), which history has shown to get out of hand too easily and threaten the power-holders. Party directives to keep a watchful eye on 'superstitious activities' in rural areas are passed down regularly, but unless there have been instances of real turmoil involving the public security bureau, they tend to be futile.

From time to time violence does break out. The daily control and mediation of all affairs involving fengshui are delegated to village leaders, of whom most are party members. It is they who must deal with complaints of destroyed fengshui around houses, marking sticks for new houses being pulled out by angry neighbours, or vicious rows threatening to turn into violence. It is also their individual policies and decisions that rule in the villages; only when a conflict gets out of hand are township government officials or police sent for.

A township official who has often been called in as a trouble-shooter is Mr Chen, the man who also started to check the People's Commune files in cases of land disputes. In his youth he was trained at the legal office of the Guomindang local government. Later he had important positions in the new government, such as head of the health clinic during the Cultural Revolution and head of the forestry department during his later career. Mr Chen has a whole arsenal of stories of families and entire lineages engaging in fierce battles over fengshui matters, after which many a wounded peasant has been taken to hospital. He describes the peasants' hot temper with biting irony when he refers to a vernacular saying, 'when people open their mouths they scold each other, when they move their hands they beat each other' (*kai kou, ma ren – dong shou, da ren*). One case refers to the rebellious village of Mudan. In 1978 two neighbouring families named Feng and Luo, Dragon and Tiger side, started building new houses simultaneously. Since the two families' old houses had been exactly the same size, it was only natural that the new houses should also match. However, both families wanted their new houses to be a bit bigger than the old ones, and they agreed upon where to put the marking sticks in the ground, outlining the layout of the houses. Then the Tiger family started digging the earth and putting down base stones, but simultaneously moving the marking sticks beyond the original layout. The Dragon family was outraged; immediately they called in relatives 'from all four directions' to have a meeting. The crowd soon agreed to pull out the sticks and remove the base stones, which they did. The Tiger family knew what was coming and had also sent for their relatives from all four directions. As soon as the Tiger family's relatives arrived and saw what was going on, fighting broke out. They fought 'young against young, old against old, women against women', using sticks as well as odd farming implements and there was a terrible bloodshed. The whole village was terrified at the escalation of events and called for Mr Chen. When he arrived, wounded and bleeding people were lying everywhere. Since there was no law that could resolve the matter, he used entirely traditional means. He commanded that the White Tiger respect the Green Dragon, and that the family refrained from building higher or bigger than their neighbours. The whole village stood behind this command, so the Tiger family withdrew their marking sticks and built a house of exactly the same size as the Dragon family.

THE LONGCHANG MONASTERY

Since many aspects of the local history and characteristics of Baohua district, particularly its eastern part, owe much to the Longchang monastery, I shall conclude this chapter with a few notes on this huge temple complex located in the mountains a few kilometres southeast of Mudan village. Temple history also shows the dubious position of fengshui practices between institutional religion and popular cosmology. The temple is the centre of the 'Vinaya' sect of Chinese Buddhism and used to serve as the leading ordination centre in central China. Thousands of monks from all over the country journeyed here for ordination ceremonies, where they would have three little dots tattooed on top of their shaven heads. The size of the temple complex, built over fourteen centuries, is best illustrated by the some 3,500 monks it could accommodate. The old kitchen hall still contains the immense pans that were used to cook rice and vegetables for the monks, the largest being 6 feet in diameter.

However, it was not only as a spiritual agency that the monastery contributed to local life. It was in fact the largest single landowning unit in the entire area until the land reform, estimated at 3,000 *mu* (Welch 1972: Table 1) and controlling the eastern part of Baohua, including several villages, whose inhabitants tilled the land. The monks were much respected by the peasants, because they were always reasonable and trustworthy and the rents were low. Since the monastery was a popular landlord, offering better conditions than most other places, landless peasants came from afar to seek tenancy of temple land or to become lay workers for the temple, for instance in the kitchen, the barbershop, the tailorshop, the vegetable gardens, or in carpentry and building activity. It is likely that the lineage organization that developed under the relatively stable conditions of temple land ownership – as compared to the exploitation, poverty and grievance of common landlordism – accounts for the internal coherence and solidarity that later became a prominent factor in the villagers' sturdy resistance to Communist control. The monastery is itself a standing testimony to the atrocities of the Cultural Revolution.

A rich symbolism always surrounded the monastery, not least sustained by the monks' mastery of Buddhist liturgy and divinatory techniques such as fengshui, which several monks practised for the villagers – and sometimes also against them. A pre-liberation story is told of the village of Liujiabie, which controlled access to the rear entrance of the temple through the Baohua Mountains. In contrast to other people the inhabitants of this village were opposed to the monks. They were very reluctant to let the monks pass through their village when they collected their rice-rents from the peasants. The village elders had gates erected and let only the monks pass at certain hours; if their donkeys dropped dung in the village, they were forced to remove it. The monks, who were knowledgeable people, noticed that when seen from above the shape of the village resembled a large ship, with two giant trees in the middle of the village resembling masts. So the monks erected a four-cornered pagoda in the mountains above the village, resembling an anchor, intending to 'stop the sailing of the ship'. It did not seem to have any impact, so the monks changed the pagoda to a larger eight-cornered structure. From that time the village started to lose its power and eventually shrank to a small hamlet. Even though the pagoda was destroyed during the Cultural Revolution, so the story goes, the hamlet is still insignificant.

Another story relates to the winding road leading up to the front gate of the monastery. Since it resembled a snake, its head pointing to the monastery, the monks feared that the snake would injure them by its bite. To offset the snake's evil influence the monastery sewing shop was placed half way up the road so that the working needles would prick the snake.

The Longchang monastery continued to flourish even in the Republican period, when many monasteries and Chinese Buddhism as such were crumbling. It had established itself both as a leading ordination centre and an important institution of traditional Buddhist education (Welch 1968: Ch. 6). It was under constant pressure, however, since successive regimes instituted political control mechanisms or attempted to exploit it economically. Under the Guomindang, powerful generals had their voluminous graves built on hillsides directly facing the temple complex from across the gorge in front, with harmful influence on its fengshui. After land reforms and religious persecution in the early years of Communism had stalled activity, the lethal blow came with the Cultural Revolution-ary attacks on the monastery in the 1960s, when shrines and inventory were smashed, including the huge engraved marble platform where the novices would receive their monkhood. Those of the 1,200 resident monks who were not immediately butchered were imprisoned. During fieldwork, an old monk who had showed me around inside the temple burst into tears when talk turned to this subject. Today, only himself and a few other monks bear witness to these atrocities.

Now the monastery is being restored. After the interior had been smashed, the monks eliminated and the entire place deprived of its soul, the same regime that ordered its destruction is now directing its reconstruction in concrete and turning it into a tourist attraction in order to show off China's glorious history. So there the monastery sits like a stuffed animal with glass eyes and artificial support, ready to admit its unknowing spectators. All around the central courtyard greedy entrepreneurs have set up stalls to sell religious paraphernalia, souvenirs and sodas, while a few innocuous monks are installed in the sidewings to create an atmosphere of authenticity. Much has already been repaired and the work continues, but priceless images, bronzes and marblework are missing. One hall closed to the public still retains the outcome of the Red Guards' indiscriminate destruction and hateful slogans daubed in red on wooden pillars, with stripes of running paint alluding dripping blood.

Despite its bloody history, the temple complex is nevertheless slowly reviving as a centre for pilgrimage since a small number of Buddhist ordination ceremonies have been allowed. Just below the temple a People's Liberation Army encampment is conveniently placed, controlling military installations as well as people and resources in the mountains.

NOTES

1   The division of fengshui into two schools generally receives stronger attention in Western literature, which tends to draw on Chinese literary sources, than it does in Chinese rural areas, where geomancers are rarely aware of the separate schools.

2   I have chosen to use pseudonyms for their surnames.

3   As reported in 1995–96.

4   A large number of such charms are depicted in Doré 1914, vol. 2: part one.

5   A funny story about the great Master Xu was told: In the village of Chendi there were two geomancers. Apart from Xu Yin-yang, the much respected apprentice and successor of an old master, there was also Wang Yin-yang. Wang often criticized the work of Xu; he said that his house positioning was wrong, that his grave sites were pointing the wrong way and that he was incompetent. Xu responded by inviting him for a contest. A scholarly geomancer from Nanjing, much greater than either of them, was invited as a referee. The contest consisted of finding the best location for a grave in the mountains east of the village. After demonstrating their skills the referee inspected the two sites, and naturally Xu was the winner. The loser had to pay for a 30-table banquet for the entire village to relish.

6   One of the first books on fengshui published in China after liberation. See Chapter 3.

6 *Fengshui Applications and Possible Interpretations*

Below is presented a collection of stories indicating the specific uses and manifestations of the fengshui tradition in the two fieldwork areas. The stories have not been selected according to a pre-conceived scheme of interpretation. On the contrary, out of a large body of material the stories included here were first of all chosen for their general representativeness, and their distribution among various types of problems and cures also matches well with the whole material. They are, of course, personal accounts or narratives, taking form as subject to the memory and interpretation of the narrator, and furthermore being told to me as a foreigner in a specific ethnographic context. I had no reason to believe that local people would differentiate between certain classes of fengshui-related phenomena which could be disclosed to a foreigner and others which should be kept secret. Hence, this compilation of stories is believed to be representative of fengshui thought and practice in the fieldwork areas and presumably in large parts of rural China, though immense local variation must be taken into account.

I shall attempt to interpret some of the most common applications of fengshui, both in terms of their ethnographic contents and their socio-political meaning as opposed to other modes of thought. This must be done with caution, however, quite similar to that which Lévi-Strauss pointed out for mythological analysis: no hidden unity may be grasped once the breaking-down process has been completed – themes can be split up *ad infinitum* (Lévi-Strauss 1969: 5). Though a number of themes are recurring, their unity is never more than tendentious and projective; in some instances I shall contextualize rather than interpret, avoiding a fuller meaning to the story than the teller presumably would have agreed to.

Apart from the conventional uses of fengshui, such as positioning houses and graves and calculating dates for funerals, weddings and so forth, fengshui specialists are called in to solve a number of problems. Today, the most frequent of such tasks belong to the broad category of 'seeing' and 'correcting' fengshui in households that suffer from illness, mental disorder, and premature death. These cases account for nearly two-thirds of the total number of incidents where geomancers are sent for. Second in importance is another broad category of 'misfortune', including miscellaneous kinds of failure, mishap and lack of prosperity. Another important category relates specifically to monetary affairs and business. A number of incidents relating to accusations of 'broken' or 'stolen' fengshui were recorded, although such village skirmishes may not involve a geomancer. Finally, there is a number of rare stories not fitting any of the categories above as well as some tales and incidents that local people recounted to prove that fengshui does not always work.

Another 'emic' typology will be referred to. It consists of the four fundamental concerns which the geomancers claim to be the aim of all their work since they derive from classical tradition. They are 'prosperity' (*cai*), 'happiness' (*fu*), 'long life' (*shou*), and 'procreation' (*zi*). Both in terms of attaining the good life and in terms of fighting off threats to this aim, these concepts represent the outlook of rural people quite well, but they are as much symbolic representations, each with a universally important Chinese character attached to them. These categories are not contradictory to those mentioned at the beginning. Rather they are translated, philosophical concepts, paralleling the rational categories from a human starting point, for instance by refusing to define disease or premature death as a category of fengshui concern, but viewing these entirely from the perspective of a good life, defining the ideal condition for human existence and discerning disorders as deviations from the ideal state. Thus prosperity, happiness, long life, and procreation are the fengshui-induced responses to the modern (and also far more abstract) Western-inspired categories used by the Chinese state: development, rising living standards, public health, medicine, mortality rates, and birth control. The two sets of categories clearly work as idiomatic translations of each other and competing conceptualizations as to what matters to human existence. One obvious difference, however, is that fengshui is a highly flexible tradition with an inborn capacity to encompass nearly any issue of concern to the rural population, also those without justification in state rationalism.

WEALTH AND COMPETITION

There is a virtually universal Chinese conviction that a good life has material satisfaction as a precondition – and not a living soul in any of the fieldwork areas would deny this. All placement of houses and graves refers to this fundamental concern. Yet popular ideology continuously stresses the confines of the Chinese world and the scarcity of its resources. Population pressure, hunger, political turmoil and social disintegration have been the common experience of successive generations, transmitted in the form of common appreciations of what to share and what to hoard. Popular notions definitely run counter to Chinese state rationality and discourse on modernity: that we all get rich if we work selflessly for the four modernizations, develop the nation, respect the state and the party and so forth. The ceaseless, vulgar roar of development, increase, wealth and power for the nation, which suspiciously resembles brainwashing, is up against a deeply ingrained belief that one man's gain is another man's loss, a fact that a wealth of ancient and modern literature, proverbs, expressions and terms indicate. This is one of the toughest aspects of popular ideology that recent regimes have been confronted with, certainly not easy to reconcile with 'socialist spiritual civilization'.

Fengshui is at the centre of all this. It has expanded and elaborated on this theme and given cosmological credence to individual pursuits of wealth as contrasted to communal enterprise. The leading notion is the interconnectedness of the social and physical environments, commonly understood as the general arena in which *qi* flows and creates. This immanent world of mutually interacting human and natural agencies can be neither expanded nor deepened and it contains a given pool of resources. From a personal standpoint it may be further exploited, but the prevalent anthropocentric outlook does not differentiate between exploitation in the natural and the social worlds. Fengshui provides techniques for furthering personal aims that operate across such boundaries. In fengshui thought everyone is expected to care for his own household and optimize his potential, while convention sets the rules for inter-household competition. Convention alone, however, does not impede differentiation. When people build bigger houses in the village, for instance, and build far bigger than they need, they appear to show off their wealth – this is implied in the mode of explanation deriving from modernity. By contrast, in fengshui terminology, which is equally applicable, they build bigger to catch more of the fortune-bringing *qi* to improve all the four aspect of the good life. Inside the village confines they inevitably do so at the expense of other people's *qi*, while on the outskirts it may interfere less. The two explanations above are clearly synonymous, but the former tends to be socially contemptuous in any respect, while the latter has cosmological backing and therefore can be posed as morally neutral.

Several stories have already been mentioned of people building bigger houses than their neighbours, causing animosity or grudge, for instance in Longquan, where a man was allotted a site for a new house inside the courtyard of an old building. Now, even though your next door neighbour builds a new house that is considerably bigger than yours, your own house should in principle remain the same size. This is the perception contained in modernity and also the view that the public authorities are meant to convey. But rural people refuse to look at things this way. Houses remain the same size, everyone knows that, but they *seem* smaller when larger ones are built next door and that is enough to trigger a response. By implication your house becomes smaller in the combined physical-social world. You may complain to find an outlet for your frustration. If it is also placed in front of your entrance, to which good fengshui is expected to flow, a complaint can even be backed by both cosmology and convention.

Following Maurice Freedman (1969), several anthropologists have accounted for fengshui in terms of an amoral system, used to explain economic difference as an alternative to Buddhist ideas of a moral order in the universe and not least in opposition to the persistent moralizing trends in Chinese state power. That is, a system for manipulation of selfish benefits in the face of moralizing entities, be it in inter-family, inter-factional, inter-village or family–state relations (Watson R. 1995: 10). Let us look at a specific instance from the Jiangsu fieldwork area, where the placement of houses in relation to others is highly restricted and surrounded by much tension due to the orientations school of fengshui.

> For many years the houses of the eastern half of the Zu village, dominated by the Wangs, had been higher than those of the western half, dominated by the Fengs. Then in the 1970s the western half started getting richer and building bigger houses, so that the western

half now became higher than the eastern half and also tended to expand. Immediately strife occurred and when it developed into violence local government also became involved. Everyone knew that before liberation these two 'halves' were independent villages and their separate identities had been preserved ever since. Most house were still located on each individual family's original plot, and only fields had been reallocated. The eastern village called in a geomancer to help them re-establish their good fengshui. The geomancer, who was also acquainted with the history of the local area, advised them to separate the two villages so that their fengshui could become complete again. With the establishment of the People's Communes in 1958, however, the original land titles had been burned and the two villages were integrated into one brigade. One local government official happened to know, however, that the commune had kept copies of the old certificates 'for their own use'. Since this official was much respected by everybody, he accompanied representatives from the two halves of the village to the township government, where they searched for old land documents to find out where exactly the lines were originally drawn between the two villages. Finding the original lines separating the two villages, a border line was established allowing families to build new houses only on their own side.

The competitiveness of local communities is felt everywhere as new opportunities open up in the market economy. With rapidly increasing differentiation fengshui is a handy device for leaving socialist ideals behind and making the best of a new beginning. Perhaps for those losing out, economic backwardness is easier to tolerate when it is shared by one's community, where a communal identity and therefore a common aspiration for future prosperity may be preserved. Yet, as noted above, fengshui is flexible enough to allow for convenient social entities to be emphasized in the face of a threat to one's relative position, which again indicates the contextual nature of the identities backed by fengshui terminology. Several incidents have been shown of inter-household skirmishes, but as evident from the meticulous calculations of cosmological correlations used in divining the correct site, involving, for instance, the astrological sign of the head of household, fengshui can be entirely individualized, casting bad luck and illness on a single family member.

Both for reasons relating to its plasticity in terms of interpretation and because of the varying scale of application, fengshui is not a system in the sense that it relates to events in a systematic way. It dictates nothing apart from simple, conventional principles for construction. As a popular cosmological resource for the actor, however, it may serve as an straightforward mode of reflection conveying an emotional state of mind and allowing for the incorporation of infinite local, political and personal considerations to be included in a 'judgement' of a geomancer or a sensation felt by a commoner. There is even a potentially reversed moralizing in feng-shui terminology instead of amoral reasoning when, for instance, large new houses are being built in the vicinity of smaller ones and people in the old house feel that the new houses are erected as acts of mockery rather than as living spaces for their owners.

In contrast to modern views, folk wisdom holds that no matter how skilfully and dedicatedly you work there is an independent variable involved in determining your success. This relates to notions of sovereign agencies such as fate, astrology and the flow of *qi*, all influencing people's luck, although neither is considered to be a given fact. Such ideas of independent and unpredictable agencies may seem inconsistent with the fundamentally undivided world, but it is nevertheless symptomatic of an anthropocentric worldview. First of all it has a foundation in neo-Confucianism as well as in fengshui cosmology, where the principles deriving from yinyang, the flow of *qi*, the Five Phases, the *bagua* and astrology all have a separate impact on a given phenomenon. (How each of them was incorporated into the cosmology over time is shown in the Appendix).

Compared to notions of a world consisting of various spheres of, for instance, the natural, the social and the psychical, to which specific laws of causality may apply, anthropocentrism tends to invert domain and agency. There is only one domain, the world that matters, but multiple agencies exercise their influence on it. There is no reductionist incentive such as in monotheistic rationalism to trans-pose these into a common formula. To some extent these agencies may be manipulated, if the pertinent knowledge and techniques are at hand, but they must be confronted one by one. So when people almost customarily express uncertainty in terms of 'maybes' rather than adherence to positive 'beliefs' (which we have seen are un-important), it is first and foremost an indication of the fundamental assumption that the given world includes a number of truly independent forces or agencies, which, again, bridge the social and the physical. There is a prominent uncertainty factor built into every human endeavour, and hence the pervading assumption of good luck as an autonomous agency – not distributed meaningfully according to morals or other forms of just deserts. Yet it may have tenuous links to other domains, which only the geomancer can see. A couple of stories illustrate this.

In Honghu a wealthy family bought a private motorcar, but on several occasions they had accidents with the car, always caused by somebody else hitting them from behind. The head of household, who drove the car, always complained: 'I don't want to collide with them, so why do they come to me.' He thought that there might be something wrong with their house. He sent for Ye, the 36-year-old geomancer who is the nephew of the famous old Ye. Ye investigated the house, but found nothing wrong. However, he found that the direction of the door did not quite harmonize with his calculations of the owner's astrological data, and advised him to change the gate slightly. 'Your forefathers are a bit unhappy', he explained, 'past generations are striking your back to remind you.' The owner of the house changed the gate and suffered no more accidents; he also felt much more comfortable when driving the car.

In the village of Woji people had felt unhappy for many years. The village was not prospering and there was much illness, many miscarriages, and a general uncomfortable feeling. At a public meeting the inhabitants decided to invite a specialist to inspect the fengshui of their village. Upon his arrival he started walking around the village for a very long time, just walking and walking without saying anything. Finally he told the villagers that the water in the village pond was still, which means very bad fengshui (flowing water means good fengshui). He told them to connect it up to a nearby stream in order to increase the water flow and bring fortune to the village: 'After that was done people felt much better and more confident. Everybody could work much harder to improve their lives and the village finally prospered', a villager commented.

Now what really works here? Is it the fengshui manipulations themselves that people regard as effective or is it the psycho-social impact of the assurance given to them by the geomancer? The answer is probably neither of them alone but instead their nexus: a combined physical and psycho-social implantation from the geomancer which is catalyst for a greater effort on the part of the villagers – a collective 'placebo' effect. Evidently such holistic reasoning produces doubts about the effect of any one factor alone and people feel compelled to express that maybe fengshui works, maybe the reason for improvement is found elsewhere. Fengshui holistic knowledge apparently blends with modern, or perhaps universal, reductionist thinking.

We meet a youthful man cutting down a small tree next to the entrance of his house on the main road. He is a friendly and talkative person, and when he eventually hears about our interest in cosmological knowledge he even claims that he himself has some knowledge of fengshui. He reports the story of his own household:

When we built this house in 1988 we invited a specialist, who is a distant relative. But after we moved in the family did not fare well. We were often sick and many of our domestic animals died. So we spent too much money on medicine, hospitals, and new animals to replace the dead ones. Money flowed out of the house. Then I thought that I could remedy the fengshui myself by fetching a large flagstone (fengshui-stone) in the mountains and placing it in front of the entrance so that the money did not flow out so easily. But it did not help; we were still not doing well. Then I realized that the stone was too close to the entrance and blocked for the good *qi*, and I moved it 50 feet down into the garden in front of the house. Since I moved the stone we have not had misfortune and all is well.

The establishment of small rural industries and the revival of many small stores in the villages have greatly increased the demand for geomantic services. Both public and private factories now tend to invite a specialist before ground plans for new buildings are drawn up, but due to the highly controversial nature of the matter, particularly when public authorities are involved in private business, it is nearly impossible to investigate. Instead we visited Yinyang Master Xiong, who is one of the trusted authorities in this field. After calling in vain several times, we finally found him at home one evening. Mr. Xiong has just built a new house for himself and his household. He shows it to us as an example of perfect fengshui. The house is placed a bit outside the village with a view over the fields and the hills in the background to block the evil influence from beyond. It is a two-winged construction, allowing the two wings placed at a right angle to catch the fengshui of the open area and making it 'spin' in front of the house. Also, when placed out here, his entrance will not face those of other houses.

Master Xiong tells about some of his recent jobs. He pretends not to be quite at ease with being asked to talk about his accomplishments as a geomancer, since he prefers, as he says, 'to be praised by his clients'. But just like all his competitors he is prone to advertise his superior skills.[1] There is little we can do in terms of analysis when the stories are told by geomancers, since they are actors with a specific professional interest in supporting one mode of explanation over others. Some brief stories may suffice:

> A man from this area built a factory for making washing machine and refrigerator bodies. He could not sell his wares, however, and facing the prospect of going broke he called me in to inspect the factory. I immediately saw that the entrance was facing a large mountain, which blocked the flow of his sales. I advised him to move the whole factory since there was no possibility of redressing the fengshui situation of that place. He moved the entire factory and soon prospered.

> Another man with a private rubber eraser factory complained that he could not sell his products and invited Xiong to come and see the place. He soon found that the gate was wrongly placed and told the

man to move it further down along the wall towards the street (such cases are very common, Xiong comments).

COEXISTING EXPLANATORY DEVICES FOR
CURING AND CONSOLING

Illness, affecting either individuals or entire households, is a common threat to happiness (*fu*). The most prevalent understanding of illness in rural areas like Longquan and Baohua is neither traditional nor modern, but a conglomerate of reasoning involving both plain physiological causes, metaphysical non-personal causes and spiritual agencies, including ancestors. Thus, amidst coexisting aetiologies or 'multi-causality', people can never be sure whether a stomach ache is due to food poisoning, to malicious *qi* ruining one's fengshui, to the independent workings of fate or to spirits pressing some message through.

To the Western observer, brought up with an expectation that a given phenomenon must be explicable along a single strand of reasoning to avoid anomaly, this may seem confusing. Yet a closer probing into private lives may reveal that also a great many Westerners contemplate several possible causes of life-threatening diseases, including astrology, fate and desert. In terms of how we *think* of disease the difference may be smaller than in terms of how we *express* disease. A particular mode of explanation, that of modern medicine, is made explicit at the expense or other modes, which presumably were more important earlier on but gradually were subordinated and internalized.

Such coexisting traditions, which each individual entertains and participates in, have been termed 'discursive universes' by Fredrik Barth (1989), but despite the appeal of the term in a Chinese context there is no evidence that people perceive them as belonging to disparate spheres or see a dilemma in their coexistence. It is presumably the coexisting realities that annoy our rational minds and induce us to see them as derived from separate 'universes'. In the Chinese context these coexisting explanations rather belong to discursive domains within a single universe of great complexity. Before relating some cases illustrating the fengshui mode of thought in regard to illness, it is pertinent to say a few words about health and medicine in rural areas.

It was in fact entirely natural visits to public latrines that aroused my interest in public health. These public conveniences are merely holes in the ground or moulded concrete containers that are regularly emptied, the contents most often still being used as fertilizer – the so-called 'night-soil'. In those instances one cannot avoid looking down, and a fairly representative portion of the villagers' calling cards will be disclosed. Most of the earlier callers' stools were runny, sometimes with worms, both indicative of stomach disorders. Moreover, this repeated itself over and over again, both in villages and towns. If people did not suffer there would be no problem, of course, but incorporating questions concerning health standards in my routine interviews gave some results. It turned out that few house-holds did not have one or more members suffering from diarrhoea or stomach ache; in most cases these ailments were either recurrent or chronic. In sum, the number of individuals that suffered from out of the ordinary stomach ailments either frequently or chronically matched well with my simple 'observations' in public latrines.

In a great number of cases, people reported that going to a hospital to see a doctor was in vain. To my astonishment this applied equally to rural people with access to only township clinics and urban people with access to both local practitioners and national top-priority university hospitals. Whenever people went to see a doctor, they would return with large quantities of medicine, usually of herbal origin. One could conclude that either Chinese medicine is frequent-ly ineffective or that the Chinese rural population in general is susceptible to illness of a kind that cannot be cured by medicine, but that needs treatment by means of alternative kinds of aetiology, for instance fengshui knowledge. I shall later return to the question of distrust in the medical system.

Ironic as it is, one very pressing reason to fight fengshui in the early years of the People's Republic was that peasants should be taught to see doctors when ill, not geomancers. Modern medicine really brought revolutionary news to the villages: old plagues like typhoid, cholera, malaria, tuberculosis, bilharzia and leprosy were brought under control, but it was primarily by means of Western medicine. National pride in both food habits and native medicine, which truly has contributed to the recognition of the complexities of the human body, are nevertheless continuous obstacles to releasing the potential for a real breakthrough in applied medicine. What apparently is to blame is the failure of Chinese medicine to practise what it preaches. The holistic approach to man's health and seeing the internal microcosmos as an analogy to the external macrocosm appear to be only vague idealizations in the concrete examination of the patient by the medical practitioner. Furthermore, Chinese traditional medicine builds on cosmological reflection, but it also embraces a power discourse in the form of an obscuritism that allows infinite manipulations beyond the patient's control: diagnosis, therapy and payment are the exclusive judgement of the practitioner, who usually maintains a monopoly on his particular style of medicine as opposed to that of others, much like the trade secrets of old Chinese crafts and the specialization and competition that are still observed among geomancers. Considering the relative wealth of modern China, the health of her people is often strikingly discordant. The nearly universal Chinese stomach and digestion problems are not even remotely linked to the greasy food, its often very low fibre content, and the addiction to monosodium glutamate. Neither are the far too common liver, kidney and spleen diseases linked to circumstances in the human environment or to the diet. What we often blame Western medicine for – primarily handling symptoms and only inconsistently incorporating the patient's diet, lifestyle, environment and so forth – is even more customary in Chinese medicine. Anybody who eats 'normal' Chinese food will never be told to change diet, even temporarily, by a Chinese doctor. Thus Chinese medicine has so far failed to put the holistic approach into practice and to adapt itself to changing societal circumstances. Chinese food may be tasty, but its total impact on the body as it is prepared today frequently appears destructive, not least due to the vastly increased content of heavy rape seed oil. A large number of people report that their regular symptoms disappear when they travel to the West – only to reappear upon returning home.

The rural health clinics, where health workers were supposed to work selflessly in the interest of public health, have been closed down long ago due to a thorough liberalization of the health sector. In Longquan, for instance, a former commune health clinic, on the facade of which was painted the WHO slogan 'Health for all by the year 2000', was shut down. In reality doctors disappeared from rural areas as soon as it became possible, since nobody with a proper education wants to live in a rural area. The medical system's discrepancy between word and practice grew tremendously after the reforms when medical personnel could no longer be retained in rural areas by means of state assignments. On top of that rural people often feel discriminated against at city hospitals. In many rural areas only geomancers remain for people to consult. Thus, there is good reason to believe that today more than previously fengshui deals with illness and mental disturbances, something which tends to be supported by historical accounts. When the local traditional doctor and traditional medicine were extinguished by the introduction of modern medicine, people lacked a local practitioner who would speak their language and maintain the rural tradition of knowledge, interpreting illness within a framework of holistic thought, involving ghosts and spirits – geomancers took over these functions.

National pride in the diet and an incoherent medical system are not alone to blame for the poor health standards. Another factor, already indicated, relates to conspicuous consumption. With the reforms rural incomes have rocketed in many places, but so have expectations. Today, only few peasants cannot afford a sound diet. Still, peasants everywhere are prone to save money by sticking to an absolute minimum of protein and dietary variation in order to put money aside for a new television set, a new house, or even an automobile.

To return to our proper subject, how illness is understood and attempted to be cured by means of fengshui, some cases will follow. As is obvious from these cases, illness may have multiple causes as well as cures, since neither cause nor cure necessarily refers to a single type of knowledge. A man in the tea house tells a story from his household:

> My sister contracted some gynaecological problems and went to hospital many times. But the drugs she got did not help her. Then she invited a yinyang specialist to her house. He inspected it and found that a large tree stood right in front of the entrance. He told the family to cut it down. They did so and my sister soon recovered.

We called on a peasant in the courtyard outside his farmhouse. Newly harvested rice is spread out to dry in the sun. The peasant has 2.4 *mu* to support four family members. Out of his harvest, a quota of 500 kilograms must be sold to local government at a fixed price. The peasant complains that even though the price is reasonable he will not get much money. Local government writes off an electrical power fee plus a number of other 'service fees' so that in the end he may get only 100 yuan, if anything at all. This kind of deep suspicion of public authorities, frequently elevated to encompass the entire system, state or the outside world, is also a crucial factor for understanding many people's attitude to the medical system. Telling us about his household, the peasant reports the following:

> Some time ago my daughter got ill. She had a terrible pain in the left side of her stomach. On advice, I went to Yinyang Master Fu, who is a geomancer specialized in driving out evil spirits. He poured water into

a bowl (*shengshui*) and then stirred it slowly with his finger. Then he said: 'You have pulled out a beam from the roof of your house, your ancestors are very unhappy about it. You have to put it back in place and honour them properly.' I remembered that shortly before my daughter got sick I had pulled out one of the sticks supporting the thatched roof, because it had become loose and was sticking out so I continually bumped my head against it. I went into town and bought plenty of wine, food, candles, incense, and strings of coloured paper. When I came back the whole family, except my daughter, gathered to honour and pray to our forefathers to make my daughter well again. Soon after my daughter recovered. She was also taken to the hospital and got some medicine ... It is difficult to say whether I believe in fengshui. The geomancer says there are ghosts, but you cannot see them, so how do you know? But fengshui *works*; that is the most important thing and I do not doubt that.

We stop to inquire about a new house built on the main road passing through Longquan town. Talking to the young man, who is the only person at home, we get confirmation that the ground plan of the house was laid out according to the directions given by a geomancer. The family has become well-off from growing fruit, mainly grapes, which may bring in as much as 4,000 yuan per *mu*. Sensing our interest in fengshui, the young man relates an episode dating back some years.

Before we built this new house our family lived in an old house near the hills. At that time we were not doing as well as now. I remember when I was 10 years old I suffered from a terrible pain in my ankle. My parents took me to hospital several times, but the medicine they gave me never worked. Then they called in a geomancer. After feeling the fengshui of the house and doing some thinking, he said to my parents: 'Your son has twelve evil gates (*guankou*, thresholds or difficult points in a person's life-course) in front of him and cannot fight his way through. I have to help him getting through.' The geomancer told the family to find a ladder with twelve steps, whereafter he left.

The next day the geomancer came back with twelve big knives (*shadao*, models of those once used for capital punishment). Then he fastened the knives on the steps of the ladder with the blades pointing upwards. He asked my parents to place the ladder horizontally on top of two chairs, thus resembling a bridge. Then he lifted me up and placed me over his shoulder and climbed on to the chair at one end of the ladder. With great difficulty he balanced over the knives, from step to step, and finally arriving at the far end. As soon as he climbed down and put me back on the ground the pain eased and it soon disappeared completely.

Stories like these above, and several of those related in the previous chapters, first of all illustrate how easily people will switch from one mode of explanation to another, unaffected by demands of consistency. What we habitually call 'pragmatism' seems to prevail, but the term itself is somewhat inappropriate because pragmatism like other terms derived from an absolutist type of reasoning tends to preclude the simultaneous deliberation of several strands of reasoning. Our shortage of terms is particularly conspicuous as people rarely express any ranking of the various modes of explanation that may apply. In the case of illness, there may be one type of causation that is found more likely than others and the proper practitioner is then consulted, but it may as well be the case that two or more types of causation are investigated simultaneously. Fengshui as a tradition of knowledge provides a vast but loosely structured frame for analysing and removing causes of illness, which is simple enough for layman's use. The basics of house design, placement and environment are common knowledge and the very general implications of breaking these common rules tend also to be commonly shared knowledge. Chinese traditional medicine and modern medicine also provide comprehensive modes of explanation, of which people understand some, enough to have general ideas, but not all, and therefore need to contact specialists in critical situations. Yet another mode of explanation derives from ancestor worship and recognition of a variety of ghosts and spirits, which may affect people's health – most clearly so in the Jiangsu fieldwork area, where ideas of a departed soul are prominent among disease aetiologies.

We observe what may be termed an agglomerative approach – building a string of possible causes and required precautions – since people will add precautions belonging to different modes of explanation until an illness is eventually cured or a problem is solved, usually without strict priorities of order, but with certain social-group patterns being recognizable. There is a discernible sociology of knowledge in relation to choices of explanation in case of illness and mental disease, corresponding to, for instance, the distinction between developed and undeveloped villages that was shown in the previous chapter.

Spotting a house on which a mirror and some cock feathers have been placed over the door, we go in to inquire about the reason for this arrangement. This is definitely one of the poorer villages in the Sichuan fieldwork area, and the interior of the house is very basic with earthen floor and few conveniences. There is nobody home, but in the garden behind the house we find a woman spraying the vines with a pesticide. When asked specifically about the mirror she says 'I don't know'. Only much later does she admit that they have many problems in her family. The crops are not good and everybody in their village has only 0.5 mu of land, which, considering the shortage of water, is below the minimum for a decent life. The family members are often sick, suffering from flues and almost chronic stomach ailments and her husband has had several strokes. The family could not afford a geomancer, but they heard from another family what a geomancer had advised them and copied this remedy. They killed a cock at the spring festival and used some of its feathers to stick on a mirror (*zhaoyaojing*) that was put up on the front of the house to reflect evil influence. The woman's attitude to us clearly indicates that the outside world spells danger to them. They have experienced no improvement from the mirror, however, and when asked about the possible impact on their health that the four different pesticides in use may have, the woman says: 'Yes, it is true that they have killed all the insects, including bees and butterflies. We have used them for many years, maybe since the 1960s, and we are afraid that they are also the reason why we are always ill. But we are not sure.'

Several of the houses in her village have mirrors over the doors. We inquire about the reason in a number of other households, but only find that people are extremely unwilling to talk. Only when asked directly if it is because they have problems, they confirm: 'exactly' (*jiu shi*). A paper poster in one house reads, 'Good behaviour will please the forefathers' (*zu de liu fang*). Such accounts immediately raise the question of primary and secondary causes of an ailment: will people attribute health problems to pesticides, to bad fengshui or to unhappy forefathers? And do people believe that fengshui acts and rituals can change the quality of polluted ground water? These questions are indeed difficult to answer. In any case people appear to be unprepared for abnormal situations such as when a single cause of illness must be pursued and eliminated. One derived question is whether the holistic fengshui thinking may be detrimental to eliminating causes of illness that stem from highly reductionist manipulations of nature such as the use of pesticides? Ecological thought and environmental protection have not made their way to these villages, where even the young are uninterested in finding the true causes of the misery, but prefer to leave.

With some caution the analysis may be taken a bit further. We discussed in the historical chapters the contradiction between orthodoxy and heterodoxy, a persistent theme in Chinese history, with every era establishing its own delicate balance. It goes without saying that orthodoxy as promoted by the state power is single-stranded and absolutist, whereas 'heterodoxy' has always covered a diversity of traditions, having only in common their opposition to the orthodox ideology of state power. According to my general argument these traditions must not be taken for anything like archaic systems of thought unconsciously transmitted into the present. They are and have always been dependent on their reproduction in the present and cannot be examined independently of their logical opposition. Viewing this set-up in terms of power structures in Chinese society, diversity is in itself in opposition to state power, disregarding its ideological content. We cannot argue on the basis of the fieldwork material alone that when local people hang on to a multitude of explanatory devices it is an intentional anti-authoritarian strategy, but we can indeed speculate that ontological diversity may serve as a weapon of the weak against state power's monopolization of ontological truth. The changing balance between state power and popular cosmology during the past one and a half centuries, outlined in the historical chapters, tends to support such argument.

As indicated in the fieldwork chapters, due to the political climate it is still difficult to admit in public that one respects something which the ruling authorities brand as superstition. When it comes to recognizing that bad fengshui around a house may cause trouble, however, most locals will proclaim that it plainly induces illness as a matter of course. In addition, most people will assume that the fengshui situation can be changed by means of a specialist's manoeuvring. These are fairly harmless aspects of fengshui knowledge, which also tend to be shared by government officials. Some applications of fengshui go much further than these basics, however, involving magic, mystery and psychic experiences. Some instances of 'building magic' were reported, quite similar to those described by Wolfram Eberhard dating back to the early 1800s (Eberhard 1970: 49); also Ronald Knapp confirms that there is an almost universal belief that carpenters possess knowledge of spells and that can inflict harm on households (Knapp 1999: 52).

> A carpenter who built a house was treated badly by the owner, who made him work long hours, gave him poor food, and always scolded him. When finishing his work he decided to take revenge on the owner by destroying the fengshui of the house. He took a little round cup and placed a dice in it with the numbers 1, 2, 3 pointing upwards. These numbers mean bad luck and misfortune, whereas 4, 5, 6 are the lucky numbers. He placed the cup in a hole above the doorframe and covered the hole. After moving into their new house, the family never fared well. Much misfortune came to them, they were often sick and their money was always spent too quickly. The wife could not understand why she always heard the 'sound' of 1, 2, 3 in her ears. Then the

family invited a geomancer to see fengshui. He heard the sound too and soon found the little cup with the dice inside. Instead of removing it, he just turned the dice so that 4, 5, 6 were now visible and put the little cup back in place. Then misfortune turned to good fortune for the family.

A carpenter was treated badly by his hosts. He was made to work until late at night and forced to get up much too early in the morning. The owner's wife would make breakfast for him before sunrise and refuse to allow him anything to eat after that time, so that he had to get up. When the carpenter was so exhausted he could hardly work any more, he decided to retaliate: he took a small piece of bamboo and carved a small image of a devil (*gui*), which he placed in the kitchen in a place where nobody could see it. From that time the woman saw a devil in the kitchen every time she went there in darkness. Soon she dared not go out there before sunrise and finally the carpenter got his sleep.

We meet a man cleaning his bicycle in the village pond and start chatting with him about the village. He confirms that everybody will use the service of a specialist when building a new house:

It is such a great event to build a new house, maybe it only happens once in a lifetime for most people. So spending a few tens of yuan for a geomancer to celebrate the event is quite natural. But many people also use geomancers when there is trouble in the household. For instance, some time ago I had a terrible pain on the right side of my stomach and it would not go away. My wife called a geomancer to inspect the house and find a reason. He came with his compass and inspected both the house and the ground around it, but found nothing wrong. Then he poured water into a bowl and stirred it with his finger, and then made me drink it. It helped me so much that after a short time the pain had disappeared. The geomancer did not tell me the reason for my illness – maybe it was his secret.

Apart from physical discomfort and illness, bad fengshui is repeatedly seen to cause mental disorders, which the geomancers commonly divide into three types of 'madness' (*fengle*): 'spiritual' madness (*shenfeng*), 'emotional' madness (*qifeng*) and 'sexual' madness (*huafeng*). One day when we pay a casual visit to Mr Xiong he wants to tell us about one of his latest jobs, concerning a young man who went mad. But instead of just telling the story, he asks us to follow him to the young man's household since it is not too far away. It proves to be a 30-minute walk along small paths, while balancing on planks serving as bridges over small creeks, jumping over dykes, and climbing through rocky gullies. The old man leads the way at a good pace without slowing down even once. When we arrive he explains to the household members that his visitors wanted to know about fengshui, to which they just nod in acceptance and place us around the table.

This son of the household (18 years of age) joined the army some months ago; it was his first time ever away from home. After only three weeks in the barracks we went mad without any clear reason. He could not speak and he could not eat, he was just lying on his bunk without any contact with people around him. After some time his superior called his parents and asked them to come and take him home. His parents then travelled to the barracks in Gansu to bring him home. As soon as they arrived home, they called on me to investigate their house. After walking around for 'half a day' (*ban tian*) I came to the conclusion that the entrance of the house, which was built in 1987, was pointing too closely towards the mountain over there. It is called the Cock Mountain (*Jigong shan*, the highest point in the horizon), because the legend has it that long ago a cock flew by and decided to settle down here, so it turned itself into a mountain. Moreover, a stone wall around the courtyard blocked the entrance, since its opening was facing another direction than the door of the house. I judged that *qi* could not flow freely in and out, and that yin and yang were the same whether the door was open or closed so they could not transform naturally. I advised them to build a proper gate at the side of the compound, where the opening in the wall already was, pointing towards the row of hills behind at a pointed angle so that it had a much larger space in front of it to catch the *qi*. Thus the actual gate was moved from the house itself to the wall surrounding the courtyard. Only three days after the gate was erected, the son was cured and he became fully normal again. Now he is on an extended leave, but will soon go back to the army.

Another story told locally is of a man in the village of Nansha who was building a brick wall around his courtyard,

When the wall was half built, he suddenly had problems with his eyes. He soon collapsed in the middle of his courtyard, paralysed with his eyes wide open, staring at the sky. His family brought him to a hospital where he had a check-up. The doctor could find no particular ailment and sent him back to rest. After some days, during which his condition had not improved, a family member went to see Wang Yinyang, who is much respected, but afraid of going out to practise. Instead Wang poured *shengshui* into a bowl and stirred it with his finger. Then he said that the gate in the new fence was wrongly placed and that this was the reason for his paralysis. He advised that the gate was moved to another position. Then he poured the water from the bowl into a bottle for the family member to take back and give the man to drink. He drank the water and the family had the gate moved, whereafter the man recovered.

We should be aware of the function of such stories told by third parties, who have not themselves taken part in the incident. We know little of the circumstances and the accuracy of the narrative, which tends to acquire a truth of its own when repeated and sanctioned by a group of people. As such it may serve to support local identities, values and conventions; narratives that confirm fengshui thought will certainly also support the standing of the geomancers, who themselves will have an obvious interest in their circulation. Another story is told by the old geomancer Li in the village of Shentou, while a number of people have gathered around us in the tea house. There is much joking about it, since everybody knows the family in question, but no one repudiates the essence of the story.

I was once called out to a family whose son suddenly went mad without reason (Li has a good reputation curing such cases). I went to the family house, where I wandered about for some time without finding anything wrong. Neither in the neighbourhood nor in the house could I find any reason for the son's ailment. Then I went to the family gravesite on a nearby hill. I immediately discovered that the gate of the house and the front of the grave were pointing directly towards each other. This is called the 'killing position' (*shazuo*) and is supposed to have a very evil influence on the household. I first urged the family to reorient the grave. After some days I went back with red paper and a brush. Then I cut out two equal-sized pieces of paper and painted the characters *qi ling* entangled together on both pieces. I placed one of them on the mad son's forehead and the other one I rolled into a ball, which I asked the son to eat. Soon after he recovered.

The geomancer Zang tells a couple of similar stories:

A man in Chengdu suddenly went mad (*qifeng*) after his wife had left him. He was in his fifties. He started walking about in his small home putting everything into his mouth and chewing it. Outside in the streets he picked up garbage and paper and chewed that too. He also went into other people's homes. A relative of the man called me to do service for him. I stirred water and found out that his heart was captured by an evil spirit. So I chanted, played my instruments, and walked about in the room to drive out the evil spirit. I chanted all night long for three consecutive nights. The first night there was no result. The second night the man got a little bit better. The third night the man greeted me when I came and he soon recovered completely. His heart had been captured by an evil spirit so that *qi* could not flow freely.

A 14-year-old girl in Hongfuxiang suddenly went out of her mind (*shenfeng*). She stopped speaking and at night she took off her clothes and went out and did 'strange things'. She was impossible to control and her father often wanted to beat her. It went on for two years. Then her parents decided to call me to do service for her. I told her parents not to beat her, since it would only make matters worse. I sat down in front of the girl, poured water into a bowl and stirred it with my finger. Then I filled my mouth with water and blew it straight into the girl's face. She was so shocked that she actually started speaking. Then I did service for her all night and several nights after in order to call gods and spirits (*jingshen*) to search for motives for their attack. The girl soon recovered and the family was very happy.

Lastly in this section I shall present a few stories of various illnesses for which geomancers are consulted. Common to them all is the attempt to explain and cure illness by means of analogy and symbolic meaning, drawing on various fragments of Chinese cosmology and fengshui thought. The first is about calling back the soul in eastern China.

Soon after the death of my husband's sister, who was only 20 years old, our little son got very ill. He had a high fever, pains in his body and a stomach ache. The doctors could not find anything wrong so they could not help. Since it happened right after the death of my husband's sister we thought that there might be a connection. We went to the geomancer who chose the stone chamber for the urn at the public graveyard and asked his advice. He examined the grave and said that the boy's soul (*hun*) had left him to go with the sister-in-law's. His advice was that the boy should go to the graveyard the very next day, and when a spider (usually a good omen[2]) came out from the chamber he should take it, fold his hands around it and hold it against his chest all night. Immediately the parents remarked: 'But it is a modern concrete chamber and all sealed up, how can a spider come out?' 'You will see', the geomancer answered. The boy went to the graveyard, and suddenly a spider really came out from a little hole in the chamber. He took it and started running home, but on the way he stumbled and the spider disappeared. The parents went to the geomancer once more. 'Go again tomorrow and you will get another chance', he said. The next day the boy went out and found the spider once more, this time taking great care not to lose it. The following night his mother held the spider against his chest all night long while he slept. The next day he immediatly started improving and he soon recovered.

A family built a house on a site inspected and approved by a geomancer – but he disapproved of their idea of extending the roof at the back of the house to make a sheltered porch. According to the *bagua* of his compass this could not be done. The family disobeyed the geomancer and extended the roof. Just two years later the grandparents both died at an early age. Another geomancer, not the one who had earlier inspected the site, was called in. This geomancer, not knowing his predecessor's judgement, also used his compass and immediately pointed to the roof. He said that according to the *bagua* the roof was corresponding to the character *sha* (meaning break, stop or the termination of life). He ordered the roof to be shortened immediately. The family did so and lived well ever after.

A family on the mountain had a 4-year-old child, who had been running a fever for a very long time. The family called Mr Fu, who specializes in curing illness. He inspected the house, but found nothing odd. Then he investigated the child's astrological data and found out that the child's year of birth was in opposition to this year, which meant a very difficult period for the child. He asked the family to buy incense and oil. Then he went home to write some charms. The next night he gathered the family for a ceremony. He brought an old book of chants, his musical instruments, and the couplet, which he stuck on the wall. From 9 o'clock in the evening until 3 o'clock in the morning he chanted and danced around on the floor in a pattern of nine spots forming a square (derived from *Luo Shu*,[3] the 'magic square'), while he simultaneously called upon all the known ancestors and asked them to assist the child through the difficult year. After some time the child got better.

Anyone becoming acquainted with the countless stories of fengshui in Chinese rural areas will inevitably ask the simple question: does it really work? It is beyond the scope of this work to attempt to answer this question with any measure of accuracy and detail, but one aspect of the possible effect of fengshui demands our attention. Most local users of geomantic services will maintain that they do really work. Critics, on the other hand, will maintain that most diseases cure themselves, with or without the interference of a geomancer. It is also necessary to take into account the possibility of somatization, amply described in a Chinese setting by Arthur Kleinman (1986: 178), who argues that somatic affect enjoys sanction by cultural norms, whereas psychologization tends to be stigmatized, since it threatens the 'socio-centric' Chinese society. In these cases the mediation of a geomancer, familiar with every detail of the individual's social background, may alleviate discomfort, pain and depression. More research on fengshui in this respect could be done, particularly taking into account its explicit antithesis to the collective ethos of Chinese state rationalism.

Although it falls beyond the scope of this work, a rapidly increasing body of cognitive neuro-psychological research on placebo medicine may contribute to a new understanding of pre-modern medical and religious traditions. Central to this research is that human perception is based not so much on, or not entirely on, outside 'objective' information, but as much on what the human mind expects to happen, for instance a cure that out of previous experience is known to work. Thus stimulated expectancy alone may be enough to trigger massive cognitive *as well as* physiological responses that in a number of cases parallel the effects of drugs or other therapies. It has been called a 'triumph of expectancy over reality' as sensory inputs and their meanings learned through experience may eventually beat objective inputs. Highly relevant to the general argument is that this research furthermore points to an inherent ambiguity in the inner states of the mind as a possible explanation of placebo phenomena. Due to the human necessity of 'acting first' in critical situations, for instance when faced with what could be an enemy, a falling object, a snake or other dangers, anticipation of danger takes precedence over objective examination of information and demands an immediate reaction in the form of a powerful physiological response, including instant production of stress hormones and increased pulse (*IHT* 14 October 1998: 1, 4).

What is of primary concern to us, however, is that *if* this 'placebo' effect is applicable to the relationship between the geomancer and his client – that is if mental energies are to be released – the patient must have some measure of *expectancy* or *faith* in the cure. Even more important, for faith to be played out on any scale it presumably necessitates the perception of cognitive *distance* – that the geomancer is believed to command a mystic knowledge that is beyond the comprehension of ordinary people. This distance needs to be maintained by both sides for the antidote to be effective. We could see it as a logical consequence that the clients, and to some extent the entire local community, more or less unwittingly create the elevated platform occupied by the professional geomancer: the community needs his embodiment of the fengshui tradition in order for it to be effective as much as he depends on the community for his livelihood. This is what Lévi-Strauss has termed a 'gravitational' field within a consensus on belief in magic: the effectiveness of magical healing has as a precondition a social field of faith and expectations, where the shaman believes in his own methods as much as the client has faith in his power, generating the complementary conditions to set psycho-somatic responses in motion (Lévi-Strauss 1967a: 162).

Paradoxically, this does not preclude the perception of the geo-mancer as a dubious figure, who is prone to exploiting people; the complex balance of credulity and scepticism is quite commonly manifested in religion. Everywhere people are exposed to doubt in their religious beliefs: they see their lamas as petty thieves, but still need them, they regard their mullahs as charlatans, but listen to their words, or they despise Catholic priests for their hypocrisy, but cling to them as an indispensable institution. It is the delicate interplay between the venerated figure of the geomancer, the fengshui tradition drawing on 'ancient wisdom' and the client seeking an external authority to deliver the stimuli that can release his inner healing powers that may change the state of affairs in his own world. The geomancer's own words, 'You cannot know how it works', gain some credibility – presumably because *if* you knew, it would not work any more! A parallel explanation following the somatization model may also point to the significance of distance: the geomancer is a figure standing decisively outside formal society, able to express symbolically and legitimize socially ego-centred motives, sentiments, discomforts and fears by means of their sanctioning in classical tradition – he makes them Chinese and permissible (the Appendix shows fengshui as a pseudo-classical tradition, though its proponents have constantly struggled to legitimize their art by means of writing it into ancient history).

The notion of cognitive distance as mutually generated within a common field of faith and expectations is further supported by material on 'feudal superstition' collected from the Chinese press. On the basis of newspaper accounts from the early 1980s – which was also the period when rural fengshui took off – Ann Anagnost (1987) shows how the Chinese state press has attempted to expose magical healers as swindlers. One such attempt is the healers' own confessions to being social creations: word may spread that certain individuals have been possessed by spirits or have extraordinary powers, where-after people start consulting them for curing. They give in to social pressure, and further motivated by their own self-interest they begin to practise while gradually building up their self-confidence. This repeats itself in the present material as a number of instances were recorded of 'geomancers' without recent experience responding to a growing market for their services. As pointed out by Anagnost, however, it is a misreading of the 'magical situation' merely to disclose that the social consensus of belief may precede the healer's own knowledge of his or her powers. By its fundamental suspicion towards all aspects of popular cosmology the Chinese state de-marcates 'feudal superstition' as a reservoir of latent counter-hegemonic elements (Anagnost 1987: 43, 58) – perhaps unwittingly investing it with a more potent means of expressing a heterodox conception of the world and thus reinforcing the preconditions for its existence.

BELIEF IN THIS WORLD

Chinese state ideology has customarily placed the strongest emphasis on a collective spirit as the basis for an orderly society and demanded that the individual submit himself to society's grand scheme and work for its common good. Fengshui, on the other hand, is really designed as a celebration of the self. It depicts a discrete, personalized and anthropocentric universe, in radical opposition to any type of communitarian ideology. Although it sets out rules for the competition for the life-giving qi in the local community, it would never recommend making sacrifices for others. Geomancers take great pride in having lifted their clients to wealth and power, while the rich fengshui allegories in Chinese literature provide powerful backing for the idea that humans inherently strive for ever higher eminence with only the position of emperor as the upper limit.

Fengshui ideology intends to mobilize the powers of mind and body – to release human energy by suppressing bonds, obligations and communitarian demands from what for centuries has presumably been an innately oppressive society. It stands for longevity (*shou*), activity until old age and rejection of fatalism, since any human condition may be altered. Once individuals and families in the local community rise to wealth and power, few restraining devices are found in fengshui ideology – on the contrary, it may provide cosmological backing for inequality. For instance, there is nothing odious in having others tilling your land or working for you for the lowest possible pay. In this respect fengshui is far from being anti-elitist, although it can be said to manifest an anti-authoritarian propensity.

All significant human values are firmly placed in a this-worldly context and human satisfaction is pursued unwaveringly, preferably enjoyed through a prolonged life. Accordingly, fengshui thought cares little about the afterlife, except for making the best of the departed. Ancestor worship is a different tradition, which fengshui cosmology may draw on, but the practice of ancestor worship is not an aim in itself since the well-being of ancestors is essentially unimportant. It is only when the unhappiness of the dead has a direct bearing on the life-course of the living that fengshui advises action to be taken.

The occurrence of death, however, is a vital concern to fengshui as a stamp of horror and danger. Longevity is invariably pursued, the causes of early deaths are looked into, burial arrangements are made, precautions for the descendants are taken, and so forth. A few stories that involve the deaths of family members serve as illustration.

A family built a new house many years ago, but was always followed by misfortune. First the oldest generation died much too early. The family called in a geomancer to inspect the house, and he advised that the direction of the door was changed by cutting the door frame. The family did so, but with no improvement. Soon their first son died and after some years the second son was killed in an accident. After another couple of years their daughter died in labour and the baby was stillborn. Finally the remaining family members chose to move out of the house. Another family rented the house for some years, without having misfortune, because 'they were not the owners'. When they moved out, however, nobody wanted to take over the house and it was finally torn down.

A family in Baoting buried a deceased family member in the public graveyard on the mountain behind the village. After the burial, however, the family's dog started digging in the grave. It went out there every day and nothing could keep it back. It was digging and scraping its snout in the soil like mad until blood was pouring from its head. Then the family went to see Yinyang Master Wang, who had selected the grave, to ask his advice. He looked in his calendar and found that the direction of the grave was contradicting the mourning periods (*fan qi*, periods of seven days). He calculated a certain day according to the deceased's birthday and asked them to go out on this particular day and put sticks on the grave. On the calculated day they went out and did what they were told, and immediately the dog stopped digging in the grave.

We are waiting for Yinyang Master Wang in the village of Jinhua, where he is going to inspect the building site for a new house. While waiting for the old man, who is known to 'come when you see him', some villagers tell us stories about his skills:

> Our neighbours lost a son in a traffic accident – it was their only remaining son at home. In their despair they sent for Wang to inspect their house. He came with his compass and soon found that a straight line pointing south from their door hit the corner of another house. This was intolerable (*bu kenengde*) since the corner of the other house was sending disaster to their house (corners are dangerous[4]). He told them to plant a garden in front of the house to ward off the effect of the corner and re-establish balance, since a corner was pointing upwards and a garden was pointing downwards. The family followed his advice and have never since had accidents.

Hepatitis and liver cancer abound and take many lives, both in the countryside and the city. Sometimes entire families are wiped out or decimated when epidemics strike.

> In a village in Jiangsu there was a family which had seven sons and two daughters. Suddenly one son was struck by liver cancer and he soon died. He was cremated and a place for his urn was selected on the mountain. Not long afterwards another son contracted the terrible disease and died, and yet another followed. They were cremated and the stone chamber on the mountain was extended to make room for them. But there was no end to the disaster. Within a short time another son died and one of the wives. Soon all seven sons had died from the terrible disease and also two of the daughters-in-law. The health authorities were notified since everybody in the village feared for their lives. Some professors from Nanjing were sent to investigate the local conditions, but returned without being able to trace anything unusual. So the family who had lost all their sons invited a geomancer. He inspected the family grave, in which all nine urns had been placed one after another, and said 'they are standing too close, they are calling out for each other. You will have to build a chamber for each one of them'. So they did and neither the two parents, nor the remaining daughters contracted the disease.

222

In cases like this, fengshui is merely used as a source of symbolism, where the conditions of the dead are likened to those of the living. The surviving family members are apparently advised to distance themselves from the dead family members and hold on to life, to resist fatalism, and to mobilize their own mental powers. The proximity analogy could also be taken as a warning: that the living family members should distance themselves from the lifestyle, house, food of the deceased or from other sources of contamination in order to stay in good health.

Imaginative geomancers sometimes use grotesque recastings of propaganda and other material from the public media:

> A young man from Shentou village was often ill and regarded as a weakling in every way. He was several times sent for medical check-ups at the hospital, but in vain. Then a geomancer was called in. He inspected the house and in the young man's room he saw a small picture from a magazine, repeating a popular slogan of the time, 'Build your body to work for China's Four Modernizations'. On the picture was a brawny American athlete running a race. The geomancer took the picture and meticulously cut out the sportsman. Then he asked the young man to boil the cutting in water and afterwards drink the water. He did as he was told.

PROCREATION, EDUCATION AND SOCIAL ASCENDENCE

Birth control programmes are a key concern to the Chinese state and a critical issue for the Chinese nation to prevent the new wealth from being swallowed up by masses of jobless, landless, and helpless people. That private notions of procreation (zi) run counter to public policy is a trivial matter. For people who have been taught by historical experience that only family and kinship are reliable institutions, it takes more than state propaganda to generate trust at a higher level. The new market economy has pushed responsibility for servicing the individual back towards the family. There should be no doubt that fengshui also in regard to genealogical continuity stands in the sharpest opposition to political correctness and a communitarian ethos. A few stories emphasize the importance that rural people attach to procreation.

> A woman from a neighbouring village once came to Fengshui Master Li for advice. She had been married for nine years but still had not given birth to a child. Her husband, who was an army officer in Beijing, scolded her every time he came home for not being with child. Once he got so mad that he even tried to kill her, but other villagers interfered and saved the poor woman. She was so depressed that she did not know what to do and eventually went to Mr Li. He told her that he was not sure if he could help her, but that he would try. He

checked the family grave sites and the birth dates of the man and wife. He found that the direction of the former household head's grave did not harmonize with their birth dates, and asked them to change the direction of that grave. They did so – and after only one year the woman bore her husband a son. After some time, another local woman, having heard about the sudden good fortune of the first, also came to seek advice. She had been married for six years and was still childless. Li told her that maybe he had only been lucky with his cure last time. Anyway, he found that also in her case a family grave had to be changed, and just a year later the woman gave birth to a boy. Yet another woman came, and after just three years she had two boys.

A young couple from Longtan had a child a year after they were married. The woman had been sick all through her pregnancy, however, and the child was not strong. Shortly after giving birth the woman got hepatitis. Instead of being hospitalized in Nanjing, where the couple ran a restaurant, they went back to their native area where hospitalization is much cheaper. She was in hospital for a week. After coming home she still felt weak and uncomfortable. Since it went on for such a long time and both herself and the child were weak, she decided to see a geomancer. In their home village they shared a house with the husband's parents, having separate entrances and separate kitchen shelters outside. The geomancer, on seeing the inside of the house, asked both families to gather in the living room. Then he strolled around the house once and came back: 'The roofs of your kitchen shelters are pointing directly towards the young couple's bed on the second floor – that cannot be. Also, the beams on which you have suspending your clothes lines are pointing towards the roof rafters – that cannot be either. But there is more than that. When did you get married?' 'The second day of the new year', they replied. 'And when is it your birthday?' he asked the wife. She told him 22 June. 'The 22nd is an unlucky day, often accompanied by ill health, and the two dates cannot go together. You have to remarry.' Then the geomancer instructed them when to remarry and how to perform the wedding ceremony. In the end he received 25 yuan and went home. The couple followed his instructions. First they moved their bed to the other side of the room and hung up a curtain as a partition in the room. The clothes lines were turned in another direction. On 20 June the young woman went back to her own family to prepare her wedding. Her family gathered, celebrated, burnt incense, and so forth, whereafter she was taken to the groom's house again on the 21st, the day indicated by the geomancer and also the day before her birthday. Moreover, the geomancer had foreseen that it would be a difficult year for her, so he had advised her to stay in their home for the rest of that year. So she did. Now, a year later, everything is reported to be well again.

With the counter-rationality of fengshui thinking common people have at their disposal an instrument to contemplate everyday occurrences and weigh rational and non-rational perspectives against each other. Nevertheless, this section also serves to demonstrate how the fengshui tradition can be used as a convenient tool to manipulate the course of events in order to find 'plausible', irrational explanations to things that could in fact be otherwise explained. In addition, this type of fengshui application illustrates how distorted our perception would be if we analysed fengshui entirely as a 'system' that responded definitely and predictably to given inputs, without any attention to the actor. Fengshui is used to divine both time and space,[5] and a cardinal theme in fengshui knowledge is the space–time continuity, which is also contained in other traditions making use of the Five Phases theory. From the Five Phases a series of cosmic correlations are made, which stretch across the time–space boundary. Elements, directions, colours, odours, forms, animals and so forth on the space side are correlated to days, months, years, seasons and similar on the time side, creating a scheme of immeasurable correlations which the geomancer may use with rich inspiration drawn from his compass. We have already seen many instances of how they are put into practice, for instance when a houseowner's birth date is likened to an animal or when certain years involve gates that people must pass.

These partly systematic, partly haphazard exercises in space–time continuity are among the geomancers' most precious appliances since any situation will have its own, unique set of correlations for the expert to analyse. People know, of course, that the geomancer is playing with obscure terms and that neither he nor his science should be uncritically believed on this issue. Instead, and perhaps inspired by the geomancer, also common people may engage in a reworking of facts to fit their objectives. Common instances of this are after-the-fact explanations – cases where people themselves participate in the construction of a fengshui-type of explanation with the purpose of eluding responsibility or preserving face, dignity or control. Let us look at a few examples.

> Some local people came to Wang and complained that their household suffered from 'bad luck' and they had long felt uncomfortable. Some time ago they had some money stolen, the wife had been sick and the husband was unhappy with his job at a shoe factory. Worse still, a week ago their 14-year-old daughter had run away and she had not yet returned. They asked Wang to inspect their house to see if maybe something was wrong.

Mr. Wang, however, the Longtan geomancer with intimate knowledge of every family in his neighbourhood, knew that at least concerning their daughter they were partly to blame themselves. After hearing the story from Wang my assistant and I waited for the daughter to return home and when she did, we took her out to a small restaurant after school to talk to her. She revealed that her parents had indeed pressed her to study hard and get good marks so she could enter university, and this was the main reason why she had gone to live with an aunt for two weeks. It had been going on for several years and at times she was so depressed that she wanted to take her own life. Her parents had very little education themselves and wanted her to do better than them 'for the sake of the whole family'. She could not cope with it because she had never been among the best in her class and had almost no chance of entering university. She would rather leave school to start earning money since 'the game was over' in school. This wish had created so much tension in her family that they could hardly have their meals together any more and that was the real issue behind her parents' fengshui concern. The other incidents which her parents had mentioned to Mr Wang were not nearly as important or had happened several years previously, for instance the theft of the money. Another case:

> A newly rich family in Chendi village were about to send their son to university. At the same time the family were nurturing plans of building a new house for themselves. To show off both their wealth and the higher status they had attained now that their son was going to university, they intended to build both higher and bigger than the house to the west of them in the alley. The walls and roofs of the two old houses were exactly flush, however. The neighbouring family protested vociferously against the plans and demanded that the lines of the new house did not deviate a single inch from the previous lines. After endless quarrels gradually involving the entire village, the wealthy family finally had to obey conventions and build so that lines were flush. At the same time the family had applied for their son's admission to one of the key national universities, but shortly after the new house was completed – so they said – they were informed that he could only be admitted to a mediocre university. The family was convinced that this was due to the average size of their new house and they continuously complained to their fellow villagers.

Again, interviewing the young man revealed a different sequence of events than told by his parents. That he did not enter the best university was chiefly because he had not gained the highest marks at the final exams in high school. Moreover, they had received the letter stating the facts several months before the new house was built, but his parents had been somewhat frustrated over his apparent 'failure' and had hesitated to tell others. Being thwarted by the village community over the new house was a convenient time to break the news.

Several other examples could be mentioned of either people themselves, the geomancer or both parties in combined efforts reworking a series of events to preserve the integrity of one or more household members. Towards the unruly young in the family, fengshui explanations supported by geomancers loyal to the paying client can undoubtedly serve a repressive function, comparable to how geomancers in the old society were frequently accused of being the landlords' instrument to maintain control. These psychological manoeuvres, however, are probably linked to other expressions of a deliberate rejection of moral introspection in Chinese culture – a conspicuous drive towards the projection of inner shortcomings out on the external world.

Before dealing with the reinterpretation of fengshui in Western culture in the next chapter, a summary of what was interpreted as the fengshui mode of thought and knowledge is useful. First of all was shown a distinct interconnectedness of the social and the physical domains, a notion of a coherent and indivisible world that matters to common people. In a number of instances this was expanded to include the human mind. A series of independent agencies, mostly of an impersonal and non-moral nature, is acting in this common world. Fengshui cannot be understood as an isolated phenomenon. It engages in a dialogue with the dominant type of reasoning as promoted by the Chinese state, particularly over the relationship between the individual and society. The fengshui terminology makes use of a number of inversions and transformations of the state rationality, for instance by playing on individuality instead of communality and by legitimizing personal motives, strategies and actions. Also in opposition to state propaganda are notions of the integrity of the self as a complete microcosmos, a self-centred universe. This may take the form of self-celebration, and may imply the projection of inner discontent outwards onto the surrounding world. Similarly, social malfunctioning may be somatized as a feeling of pain, which either doctors or geomancers, or both, are consulted to cure. Many original features of the old Chinese cosmology are maintained, for instance the space–time continuity, which provides a vehicle for constructing infinite correlations in both the perceptible and imperceptible domains.

FENGSHUI AND POPULAR RELIGION

After exposing the immense repertoire of fengshui applications and indicating feasible interpretations, it remains to discuss the relationship between modern fengshui and the broad field of 'popular religion'. Following Catherine Bell and others there are several possible readings of popular religion, respectively drawn from second or third generation studies of Chinese religion (see Chapter 1). Stephen Teiser has outlined the common readings of popular religion as comprising three distinct interpretations. The first derives from older studies of the religion of the lower classes as opposed to elite religion, the religion of the *popolaccio* (Teiser 1995: 378). A second version includes what is shared by the people in general, across all social boundaries, thus emphasizing the unity aspects of popular religion. A third perspective integrates modern views of culture in a much more profound way, turning attention towards dynamic processes involving difference and dispute, with popular religion becoming less of an entity than an activity, an arena for different meanings to be played out.

Scholars agree, however, that popular religion should be defined as a positive category, not as a failure to be something else, and that the phenomenon is so extensive in space, time and demography that it is perhaps better analysed in narrower categories of spirit-possession, morality, cosmology, family religion, and so forth (Teiser 1995: 378). Yet there is no doubt that Chinese popular religion must be understood according to the religious aspects of the Chinese kinship system. Family religion is a social glue, with meaningful roles created for all family members in a dynamic hierarchy, including positions assigned for ancestors.

In a certain sense we may associate fengshui with religion in a stricter interpretation. It was shown in Chapter 1 how fengshui cosmology forms an ego-centred universe, by which the individual may order both social and physical or metaphysical forces. For the individual, this universe, which is centred on the home, may be inhabited by a number of beings, including household gods, spirits and ghosts. Thus fengshui may be seen to operate around a personal pantheon of significant beings, for which reason the individual may not perceive any profound division between fengshui and religion. As noted in the fieldwork chapters, native categories are vague in the spiritual field. In modern times we have noted even less of a distinction between fengshui and popular religion, as geomancers were seen to take over certain functions of other religious practitioners, for instance spirit mediums. The position of ancestors is dubious in fengshui, however, and does not relate to ancestor worship or filial piety as such. In Maurice Freedman's terms, fengshui is complementary to ancestor worship, being in itself an amoral system of interpretation and action.

Apart from these general problems of distinction we are faced with the Chinese concept of religion as such – or rather the Chinese conception of religion, which we have shown in the preceding chapters to be heavily influenced by 'pragmatism', and far removed from questions of belief as derived from a monotheist context.

We commonly assert that belief in superhuman beings constitutes the core variable in religion, which accordingly is associated with worship of gods, spirits and deities, including ancestors. Yet some scholars feel that even this is a biased view, generating unnecessary distinctions between personalized subjects and impersonal objects of veneration and worship. Fengshui is really a case in point as it maintains no distinction between spiritual and mundane affairs or between personal and impersonal forces to be reckoned with. Furthermore, fengshui is considerably more activist oriented than we usually expect from a religious creed. We have interpreted fengshui *here* as a means of native reflection, a mode of thought, and a tradition of cosmological knowledge rather than a system of belief and worship, since both historical material and fieldwork suggested these to be the crucial characteristics.

The discussion as to whether fengshui belongs to popular religion or other areas of thought and reflection will continue. Someone may see the resemblance to earlier discussions of possible interpretation of Confucianism as morality, philosophy or religion. If we must conclude, it is not so much Confucianism and fengshui that evade our attempts at clear definitions – it is the phenomenon of Chinese religion as such that challenges our conceptions.

In this connection we may ask if there is any resemblance between the three popular cosmological or religious trends in China during the last twenty years, fengshui, *qigong* and *falungong*. They have obviously in common a great number of concepts and elements derived from classical Chinese cosmology, but each has creatively been adapted to modern society. The Chinese state has acted differently but intentionally in each case: fengshui has been largely ignored, presumably because of its mainly rural significance; *qigong* was accommodated in state-sponsored research centres and organizations; and *falungong* has been criminalized and subjected to purges, apparently because of its attraction to urban people as mass events, its foreign connections and elusive human rights messages. Yet there are important similarities. Nancy Chen has pointed out how *qigong* expresses a longing to transcend the prescribed mentality of the state and the cramped spaces of urban life; it gives individuals the opportunity to experience their minds and bodies in a time and space outside the ordinary present. Hidden transcripts of identity and meaning are forged and the self is disembodied from the state (Chen N. 1995: 358). Common for all three movements is that they seek to carve out independent domains of alternative experiences and moralities, sharing at least their antithesis in orthodoxy, the modern Chinese state ideology.

NOTES

1   According to de Groot (1897: 951) each of them 'is imbued with professional jealousy and cherishes the rather arrogant conviction that his own wisdom is always necessary for the correction of the opinions pronounced by his colleagues.

2   The spider may symbolize 'good luck descending from heaven', for instance the return of a son from far away (Eberhard 1988: 271).

3   For an interpretation of Luo Shu as a cosmological model, see Berglund 1990.

4   Corners are associated with 'secret arrows', which may send injurious *qi* (*sha*) to other houses.

5   This is obvious from both the fieldwork material and historical uses. For the latter, see, for instance, Huang Y. 1991.

7 The Construction of a Discourse: Fengshui as Environmental Ethics

Eastern wisdom brought to a Western audience: Chinese fengshui, a holistic folk tradition interpreting the influence of the 'cosmic breath' (*qi*) on humans, has established itself in the United States and now also in Europe as an instrument to harmonize humankind and the environment and ultimately to achieve a happy life. Environmentally conscious citizens build houses and mansions situated in lush greenery according to 'ancient' fengshui principles and offices are re-orientated to improve performance – while a growing number of fengshui priests, experts and manual authors generate handsome incomes for themselves. Numerous manuals are now available in airports and common bookstores, competing in their appeal to people wanting quick changes in their lives, introductions are available on the internet and Chinese professors arrange study tours to 'The Country Where Fengshui Began'. What is going on here? These are indeed complex matters, because the variant now practised in the West is a far cry from what it ever was in its country of origin. In the present era of global intellectual exchange, ideas and concepts travel freely between regions of the world to become adopted by systems of thought far removed from that of their origin. Ideologies with reference to nature in particular have inspired new thought across cultures and between East and West, although frequently seen to undergo a process of de-contextualization, fragmentation, and re-contextualization into a new social and political reality.

This chapter will investigate how fengshui was adopted as Oriental wisdom by subcultures in the West in the 1970s and credited with showing the way to a harmonious relation between man and environment, while, at the same time, it was banned as feudal superstition by the Chinese regime. Before this happened, however, it was exposed to the impulsive interpretations of a few but influential writers, who gradually infused it with new meaning, positively inspired by the cultural trends of their own society. This has not happened as a one-way process only. Within the past few years serious pollution and a rising environmental awareness in China have inspired young Chinese intellectuals to look for remedies in their own cultural tradition. Strikingly, the emergent reading of traditional Chinese cosmology includes the version of fengshui forged in the West. Thus fragments of Western counter-culture contribute to a neo-traditionalist movement among young intellectuals in China.

It is perfectly sound to explore the fengshui tradition's role in resource management and its capacity for environmental protection. Too hastily, however, much Western literature conveys the simplified message that fengshui is an ancient tradition that moralizes harmony between man and environment. Taken as a conclusive statement this is an absurdity, fabricated for an environmentally conscious Western audience. What fengshui means to the individual in its Western intellectual interpretation is not my concern, since any tradition is subject to change and reinterpretation. I shall emphasize, however, that if Chinese peasants destroy their environment but get rich in the process, they are most likely seen to have auspicious fengshui. And if mountain villagers make a fat living from selling endangered species of plants, birds and wildlife, they can look out from their south-facing doorways and praise the mountains for their generous fengshui. Yet it is also clear that, for instance, serious pollution from a factory chimney or contaminated groundwater affecting people's health may be interpreted as malicious fengshui. As a medium of expression, this holistic tradition may work both in favour of development at the expense of the environment and against environmental degradation. So far, however, fengshui as practised in the People's Republic has encouraged the former rather than prevented the latter.

We shall first look at the intellectual process that induced Western writers to rediscover fengshui as environmental ethics in the 1960s and 1970s as well as the sources they used. Subsequently there will be offered some reflections on the practical role of fengshui as environmental ethics in the fieldwork areas.

THE WAY BACK AND FORTH

The historical chapters described how fengshui in the years following its 'discovery' in the 1860s was classified as superstition, fortune-telling, folk religion, proto-science, and so forth. Comparison with 'scientific geomancy' was made by some, but rejected by others, and allusions to 'terrestrial magnetism' were possibly inspired by the popular beliefs in the healing properties of magnetic devices in the West, following the work of the magical doctor Mesmer in the 1700s. In the debate of the 1860s it was even compared to Western superstitions of everyday life. At this time no Westerner had ever made allusions to the possible protection of landscape, environment or natural objects in fengshui. The dismantling of a telegraph line by a Chinese local governor in Shanghai in 1865, allegedly because the line disturbed the fengshui of nearby tombs, and the continued Chinese refusal to allow the erection of telegraph lines had caused some concern in the foreign community. Behind the scenes, Chinese policy built on a firm determination to prevent foreign influence from spreading into the Chinese interior (Sturdevant 1976). The mass raids on railways, factories and telegraph lines that followed in the wake of technological innovation had clear parallels in Europe. While machine breaking in Europe was primarily guided by economic motives, similar action appeared to be of a nationalistic nature in China since the machines symbolized foreign influence (Chesneaux 1973: 50), and the resistance to them became a focus for various local interests.

It was such nationalistic sentiments, in their popular form frequently dressed up as concern for the fengshui situation of a local area with reference to the 'living *qi*' or the 'breath of the dragon', which were later noticed by environmentally conscious groups and individuals in the West. E.J. Eitel, writing his famous book on fengshui during this intense historical period, opens with an account of all the impossibilities of modernization in China. According to Eitel, Chinese officials would make a polite bow and declare the erection of telegraph poles, construction of railways, opening of coal mines and so forth impossible on account of fengshui (Eitel [1873] 1984: 1). Being the first on the subject and containing these references to the Chinese opposition to industrialization, Eitel's book was also among the central sources on Chinese geomancy to be studied later by the environmentally conscious in the West, although they generally ignored his conclusions.

During the following decades, fengshui was treated in Western sources in accordance with the prevailing preoccupations as regards the overseas world. While it was the subject of curiosity in the 1860s, it became described as a major pest in the 1880s, although sound accounts of its philosophy and practice were also provided (Hubrig 1879). Around the turn of the century Isabella Bird merely terms it the 'mystery of mysteries' (Bird 1899: 96). In the early twentieth century, however, after the Boxer Uprising had died down and foreigners returned to the Chinese interior, a number of new writers delivered accounts of Chinese culture to Western readers. In addition to the works of sinologists, books by ordinary travellers and so-journers became more numerous and many were written with a poetic or romantic strain. It became increasingly common among these writers to express admiration for the beauty of the Chinese landscape, to describe fengshui pagodas and perhaps implicitly to link landscape properties to fengshui. The role of fengshui in architecture and the layout of cities, towns and villages was also intimated. Well into the new century, fengshui had become a standard topic for anyone wanting to boast a deep acquaintance with Chinese 'culture'.[1] A whole new set of keywords were introduced in the new century, including landscape, beauty, architecture, aesthetics and culture.

At this point Western sources on the topic had attributed merely aesthetic properties to fengshui. Nor did J.J.M. de Groot (1897) mention anything that might connect fengshui to an early Chinese environmentalist inclination. Taken together, Westerners' obser-vations from the pre-liberation period interpret fengshui as em-bedded in Chinese cosmology and religion without either explicitly or implicitly sustaining concern for the natural surroundings in their own right.

FENGSHUI REDISCOVERED

After World War II, a number of writers from various disciplines laid the foundation for a new reading of Chinese cosmology. An interesting figure in this respect is Joseph Needham, unfolding his tremendous amalgam of Marxism, Christianity and modern science in the progression of his monumental work, *Science and Civilization in China*. While himself a late example of how Westerners have read the Chinese sources through glasses tinted by their own personal con-victions, Needham nevertheless sought to raise the standing of Chi-nese science and civilization in the West. He paid limited attention to fengshui, but examined it sufficiently to conclude that it belonged to superstition (pseudo-science) rather than early Chinese science. However, a small passage that he wrote on the subject is widely quoted and has probably gained a significance far beyond its intention:

> In many ways 'feng shui' was an advantage to the Chinese people, as when, for example, it advised planting trees and bamboos as windbreaks, and emphasized the value of flowing water adjacent to a house site ... [A]ll through, it embodied I believe, a marked aesthetic component, which accounts for the great beauty of the siting of so many farms, houses and villages throughout China. (Needham J. 1962: 402)

We here sense a rising awareness of the environment and suggestions of fengshui being a regulating agent between man and nature. A few years later, in 1968, the emerging environmentalist reading of fengshui took a further step forward. Andrew March, a geographer, wrote the essay 'An Appreciation of Chinese Geomancy', in which he criticizes early sinologists such as de Groot, Hubrig, Dyer Ball and Eitel for their scorn and patronizing tone against the Chinese beliefs in fengshui. Several other contemporary writers take fengshui seriously – Needham, as already mentioned, in terms of its possible contribution to the evolution of science and Maurice Freedman (1969) from an anthropological perspective – but March opens a new era in the Western approach to fengshui by investigating it as 'a kind of integral experience', to which 'certain meanings' are given. He sees fengshui as dealing with 'landscapes' and 'sites' as manifestations of the natural world, while concerned with 'the psychic properties of the material world' (March 1968: 253, 256).

By focusing particularly on the issue of the interaction between psyche and landscape, March wrote entirely in accordance with specific Western preoccupations of the time, communicated in the keywords of psyche, holism, nature, cultural extroversion and alternative beliefs. There was a subcontextual message of holistic 'truths' to be found in the natural world and, accordingly, an implicit reverence for the landscape to be attributed to fengshui. In this interpretation the geomancer's art was to 'discover places' and 'ascertain their individual properties' in terms of their life breath (qi) (ibid.: 256). March even vented the hypothesis of certain 'meanings' being properties of the natural world, with reference to C. G. Jung.

Jung himself was not working with Chinese cosmology in its own right, but still found in it much inspiration since it somehow constituted 'the missing piece' in his grand puzzle. Jung obviously had a great impact on the generation of young who tried out new ways and sought intellectual alternatives up through the 1960s to 1980s. When he wrote the introduction to a new edition of the Richard Wilhelm translation of the *I Ching or Book of Changes* (*yijing*),[2] he confessed that in old age, 'the thoughts of the old masters are of greater value to me than the philosophical prejudices of the Western mind' (Jung 1968: xxxv). With the writings of Joseph Needham, Andrew March, C.G. Jung, Lynn White[3] and many others, Chinese cosmology gradually gained prominence. From previously being seen as a collection of absurdities it now re-emerged as a source of holistic truths with direct relevance for the individual in modern Western society.

There is no immediate link between the rising science of human ecology and the contemporary interest in Oriental philosophy, but several writers ventured to bring them together, having a foundation in one while using the other for reference. In the early 1970s some Berkeley anthropologists, evidently inspired by Terence Glacken, Wolfram Eberhard and other prominent professors of the time, provided studies that affirm the link. E. N. Anderson wrote an essay explicitly linking fengshui to ecology, arguing that fengshui design 'is a matter of sound ecological principles', restraining people from doing things that are 'ecologically unwise' and enabling the Chinese to 'survive and flourish and preserve their environment in spite of fantastic population densities' (Anderson 1973: 139–143). There was a subcontextual message, clearly spelled out towards the end, of modern civilization having failed. Another anthropologist, Armando da Silva, contends that the complex Chinese lore, including fengshui, 'is really an attempt to harmonize everything, astrology, astronomy, landforms, and the life-giving seeds planted by man, into a unified cosmic ecosystem' (da Silva 1972: 64).

Interestingly – although some would question its relevance – March, White and Anderson all wrote in an era when the Chinese environment was degrading faster than ever due to human intervention. A significant part of all Chinese forest reserves was depleted during the few years of experimentation with village furnaces, wild life was extinguished from both forest felling and hunting in a period of unprecedented hunger disasters, and in the search for easy political targets campaigns would even be directed towards rats and sparrows. Through the 1970s and 1980s, when heavy pollution became conspicuous in China, a number of writers in the West again began to praise the messages of Chinese natural philosophy.[4] The new concepts that were transplanted into fengshui on an experimental basis in the 1960s and early 1970s made it appeal to large sub-cultures as well as to the rising ecological science through the 1970s and 1980s.[5]

The environmental reading of fengshui further took shape with a number of popular and easily digestible works on the topic, all affirming the myth previously established by writers such as Lynn White of Eastern harmony with nature as contrasted to Western domination of nature. Chinese fengshui has now become 'environmental science': 'It is an attitude to life in the land that has enabled China to feed one of the densest populations in the world without doing great violence to the earth' (Skinner 1982: 1), '[F]engshui supports the idea of ecology and conservation. Its message is: Harmonize with, do not disrupt, nature' (Rossbach 1983: 9). Or expressed by book titles such as Derek Walter's, *The Fengshui Handbook: A Practical Guide to Chinese Geomancy and Environmental Harmony* (1991) and Evelyn Lip's *Fengshui: Environments of Power: A Study of Chinese Architecture* (1996).

The Western markets for alternative philosophies of life and life sciences were insatiable and the popular writers to a large extent just pleased their audience by confirming vague notions of existing alternatives. In the 1990s this market exploded, with several new titles on fengshui each year being available in English. The popular material even started a wave of applied fengshui, which since the early 1990s till the present has reached sensational proportions; the masters now practising in all major cities in the West have back-grounds as dubious as those of their contemporaries in China.

Also more recently, anthropologists working in the field of ecology have made their contributions, perhaps finding in fengshui confirmation of the human ability to address the environment successfully by a poetic approach. Political statements addressing issues of Western concern are typically of paramount importance to the view of fengshui. One example:

> China in eight thousand years of farming did little or no more damage to its farmland ecology than the United States has in two hundred years ... Compared to the almost total failure of environmental planning in the United States – with its superior scientific establishment and law enforcement capabilities – *feng-shui* was nothing short of miraculous. (Anderson 1980: 26)

Some common assumptions form the background for such naive and ahistorical statements: first, that the obvious environmental damage in China was done by monstrous Communism in recent times, not by the prevailing environmental attitude of the people, and second, that fengshui as an ideology is concerned with ecology (or as described by Anderson above a fusion of religion and ecology). Apparently the science of ecology inspires such eager criticism of the Western world that it neglects to see Oriental ideologies in a critical light; fengshui simply becomes folk wisdom born out of ecological experience, again in the words of E.N. Anderson, 'harnessing emotional involvement to motivate people to good land use and reasonably sound architectural principles' (ibid.: 27). By picking among classical Chinese sources while attacking Cartesian duality as a symbol of Western alienation from nature, also Stephen Field manipulates fengshui in the service of ecological advocacy, characterizing it as the longest-lived tradition for environmental planning in the world: 'The vision of integrated *qi* preserved the ecology of China for centuries, and a similar vision is needed in the West' (Field 2001: 196–197). Fengshui fills an imaginative space created by the now dominant ecology-culture and has emerged as 'a powerful and coherent intellectual system [which] guided people in understanding the landscapes of nature and in creating a built environment' (Walton 1998: 23–24).

FENGSHUI RECLAIMED

In recent years, a profound nativization of culture has begun in the PRC, perhaps as a reaction to the pursuit of foreign culture in the reform decades (*CF* vol. 2, 9: 6). China's economic success has certainly also boosted national self-assuredness and induced ordinary Chinese to look at 'tradition' with greater complacency, including those elements, such as Confucianism, that were earlier associated with economic backwardness. Recently, a number of celebrated home-produced films, television series and novels have also prepared the ground for a growing intellectual interest in indigenous cosmology, medicine, healing and so forth, with the art of *qigong* perhaps as the most celebrated example.

In Chapter 3 it was mentioned how a whole range of new books on fengshui appeared in the bookstalls in China after 1990. These books, perhaps in self-justification, have applied a modern 'scientific' terminology to fengshui as a 'learning', a sort of proto-science oriented towards people's selection and handling of the 'environment', a new term used by the young generation of scholars. Since around 1990 young Chinese intellectuals have also started dabbling with traditional cosmology in a new guise of modern science, seeing explicit links between fengshui and modern geography, human ecology, psychology and other sciences (Hong 1993: 1). The number of books addressing fengshui as well as other elements in Chinese traditional cosmology from this angle has increased steadily,[6] as has the entire book market on cosmology and the relationship between man and nature. In several of these works the opening chapters contain explicit references to environmentalism and ecology. Presumably this is expressive of a rising environmental awareness in China, although we can barely see the outline of the orientations emerging.

What is of particular significance in this context, however, is that the young Chinese writers find considerable inspiration in Western works on fengshui. These scholars find reason to complain, for instance, that although fengshui has accompanied Chinese architecture for more than two thousand years, 'now the West sets a fashion of studying and imitating it while in China it is almost neglected' (He X. 1990: 158). Specifically, it is the reading of fengshui that originated in the West in the 1960s and 1970s that appeals to Chinese scholars, since it tends to convey simple messages and absolute truths well in accordance with the intellectual climate prevailing under Communism in China. This brings us back to Joseph Needham, this curious cross-civilization mediator, and again despite his limited interest in the subject. Those few pages of his monumental work dealing with fengshui are in fact also quoted in countless Chinese works, used as a reference to hard science in order to justify a renewed interest in a field conventionally classified as superstition (Hong 1993: 408). Specifically cultivating this propensity is a compendium on fengshui published in China in 1992, which contains translations of the works of Joseph Needham and E.J. Eitel, together with new interpretations by Chinese scholars (Wang Q. 1992).

Another important figure serving as a intermediary between Western and East Asian intellectuals is Hong-key Yoon, a young Korean who came to Berkeley as a student of cultural geography in 1971. Under the influence of Wolfram Eberhard and Clarence Glacken,[7] who both showed a keen interest in fengshui, he wrote his dissertation on 'Geomantic Relations between Culture and Nature in Korea' (Yoon 1976). Originally serving as an account of Korean and Chinese geomancy for a Western readership, his work clearly reflects the point in time when it was written. By developing the assumption that fengshui is closely related to the natural environment, he defines the art as 'a unique and comprehensive system of conceptualizing the physical environment which regulates human ecology by influencing man to select auspicious environments and to build harmonious structures (i.e. graves, houses, and cities) on them' (Yoon 1976: 1). Yoon concludes as he begins and with statements like 'this naive but stable and harmonious culture–nature relationship has been ignored and overcome by so-called "modern civilization"' (ibid.: 231), he contributes forcefully to inflating the environmentalist reading of fengshui. Despite being produced by a Korean, Yoon's work has nevertheless become prominent among the 'Western' works on fengshui cited in the recent wave of Chinese works on the subject.[8] Thus regarded as an Eastern writer in the West and as a Western writer in China, Yoon has had a considerable impact not only in conveying ideas between East and West, but as much in adapting Chinese philosophy to a Western mindset and later bringing new inspiration to Chinese writers; his work is commonly cited along with those of Needham, Eberhard and Rossbach.

Thus, in China as in the West, fengshui has been infused with a range of new concepts relating to environmental ethics: nature, environment, system, harmonious relationship, managing the environment, and so forth. Another example is an article by Fan Wei, who despite a sceptic attitude concludes that 'fengshui no doubt has helped restrain Chinese villages from unwise ecological decisions, nurturing reasonably sound ecological practices and leading to 'planned' settlements far ahead of their time' (Fan 1990: 45). A further example is provided by Pan Haoyuan and Zhao Chunlan, who see in fengshui 'something compatible and compensative to modern technique', expressive of a unique culture with a traditional worship of nature and 'one way to preserve and ameliorate the living earth' (Pan and Zhao 1997: 34–35).

Of the new vocabulary adopted by environmentalists in the West, particularly those concepts that resemble Taoist and Neo-Confucian cosmology have appealed to their Chinese counterparts. When Western ecologists propagate concepts like 'living with nature' or when Western architects speak of 'designing with nature' (McHarg 1969), Chinese scholars will immediately point to the concepts of harmony and immanence in the holistic Chinese cosmology. An example from the Chinese architect Yu Kongjian:

> The ecological and environmental crisis awakens us to consider man
> and his environment as an integrate system ... From the concept of
> ecosystem (Tansley 1935) to that of ... the total human ecosystem
> (Egler 1970, Naveh and Lieberman 1984), one may find that the ways

> modern ecologists deal with the relationship of man and nature have been progressing increasingly closer towards what had been stated in the theory and practice of Feng-shui. (Yu 1992: 2)

Particularly during the 1980s, the prevalent international discourse on sustainable development as well as the Western ecologists' search for 'indigenous knowledge' in non-Western cultures have inspired the adoption of ecological concepts as well as a redefinition of indigenous cultural values among countless nations across the world. New images of indigenous ecological-mindedness are constructed, drawing their explanatory power and credibility from the international vocabulary and political attention to the subject. In the Chinese case, cooperation between Chinese and Western scholars along such lines has frequently resulted in a kind of unwitting conspiracy, where historical facts are distorted and fieldwork neglected in order to reach popular conclusions – for instance, when the Chinese peasant is attributed an innate ecological consciousness and Chinese agricultural history is reinterpreted accordingly:[9]

> In other countries, especially those of the West, they use a great amount of inorganic fertilizers ... This we must avoid in China: we must practice organic, or ecological agriculture. This is in accordance with traditional agricultural practices over many centuries. (Zhong 1989: 123)

Modern Western agriculture is here compared to Chinese historical practices – not the present ones, which would produce a discouraging picture. Similarly, when certain Western philosophers see Asian traditions as a 'conceptual resource' for environmental philosophy (as, for instance, Callicott and Ames 1989: xi), some Chinese scholars instantly seize the opportunity to elevate the position of Chinese philosophy. The before-mentioned Yu Kongjian, for instance, read the elusive qi of Chinese cosmology as the 'flow of the total human ecosystem', whereafter he asks, 'can qi bring enlightenment to modern human ecology?' (Yu 1992: 3, 8).

The renewed Chinese intellectual attention to fengshui has emerged simultaneously with the adoption of the ecological vocabulary.[10] Although the renewed interest in indigenous cosmology in general and the reinterpretation of its fundamental tenets in particular reflect processes that have barely started, they will presumably merge with other significant currents of intellectual and political change in China. It was in fact the Chinese party-state that already in the late 1980s gave Confucianism its blessing as a means of fighting moral disintegration in contemporary society. The vast number of books on indigenous cosmology that have been published by the public printing houses in recent years may therefore enjoy a certain official patronage, or at least be seen as a lesser evil than the continued influx of foreign culture, in the push for moral and intellectual rearmament.

A GLOBAL DIALOGUE?

Above I have outlined how traces of fengshui ideology have inspired new thought as a two-way process between East and West. To sort out and analyse such complexities we should, as a critical first stage, distinguish between the specific historical process in China, during which fengshui may gradually have taken on new meanings, and the way fengshui has been exposed to readers in the West, since these have followed their own independent sequences, closely tied to the workings of their respective intellectual, cultural and political milieus. Only then does it become possible to investigate how description and practice have come to interact and finally address the crucial questions of why and how, at a certain point in time, these separate sequences of fengshui meanings have merged or been linked together.

In China, a long-standing state policy aimed at restraining the societal position of geomancers and their trade was temporarily reversed when an imperial edict in 1871 legalized fengshui when specifically turned against foreigners. Although sources are scarce, we may assume that this move coincided with anti-foreign and nationalistic sentiments of the time, so that the fengshui practised in areas with intensified cultural contact in the late nineteenth century is likely to have acquired a somewhat different character than was the case earlier in that century: while it previously contained a metaphoric idiom that mediated social competition between individuals and local areas, it became infused with the nationalistic discourse to be used as a weapon in the Chinese struggle against the Western colonial powers. Since fengshui was already a convenient means of expression in terms of social resentment, challenge and grudge, redirecting it from the inner to the outer enemy was merely a question of elevating accusations to a higher plane. We have many examples of changes in cosmologically significant rituals taking place elsewhere in colonial areas in the face of Western intrusion, although some cases involve specifically anti-foreign expressions while others may show that a new order was accommodated fairly smoothly. A well-described instance of ritual change was the decentralization and gradual disappearance in the eighteenth and nineteenth centuries of the *rampokan,* the ritual tiger fights in Java aimed at the metaphoric purification of the political centre (Wessing 1992). Other examples were the British attempts to curb *sati,* hook swinging, *suttee* and other ceremonies involving self-mutilation, which from time to time reappeared in colonial India, by means of establishing their lack of authenticity and proper sanction in Hindu religion, and thereby favouring classical tradition and Brahmanic values at the expense of folk tradition.[11]

Conventional history writing has paid very limited attention to these changing ritual practices in response to changes in the local experience. Thus, when traditional power structures collapse and entire experienced worlds fall into disarray, the outcome is usually mirrored only in the domain of the state. In China, foreign intervention and cultural exchange in general terms advanced the collapse of the Qing empire and with it the Chinese traditionalist politico-intellectual universe. But the local traditions, usually drawing more on popular cosmology than on Confucian learning, responded to the new order at their own pace, presumably meeting Chinese and foreign power with equal scepticism. Both the new Republic of 1911 and the Communist state after 1949 fought fengshui beliefs, through an entire century unanimously classified as superstition. Particularly the latter regime has adopted a harsh persecution of practitioners during several campaigns. As a consequence, during most of the twentieth century the fengshui tradition was under pressure, effecting it to be either played out in a narrowly local and usually quite private context, mainly in rural areas, or perhaps in some instances to be turned against the Communist state. In any case, in modern times its application has had no resonance with the rising ecological connotation that it simultaneously gained in the West.

It has been shown how a sequence of Western interpretations of Chinese fengshui occurred during a historical period of intensified cultural contact. It has also been demonstrated how a new and radical reading of fengshui originated in the West in the post-war period, intimately connected to a critique of Western civilization and a zealous exploration of intellectual alternatives in the outside world. Apparently, however, the alternative ideologies that were introduced as Oriental, time-honoured wisdom were deprived of both their historical and cultural contexts, and the critical questions of their applicability and possible implications in the present Chinese society were purposely avoided. By means of scattered references, selected accounts and avoidance or even defiance of authoritative sources,

Chinese fengshui was re-contextualized to fit the specific needs of an emerging subculture in the West. It became a mere reflection of Western intellectual processes. Even though China was mostly inaccessible, accounts of fengshui practices in modern society were available. The official Chinese news agency would gladly have contributed stories of, for instance, how a mad geomancer in a remote mountain village made the entire village population jump down a cliff into a creek, killing scores of people, to avoid a natural catastrophe or how local peasants on account of fengshui would bury their corpses in the field instead of cremating them and thereby occupied scarce land.

This new reading of Chinese cosmology has nevertheless served as an inspiration for a new generation of intellectuals in China. For many, the Western writings on the subject have provided the legitimization to take fengshui seriously – and to oppose state policy on alleged scientific grounds. In writing about their own culture, Chinese intellectuals have long neglected those appearances that were in discord with the learned high-Chinese ideals, for instance when classified as superstition or popular religion. The Chinese modern intellectual treatment of fengshui came very late, since representatives of the old elite – especially those who wrote for a Western audience – never took it seriously and even appeared to be ashamed of its popular support. To them, it embodied backwardness.

With the waning of Communism, the reformulation of the Chinese national identity has been seen to give rise to nationalism. Because of the tremendous inertia of the political system, however, this manifests itself along different lines in various spheres of public life, although some basic tenets may be commonly shared. Owing to the ideological climate in China, Westernization is usually frowned at while modernization in a neutral sense is promoted. There are strong cultural codes at work, demanding writers to adopt the leading notion that the Chinese civilization is unique. Expressions of patriotism are essential in any aspect of public discourse in China, also when only nominal, since there seems to be no middle ground between patriotism and treason.[12] After a long period of de facto Westernization many Chinese intellectuals have found it imperative to search for Chinese roots and Chinese contributions to modern philosophy and science; an undercurrent of inter-racial competition can be sensed in much modern Chinese literature. In the philosophy of fengshui young Chinese intellectuals find indigenous ecology, even 'expressive of a deep layer of the Chinese mind in the form of a biologically inherited environmental consciousness' (Yu 1990: 87–90). Periodic Western self-criticism in regard to materialism, modernism, imperialism and so forth is readily absorbed in the Chinese nationalist discourse to be used as proof of their own cultural superiority or of historical wrongs inflicted upon China by the West.

Again we may look to similar experiences from other countries. A close parallel to the attempts of raising the position of Chinese cosmology is found in the Japanese revivalist treatment of *fudo* (a holistic term referring to aspects of both natural and cultural environments). In Japan, this process has been closely tied to the construction of a new national identity and also evidently inspired by an array of Western philosophers from Hippocrates to Heidegger (Befu 1997). In Japan, however, the more unobstructed and continuous interaction with foreign academia has sustained the popularity of indigenous philosophy since Watsuji published his famous work on *fudo* in 1935.

There remains to be discussed the interaction between fengshui as (described) exotic cosmology and fengshui as a practised craft. Text and practice have always interacted in China, since intellectual production in the form of manuals and popularized philosophy has been the backbone of practised fengshui, thereby bridging elite and popular cosmologies. What we see now, however, is an exchange across a very different set of boundaries. The rapidly increasing flow of information and people in the modern world break down geographical boundaries and change the sense of distance; it may even transfigure class and social group distinctions. For instance, avant-garde intellectuals in China may now feel more closely affiliated to the American university campuses, where they studied for years, than to the rural hinterlands of China. Other factors play important roles in the new exchange: most prominent are the increasing language abilities in China and the intermediary role of Chinese communities in the West.

In anthropology there has been a rising awareness of the interaction between exoticized descriptions of local groups and their own identity formation. Prominent examples are Edward Bruner's depiction of a common 'narrative' shared between ethnographers and the American Indians, a sort of unwitting conspiracy that shapes both the description and the self-image of the groups in question (Bruner 1986), and Allan Hanson's account of the modern construction of Maori identity on the basis of an idealized interpretation of their history by foreign actors (Hanson 1989). Another very prominent example is that of indigenous peoples in general terms being described as custodians of nature, which has slowly worked its way into both local identities and the terminology of international organizations. Undoubtedly, similar processes are at work in the modern resurgence of traditional cosmology in China, although the actors are more numerous and the story has more facets. In particular, the interaction between practice and representation has been complicated by the fact that fengshui is no longer just practised in China and interpreted in the West. As a spin-off from the intellectual debate among avant-garde theorists, subgroups have started applying the system to a modern Western setting. What is perhaps most striking is the fact that Western intellectuals have such a profound impact on other peoples' cosmologies, be it small indigenous groups or entire civilizations like the Chinese.

There remains to be considered whether the new correspondence we see between fengshui in China and the West is a lasting phenomenon. Up until now, despite growing academic exchange, very different processes have been at work as to how the foreign material was adopted in China and the West. Whereas the Western academics in question allegedly found alternatives in foreign philosophies, their Chinese counterparts were informed by convention to find remedies for societal ills in Chinese history. However, one conclusion to be drawn from the present material is that such difference may only be apparent and nominal.

Fengshui as understood in China and the West had their separate sequences. It is only recently that these sequences were reconnected when a new radical interpretation in the West had a direct influence on the revitalization of traditional cosmology in China. Yet it is only when the ideological conditions for intellectual production are comparable that these sequences of changing interpretations in China and the West will join in a more durable relationship. Until then, intellectual trendsetters and New Age philosophers in the West will keep translating and re-contextualizing exotic traditions of thought while at the same time inadvertently challenging cultural identities in their places of origin.

Created in China as a conglomerate of diverse philosophical and popular religious ideas with only vague reference to nature in the strict sense, then at a point in history having been adopted and infused with environmentalist ideas in the West, and finally being reimported into China in an avant-garde guise, fengshui adequately illustrates the complexities of the East–West environmental debate.

246

NATURE AND ENVIRONMENT IN CHINA

Any social scientist who has been working at length in China knows that the written tradition and the everyday life of the Chinese are often worlds apart. The Chinese social ethos is able to embrace considerable tension between these disparate realities. When we investigate the Chinese relationship to nature (*ziran*), these problems are even amplified. The Chinese have an extensive literary tradition venerating nature, but we have few means of investigating how this was applied in practice; John B. Cobb (1972) and other, later writers have stressed that the Chinese natural philosophy has not prevented deforestation and destruction of the environment through history. We should keep in mind that Chinese natural philosophy is a domain of thought in which the social metaphor is a constant subject or even the object for creation of meaning with an inherent discrepancy between word and practice, with natural philosophy being a moralizing agency stressing ideal culture rather than observed reality. Tension is obvious when, for instance, Confucianism maintained that 'wealth and honour are from heaven', while common ancestor beliefs and geomantic practices indicated how men may alter heaven's doom.

The Chinese are known for anthropocentrism in their philosophy and sociocentrism in basic orientations – meaning that by far the greater part of the 'world that matters' is made up of humans and human society – which still holds true. Yet I will not argue that the Chinese perception of what belongs to 'nature' is totally different from our own. Today we may also speak in Chinese of the 'natural world' (*ziranjie*), 'natural environment' (*ziran huanjing*), 'nature preserve' (*ziran baohuqu*), 'natural resources' (*ziran ziyuan*), 'natural behaviour' (*ziran xingwei*), and even 'naturalism' (*ziran zhuyi*). The term signifying nature, *ziran*, indicates spontaneity, however, while the natural sciences (*bowu*) refer to the study of the 'abundant matter'. Also nature in a pure, material sense – like untouched ground and landscape, wild animals and life hidden in the depths of the ocean – is understood and signified in terms comparable with those in the West. However, the closer we get to the zone where nature and culture combine, the sharper the differences in a cross-cultural perspective.

China has also a long tradition of writing symbols into nature, for instance in landscape painting. A rich 'vocabulary' of symbols, of which many apparently had erotic content (Eberhard 1988: 10–12), was depicted in art by means of interpreting natural forms, forces and

247

constellations. A great number of word collocations such as mountain–water (*shan-shui*), mountain–spirit (*shan-jing*) and the Emperor's court–wilderness (*chao-ye*), which all build on extensions of the yinyang pair, constitute a huge and rather poorly investigated semantic field. Also in fengshui the sexual connotations of yinyang often become explicit when the feeling of liveliness and diversity in the landscape is represented as the coupling of male and female elements (March 1968: 258).

Yet natural symbolism has no immediate impact on the concrete activities of resource management and environmental practices in general. Concerning the general role of environmental care in Chinese history, the historian Peter C. Perdue deducts:

> As a historian of China, however, I must reluctantly conclude that the force of material gain has been persistent, pervasive and pernicious in its effect on the Chinese environment for many centuries. Chinese peasants have long sought to improve their livelihoods by clearing the next wetland, cutting down the neighbouring forest for fuel and arable fields, or tearing up the grasslands for wheat and millet. Noble cultural ideals of Taoism or fengshui have had little restraining effect, especially since the population boom of the eighteenth century. (Perdue 1994: 6)

Amazingly, a very similar view has been purported by some of China's most respected ecologists. Li Wenhua and Zhao Xianying, for instance, note that Chinese history saw the unheeded exploitation of natural resources take a heavy toll as China was very late in forming a conservation strategy (1989: i–ii, 1–2). Early Western sources of fengshui reveal that protection of the 'environment' (a term first really developed in the republican period) was neither a concern to Western onlookers nor to Chinese users. Nature was most commonly denoted as the resource base that should be brought under control in the service of mankind.

FIELDWORK EXPERIENCES CONCERNING FENGSHUI AND THE ENVIRONMENT

When doing fieldwork in rural China one is immediately struck by the degree to which the Chinese state has penetrated all local affairs, though it is not necessarily able to exercise control at all times. The state as an institution, represented by local government, still plays a vital role in agriculture by regulating production, supervising markets and providing a number of inputs such as energy, chemical fertilizers and pesticides. The same apparently goes for the environment. Since China is an ancient hydraulic society, a number of crucial functions in agriculture were always communal tasks and continue to be so, with either local or higher level governments in charge. The decades of experimentation with Communism and continued public land ownership may have moved responsibility for support functions further away from the individual. This includes management of those factors we usually associate with the 'environment' in agriculture: inputs of chemicals, emissions of toxicants, protection of waterways, monitoring drinking water and care for the wild flora and fauna. Vaclav Smil quotes a Chinese expert as saying that the peasants' management style is that of a plunderer, without enthusiasm in long-term planning. Evidently government policy must also take its share of the blame (Smil 1993: 161). So today the primary caretaker of the environment is the state. As a consequence, only state institutions, usually with very weak local foundations, have precise knowledge of the true state of affairs concerning pollutants in air, soil and water. Mark Elvin has presented the hypothesis that in a historical sense, the central driving force of environmental degradation in China, where growth is so often pushed beyond the limits for sustainability, has been the intensified exploitation of nature linked to the parallel drive to acquire the means of political, economic and military power (Elvin 1999: 739). Totalitarian power threatens the environment as much as it threatens humans.

One early component of the fieldwork concerned rural people's views of their natural environment, including their possible linking of fengshui to their own environmental practices or to the overall state of the natural environment, be it implicit or explicit. In the Chinese interior many rural communities have virtually done away with all uncertainty factors in agriculture to the extent that the visible organic habitat consists entirely of items that are deliberately grown and raised for the sake of humans; in this scheme even birds have become rare and insects are mostly under control. This was not quite the case in the fieldwork areas, where it did make sense to ask questions about a natural environment outside the intensively cultivated farmland. Both fieldwork areas included hilly stretches, being unsuitable for intensive agriculture and instead giving the inhabitants access to other resources.

But even in the hills nothing is left untouched if it has just the slightest use-value. The green cover of grasses and herbs between the rocks is cut for hay at regular intervals and occasional small trees are likewise cut for firewood or building materials when grown to a proper size. Practically all wildlife that previously inhabited the hills is gone, including snakes and reptiles, having all served as a supplement to the overtly monotonous rural kitchen. Any creature that may venture a comeback will be sure to suffer the same fate again. Only in the Jiangsu fieldwork area, which bordered on forest farms owned by the Forestry University in Nanjing and included some stretches of forest surrounding the Longchang Buddhist temple (but presumably managed by the army), could the peasants still make occasional hunting expeditions and, if lucky, bring back a rabbit. Otherwise, wildlife simply does not exist after an entire century of civil war, recurring periods of starvation following disastrous political campaigns and, on top of all this, inadequate interest in preserving whatever species that may be left. Thus, to make it absolutely clear, fengshui does not entail making the earth a suitable living space for other creatures than humans and their domesticated animals.

Some rural areas near Yaan in southwest Sichuan were included in the early fieldwork. These areas had actually been surrounded by dense forest as late as the 1950s. The older generation would still recall a time when hunting for deer, fox, wolf and even tiger was good in the forest, while at times the beasts would bite back: hungry tigers were known to scramble around villages, preying upon children or feeble elderly persons if possible. But all wildlife succumbed together with the forest during the experimentation with village furnaces during the Great Leap Forward. It took but a year and a half of centrally guided mass campaigning to wipe out both the forest and its animal inhabitants.

Now one does not expect to see tigers or other large game in heavily populated areas anywhere in the world, but the Chinese countryside nevertheless distinguishes itself from that of many other countries. When standing on a hilltop in either of the fieldwork areas I always wondered why I felt something was missing. The lush green vegetation with clusters of trees and bamboos around farmhouses was indeed a pretty sight for the eye, particularly in Sichuan, but the visual sensation lacked a corresponding auditory sensation: the landscape was silent. In the whole panorama one could oversee there would be fewer birds than in my average-sized suburban garden at home. On inquiry, locals would confirm that maybe there had once been more birds, but that was a very long time ago. However, inquiry substantiated that the introduction of pesticides along with the market economy could have been the reason for a further decline in the bird population since they occurred simultaneously. And what pesticides, including widespread use of DDT, did not destroy would be finished off by humans. In one of the Sichuanese villages, people related that where birds could be found, young men from the city would come out and shoot them for fun. So the birds were gone, too, and nobody seemed to miss them much. 'If you want a bird that sings, you can buy one in a cage', seemed to be a routine commentary. A few households in either fieldwork area had small singing birds in tiny cages suspended from the roof outside the door or in the courtyard. As elsewhere, children are seen to play with occasional grasshoppers, but they are hard to come by.

To the failure of Chinese medicine to come to grips with common diseases like diarrhoea, gallstone, hepatitis, and liver cancer (as outlined in Chapter 6) must be added the failure of linking the use of pesticides to public health. DDVP (*didiwei*) and DDT are frequently sprayed directly on vegetables before cooking. In the two fieldwork areas, the use of pesticides had started from five to twelve years prior to fieldwork depending on local conditions, crops, and initiation of local government programmes. Although applied for fairly short periods, the effect on the environment had everywhere been dramatic. Bees and butterflies, supposed to be good indicators of the state of the environment, have become very rare in some areas and totally extinct in others. Birds, which were already scarce after hunting campaigns in the 1960s, are particularly sensitive to an environment overloaded with pesticides. As a result, birds are only occasionally seen in the most heavily affected areas and flocks of birds are not seen anywhere. When interviewing a woman whom we met while spraying the vines in her orchard, the conversation came to insects. She informed us about a dramatic decline in their presence: 'All the butterflies and most of the insects disappeared when we started using pesticides; that was in the late 1980s. But they were such a nuisance anyway.' Indeed, some enormous Sichuanese species of wasps and biting flies are not only terrifying sights but some are even highly dangerous. Yet, with these disappeared also a wealth of beautiful butterflies.

Of course we can only presume that the use of pesticides is excessive since there is no farm-level monitoring of pesticide application whatsoever. Those technicians of the agricultural extension service who possess the proper training will hardly ever descend to visiting the villages; they tend to spend most of their time in the cities, frequently even departing with the station's only means of transport. Those 'village technicians' who are trained and stationed locally will neither have the skills nor the equipment to carry out tests. Thus, judging the quality of soil and water is generally left to the peasants.

The township government receives centrally devised radio programmes which it broadcasts locally through the propaganda system that includes loudspeakers in all hamlets. Such broadcasts include information on the correct application of chemical fertilizers and pesticides. The peasants, however, only shrug their shoulders and say 'we never listen'. After years and years of political campaigning, trying to reach the peasants has backfired. People automatically shut off their minds when the loudspeakers roar. Thus, in terms of environmental protection the propaganda system has had dangerously adverse effects. When loudspeakers may start as early as six o'clock in the morning and go on and on for twelve hours, not using local dialects or even Sichuanese but Beijing dialect, most people simply refuse to listen.

So much for the fauna – or perhaps one should say the missing fauna. On the other hand, at least in the classical literature on fengshui, vegetation plays an important part. For centuries, and certainly since Chinese landscape painting came into being, the presence of vegetation in the form of trees, bamboos, bushes and groves is clearly indicative of the auspicious fengshui qualities of a landscape. So to what extent has this view survived today?

Trees around houses are still associated with good fengshui, but the material circumstances of life forbid most peasants to plant other than a few trees or a cluster of bamboos. Particularly the old villages with small houses crammed together are often clad in lush greenery that provides both shelter and coolness in the hot summer season. However, fengshui is not seen to inspire more vegetation than quite practical considerations will any way produce.

For graves and tombs similar deliberations apply. Anything that obstructs the prospect in front of a grave is considered a bad influence and whenever possible removed or levelled out. Trees growing behind or along the flanks of graves are on the other hand considered beneficial, pertaining to the ideal layout of a grave in an 'armchair' position. As a consequence, fengshui theory will advise the planting of trees in some positions and warn against them in others. Therefore, again in theory, if a grave is placed in solitude on a hillside it will contribute to the preservation of trees and greenery at least in some positions. In real life, however, favourable burial grounds are scarce and almost any serviceable hillside will be sprinkled with graves, old and new higgledy-piggledy. To obtain the best fengshui people scatter their graves (Freedman 1979: 197), and since the trees which are beneficial to the grave in front will be intolerable to the grave behind, the compromise is usually no large trees at all, but only shrubs and bushes. In some regions, for instance in Fujian, vegetation is commonly removed in front of graves, frequently turning hillsides into dreary wastes (noted in de Groot 1901: 945).

In very general terms few people show concern for such environmental factors as outlined above. For common peasants, a care for the natural environment outside those factors on which humans immediately depend is a predominantly intellectual pursuit – and why should Chinese peasants be different from peasants and farmers elsewhere in these matters? Moreover, the vast number of inhabitants in the villages would not recognize any direct connection between the disappearance of bees, butterflies and birds and increasing local health hazards. Neither did anyone suspect that health problems could arise from polluted drinking water or contaminated foodstuffs, let alone interpret such issues in fengshui terminology. Still there are no rules without exceptions. Just a few individuals in the villages showed a genuine interest in the natural environment outside the cultivated domain. One was an elderly barefoot doctor, who deplored the disappearance of butterflies which he once had collected, and another was a fengshui specialist, who had developed a 'professional' interest in vegetation around houses. Otherwise, the common view of the natural surroundings is unaffected by the rising environmental concern in the higher echelons of Chinese society. There is most certainly an outward movement of individuals leaving agriculture, but no influx of educated individuals, who could serve as cultural and political mediators between the powerful and the subservient.

NOTES

1 A few examples are Ball 1893; Wiegers 1913; Headland 1914; Moule 1914; Myron 1915; Willoughby-Meade 1928; and Crow 1933.

2 Jung had previously written an introduction to Wilhelm's translation of *The Secret of the Golden Flower*.

3 Lynn White stressed the influence of Chinese inventions and discoveries on the pre-Renaissance world in his celebrated work *Medieval Technology and Social Change*.

4 The question of the consistency between ideology and practice seemed of little relevance through this period: see Bruun and Kalland 1995.

5 A number of works on ecology mention Chinese cosmology, for instance Forman and Godron 1986.

6 For a few common books, see Chapter 3.

7 Wolfram Eberhard was a folklorist while Clarence Glacken was working with comparative philosophy and ideas relating to nature and culture.

8   Referred to by the Chinese name Yin Hongji in, for instance, Wang Y. 1991: 4.

9   Some examples are Wen and Pimentel 1986; Ruddle and Zhong 1988.

10   For a critical analysis of the Chinese eco-wave, see He B. 1991.

11   In the case of 'hook swinging', see, for instance, Dirks 1997.

12   The late Chinese philosopher Feng Yulan, for instance, was denounced for insisting that Chinese civilization was not unique but subject to common evolutionary development (Fung 1960).

8

Conclusion

A number of themes have guided the creation of this book, spanning both empirical expositions of fengshui in China and arguments of a more conjectural nature concerning the coexistence of diverse traditions in any given society. Let me first recapitulate some of the historical and empirical material before setting off to condense the general argument and finally attempt to answer the principal questions formulated along the way: first, why geomancy retained such an important role in China while it faded elsewhere and secondly, why grave divination remained so controversial to Chinese state power while house divination was viewed with greater complacency. Apart from the generic relevance of these questions it is my hope that pondering them will also serve to put the present fengshui fashion in the Western world into an appropriate perspective.

The overall implications of the fengshui mode of thought have been subject to substantial change during the period covered in this work. That fengshui is a living tradition with an inborn capacity to survive changing societal circumstances is obvious from its countless historical and geographical modifications. Yet, to come to terms with its seemingly haphazard manifestations and gushes of publicity we should search for possible patterns of change in response to other significant factors and events. Apart from obvious material and technological circumstances that inevitably will have a bearing on the rural existence, I believe that the fundamental driving forces accounting for the continuation of the fengshui tradition during the period studied are found in its complex relationship with the dominant tradition – that of the authoritarian Chinese state.

The changing attitude of Chinese state power to fengshui is itself remarkable and bears witness to a proceeding 'authoritarian rationalism' from Confucian roots. From scepticism towards popular fengshui as an unorthodox recasting of classical divination, Chinese state power has steadily moved towards increasing coherence and growing intolerance in the politico-religious field. Still in the imperial era, the Chinese government in 1871 recommended the legalization of fengshui when turned against foreigners, while at the same time orthodox divination was authorized and used by the imperial government. With the modernization movement from the 1890s onwards a number of new orientations and conceptions were introduced into Chinese state craft, including futuristic thought, social change, secularization and international competition. These were further developed in the May Fourth movement, now including explicit emphasis on modern science, democracy, and social management. Equally significant were the manifestation of a new urban elite and a rising discrepancy between rural and urban lifestyles, outlooks and expectations for life. In this process, during which democratic forces quickly lost out, the rural 'superstitions' were progressively criminalized by government and despised by the urban elite as an intrinsic sign of backwardness.

Attacks on rural superstition and popular cosmology as such were taken to new heights when the Communists consolidated their power, with parallel attacks on the Chinese family organization. As we approach the present era it becomes easier to detect changes in the fengshui tradition as a response to these double assaults on family and religion, primarily because field observation has become possible. What did the Communist epoch mean for fengshui related beliefs and practices – did the entire tradition, in concurrence with its plasticity and capacity for adopting new issues, develop a new orientation? It seems beyond doubt that the increasing antagonism between state power and popular cosmology also affected that fengshui acquired the role of an anti-authoritarian medium of expression. It stood out as an amoral scheme of interpretation as opposed to public and collective morality. I have consistently rejected that fengshui compare to a system, for which reason we should not ascribe to it any systematic form of resistance, apart from what arises out of everyday experience and private considerations for material, social and psychological survival, or as couched in fengshui terminology, for prosperity, happiness, longevity and pro-liferation.

To a much higher extent than earlier, fengshui in the Communist era began to address disease and mental disturbances. First of all, when traditional medical specialists, including Taoist priests and a host of other diviners were extinguished, people still needed a local practitioner who would speak their language and explain disease within a framework of holistic thought, involving ancestors, ghosts and spirits. Moreover, after the economic reforms the medical system's discrepancy between word and practice enlarged as medical staff could no longer be retained in rural areas by means of public assignments. Medicine became another manifestation of the rural-urban divide.

Chinese geomancy, in all its conceptual and operational broad-ness, more than anything else denotes an archetypical mode of thought and explanation, arising spontaneously out of the human intellect as a response to the inescapable pondering of the innate human condition. It considers fate and chance events and explores possible correlations in the combined psycho-social-material world. It is highly activist in outlook and suggests remedies for all ills and imbalances. It may even be seen to serve as a matrix for rewriting and reconstructing reality. Variations on the same theme may be found in India, in large parts of Southeast Asia, in the old Confucian world including China, Korea, Vietnam and Japan, as well as in medieval times in Europe, where its is now returning in the curious version of Chinese fengshui reworked in the USA. It is something we share in one form or another as a countermeasure to political, intellectual or religious attempts at bringing the world to 'one', the relentless economic compulsions and political forces attempting to monopolize rationality and restrict our freedom of reasoning. To recapitulate the quotation opening the introduction, 'we too have our fungshuis, even though we attend to them with less cost of our purses'. But one could say that with rising fengshui fever in the Euro-American world, even this difference diminishes. And yet, if all places have their independent fengshuis contradicting mainstream reasoning this is also where the similarity ends. For each culture and, as we have seen in the case of Chinese fengshui, each era is seen to develop its own constituency of positioned actors and an assortment of keywords denoting the chief political and socio-economic issues of that particular period. To argue that the same scope of thought is covered by the array of traditions at play in any given society, that they together constitute a common, 'complete' set of cognitive possibilities, is too obviously contradicting our sense of cultural difference.

So how can we explain the coexistence of so strikingly parallel traditions of thought across large regions of the world, without reverting to abstruse notions of developing world systems and rising globalization? I think we can escape this dilemma by identifying a combination of static and dynamic constituents in any cultural formation under focus. The static component consists of a number of archetypical positions in the joint politico-religious field where ideological antagonisms are played out – frequently recognizable within an ecumenical cleavage between individual salvation and public morality, between state orthodoxy and popular cosmology, between world religions and anthropocentric outlooks, between monotheism and religious pragmatism, and between communal worship and self-deification. This is not to say that such dualism is the true essence of religious discord and that individual and community are the genuinely basic entities; indeed, many religions attempt to synthesize such antagonistic positions in their appeal to power and the public. The dynamic component, on the other hand, consists of a process of displacement over time, whereby a tradition retains much of its original, relative position, but its defenders are compelled to adopt new issues and formulate new paroles to meet new material circumstances of life and confront new political issues, for instance threats from authority. In this scheme of interdependent modes of thought and justification for action there is ample room for rising or declining tensions. We see some reconciliation of oppositions or the radicalization of ideology, for instance with the sudden, mysterious restoration of an archetypical mode of thought that has been quelled or overshadowed for some time. Thus in the cross-cultural comparison we can identify likeness and affinity across all imaginable borders, but not similarity. For these reasons it is also clear that Chinese fengshui will never retain its original characteristics when transposed into either a Western setting or a Chinese avantgarde city culture.

But it is also very obvious that the issue of dominant and subordinate traditions is a complex one, as there is no domination without the dominated, no pressure without counter-pressure, no authoritarian rule without a constant need of repression. Mind control and censorship is only needed in the face of continued resistance, that is, a consistent threat of insurrection that will invert the dominant and the subordinated paradigms.

CONCLUSION

After the submission to a 'market oriented socialism' in China, state and public expression are becoming more aligned in some localities, mostly the better-off, while neighbouring villages may have been left unaffected. Chinese fengshui has grown to prominence in a high-tension, low-trust environment and its continued vitality as an all-embracing perspective on the man–cosmos–community relation bears witness to the immanent disability of Chinese state power to create trust and reconciliation, particularly between state power and those segments of the peasant population, for whom economic development has either passed by or has stalled. The Chinese rural villages are sadly neglected as the new wealth of the nation is exclusively allocated into industrial development and urban planning, development, infrastructure and environment. The dismal contrast between the elite's obsession with emblems of wealth and power and the rural population's scramble for a simple existence unites Chinese history across several epochs. At least for the period covered in this study we have seen a neglect of the rural masses, who, except for brief intervals of Chinese history when new elites have consolidated their power, have been viewed as a resource for the 'nation' rather than a rightful population segment with legitimate demands for participation in nation-building. The differentiated access to resources, education, information, medical care, social justice and so forth wears on.

The combined historical-anthropological approach employed in this work has been an ambitious one, and some detail has been sacrificed in the process, but its purpose has been obvious. A purely anthropological approach would merely have produced a partial picture: fengshui as experienced in rural villages would possibly have stood out as a relic of the past, a sturdy remnant of pre-liberation society and a livelihood for a group of elderly practitioners, maintaining their art to be orthodox and authentic. The historical material has informed us where to look for change in practice and outlook, and it has induced us to reconsider the entire conception of religion and belief in China. A narrowly historical approach, on the other hand, would have missed the ethnographic detail, particularly concerning the interplay between individuals, positions and knowledge traditions. The simultaneousness of various modes of thought in a single locality would not have become clear and fengshui could easily and erroneously have been depicted as the local religion, the 'religion of the masses' – a religious system, likely to be heading for distinction.

It is my hope that others will investigate Chinese fengshui to fill in the holes left here or to approach it from different angles, for instance by means of Chinese historical sources, which have only been sporadically consulted here. In particular, local Chinese sources on the meticulous interplay between gentry interest and popular fengshui in the formative period from 1860 onwards would greatly enhance our understanding of the dynamics of popular cosmology and its interplay with major political issues. Similarly, our knowledge of fengshui practices during the period of heavy campaigning that continued into the Cultural Revolution is very scant, based on contemporary Chinese media reports, foreign analyses and local people interviewed. Altogether, the present account has attempted to make use of all sources that were within reach, but it can easily be accused of eurocentrism and a political bias against the ruling authorities in Beijing – if some researchers feel this way it is my sincere hope that they will strive to present new material to prove their point.

Finally, I shall seek to answer the two questions raised earlier: first, why fengshui remained prominent in China while it has tended to fade elsewhere and secondly, why particularly grave geomancy has remained so controversial to Chinese state power. In fact, the two questions are intimately linked, as fengshui entails cosmologically informed resistance to theocratic state power and the most distinctly religious element in fengshui is exactly grave divination. Thus we suggest the answer to both to be found in a quasi-religious rationale for Chinese state power, which is continued today despite pragmatism in the economic field. Any authoritarian, one-party state must assert the sacred foundation of its policy, maintain reverence for the deified fathers of the nation and insist on sacramental procedures of government – in order to justify its monopoly on both power and truth, as these inevitably are brought together. The difference between fengshui of the dead (*yin*) and of the living (*yang*) is obvious. Dwelling divination manipulates inherent forces – grave divination transcends this-worldly affairs and reaches out to the world beyond. It forecasts the fate of men as well as of society and attempts to manipulate both history and the future. These are among the most sacred pillars of Chinese state power, which since time immemorial has monopolized both historiography and prophecy on the fate of the nation and its leaders. Without the sincere secularization of state power the tension between state cult and popular ideology remains irreconcilable. We could reverse the argument by predicting that as long as China remains under authoritarian rule, popular cosmology will be held in contempt and from time to time be scapegoated by state power for obstructing progress. Only pluralism in politics will eventually bestow equal ranking and legality of the coexisting traditions of knowledge in the Chinese countryside.

Fengshui sanctions egotism, markedly at odds with the most celebrated paroles of high-Chinese civilization, such as the common good, the wealth of the nation, a glorious past projected onto the future, a humble nation devoted to Communism and a collectivist ethos; no wonder that Chinese leaders have always tried to keep auspicious graves and perfectly situated houses exclusively for themselves. Endemic hypocrisy has been the reason for rural people's common distrust in the outside world and its representatives, as well as suspicion towards political initiatives, mostly seen to be formulated by and serving the interests of city people. Lack of trust in the intentions of people from the outside world also generated distrust in the dominant traditions they conveyed. Xenophobia has its domestic pendants in the common requirement to ritually appropriate and transpose elements of non-local culture: everywhere there has been a desire to add local characteristics to universal traits. Government neglect and lack of protection have affected the rural-urban divide which has gradually turned into a cleavage, while prioritizing urban life simultaneously accounted for the disappearance of fengshui in Chinese cities in the period after the May Fourth movement.

In the overseas Chinese communities, on the other hand, the situation was very different. There fengshui was driven forward by a kind of nostalgia for the old country combined with cultural performance for the strengthening of ethnic self-identity; it was further stimulated by the rise to power of entrepreneurial groups as opposed to formal literati power.

What fengshui has become in the West is yet another question. Having read this book any fengshui admirer in the Western world will admit the difference – that they are, in fact, worlds apart. Yet ambiguousness and tension between some archetypical positions penetrate this new fengshui mutation as well as its bearers. Being brought up in the Euro-American world we need not be devoted Christians to sense the faint echoes of the leading premises of nineteenth century missionary work in China: that defection from God leads to self-deification and deification of one's own kind... It is not for me to upbraid the modern fengshui believers, but only to point out that while Chinese peasants have taken to celebration of the self in resistance to oppression and arrogance, the modern adherers of fengshui tend to practice self-deification in reaction to human indifference and social impoverishment.

Our perception of fengshui has indeed come a long way from the curiosity that surrounded it in the 1860s, through its depiction as a major pest in 1880s, its investigation as a possible native science around 1900, an expression of Chinese native culture in the pre-1949 era, its anthropological attention in the 1960s, its rising ecological interpretation in the 1970s and 1980s, finally to its explosion as an Oriental wisdom of life in the 1990s, continuing into the 2000s. Perhaps future expositions of this diverse tradition will be more balanced and informed, realizing the intimate association between a given tradition and its political and cultural setting. Thus, instead of translating it into abstract Western categories, we may satisfy out inquisitiveness by simply comparing it to our own fengshuis of everyday life.

Appendix On the 'Origin' of Fengshui and the History of Its Literature

Chinese site divination has a long unbroken history dating back several centuries BC, moulded on ancient vitalistic stock.[1] Taking omens from all natural phenomena also has an archaic background where heaven was seen as personal and all-powerful (Yosida 1979: 72). Taking omens as well as divining both time and place were crucial to the imperial court right up to the fall of the Qing. A long series of classical works on *yinyang xue* (yinyang studies) *dili* (land divination), *kanyu* ('Heaven and Earth') and later fengshui served the purpose of a technical framework for planning buildings, cities and graves as well as for imperial forecasting and policy formation. Divination was gradually popularized and came to bridge classical literary works and utilization by all strata of Chinese society (Freedman 1979). At the same time it was subject to interpretation by a number of factions, each claiming to be the orthodox form (Huang Y. 1991: 18–20). Although Confucianism repeatedly opposed site divination as overblown magic, it was taken seriously by many eminent Chinese thinkers, who thus contributed to its popularization (March 1968: 1). Site divination has been controversial to Chinese state power throughout recorded history, although supported by imperial rulers from time to time. It should also be pointed out that geomancy has mostly been shunned by orthodox Chinese philosophy and it has no firm place in the classical tradition, just as Western works on Chinese philosophy tend to neglect it. Instead, it lurked on the sidelines of Chinese history as it emerges from imperial records, but certainly gained prominence in popular cosmology, particularly from the Song period (960–1279) onwards. Today, geomancy is geographically spread all over the Chinese world, including Hong Kong, Taiwan and Singapore, while increasing its influence on the mainland. Surely, however, the macro-historical continuity of site divination does not in any way imply that its present practices are simple derivations of ancient forms.

Fengshui is a complex concoction of cosmological speculation and practical techniques, manifested in a huge literary production and countless popular varieties that were always in continuous interaction. We can only see the contours of this giant tradition, which may be approached from many angles. The questions that occupied ancient and more recent Chinese writers of fengshui manuals were clearly of a different nature than the issues of the early sinologists, who first investigated the subject of fengshui, which again are significantly different from the issues that guided my fieldwork. Let me present some of the themes that occupied early sinology before outlining the history of fengshui.

THE 'ORIGIN' OF FENGSHUI

Early sinology attempted to answer the most obvious question – What is fengshui? – in an effort to explain it to a Western audience. The sinologists' methodology requested them to explore its origin in Chinese antiquity, and primarily in the classical literature, since they largely defended the notion that Chinese civilization had descended from a former state of glory to a present state of economic stagnation and political dissolution.

Several theories on the origin of fengshui were put forward in the early accounts. The Protestant missionary and sinologist, J. Edkins, first addressed the issue in a series of outstanding papers in *The Chinese Recorder and Missionary Journal* in 1872. Motivated by the growing concern over the 'obstacles to the progress of civilization' among the Chinese on the grounds of fengshui disturbance, Edkins attempted to make fengshui comprehensible to Western sojourners from the standpoint, as in the opening of the first essay, that 'everything can be made plainer by investigation'. He compared fengshui to the system of magic and fortune-telling of the Chaldeans which Christianity once had to fight, suggesting that it eventually would go much the same way.

Very peculiar to Edkins, however, especially in relation to many later writers, was his relaxed view of both filial piety and superstition among the Chinese. He described filial piety as less sincere than supposed by many, more selfish than generous and more calculating than spontaneous, resulting from the sense of morality being deadened by the prevailing desires for riches and rank. Therefore all beliefs were dubious: 'It is often the case that the care bestowed by the Chinese on the graves of their ancestors may be less from respect for the deceased than from fear of ill consequences to themselves and their descendants' (Edkins 1872: 291). Perhaps associated with this view, he saw the roots of fengshui in a theological light:

> When God as governor is banished from the world, atheistic philosophers substitute an impersonal Fate, whose decrees sometimes are in harmony with the moral sense in man, but are perhaps much oftener influenced by low motives such as are believed by the superstitious to control the acts of the Fetish. In this sense it may be said that the Chinese have retrograded in proportion as the Feng Shui and similar superstitions have extended among them. In the days of Confucius the moral sense was probably brighter than it is now and there was less superstition. (Edkins 1872: 291)

Edkins traced a strong Indian influence in Chinese geomancy, which was not entirely unwarranted, and speculated that the concept of 'wind and water' itself could be of such origin since it paralleled a native Indian term for climate, transferred by the Hindu philosophy on the elements (which he again saw as inspired by Greek Ionian philosophy during the last centuries BC). In accordance with these common diffusionist ideas of his time, he believed fengshui to have developed with the subsequent spread of Hindu and Buddhist thought in China, which produced the new philosophical era in the Song dynasty. Although most of his Chinese sources claimed fengshui to originate in the classics, primarily the *Yijing* (Book of changes), Edkins refused to see it in an exclusively historical light; he believed the 'real fengshui of the present generation' to be of modern date, having developed chiefly in the last dynasty. Both in his view of filial piety and in that of the origin of fengshui Edkins showed a far more sophisticated criticism of the Chinese sources than many of the later sinologists. The works and insights of other theologists confirmed this trend. In 1871 in the same journal Reverend Carstairs Douglass had called fengshui 'a modern superstition unknown to the classics, and actually condemned by Imperial edicts' (*CRMJ* September 1871: 111), presumably a lasting perception in missionary Chinese studies (e.g. Moule 1914: 215).

The German sinologist E. J. Eitel, who was working as a schoolmaster in Hong Kong and writing almost contemporaneously with Edkins, was the first proponent of the straightforward view that fengshui was of ancient origin and developed from ancestor worship, which he, somewhat contradictory to Edkins, supposed to have acquired an intensity peculiar to China:

> The deepest root of the Feng-shui system grew out of that excessive and superstitious veneration of the spirits of ancestors, which, though philosophical minds like that of Confucius might construe it on an exclusively moral basis as simply an expression of filial piety, was with the mass of the Chinese people the fruitful soil from which the poisonous weed of rank superstition sprang up in profusion. Ancestral worship naturally implied the idea that the spirits of the deceased ancestors could and would some how influence the fortunes of the descendants. This superstitious notion, the existence of which can be shewn in the most ancient records of Chinese thought that we possess, is the moving spring and leading instinct of the whole Feng-shui system. (Eitel 1984: 51–52)

After working his way through the historical sources of fengshui, noting the continual adoption of ideas from mainstream Chinese philosophy, Eitel still defends the notion that fengshui can be seen as a complete amalgamation of religion and physical science – religion distorted into gross superstition and science in the form of rough guesses about nature:

> What is Feng-shui, then? It is simply the blind gropings of the Chinese mind after a system of natural science, which gropings, untutored by practical observation of nature and trusting almost exclusively in the truth of the alleged ancient tradition and in the force of abstract reasoning, naturally left the Chinese mind completely in the dark. (Ibid.: 1984: 69)

From Eitel's reasoning it followed that the entire system was marked for dissolution with the coming of enlightenment to the Chinese, a common view among contemporary sojourners in China, and also the stand of later Chinese governments in their drive against 'superstition'. What the sinologists of his time lacked in comparison with the Christian missionaries in China was presumably the close interaction with the Chinese population below the scholarly class. This manifested itself in the early sinologists' ready acceptance of some common dogmas of the Chinese elite, taken out of the classics: cultural uniqueness, historical continuity and literary authority.

Some twenty years later, Eitel's naive assumptions about the origin of fengshui were meticulously developed by another sinologist, J.J.M. de Groot, in his monumental work *The Religious Systems of China*. He argued that already in early antiquity the worship of the dead was the religion proper of the Chinese and since the deceased ancestors were their principal patron divinities, the first form of geomancy was grave geomancy. Filial piety was supposed to have a material reward, involving wealth, position, health and descendants: 'By Fung-shui the graves are turned into mighty instruments of blessing or punishment.' The intermediate step in the development of fengshui was domestic worship:

> But souls do not dwell in graves only. They also reside in tablets exposed for worship on domestic altars, and in temples specially erected to shelter them. There, too, precisely for the same reasons, they ought to be made to live under the favourable influences of nature. Consequently, Fung-shui is firmly entwined with house-building and the construction of ancestral temples. (de Groot 1897: 937)

Since both Eitel and de Groot were well read in the classics and could demonstrate the off-shooting of fengshui works from the classics on burial rites and dwelling orienting, few scholars found reason to doubt at least their fundamental claim concerning origin and historical development from burial geomancy to dwelling geomancy. Particularly de Groot carried the historicist interpretation of fengshui to an extreme, exposing a view of history as the biology of society, under the sway of which each generation had only negligible capacity for change. Presumably Eitel's and de Groot's assumptions were largely both inspired and supported by their contemporary Chinese scholars. They confirmed the ancient origin of Chinese civilization and early development of the essential literature – but while backdating the roots of civilization served the purpose of granting authority to tradition and convention for the Chinese literati, their Western counterparts were perhaps more informed by the growing romanticism of their audiences at home.

Both Eitel's and de Groot's theories rather endorsed the importance that the Chinese themselves granted to filial piety as a crucial element in their national self-identity. The delicate equilibrium between the Chinese glorification of tradition and sinology's historicism, which both met in the sentimental exhibition of ancient Chinese glory, lasted for decades. In 1937 the Chinese scholar Chen Huaizhen repeated de Groot's argument by and large, though expressed with a different compassion for his own cultural heritage:

> The concept of geomancy (*feng-shui*) has a very long history in China. The concept originated in the system of ancestor worship. The Chinese have always emphasized the importance of filial piety. Therefore, when parents are alive, the children must express their filial devotion by serving them properly; after their death they bury them properly and offer sacrificial services for them in the proper way. Besides the concept of filial piety, the Chinese also believe that after

their death, their spirits remain in this world ... In short, most Chinese
believe that deceased parents could determine the prosperity of their
children. This belief has been very popular since the middle ancient
time ... Not until after the custom of burial had already been
established did the art of geomancy become popular. (Cited in Yoon
1976: 246)

This Chinese interpretation of de Groot's theory saw the pure and
persistent filial piety, a devotion even stretching into the afterlife in
the form of worship of spirits, as the true origin of Chinese geomancy.

Another important figure, who had a few pertinent statements to
offer on the origin of fengshui, was Max Weber. Weber did not
entirely reject the evolutionary perspective on religion, but he subordinated evolution to ideological processes in the present manifestations of religious practices. In his comparative scheme of
rationalization the failure of Confucianism to establish monotheism
– seen, for instance in the want of an efficient impersonal bureaucracy and in the continued role of magic – was to blame for the
persistent prominence of fengshui in his day:

> It is crystal-clear that defects of technical and inventive genius cannot
> be attributed to the Chinese. The backwardness of mining ... the
> failure to use coal for the production of iron ... and the increasing
> restriction of shipping to river traffic in traditional forms and along
> traditional routes were not due to lack of inventiveness. Fêng shui
> (magicians) of all sorts, prebend interests – products of magic and the
> form of state – were the decisive factors. (Weber 1968: 296–297)

Weber argued that all great religions had made attempts at monotheism since political and religious unity were synonymous: 'Bigger
gods conquer the smaller ones.' As the product of Confucianism's
stalled rationalization it was only predictable that magic tended to
grow in later dynasties and that arts like fengshui developed late and
tended to be criminalized by orthodoxy. Weber's approach represented a radical and forceful opposition to historicism.

It is still striking how countless sinologists through the twentieth
century asserted as a leading notion that the origin of all possible
aspects of 'Chinese civilization' were to be found in antiquity. It is
perhaps best understood as a coincidence of their own evolutionary
predisposition and a Chinese inspired inclination to accord authority
to everything archaic. But there is more than this at work; by viewing
aspects of Chinese civilization as discrete entities, each with clear links
to its archaic roots, they came to depict China as inherently static. The
process brought about the rise of the Orientalist tradition, which
tended to homogenize both time and social space in the exploration

of Chinese culture.[2] Hence fengshui was described as a continued system, inviting the obvious questions as to its origin and evolution. Arthur C. Wright, for instance, traces its origin as 'a system' to the 'Han synthesis', later expressed in the text of Guo Pu (276–324), who applies a number of principles to the siting of graves to ensure good fortune (Wright 1977: 54). Strikingly in disagreement with his own prediction, however, Wright admits that 'the application of ... the feng-shui system to the siting of cities is only partially and uncertainly reflected in the sources'. Yet this does not prevent Wright from regarding fengshui as a comprehensive, continued system, which ramified its influence among common people in later dynasties. Here we have a lucid example of concepts and ideas, of which many of those used in fengshui evidently have ancient roots, being mistaken for a consciously constructed system. By contrast, the early missionary theologists seemed to possess a much more refined epistemology, inspired by early hermaneutics, that sharpened their awareness of the interplay between text and social process.

From the time Eitel wrote his treatise it took a hundred years before anyone seriously challenged the notion that fengshui spontaneously grew out of ancestor worship. In 1976, greatly inspired by the rising environmentalism in the West (see Chapter 7), Hong-key Yoon wrote his *Geomantic Relationships between Culture and Nature in Korea*, in which he strongly denounced de Groot's theory for being 'illogical and uninformed' and in want of evidence (Yoon 1976: 246). Instead he proposed a theory taking its outset in a series of postulates about man's inborn knowledge about his environment. For instance,

> Chinese geomancy represents an instinctive response to the environment ... at first, Chinese geomancy may have existed as simple knowledge about the environment ... This knowledge was probably handed down from generation to generation by elders ... (Ibid.: 252)

> Probably few ideas in the world are more closely related to the natural environment than is geomancy ... geomancy is defined as a unique and comprehensive system of conceptualizing the physical environment which regulates human ecology. (Ibid.: 1)

Thus, all of a sudden, with Yoon's work fengshui had been transferred from the sphere of superstition to that of ecology, a comprehensive field of studies without definite borders between science and human intuition. While early writers such as Eitel had speculated whether fengshui, under the right intellectual circumstances, *could* have developed into true science, Yoon, by making the concepts of ecology and environmental knowledge the cornerstones of his argument, simply evaded any question of verification. Fengshui was alternative wisdom, created by the instinctive feel for the environment of the ancient Chinese. Perhaps in his stance can even be traced the uncritical belief in the true knowledge of the classics and instinctive intelligence of the people who created them.

FAILED PREDICTIONS

Something went wrong with these theories on Chinese fengshui. Sinologists believed in the forces of modernization, theologists in those of enlightenment, and Chinese intellectuals in those of national mobilization around 'self-strengthening' in the face of foreign aggression. Why did they all foresee the rapid disappearance of the fengshui tradition as Chinese society modernized? And were they ever close to revealing the true character of the 'system' when they could not correctly judge its vitality and endurance? I shall put forward some assumptions as to why these theories failed, focusing on their depiction of fengshui as something having a definite origin, a linear evolution and a specific outlook, a view exposing a rather rigid perception of Chinese culture.

The phrases used in predicting the extinction of fengshui were rich and bountiful. Edkins saw its elimination as a necessity for the sake of progress, but obviously believed in the power of the light itself when he wrote that 'the shining of true science may pale its ineffectual fire and cause it to disappear as a thing of darkness without special effort to bring about its extinction' (Edkins 1872: 320). Herbert Giles described a system that, after having presented a series of obstacles, 'in the last years [has] been shaken to its centre, and is now destined very shortly to collapse' (Giles [1878] 1974: 71). In a similar vein, Eitel remarked that the system, 'based as it is on human speculation and superstition and not on careful study of nature, is marked for decay and dissolution' (Eitel [1873]1984: 69), while de Groot mocked it as 'a mere web of speculative dreams and idle abstractions, the product of a credulous faith in absurd vagaries' (de Groot 1897: 979), bound for destruction along with the petrified culture that produced it. Although Yoon wrote more than half a century later and from a totally different perspective, deploring its ancient wisdom being eradicated by development, his forecast for the system was little brighter: 'This naive but stable and harmonious culture–nature relationship has been ignored and overcome by so-called "modern civilization"' (Yoon 1976: 231). Most onlookers to the Communist revolution tended to agree; in the 1950s the anthropologist Wing-tsit Chan simply noted that fengshui 'is fast becoming a thing of the past' (Chan W. [1953] 1978: 145).

The Chinese people held on to the fengshui tradition. What further discredited the theories of its extinction was the fact that throughout the Communist era in mainland China it showed the greatest vitality in the more developed parts of the Chinese world, notably Taiwan, Hong Kong and Singapore, while in the shattered and impoverished People's Republic it only lived on clandestinely.

So what went wrong? Was it the firm belief in the power of progress among these writers? Or was it a methodological flaw that induced them to formulate the wrong questions with consequently little chance of obtaining the right answers? Although the former is not to be ignored, the latter is probably far more serious. They observed a stagnant literary tradition and assumed that the entire civilization was static; they observed an educational system having used the same curriculum for centuries and assumed that the society was incapable of change; they observed a system of geomancy with explicit reference to ancient classics and assumed that the system had a single origin and evolved along a fairly linear path; and they noticed references to fengshui throughout the second half of the Chinese dynastic record and assumed that it had meant the same to people then as in contemporary Chinese society. It was of course tempting to answer the question so frequently formulated, 'what is fengshui?', by means of such assumptions, but apparently the question itself induced an inappropriate methodology.

Interestingly enough, the early missionary writers whose thinking was firmly embedded in theology were far more inclined to a dynamic interpretation of fengshui than those writers, mostly of later days, who strove to emancipate humanistic studies from religion, but in that process tended to substitute theology with historicism and cross-cultural comparison with a narrow Chinese focus.

To better appreciate the rationality of the fengshui tradition we must free ourselves from notions of its 'nature', associated with biology and related modes of thought. Fengshui does not have a single 'origin', since its historical evolution is multifarious and diffuse with shifting contents; in terms of understanding the present manifestations the origin is relatively unimportant. It must be seen as a dynamic tradition, a social construct maintained primarily by ideological and social factors in the present. Following an anthropological approach, as outlined in Chapter 1, implies a processual account of the articulation and formation of traditions in their social contexts, an awareness of interacting or competing world views and an examination of power relations and clash of interests in the articulation of cosmology.

In the greater perspective we must formulate a new set of questions to replace those asked by early sinology in order to grasp the total significance of fengshui, replacing dry historical data with social processes. It is an empirical fact that geomancy developed in large parts of the world (Skinner 1980: 1–7). So instead of asking about its origin we must investigate the factors that served to maintained its importance and vitality through late imperial Chinese history as well as in the present, while it disintegrated elsewhere. It even rose to prominence in China despite continuous attempts by the Chinese state to quell it. Secondly, we should ask why it took that particular course in China, involving those particular social groups, sets of beliefs, and contradictions to state orthodoxy. Thirdly, in terms of societal and cultural processes another important question is why Chinese governments, ancient and modern, have striven to eradicate grave geomancy, but have looked at house geomancy with greater complacency.

THE HISTORY OF THE LITERATURE AND LEADING IDEAS

Following the work of de Groot and many Chinese scholars it has been the common assumption that fengshui grew out of worship of the dead, often portrayed as the true religion of China in remote antiquity. Yet the sources are indefinite as to whether building site or burial divination came first.[3] It has often been said that the history of its leading ideas and practices is the history of Chinese philosophy (e.g. Eitel 1984: 51; de Groot 1897: 997). The further we go back in time from the Song period, the more fengshui philosophy merges with natural philosophy in general and its practice with ancestor worship in particular. Critical examination of available sources reveals that it was quite late on in Chinese history, more specifically during the early Song (960–1126), when the court patronized popular religion, and Late Song (1127–1279), that fengshui was constructed as a separate branch of study while simultaneously a new profession emerged from its practical implications.

From archaic times ancestor worship meant not only revering the deceased but also implied notions of their spirits being active agents capable of influencing the fortunes of the living. The immanent order of the universe and the intimate connectedness of its various aspects are expressed in the ancient classic *Yijing* (Book of changes).

272

It takes but little imagination to connect the potency of ancestors with the locality, appearance and other qualities of their tombs; this step was presumably taken at the dawn of Chinese history. Already in the Zhou dynasty (c. 1030–722 BC), the elementary principles of grave divination may have been applied (de Groot 1897: 983). At this time commoners were reportedly buried on level ground, princes on low hills and emperors under mounds constructed on mountain tops. The Book of Rites (*Liji*) indicates that ancient graves were oriented so that 'the dead have their heads placed towards the north', since the north was conceived as ruled by the female principle, while 'the living face the south', ruled by the male principle (Chapter 30, line 20), yet this is not universal (Field 1999: 13–14). Thus the fundamental male and female principles as well as the compass points were already indicating distinctions between the living and the dead (Wang F. 1992: 93). The still commonly held assumption, which repeats itself both in fengshui and countless other folk traditions across the world, that houses should face the south refers to this and other passages of The Book of Rites. In the course of time the mound over the grave, originally maintained for the rulers, was adopted by all strata.

By the time of Confucius we have ample evidence of conflicts over the construction of graves and the role of popularly held beliefs connected to ancestor worship. Both Confucius himself and his disciples were much concerned with the firm hold that superstitious notions had on their countrymen, but chose to remain neutral and instead concentrate their efforts on moral reform modelled on the pattern of the ancient sages in order to reach a new golden age. Their cautious position clearly indicates the limits of their own power over people's minds, as illustrated by an anecdote: Confucius, after some difficulties locating the grave of his father, finally had it opened and the remains of his mother buried together with those of his father. On this occasion it was suggested that, in accordance with the custom of the time, a mound should be raised over the grave. Confucius did not oppose it, though he remarked that this was not in accordance with the rules of the ancients, but, so it is said, soon after the mound had been raised a sudden fall of rain washed it away and levelled the ground to his satisfaction (Eitel 1984: 55).

Confucius' followers observed what has been called a studied neutrality. They allowed the application of diagrams for divination although they did not believe in this themselves; they quietly accepted that polytheistic popular beliefs supplanted the monotheism of the ancient sages and even though they disproved of the cosmogonic

273

speculations of their contemporaries, they offered no alternative explanations of how the world came into being.

Mohism, although speaking of salvation through doing good and in principle believing in ghosts' and spirits' power to reward and punish men, also maintained a sceptical attitude in the pursuit of facts:

> If there are ghosts and spirits, then our sacrifices are offered to feed and feast our own (dead) fathers, mothers, brothers and sisters. Is that not a fine thing? And even if there be no ghosts and spirits, we are at most spending a little money on our offerings. Even so, we do not waste it in the sense of throwing it into the ditch. We can still gather our relatives and neighbours and participate in the enjoyment of sacrificial victuals and drinks. Therefore, even if there be no ghosts nor spirits, this may still enable us to enjoy conviviality and give pleasure to our relations and neighbours. (Quoted in Hu S. 1968: 75)

Despite the impact of Confucianism, Mohism and other pragmatic philosophies, early geomantic philosophy appears to have enjoyed considerable popularity. During the Han Dynasty (206 BC–220), this popularity continued. After the book-burning mania and suppression of ancient classics under the despot Qin had ceased in 190 BC, Confucianism flourished anew. Under imperial auspices all remaining pieces of literature were collected and studied and the classics were reconstructed. Despite its privileged position, however, Confucian learning once again found itself impotent in the spiritual field. While Confucian scholars became absorbed in literary criticism and the meticulous study of the ancient classics, Taoism readily seized the opportunity that the reawakening national interest for literature offered. An immense speculative Taoist literature arose as a result, abounding in alchemist, astrological and cosmogonic mystics. As far as the development of geomancy is concerned, the combination of the Twelve Branches (denoting compass directions as well as years, months, days and hours), the cycle of the Twelve Animals (also denoting elements), and the concept of the 28 constellations were used for divination at this point.

It is also under the Han dynasty that the first incident was recorded of imperial opposition being eliminated by geomantic means. The Confucian scholar Liu Xiang, who successfully re-edited the lost Confucian classics, reported to the throne that a certain family's grave showed such remarkable features that it indicated that a descendent would become emperor; such a hint clearly intimated the extinction of the entire family in question (Eitel 1984: 57).

Historical records suggest that a substantial literature of grave divination existed under the Han (Song 2000: 51–57). Among a large number of titles on divination mentioned in these records is one book called *The Golden Kan-yu Thesaurus, in Fourteen Chapters* and six works of 'authors on the rules concerning forms', of which one is titled *On the Configurations of Grounds for Mansions and Houses, in Twenty Chapters* (de Groot 1897: 995).

Thus historical texts and records suggest that the literature on site divination coincides with that on Taoism. Under Taoist influence a first attempt to bring popular geomantic notions together into a unified scheme was made under or shortly after the Han dynasty (Wang F. 1992: 94–96). The *Classic of Dwellings* (*Zhaijing*), which for purposes of authority was ascribed to the legendary Yellow Emperor, is a true exponent of early geomancy. In addition to an outline of the theories of earlier ages the book provides a new theory of geomantic influences based on the concept of male (*yang*) and female (*yin*) dwellings, thereby for the first time extending geomantic cosmology to the dwellings of the living. Similarly, the book divides the diagrams formerly used for divination into male and female diagrams and applies them to determine the geomantic characteristics of male and female dwellings. Of the eight trigrams (*bagua*), those of the west to the southeast were said to work in accordance with the female energy and those of the east to the northwest were said to work in accordance with the male energy. Theories relating to the five phases (*wuxing*), refined into the theory of mutual construction and mutual destruction, are also commonly applied from the Han onwards (Wang F. 1992: 94; Song 2000: 52).

During the following periods of the Three Kingdoms (221–277) and the Six Dynasties (265–618), we find numerous references to the connection between favourable grave sites and high position for the descendants. Furthermore, geomancy became infused with Hindu astronomy and Buddhist cosmology. Particularly during the Jin Dynasty (265–419), when Buddhism was adopted by the state power, divination philosophy rose to a golden era after it received a new impetus, not least from the Buddhist cosmological concepts of ceaseless cycles of construction and destruction of the material world. This period also gave birth to several renowned figures in the art of geomancy, including the outstanding diviner Guan Lu and the famous scholar Guo Pu (276–324). The latter has frequently been credited with being the great patriarch and founder of modern fengshui – this common backdating of traditions has no historical value, but is merely ritual.

One of the principal classics of geomancy, the *Burial Book* or *Book of Interment*, (*Zangshu*), which has a strong orientation towards topography, originates from this period. It is ascribed to Guo Pu, although it is not mentioned in his contemporary bibliography (de Groot 1897: 1004). However, three other titles are attributed to his authorship. It is also during the Qin Dynasty that references to fengshui matters grow substantially in numbers in the official annals to remain prominent in the following dynasties; many such references allude to the potential of auspicious graves to produce emperors, kings and ministers.

While fengshui philosophy apparently was promoted during the reign of the Six Dynasties, and imperial annals from this period contain special sections on benign geomantic influences, it is also gradually seen to become an issue of political significance. The official histories of this period relate stories of geomantic prophesies coming to pass when exceptional tombs and omens lead descendants to wealth and dignified state positions.[4] It is also reported that Wendi, the first emperor of the Sui Dynasty (581–618), argued against the truth of grave divination while fighting for the throne. His enemies then violated the tombs of his ancestors to inflict misfortune upon him. He nevertheless ascended to the throne although he lost a brother on the battlefield. The imperial historiographer credits him with the words: 'If the tombs of my ancestors are not in a felicitous position, why did I attain to the throne? But if their position is felicitous, why was my brother killed?' (Eitel 1984: 60). Later elaborations of grave divination have perhaps considered this legend when they came to the conclusion that the same tomb may give blessings to one and cause misfortune to another among the descending family members.

The Tang Dynasty (618–905) marked a further propagation of the mystical doctrines of Taoism and Buddhism, which again created a favourable environment for geomantic philosophy. Literature, both philosophy and poetry, flourished during the Tang and also a large body of Buddhist literature was translated from Sanskrit into Chinese. Again, new concepts and ideas were transplanted into divination literature, not to replace the existing ones, but to supplement them in an agglomerative pattern. From Sanskrit literature was borrowed the notion of the Five Planets influencing the earth and its inhabitants and in addition some works adopted ideas of the Nine Stars/Palaces (*jiugong*) influencing the propitiousness of dwelling sites. Important works on divination arose from this new influx of foreign ideas. Three books are ascribed to the geomancer Yang Yunsong, who in particular developed those aspects referring to the ancient symbols of Dragon and Tiger as well as the direction of watersheds and influence of watercourses. These classics are the *Classic on the Art of Rousing the Dragon* (*Han long jing*), which in addition to the influence of the Five Planets develops a theory on the influence of the Nine Stars on the dwelling site, the *Classic of the Green Bag* (*Qingnang jing*), which speculates in numerologic correlations between heaven and earth, and the *Classic of the Doubtful Dragon* (*Yilong jing*), which develops theories as to which land forms and outlines of nature may accommodate Dragon and Tiger.

Both recurrent criticism of 'unauthentic' geomancy during the Qin and an imperial initiative to curb it during the Tang testifies to growing imperial concern over the popular beliefs in divination, which in its literary form increasingly takes the appearance of a cosmology. In the sixth century the scholar Yan Zhitui wrote the following, presumably representing well the ambivalence of the literary class:

> The art of utilizing the two breaths of nature having sprung up with Heaven and Earth themselves, confidence must be placed in the indications of that art with respect to good luck and ill, weal and woe. But a long time has elapsed since the ancients lived. Therefore the writings on that art, transmitted from one generation to another, are altogether the product of unsettled popular notions, and contain gossip of a vulgar and superficial kind; little therein is trustworthy, much is pure nonsense. Yet, by contravening the art in question, by deviating from it, or by refusing to utilize it, calamity might finally be incurred. Infelicitous results cannot be always eluded by attending to it with anxious carefulness or by entirely relying upon it; but advantage is just as little to be secured by sticking to it with very great anxiety. (de Groot 1897: 1005–1006)

Then in the seventh century the imperial annals report that the emperor Tai Zong appointed a commission to screen a large number of popular works on divination and geomancy with a view to sorting out the orthodox and useful elements from the unauthentic. The commission, consisting of more than ten scholars under the leadership of a famous scholar, Lü Cai, passed a harsh sentence on the existing literature, condemning in particular the selection of auspicious graves and lucky times for burial. Although this was obviously an official attempt to curb the booming trade in divination, its effect was doubtful; the literature on the subject continued to grow during the following centuries, from a dozen in the catalogue of the Sui to over a hundred in the Song. In this period both divination and meditation gained increasing popularity among all classes of people, for which there is evidence that it reached even into the court (Song 2000: 53). A long tradition of state attempts to control folk religion and curb the unorthodox elements was founded, however; this is simultaneously the history of the growing rationalization of the Chinese state and suppression of alternative rationalities. Not only the Chinese state felt compelled to take action, however. From around 900 onwards there is ample evidence of efficient and determined clan organizations establishing meticulous clan rules to prevent their members from playing with geomancy and other superstitious activities (Eberhard 1962 : 40–44; Yen 1968: 204).

It was not until the Song and Late Song Dynasties, however, that attempts were made to synthesize all the previously mentioned elements into a single scheme for interpreting the exhaustive influence that heaven and earth may exert on humans and their society, presumably close to what we now know as fengshui in its more literate form. While previously the imperial court's Directorate of Astronomy carried out the Three Methods of Divination (*san shi*), it was not until the Yuan dynasty (1271–1368) and onwards that the government ran district schools of divination (*yinyang xue*) to train functionaries in this specific discipline in order to 'divine auspicious days, and related matters of topography and orientation' (Huang Y. 1991: 4). With a philosophical basis in the writings of the great neo-Confucian thinkers of the time such as Shao Yong, later Wang Yangming, but particularly Zhu Xi (1130–1200), the fengshui tradition was infused with a single scheme for applying a great variety of originally independent notions. Zhu Xi's philosophy, mainly in the form of commentaries on the Four Books of Confucianism, provided the necessary synthesis. He incorporated the Principle of the Great Ultimate, the theory of Celestial Breath (*tian qi*) and the Terrestrial Breath (*di qi*) which by uniting produce and reproduce everything, the distinction between Principle (*li*) and 'Ether' (*qi*),[5] and the distinction between the Way (*dao*) and 'instrument' (*qi*).[6] Also the very premises of Zhu Xi's teachings, that man and cosmos are bound together and human nature therefore derives directly from cosmological principles, had strong appeal to fengshui advocates.

As the neo-Confucian philosophy was adopted as state orthodoxy and sanctified as the national faith in the state examination system greater coherence between literary learning and popular religion was probably achieved; the fengshui masters of the time closed the gap. By adopting everything that was appealing to common people and making it directly applicable to the routines of daily life, fengshui rose to a new 'golden age'. Competition between individual writers could never be ruled out, however, and each one had his own scheme of interpretation. Moreover, what is usually termed a 'synthesis' could as easily be depicted as a confusing array of disparate theories without common consistency. Thus, the diversity and fluidity of siting theories allows for a wide range of siting practices and in any case the human factor remains decisive (Bennett, S. 1978: 21).

Both of the two major schools of fengshui draw much of their philosophy from the neo-Confucian learning that arose with Zhu Xi and his contemporaries. Yet the two schools developed on top of an existing division between competing factions in Chinese divination: *Hong fan* Five Phases (Fujian) and Orthodox Five Phases (Jiangxi) (Huang Y. 1991: 19). One school, namely the one usually termed the School of Forms, shows greater continuity with the earlier divination philosophy. This school is primarily concerned with the influence of 'forms and outlines' (*jing shi*) or 'forms and terrain' (*xing shi*), including mountains, hills and water courses, and recognizes as its founder the famous ninth-century geomancer Yang Yunsong. Yang wrote a number of books, many of which carry titles emphasizing the influence of the Dragon: *Classic on the Means to Set Dragons in Motion, Book of Thirty-six Dragons* and *Classic for the Approximation of Dragons.* Another work of his, the *Method of the Twelve Lines,* remained a standard work through the imperial era. Yang even held the office of Imperial Geomancer during the reign of Ji Zong (874–888). The School of Forms is also termed the Jiangxi School or *kanzhou* after the department in Jiangxi Province where Yang Yunsong worked.

Under the influence of Zhu Xi's school of metaphysics a second school of fengshui came into being. By granting principal importance to the *bagua*, the Branches and the Constellations, it became closer attached to the compass and derives its name, the 'Compass School', 'School of Orientations' or 'directions and positions' (*fang wei*), from this – yet another name is *liqi*, 'pattern of *qi*' school (Field 1999: 15). This school is also termed the Fujian School after the place of work of its principal representative Wang Ji (Wang Zhaoqing), to whom several works are ascribed: *Classic of the Core and Centre* and *Disquisitions on the Queries and Answers.* These two schools prevailed ever after without any significant competition from other denominations. Yet a number of texts combine theories supposedly unique to one denomination, just as late classical siting literature often attempts to include them all (Bennett, S.: 1978: 4). To some extent geography has determined which school will predominate regionally since the School of Forms is far better adapted to the mountainous regions of south and west China, whereas the School of Orientations obviously fits better into the flatter land.

A golden era for fengshui philosophy is not at all synonymous with a prosperous society, however. The growth of fengshui philosophy must be seen in conjunction with a growing destitution of the Chinese peasant, a massive drive from north to south due to population pressure, famine, invasion and unrest (Buchanan 1970: 19–23), and increasingly despotic state power in the later dynasties (Wittvogel 1957; Gates 1996: Ch. 3).

Both Western and Chinese texts support the assumption that very little happened in the evolution of fengshui philosophy during the entire period after the Song, comprising the Yuan (1271–1368), Ming (1368–1644) and Qing (1644–1911) dynasties. Large numbers of new manuals, mainly drawing on the classics mentioned above, were produced and reproduced, and commentaries on the old works were written. The imperial court also had a series of standard guides made, trying to sort out orthodox from unorthodox divination; one such guide from the seventeenth century is the *Qinding xie ji pian fang shu*, which still remains the basis for popular almanacs in Taiwan (Huang Y. 1991: 17). But was the tradition really stagnant or is this just a common prejudice? It is a matter of fact that Zhu Xi's learning remained authoritative in the state examination system throughout most of this period and that little foreign influence could be detected in the indigenous cosmology during much of the same period, but such facts accounted perhaps more for stability in the outer framework than for the inner dynamics of the tradition; we know very little of its practice and interpretation in the daily life of common people during this vast expanse of historical time.

THE PAST IN THE PRESENT

Western sinologists writing in the second half of the nineteenth century and at the beginning of the twentieth century mention with disdain the countless geomantic volumes in existence, as well as the common belief in fengshui among Chinese scholars (Doré 1914: 412), but rarely pay attention to the contemporary material other than assuming it to be merely reproductions of classical writings. J.J.M. de Groot, however, provides a characterization of the common composition he found to prevail among them. According to him, three sections are usually provided, dealing with 'rules of the Dragon' (topography and watercourses), the Five Elements or Planets (including how to detect their influence on the earth and in the sky), and the technical applications. The last section provides long lists of common rules and warnings as well as an abundance of illustrations.

Today, not much of this large body of literature remains. Some Western libraries may have a few copies, but apart from these sporadic occurrences no larger collections seem to be available, either in China or in the West. Of the abundance of manuals that were in the possession of Chinese practitioners up until the cultural revolution, also very little survived the Red Guards' delirious book burning; those few pre-liberation works that were found in the fieldwork areas have already been mentioned. On various occasions I have contacted old Chinese intellectuals who were knowledgeable on the subject and had possessed books on it before liberation, but all in vain; a scholar in Shanghai, for instance, told with heartache that to his knowledge not a single copy of the books he himself had written in the 1930s and 1940s had survived.

If fengshui philosophy had remained stagnant for a period as long as the last three dynasties, what then about its political implications? It would be an appalling generalization to assume that the shifting ruling houses would stick to a consistent policy just because the fengshui literature became less innovative or to assume that the social implications of fengshui cosmology were constant just because the literature stagnated. When the early sinologists saw the canon of classical literature taking up issues of divination, slowly built through the Chinese golden ages of literary production and expressing an accumulative and synthesizing theoretical orientation, they judged the cultural practices beneath them along a similar vein. The real problem, however, arises from the indiscriminate translation of everything related to site divination into 'geomancy' and the application of a systems conception on this general category. By covering everything from *yinyang* studies, to *dili*, to *kanyu*, and so forth,[7] to fengshui, and by being stretched over the entire Chinese imperial history it really is a construction. For instance, the separation of the major schools of fengshui is in this way frequently dated back to the fourth century AD or even further (March 1968: 261; Needham J. 1962: 242), as previous types of divination are taken for its natural ancestors. The evolutionary conception of a single-stranded progression or regression from a common origin has framed sinology's competition in roots-finding, closely resembling and unwittingly supporting the Chinese literati's political attempts at backdating traditions for the sake of granting them undisputed authority.

If we review critically the theories of the origin of fengshui that were outlined in the beginning of this chapter, two separate strands of reasoning stand out as relevant today. First of all, the theological axiom that 'secession from God leads to the deification of man', and further entailing a wide array of 'superstitious' endeavours, appears curiously analogous to what we discerned from the fieldwork material. Secondly, Max Weber's conception of progressive rationalization, implying criminalization of deviating rationalities, is not only relevant for the growth of fengshui in the last dynasties, but provides a momentous framework for analysing Chinese state policy throughout the twentieth century. I shall avoid coming up with a new theory on the origin of fengshui, as the tradition undoubtedly had its own dynamics in each era. However, much points to fengshui rising as a counter-current to the progressive attempts of the Chinese state, in Benedict Anderson's terms (1983), to defend an elitist class's monopoly on ontological truth. Monopolizing ontology and bringing the world to 'one' (Fitzgerald 1996) – a persistent 'Universismus' in de Groot's terms (1918) – is indeed a strong predisposition of Chinese ruling classes in historical time, including the most recent political formations. Also the agglomerative development of fengshui philosophy itself may account for a rebellious opposition to state rationalism. Roland Barthes has described how the language of power intends to subjugate other languages, resulting in battles of meaning: 'The force of meaning depends on its degree of systemization: the strongest meaning is the one whose systemization includes a large number of elements, to the point where it appears to include everything noteworthy in the world' (Barthes 1974: 154–155). Particularly in a society so intensely aware of the power of linguistic representation, a confrontation of languages is a convincing token of social conflict.

We can only catch glimpses of what fengshui meant to different groups through the Chinese imperial history. With the coming of foreigners after the late fifteenth century, however, the Chinese elite's monopoly on representing Chinese culture was broken and the self-representation of the Chinese state seriously challenged. It is, of course, a heedless postulate that we only get a sense of the dynamics of Chinese society through the writings of Westerners, but it is still beyond doubt that these writers provided a novel perspective on Chinese society and that their diverse approaches and backgrounds induced unprecedented debate and criticism, both internally in China and abroad. To this day Chinese scholarship on fengshui remains hampered by futile attempts to sort 'superstition' from 'proto-science' in order to legitimize itself.

NOTES

1   For a discussion of several theories on the origin of 'Chinese geomancy', see Yoon 1976: 245–259.

2   For a critique of this tradition, see Dirlik 1993: 70.

3   Andrew March, for instance, cites eighteenth-century Chinese sources for saying that burial geomancy only spread from Eastern Han onwards (1968: 260). Evidence of early fengshui is also discussed in Field 1999: 13–33.

4   Two such stories from this period are translated in de Groot 1897: 980, 981–982.

5   This distinction has been interpreted in terms of modern science as one between organisation and basis of a system (Yosida 1973: 81) or between structure and mass/energy (Needham, J. 1969: 251).

6   These are the terms used by Fung Yu-lan in his resumé of Zhu Xi's philosophy.

7   Several other concepts may be included in the list. In addition to those mentioned a recent Chinese work comprises *xingfa, qingwu, buzhai, xiangzhai* and *tuzhai* in the prehistory of fengshui (Shi 1992: 11–24).

List of Chinese Terms

bagua	八卦	fuji	扶乩
bai hu	白虎	fuqiang	福强
baijiu	白酒	guankou	关口
Baohua	宝华	gui	鬼
baohuqu	保护区	Han long jing	撼龙经
bowu	博物	hanhun	喊魂
bu	卜	hongfan	洪范
buluo	部落	huafeng	花疯
buzhai	卜宅	huanjing	环境
cai	财	hun	魂
chaoye	朝野	jingshen	精神
Cihai	辞海	jing shi	境式
da chang	打厂	jiugong	九宫
Daqing lüli	大清律例	kaifaqu	开放区
dao	道	kan	看
daojiao	道教	Kanzhou	赣州
didiwei	敌敌畏	kanyu	堪舆
dili	地理	li	理
diqi	地气	li	礼
duangong	短工	Liji	礼记
duilian	对联	liqi	理气
falungong	法轮功	Longquan	龙泉
fang wei	方位	luan	乱
fen	分	Luo shu	洛书
fengle	疯了	luopan	罗盘
fengjing	风景	malu qian	马路钱
fengshui	风水	mixin	迷信
fo	佛	mu	亩
fojiao	佛教	nongli	农历
fu	福	nongmindui	农民队

nongmin weiyuanhui	农民委员会	wuxing	五行
poxu mixin	破嘘迷信	xiang	乡
qi	气	xiangzhang	乡长
qi	起	xiangxin	相信
qifeng	气疯	xiangzhai	相宅
qigong	气功	xiansheng	先生
Qin ding xie ji bian fang shu		xifang	西方
	钦定协纪辨方书	xing shi	形势
qinglong	青龙	xingfa	形法
Qing nang jing	青囊经	xingwei	行为
Qingming	清明	xuewen	学问
qingwu	青乌	yang	阳
san shi	三式	Yi long jing	疑龙经
sha	刹	Yijing	易经
shadao	杀刀	yin	阴
shangdi	上帝	yinyang	阴阳
shanjing	山精	yu	鱼
shanshui	山水	yu qian	余钱
shazuo	杀座	Zangshu	葬书
shenfeng	神疯	zhaijiao	斋交
shengshui	圣水	Zhaijing	宅经
shenxian	神仙	zhaohun	找魂
shicun	世村	zhaoyaojing	照妖镜
shou	寿	zhenli	真理
Shui hu zhuan	水浒傳	zhenzhu	真主
tiandi	天帝	zhuyi	主义
tianqi	天气	zi	子
tianzhu	天主	ziran	自然
tuzhai	图宅	ziranjie	自然界
Wanguo gongbao	万国公报	ziyuan	资源
wenhuazhan	文化站	zongjiao	宗教
wenyidui	文艺队	zongli yamen	总理衙门

List of Chinese names

Chen Changheng	陈昌亨	Wang Fukun	王复昆
Chen Duxiu	陈独秀	Wang Ji	王伋
Chen Yonggui	陈永贵	Wang Qiheng	王其亨
Ding Richang	丁日昌	Wang Yangming	王杨明
Fei Xiaotong	费孝通	Wang Yude	王玉德
Guo Pu	郭璞	Yang Wenheng	杨文亨
Guan Lu	管辂	Yang Yunsong	杨筠松
He Xiaoxin	何晓昕	Yeji Laozi	野鹤老子
Hong Pimo	洪丕谟	Yi Ding	一丁
Hong Yong	洪涌	Yan Zhitui	颜之推
Hu Shi	胡適	Yu Lu	雨露
Kang Liang	亢亮	Yuan Shushan	袁树三
Lü Cai	吕才	Zhang Huimin	张惠民
Li Hongzhang	李鸿章	Zhang Zhidong	张之洞
Li Wentian	李文田	Zhao Zhixin	赵执信
Liu Xiang	刘向	Zhou Dunyi	周敦颐
Luo Longji	罗隆基	Zhou Wenzheng	周文铮
Shao Yong	邵雍	Zhu Xi	朱熹
Shi Zhen	史箴	Zuo Zongtang	左宗棠
Song Dachuan	宋大川		

Bibliography

Anagnost, Ann, 'Politics and Magic in Contemporary China'. *Modern China*, vol. 13, no.1, 1987, pp. 40–61.

Anonymous, *Zhuzhai fengshui qin jixiong* [Attendance to good or ill luck in dwelling fengshui]. Sichuan, 1980s.

Anderson, E.N., 'Feng-shui: Ideology and Ecology'. In E.N. Anderson, *Mountains and Water: Essays on the Cultural Ecology of South Coastal China*. Taipei: The Chinese Association for Folklore, 1973.

—— *Ecologies of the Heart: Emotion, Belief, and the Environment*. New York: Oxford University Press, 1980.

Appadurai, Arjun, 'Disjuncture and Difference in Global Cultural Economy'. In M. Featherstone (ed.), *Global Culture: Nationalism, Globalization and Modernity*. London: Sage Publications, 1990.

Aslan, Adnan, *Religious Pluralism in Christian and Islamic Philosophy: The Thought of John Hick and Seyyed Hossein Nasr*. London: Curzon Press, 1998.

Baker, Hugh, 'Burial, Geomancy and Ancestor Worship'. In Marjorie Topley (ed.), *Aspects of Social Organization in the New Territories*. Hong Kong Branch of the Royal Asiatic Society, 1965.

Ball, J. Dyer, *Things Chinese, Being Notes on Various Subjects Connected with China*. Shanghai: Kelly and Walsh, 1893.

de Bary, Wm. Theodore, *The Unfolding of Neo-Confucianism*. New York: Columbia University Press, 1975.

Barnett, A. Doak (ed.), *Chinese Politics in Action*. Seattle: University of Washington Press, 1969.

Barth, Fredrik, 'The Analysis of Culture in Complex Societies'. *Ethnos*, 54, 1989, pp. 120–142.

—— *Balinese Worlds*, London: Routledge, 1993.

Barthes, Roland, *S/Z: An Essay* [1970]. New York: Hill and Wang, 1974.

Bell, Catherine, 'Review Article. Religion and Chinese Culture: Toward an Assessment of "Popular Religion"'. *History of Religion*, vol. 29, no. 1, 1989, pp. 35–57.

Befu, Harumi, 'Watsuji Tetsuro's Ecological Approach: Its Philosophical Foundation'. In Pamela J. Asquith and Arne Kalland (eds), *Japanese Images of Nature*. Richmond: Curzon Press, 1997.

Bennett, Gordon, *Huadong: The Story of a Chinese People's Commune*. Boulder: Westview Press, 1978.

Bennett, Steven J., 'Patterns of the Sky and Earth: A Chinese Science of Applied Cosmology'. *Chinese Science*, 1978, no. 3, pp. 1–26.

Berglund, Lars, *The Secret of Luo Shu. Numerology in Chinese Art and Architecture.* Lund: Lund University, Department of Art History, 1990.

Bernard, Henri, *Matteo Ricci's Scientific Contribution to China.* Translated by Edward Chalmers Werner. Beijing: Henri Vetch, 1935.

Bird (Bishop), Isabella Lucy, *The Yangtze Valley and Beyond.* London: John Murray, 1899.

Bodde, Derk, 'Basic Concepts of Chinese Law: The Genesis and Evolution of Legal Thought in Traditional China'. In Der Bodde, *Essays on Chinese Civilization.* Princeton: Princeton University Press, 1981.

Bohr, Paul Richard, *Famine in China and the Missionary: Timothy Richard as Relief Administrator and Advocate of National Reform, 1876–1884.* Cambridge: East Asian Research Center, Harvard University Press, 1972.

Bredon, Juliet, *Peking: A Historical and Intimate Description of Its Chief Places of Interest.* Shanghai: Kelly and Walsh, 1931.

Bruner, Edward M., 'Ethnography as Narrative'. In Victor W. Turner and Edward M. Bruner, *The Anthropology of Experience.* Urbana: University of Illinois Press, 1986.

Bruun, Ole, *Business and Bureaucracy in a Chinese City: The Ethnography of Individual Business Households in Contemporary China.* Berkeley: Institute of East Asian Studies, 1993.

—— and Arne Kalland, 'Introduction: Images of Nature'. In Ole Bruun and Arne Kalland (eds), *Asian Perceptions of Nature – A Critical Approach.* London: Curzon Press, 1995.

Buck, Pearl S. (translator), *All Men Are Brothers (Shui hu zhuan).* New York: The John Day Company, 1933.

—— *My Several Worlds.* New York: The John Day Company, 1954.

Burden, J.S., 'Causes of Hostility to Missionaries', *The Chinese Recorder and Missionary Journal,* March 1872.

Burns, John P., *Political Participation in Rural China.* Berkeley: University of California Press, 1988.

Bush, Richard C., *Religion in Communist China.* New York: Abingdon Press, 1970.

Cadell, T. and W. Davies, *Ta Tsing Leu Lee* [Qing dynasty legal code] [London 1810]. Taipei: Cheng-Wen, 1966.

Callicott, J. Baird and Roger T. Ames, *Nature in Asian Traditions of Thought: Essays in Environmental Philosophy.* Albany: State University of New York Press, 1989.

Cameron, Nigel, *Barbarians and Mandarins. Thirteen Centuries of Western Travellers in China.* Chicago: The University of Chicago Press, 1976.

Carlson, Ellsworth C., *The Foochow Missionaries, 1847–1880.* Cambridge, Mass.: Harvard University Press, 1974.

Chan, Anita, Richard Madsen and Jonathan Unger, *Chen Village: The Recent History of a Peasant Community in Mao's China.* Berkeley: University of California Press, 1984.

Chan, Wing-tsit, *Religious Trends in Modern China*. New York: Octagon Books, (1953) 1978.

Chang Kia-Ngau, *China's Struggle for Railroad Development*. New York: John Day, 1943.

Chang Kuo-sin, *A Survey of the Chinese Language Daily Press*. Hong Kong: International Press Institute, 1968.

Chen Changheng, *Zhongguo renkou lun* [Discussing Chinese population issues]. Shanghai: Shangwu yinshuguan, 1922.

Chen, Nancy N., 'Urban Spaces and Experiences of Qigong'. In Deborah S. Davis, *et al.* (eds), *Urban Spaces in Contemporary China. The Potential for Autonomy and Community in Post-Mao China*. New York: Cambridge University Press, 1995.

Chesneaux, Jean, *Peasant Revolts in China 1840–1949*. London: Thames and Hudson, 1973.

Chu, Godwin and Yanan Ju, *The Great Wall in Ruins. Communication and Cultural Change in China*. New York: SUNY, 1993.

Clifford, James and George Marcus, *Writing Culture*. Berkeley: University of California Press, 1986.

Cobb, John B., *Is it too late?: A Theology of Ecology*. Los Angeles: Beverley Hills Cop., 1972.

Cohen, Paul A., 'Christian Missions and Their Impact to 1900'. In John K. Fairbank (ed.), *The Cambridge History of China*, vol 10: Late Ch'ing. 1800–1911. Cambridge: Cambridge University Press, 1978, pp. 543–590.

Cooke, George Wingrove, *'The Times' Special Correspondence from China in the Years 1857–58*. Wilmington: Scholarly Resources Inc. 1972.

Crook, Isabel and David Crook, *Revolution in a Chinese Village: Ten Mile Inn*. London: Routledge & Kegan Paul, 1959.

Crow, Carl, *Handbook for China*. Hong Kong: Kelly and Walsh, 1933.

Davis, Fei-Ling, *Primitive Revolutionaries of China: A Study of Secret Societies in the Late Nineteenth Century*. London: Routledge & Kegan Paul, 1971.

Davis, John Francis, *The Chinese: A General Description of the Empire of China and Its Inhabitants*. Two volumes. New York: Harper, 1836.

Davis-Friedman, Deborah, *Long Lives: Chinese Elderly and the Communist Revolution*. Stanford: Stanford University Press, 1991.

Dean, Kenneth, *Lord of the Three in One: The Spread of a Cult in Southeast China*. Princeton: Princeton University Press, 1998.

D'elia, Pashal M., *The Tripple Demism of Sun Yat-Sen*. Wuchang: The Franciscan Press, 1931.

Dennys, Nicholas B., *The Folk-lore of China, and Its Affinities with That of the Aryan and Semitic Races* [1876]. Detroit: Tower Books, 1971.

Dirks, Nicholas B., 'The Policing of Tradition: Colonialism and Anthropology in Southern India'. *Comparative Studies in Society and History*, vol. 39, no. 1, 1997, pp. 182–212.

Doolittle, Justus, *Social Life of the Chinese: With Some Account of their Religious, Governmental, Educational, and Business Customs and Opinions*. New York: Harper and Brothers, 1865.

Doré, Henry, *Researches into Chinese Superstitions*, vol. 2. Shanghai: T'usewei Printing House, 1914.

Durkheim, Emile and Marcel Mauss, *Primitive Classifications* [1903]. Translated by Rodney Needham. London: Cohen and West, 1963.

Eberhard, Wolfram, *Social Mobility in Traditional China*. Leiden: E.J. Brill, 1962.

—— *Guilt and Sin in Traditional China*. Berkeley: University of California Press, 1967.

—— *Studies in Chinese Folklore and Related Essays*. Bloomington: Indiana University Research Center, 1970.

—— *A Dictionary of Chinese Symbols*. London: Routledge, 1988.

Edkins, Joseph, 'Feng Shui: The Wind and Water Superstition of the Chinese' (part 1). *CRMJ* March 1872, pp. 274–277.

—— 'On the Chinese Geomancy Known as Feng-Shui' (part 2) *CRMJ* April 1872, pp. 291–298.

—— 'Feng Shui', *CRMJ* May 1872, pp. 316–320.

—— *Chinese Buddhism: A Volume of Sketches, Historical, Descriptive and Critical*. London: Trübner and Co., 1880.

Eitel, Ernest. J., *Feng-shui, or, The Rudiments of Natural Science in China* (1873), Singapore: Graham Brash, 1984.

Eliade, Mircea (ed.), *The Encyclopedia of Religion*. New York. Macmillan, 1987.

Ellen, Roy, Peter Parkes and Alan Bicker (eds), '*Indigenous Environmental Knowledge and Its Transformations: An Introduction*. Amsterdam: Harwood Press, 2001.

Elvin, Mark, 'The Environmental Legacy of Imperial China'. *China Quarterly*, no. 156, 1999, pp. 733–756.

Fairbank, John K., *Trade and Diplomacy on the China Coast*. Cambridge: Harvard University Press, 1969.

—— *China: A New History*, Cambridge, Mass: The BelKnap Press of Harvard University Press, 1992.

Fan Wei, 'Village Fengshui Principles'. In Ronald G. Knapp, *Chinese Landscapes, The Village as Place*. Honolulu: University of Hawai'i Press, 1990.

Fardon, Richard, 'Introduction'. In Richard Fardon (ed.), *Counterworks*. London: Routledge, 1995.

Farmer, Edward L., *Early Ming Government: The Evolution of Dual Capitals*. Cambridge, Mass: Harvard University Press, 1976.

Fei Hsiao Tung, *Chinese Village Close-up*. Beijing: New World Press, 1983.

Feuchtwang, Stephan, *An Anthropological Analysis of Chinese Geomancy*. Vientiane: Vitagna, 1974.

—— *The Imperial Metaphor*. London: Routledge, 1992.

—— *Popular Religion in China: The Imperial Metaphor*. Richmond: Curzon Press, 2001.

Fevour, Edward le, *Western Enterprise in Late Ch'ing China: A Selective Survey of Jardine, Matheson and Company's Operations 1842–1895*. Cambridge: Harvard University Press, 1970.

Field, Stephen L., 'The Numerology of Nine Star Fengshui'. *Journal of Chinese Religions*, no. 27, 1999, pp. 13–33.

—— In Search of Dragons: The Folk Ecology of Fengshui'. In N.J. Girardot, James Miller and Liu Xiaogan (eds), *Daoism and Ecology. Ways Within a Cosmic Landscape*. Cambridge, Mass.: Harvard University Press, 2001.

Fitzgerald, John, *Awakening China. Politics, Culture and Class in the Nationalist Revolution*. Stanford: Stanford University Press, 1996.

Forman, R.T. and M. Godron, *Landscape Ecology*. New York: John Wiley and Sons, 1986.

Fortune, Robert, *Three Years' Wanderings in Northern China* [London 1847]. New York: Garland Publishing, 1979.

Frazer, James, *The Golden Bough*. New York: St. Martin's Press, 1966.

Freedman, Maurice, *Chinese Lineage and Society: Fukien and Kwangtung*. London: Athlone Press, 1966.

—— 'Geomancy'. Presidential Address 1968. *Proceedings of the Royal Anthropological Institute of Great Britain and Ireland*, 1968–70. London 1969, pp. 5–15.

—— 'On the Sociological Study of Chinese Religion'. In Arthur P. Wolf, *Religion and Ritual in Chinese Society*. Stanford: Stanford University Press, 1974.

—— *The Study of Chinese Society*. Stanford: Stanford University Press, 1979.

Friedman, Jonathan, *Cultural Identity & Global Process*. London: Sage Publications, 1994.

—— 'Simplifying Complexity: Assimilating the Global in a Small Paradise'. In Karen Fog Olwig and Kirsten Hastrup (eds), *Siting Culture. The Shifting Anthropological Object*. London: Routledge 1997.

Fung Yu-lan, *A Short History of Chinese Philosophy*. New York: Macmillan, 1960.

Gamble, Sidney D., *North China Villages. Social, Political and Economic Activities Before 1933*. Berkeley: University of California Press, 1963.

Gao Youqian, *Zhongguo fengshui* [Chinese fengshui]. Beijing: Zhongguo huaqiao chuban gongsi, 1992.

Gates, Hill and Robert P. Weller, 'Hegemony and Chinese Folk Ideologies. An Introduction'. *Modern China*, vol. 13, no. 1, 1987, pp. 3–16.

Gernet, Jacques, *China and the Christian Impact: A Conflict of Cultures*. London: Cambridge University Press, 1985.

Giddens, Anthony, *Central Problems in Social Theory*. Berkeley: University of California Press, (1979) 1994.

Graham, David Crockett, *Folk Religion in Southwest China*. Washington: Smithsonian Press, 1961.

Granet, Marcel, *The Religion of the Chinese People*. Oxford: Oxford University Press, 1975.

Gray, John Henry, *China – History of the Laws, Manners and Customs of the People*. London: Macmillan, 1878.

de Groot, J.J.M., *The Religious System of China*. 6 volumes [Leyden, 1892–1910]. Taipei: Literature House, 1964.
Volume 1 [1892]; Volume 3, 1 [1897]; Volume 4, 1 [1901]; Volume 5 [1907]; Volume 6 [1910]

—— *Sectarianism and Religious Persecution in China.* 2 volumes, Amsterdam: Johannes Muller. 1903–1904.

Gutzlaff, Charles, *The Journal of Two Voyages along the Coast of China.* New York: John P. Haven, 1833.

—— *The Life of Taou-Kwang, Late Emperor of China.* [1852]. Wilmington: Scholarly Resources Inc., 1972.

Halde, J.B. du, *Description géographique, historique, chronologique, politique, et physique de l'empire de la Chine et de la Tartarie Chinoise.* La Hare: Henri Scheurleer, 1736.

Hamilton, Gary G., 'Why No Capitalism in China? Negative Questions in Historical, Comparative Research'. *Journal of Developing Societies,* vol. 1, pp. 187–211.

Hanson, Allan, 'The making of the Maori. Culture invention and its logic'. *American Anthropologist,* vol. 91, no. 4, 1989, pp. 890–902.

Harrell, Steven, 'The Concept of Fate in Chinese Folk Ideology'. *Modern China,* vol. 13, no. 1, 1987.

He Bochuan, *China on the Edge: The Crisis of Ecology and Development.* China Books and Periodicals, 1991.

He Xiaoxin, *Fengshui tan yuan* [Exploring the source of fengshui]. Nanjing: Dongnan daxue chubanshe, 1990.

Headland, Isaac Taylor, *Home Life in China.* London: Methuen & Co., 1914.

Hinton, William, *Fanshen: A Documentary of Revolution in a Chinese Village.* London: Monthly Review Press, 1966.

Hong Peimo, *Zhongguo fengshui yanjiu* [Chinese fengshui research]. Wuhan: Hubei kexue jishu chubanshe, 1993.

Horton, Robin and Ruth Finnegan (eds), *Modes of Thought.* London: Faber, 1973.

Hosie, Alexander, *Three Years in Western China.* London: Foreign Office, 1890.

Howell, Signe, 'Whose knowledge and whose power? A new perspective on cultural diffusion'. In Richard Fardon (ed.), *Counterworks.* London: Routledge, 1995.

Hsu, Francis, *Under the Ancestors' Shadow.* New York: Columbia University Press, 1948.

—— 'Psycho-social Homeostasis and the Concept of "jen": Conceptual Tools for Advancing Psycological Anthropology'. *American Anthropologist,* vol. 73, no. 1, 1971, pp. 23–44.

Hu, Chang-tu, *China: Its people, its society, its culture.* New Haven: HRAF Press, 1960.

Huang Liu-hung, *A Complete Book Concerning Happiness and Benevolence: A Manual for Local Magistrates in Seventeenth-Century China.* Tucson: The University of Arizona Press, 1984.

Huang, Mab, 'Universal Human Rights and Chinese Liberalism'. In Michael Jacobsen and Ole Bruun (eds), *Human Rights and Asian Values: Contesting National Identities and Cultural Representation Rights in Asia.* Richmond: Curzon Press, 2000.

Huang Yi-long, 'Court Divination and Christianity in the K'ang-Hsi Era'. *Chinese Science*, no. 10, 1991, pp. 1–20.

Hubrig, Herr Missionär, 'Fung Schui oder chinesische Geomantie'. *Zeitschrift für Ethnologie* (Berlin: Verlag von Wiegandt, Hempel & Parey), Elfter Band, 1879.

Jacobsen, Michael and Ole Bruun (eds), *Human Rights and Asian Values: Contesting National Identities and Cultural Representation Rights in Asia.* Richmond: Curzon Press, 2000.

Jaschok, Maria and Shui Jingjun, *The History of Women's Mosques in Chinese Islam.* Richmond: Curzon Press, 2000.

Johnson, David, 'Communication, Class and Consciousness in Late Imperial China'. In David Johnson, Andrew J. Nathan and Evelyn Rawski (eds), *Popular Culture in Late Imperial China.* Berkeley: University of California Press, 1985

Johnson, David, Andrew J. Nathan and Evelyn Rawski (eds), *Popular Culture in Late Imperial China.* Berkeley: University of California Press, 1985

Jordan, David K., *Gods, Ghosts and Ancestors: Folk Religion in a Taiwanese Village.* Berkeley: University of California Press, 1972.

Jung, C.G., 'Introduction'. In Richard Wilhelm (trans.), *I Ching or Book of Changes.* London: Routledge and Kegan Paul, 1968.

Kang Liang *et al., Fengshui yu chengshi* [Fengshui and cities]. Sanhe: Baihua wenyi chubanshe, 1998.

Kipp, Rita Smith, *Dissociated Identities: Ethnicity, Religion, and Class in an Indonesian Society.* Ann Arbor: The University of Michigan Press, 1996.

Kleinman, Arthur, *Social Origins of Distress and Disease. Depression, Neurasthenia, and Pain in Modern China.* New Haven: Yale University Press, 1986.

Knapp, Ronald G., *China's Living Houses. Folk Beliefs, Symbols, and Household Ornamentation.* Honolulu: University of Hawai'i Press, 1999.

Kuhn, Philip A., *Rebellion and Its Enemies in Late Imperial China. Militarization and Social Structure, 1796–1864.* Cambridge: Harvard University Press, 1970.

Lai, John Yung-hsiang (compiler), 'Catalog of Protestant Missionary Works in Chinese'. Harvard-Yenching Library. Boston, Mass.: Harvard University, 1980.

Lee, Hui-chen Wang, 'Chinese Clan Rules'. In David S. Nivison and Arthur F. Wright (eds), *Confucianism in Action.* Stanford: Stanford University Press, 1959.

Lévi-Strauss, Claude, 'The Sorcerer and his Magic', in Claude Lévi-Strauss, *Structural Anthropology.* New York: Doubleday, 1967a.

—— *Totemism.* A.S.A. Monographs, London: Tavistock Publications, 1967b.

—— *The Raw and the Cooked.* New York: Harper and Row, 1969.

Li Wenhua and Zhao Xianying, *China's Nature Reserves,* Beijing: China Books and Periodicals, 1989.

Li Zhisui, *The Private Life of Chairman Mao.* London: Chatto and Windus, 1994.

Lieberthal, Kenneth, *Revolution and Tradition in Tientsin, 1949–1952.* Stanford: Stanford University Press, 1980.

Ling, Ken, *The Revenge of Heaven: Journal of a Young Chinese*. New York: G. P. Putnam's Sons, 1972.

Lip, Evelyn, *Fengshui: Environments of Power. A Study of Chinese Architecture*. London: Academy Editions, 1996.

Lutz, Jessie Gregory, *Chinese Politics and Christian Missions: The Anti-Christian Movements of 1920–28*. Vol. 3, *The Curch and the World*. Notre Dame, Indiana: Cross Cultural Publications, 1988.

MacInnins, Donald E., *Religious Policy and Practice in Communist China*. London: Hodder and Stoughton, 1972.

MacNair, Harley Farnsworth, *Modern Chinese History: Selected Readings*, vol. 1. Shanghai: The Commercial Press, 1927.

Malinowski, Bronislaw, *Coral Gardens and their Magic*. London: Allen & Unwin, 1935.

Mao Tse-tung, *Selected Works of Mao Tse-tung*, vol. 1. Beijing: Foreign Languages Press, 1982.

March, Andrew L., 'An Appreciation of Chinese Geomancy'. *Journal of Asian Studies*, vol. 27, no. 2, 1968, pp. 253–267.

Marcus, George and Michael Fisher, *Anthropology as Cultural Critique*. Chicago: University of Chicago Press, 1986.

McHarg, Ian L., *Design with Nature*. New York: Doubleday, 1969.

Monina, A. A., 'The Missionary Question in Qing Policy (the Zongliyamen Memorandum of February 9, 1871)'. In David Skvirsky (trans.) and S.L. Tikhvinsky (ed.), *Manzhou Rule in China*. Moscow: Progress Publishers, 1983.

Moody, Peter R., *Opposition and Dissent in Contemporary China*. Stanford: Hoover Institution Press, 1977.

Morrison, G. E., *An Australian in China. Being the Narrative of a Quiet Journey Across China to British Burma*. Sydney: Angus and Robertson, 1895.

Mosher, Steven W., *Broken Earth: The Rural Chinese*. New York: The Free Press, 1983.

Moule, Arthur E., *The Chinese People. A Handbook on China*. London: Society for Promoting Christian Knowledge, 1914.

Mungello, D.E. (ed.), *The Chinese Rites Controversy. Its History and Meaning*. Nettetal: Steyler Verlag, 1994.

Murphy, Robert F., *The Dialectics of Social Life. Alarms and Excursions in Anthropological Theory*. New York: Columbia University Press, (1971) 1980.

Myron, Paul, *Our Chinese Chances through Europe's War*, Chicago: Linebarger Brothers Publishers, 1915.

Naquin, Susan, 'The Transmission of White Lotus Sectarianism in Late Imperial China'. In David Johnson, Andrew J. Nathan and Evelyn Rawski (eds), *Popular Culture in Late Imperial China*. Berkeley: University of California Press, 1985.

—— and Evelyn S. Rawski, *Chinese Society in the Eighteenth Century*. New Haven: Yale University Press, 1987.

Needham, Joseph, *Science and Civilization in China*, vol. 4, part 1. Cambridge: Cambridge University Press, 1962.

Needham, Rodney, *Belief, Language and Experience.* Chicago: The University of Chicago Press, 1972.

Nevius, John L., *China and the Chinese.* New York: Harper, 1869.

Olson, David R. and Nancy Torrence (eds), *Modes of Thought. Explorations in Culture and Cognition.* Cambridge: Cambridge University Press, 1996.

Overmyer, Daniel L., *Folk Buddhist Religion: Dissenting Sects in Late Traditional China.* Cambridge, Mass.: Harvard University Press, 1976.

Pan Haoyuan and Zhao Chunlan, 'Fengshui and Ancient Chinese Landscape'. *IIAS Newsletter,* no. 13, 1997.

Paper, Jordan, 'Religion'. In Wu Dingbo and Patrick D. Murph (eds), *Handbook of Chinese Popular Culture.* Westport: Greenwood Press, 1994.

Parish, William L. and Martin King Whyte, *Village and Family in Contemporary China.* Chicago: The University of Chicago Press, 1978.

Perdue, Peter, *Chinese Environmental History Newsletter,* 1994.

Potter, Jack M., 'Wind, Water, Bones and Souls: The Religious World of the Cantonese Peasant'. *Journal of Oriental Studies,* vol. 3, no. 1, 1970.

Rawski, Evelyn, 'Introduction'. In David Johnson, Andrew J. Nathan and Evelyn Rawski (eds), *Popular Culture in Late Imperial China.* Berkeley: University of California Press, 1985.

Ricci, Matthew [Matteo], *China in the Sixteenth Century: The Journals of Matthew Ricci: 1583–1610.* Translated by Louis J. Gallagher. New York: Random House, 1953.

Richards, I.A., *Mencius on the Mind.* London: Kegan Paul, 1932.

Rosaldo, Renato, *Culture and Truth: The Remaking of Cultural Analysis.* Boston: Beacon Press, 1989.

Rossbach, Sarah, *Feng Shui. The Chinese Art of Placement.* New York: Penguin Books, 1983.

Ruddle, Kenneth and Zhong Gongfu, *Integrated Agriculture-Aquaculture in South China.* Cambridge: Cambridge University Press, 1988.

Sahlins, Marshal, 'What is Anthropological Enlightenment? Some Lessons from the Twentieth Century'. *Annual Review of Anthropology,* vol. 28, 1999, pp. i–xxii.

Said, Edward, *Culture and Imperialism.* London: Vintage, 1993.

Service, John S. (ed.), *Golden Inches. The China Memoir of Grace Service.* Berkeley: University of California Press, 1989.

Shahar, Meir and Robert P. Weller (eds), *Unruly Gods: Divinity and Society in China.* Honolulu: University of Hawai'i Press, 1996.

Sharman, Lyon, *Sun Yat-sen. His Life and Its Meaning.* Stanford: Stanford University Press, 1968.

Shi Zhen, '*Fengshui dian gu kao lüe*' [The textual research of ancient codes and records of fengshui]. In Wang Qiheng (ed.), *Fengshui lilun yanjiu* [Theoretical studies on fengshui]. Tianjin: Tianjin daxue chubanshe, 1992.

Shih, Vincent Y.C., *The Taiping Ideology: Its Ideology, Interpretations, and Influences.* Seattle: University of Washington Press, 1967.

Shore, Bradd, *Culture in Mind. Cognition, Culture and the Problem of Meaning.* New York: Oxford University Press, 1996.

da Silva, Armando, *Tai Yu Shan: Traditional Ecological Adaptation in a South Chinese Island.* Taipei: The Orient Cultural Service, 1972.

Siu, Helen, 'Recycling Rituals. Politics and Popular Culture in Contemporary China'. In Perry Link, Richard Madsen and Paul G. Pickowicz (eds), *Unofficial China. Popular Culture and Thought in the People's Republic.* London: Westview Press, 1989.

Skinner, Stephen, *Terrestrial Astrology. Divination by Geomancy.* London: Routledge & Kegan Paul, 1980.

—— *The Living Earth Manual of Feng-Shui: Chinese Geomancy.* London: Routledge & Kegan Paul, 1982.

Smil, Vaclav, *China's Environmental Crisis. An Inquiry into the Limits of National Development.* London: M.E. Sharpe, 1993.

Smith, Howard, *Chinese Religions.* London: Weidenfeld and Nicolson, 1968.

Smith, Richard J., *Fortune-tellers and Philosophers. Divination in Chinese Society.* Boulder: Westview Press, 1991.

—— *et al.* (eds), *Robert Hart and China's Early Modernization.* Cambridge, Mass.: Harvard University Press, 1991.

Snow, Edgar, *The Long Revolution.* London: Hutchinson, 1973.

Song Dachuan, '*Zhongguo chuantong fengshui xueshuo de yuanliu ji shehui yingxiang*' [The origin and development of Chinese traditional fengshui and its social influence]. *Beijing Wenbo,* no. 1, 2000, pp. 51–57.

Strathern, Andrew, *Landmarks: Reflections on Anthropology.* London: Kent State University Press, 1993.

Strathern, Marilyn, *Shifting Contexts.* London: Routledge, 1995.

Sturdevant, Saundra, 'Imperialism, Sovereignty, and Self-Strengthening: A Reassessment of the 1870s'. In Paul A. Cohen and John E. Schrecker (eds), *Reform in Nineteenth-Century China.* Cambridge, Mass.: Harvard University Press, 1976.

Tambiah, Stanley Jeyaraja, *Magic, Science, Religion, and the Scope of Rationality.* Cambridge: Cambridge University Press, 1990.

Teiser, Stephen F., 'Popular Religion'. *Journal of Asian Studies,* vol. 54, no. 2, 1995, pp. 378–395.

—— 'Religions of China in Practice'. In Donald S. Lopez, Jr. (ed.), *Asian Religions in Practice.* Princeton: Princeton University Press, 1999.

Valeri, Valerio, 'Fredrik Barth: *Balinese Worlds*'. Review in *American Anthropologist,* vol. 97, no. 4.

Wagner, Rudolf G., 'Reading the Chairman Mao Memorial Hall'. In Susan Naquin and Chün-fang Yü (eds), *Pilgrims and Sacred Sites in China.* Berkeley: University of California Press, 1992.

Walters, Derek, *The Feng Shui Handbook.* London: Aquarian, 1991.

Walton, Linda A., 'Southern Sung Academies and the Construction of Sacred Space'. In Wen-hsin Yeh (ed.), *Landscape, Culture, and Power in Chinese Society.* Berkeley: Institute of East Asian Studies, 1998

Wang Fukun, 'Fengshui lilun de chuantong zhixue kuangjia' [The traditional philosophical framework of fengshui theory]. In Wang Qiheng (ed.), *Fengshui lilun yanjiu* [Theoretical studies on fengshui]. Tianjin: Tianjin daxue chubanshe, 1992.

Wang Qiheng (ed.), *Fengshui lilun yanjiu* [Theoretical studies on fengshui]. Tianjin: Tianjin daxue chubanshe, 1992.

Wang Yude, *Shenmide fengshui* [Mysterious fengshui]. Nanning: Guangxi renmin chubanshe, 1991.

Watson, Rubie, 'Issues of identity in the 1990s'. Unpublished AAS conference paper, 1995.

Weber, Max, *The Religion of China: Confucianism and Taoism* [1920]. New York: The Free Press, 1951.

Welch, Holmes, *The Buddhist Revival in China*. Cambridge, Mass.: Harvard University Press, 1968.

—— *Buddhism under Mao*. Cambridge: Harvard University Press, 1972.

Weller, Robert P., *Unities and Diversities in Chinese Religion*. Appendix A: 'Geomancy'. Seattle: University of Washington Press, 1987.

Wen Dazhong and David Pimentel, 'Seventeenth Century Organic Agriculture in China'. *Human Ecology*, vol. 14, no. 1, 1986.

Wessing, Robert, 'A tiger in the Heart'. *Bijdragen*, vol. 148, no. 2, 1992, pp. 287–308.

White, Lynn, *Medieval Technology and Social Change*. Oxford: Clarendon Press, 1962.

Wiegers, L., *Moral Tenets and Customs in China*. Ho-Kien-fu: Catholic Mission Press, 1913.

Williams, Samuel Wells, *The Middle Kingdom; A Survey of the Geography, Government, Education, Social Life, Arts, Religion & c., of the Chinese Empire and Its Inhabitants*. New York: Wiley and Putnam, 1848.

Willoughby-Meade, G., *Chinese Ghouls and Goblins*. London: Constable, 1928.

Wong, J.Y., *Yeh Ming Ch'en: Viceroy of Liang Kuang 1852–58*. London: Cambridge University Press, 1976.

Wright, Arthur F., 'The Cosmology of the Chinese City'. In G. William Skinner (ed.), *The City in Late Imperial China*. Stanford: Stanford University Press, 1977.

Yang, C.K., *A Chinese Village in Early Communist Transition*. Cambridge, Mass.: M.I.T. Press, 1959.

—— *Religion in Chinese Society*. Berkeley: University of California Press, 1970.

Yang Wenheng, *Zhongguo di fengshui* [Chinese fengshui]. Beijing: Beijing guoji wenhua chubanshe, 1993.

Yeji Laozi, *Minsu dili fengshui* [Fengshui as folk geography]. Chengdu: Sichuan daxue chubanshe, 1993.

Yen Chih-t'ui, *Family Instructions for the Yen Clan*. Leiden: E.J. Brill, 1968.

Yi Ding, Yu Lu and Hong Yong, *Zhongguo gudai fengshui yu jianzhu xuanzhi* [Ancient Chinese fengshui and imperial construction]. Baoding: Hebei kexue jishu, 1996.

Yoon, Hong-key, *Geomantic Relations between Culture and Nature in Korea*. Taipei: The Orient Cultural Service, 1976.

Yu Kongjian, 'Exploration of the deep meaning of the ideal feng-shui landscape model'. *Exploration of Nature*, vol. 9, no. 1, 1990, pp. 87–90.

—— 'Keep the Living Qi: Theory and Practice for Sustainable Environment'. Beijing: Beijing Forestry University, Landscape Architecture Department, 1992.

Yuan Shushan, *Zhongguo lidai buren zhuan* [Biographies of diviners in China by period], 1948.

Zhang Huimin, *Zhongguo fengshui yingyongxue* [Applied Chinese fengshui], Beijing: Renmin Zhongguo chubanshe, 1993.

Zhong Gongfu, 'The Structural Characteristics and Effects of the Dyke-pond System in China'. *Outlook on Agriculture*, vol. 18, no. 3, 1989.

Zhou Wenzheng *et al.*, *Dili zhengzong* [Orthodox geography]. Guangxi: Guangxi minzu chubanshe, 1993.

JOURNALS

BW	*Beijing Wenbo*
CD	China Daily
CF	China Focus
CL	China Law
CNA	China News Analysis
CR	The Chinese Repository
CRMJ	*The Chinese Recorder and Missionary Journal*
FR	*Fazhi Ribao* [Legal forum]
HQ	*Hong Qi* [Red flag]
IHT	International Herald Tribune
JAS	Journal of Asian Studies
JCR	Journal of Chinese Religions
NCHM	The North-China Herald and Market Report
NCHS	The North-China Herald and Supreme Court & Consular Gazette
NQ	Notes and Queries
RR	*Renmin Ribao* [The people's daily]
SCMP	South China Morning Post
SWB	Summary of World Broadcasts
SCMP	Survey of China Mainland Press
ZQB	Zhongguo Qingnian Bao [China youth]

Index

Wright, Arthur C. 269

xenophobia 50, 261

Yang, C.K. 9, 65, 68, 85, 95, 103, 106
yang dwellings 3
Yang Yunsong 279
Yijing 58, 108, 236, 265, 272
yin dwellings 3
yinyang 248, 263, 278

Yoon, Hong-key 239–240, 269–270
Yu Kongjian 240
Yuan Dynasty 34, 51, 280
Yuan Shushan 35

Zhang Zhidong 66
Zhao Xianying 248
Zhao Zhixing 66
Zhu Xi 278–279
Zuo Zongtang 62